THE MEANING AND MEASUREMENT OF SOCIAL SUPPORT

THE SERIES IN CLINICAL AND COMMUNITY PSYCHOLOGY

CONSULTING EDITORS
Charles D. Spielberger and Irwin G. Sarason

Auerbach and Stolberg Crisis Intervention with Children and Families
Burchfield Stress: Psychological and Physiological Interactions
Burstein and Loucks Rorschach's Test: Scoring and Interpretation
Diamant Male and Female Homosexuality: Psychological Approaches
Fischer The Science of Psychotherapy
Hobfoll Stress, Social Support, and Women
Krohne and Laux Achievement, Stress, and Anxiety
London The Modes and Morals of Psychotherapy, Second Edition
Muñoz Depression Prevention: Research Directions
Olweus Aggression in the Schools: Bullies and Whipping Boys
Reisman A History of Clinical Psychology, Second Edition
Reitan and Davison Clinical Neuropsychology: Current Status and Applications
Rickel, Gerrard, and Iscoe Social and Psychological Problems of Women: Prevention and Crisis Intervention
Rofé Repression and Fear: A New Approach to the Crisis in Psychotherapy
Savin-Williams Gay and Lesbian Youth: Expressions of Identity
Spielberger and Diaz-Guerrero Cross-Cultural Anxiety, Volume 3
Spielberger, Diaz-Guerrero, and Strelau Cross-Cultural Anxiety, Volume 4
Suedfeld Psychology and Torture
Veiel and Baumann The Meaning and Measurement of Social Support
Williams and Westermeyer Refugee Mental Health in Resettlement Countries

IN PREPARATION

Auerbach Clinical Psychology in Transition
Diamant Homosexual Issues in the Workplace
Erchul Consultation in Community, School, and Organizational Practice: Gerald Caplan's Contribution to Professional Psychology
Spielberger and Diaz-Guerrero Cross Cultural Anxiety, Volume 5
Spielberger and Vagg The Assessment and Treatment of Test Anxiety

THE MEANING AND MEASUREMENT OF SOCIAL SUPPORT

Edited by
Hans O. F. Veiel
Central Institute of Mental Health, Mannheim, Germany

Urs Baumann
Universität Salzburg, Austria

Routledge
Taylor & Francis Group
LONDON AND NEW YORK

First published 1992 by Hemisphere Publishing Corporation

2 Park Square, Milton Park, Abingdon, Oxon OX14 4RN
711 Third Avenue, New York, NY 10017, USA

Routledge is an imprint of the Taylor & Francis Group, an informa business

First issued in paperback 2016

THE MEANING AND MEASUREMENT OF SOCIAL SUPPORT

This book was set in Times Roman by Hemisphere Publishing Corporation. The editors were Heather Jefferson and S. Michele Nix; the production supervisor was Peggy M. Rote; and the typesetter was Laurie Strickland. Cover design by Sharon M. DePass.

A CIP catalog record for this book is available from the British Library.

Library of Congress Cataloging-in-Publication Data

The Meaning and measurement of social support / Hans O. F. Veiel & Urs Baumann (eds.).
p. cm.
Papers from an international symposium held in May 1990 in Bad Homburg, Germany,
Includes bibliographical references.

1. Social networks—Congresses. I. Veiel, Hans O. F.
II. Bauman, Urs.
HM131.M383 1991
302-dc20 91-18354
CIP

ISBN 978-1-56032-220-7 (hbk)
ISBN 978-1-138-99572-7 (pbk)

Contents

VI
SUPPORT INTERVENTIONS

VII
CONCLUSION

Contributors

MICHAEL ARGYLE, Oxford University, United Kingdom
URS BAUMANN, Universität Salzburg, Austria
GEORGE W. BROWN, University of London, United Kingdom
SHELDON COHEN, Carnegie Mellon University, Pennsylvania, USA
BENJAMIN H. GOTTLIEB, University of Guelph, Ontario, Canada
TIRRIL O. HARRIS, University of London, United Kingdom
A. S. HENDERSON, The Australian National University, Canberra, Australia
STEVEN E. HOBFOLL, Kent State University, Ohio, USA
ANITA P. JACKSON, Kent State University, Ohio, USA
SHERI L. JOHNSON, University of Oregon, USA
RONALD C. KESSLER, University of Michigan, USA
ANTON LAIREITER, Universität Salzburg, Austria
ANJA LEPPIN, Freie Universität Berlin, Germany
ROY S. LILLY, Kent State University, Ohio, USA
SCOTT M. MONROE, University of Oregon, USA
GREGORY R. PIERCE, University of Washington, USA
KAREN S. ROOK, University of California-Irvine, USA
BARBARA R. SARASON, University of Washington, USA
IRWIN G. SARASON, University of Washington, USA
RALF SCHWARZER, Freie Universität Berlin, Germany
PEGGY A. THOITS, Vanderbilt University, Tennessee, USA
R. JAY TURNER, University of Toronto, Canada
ALAN VAUX, Southern Illinois University, USA
HANS O. F. VEIEL, Central Institute of Mental Health, Mannheim, Germany

Preface

This volume grew out of an international symposium held in May 1990 at the Werner Reimers Foundation in Bad Homburg, Germany. The primary reason for the symposium was the strong suspicion that the rapidly expanding field of social support research is losing its cohesiveness and that its conceptual foundations and underlying assumptions need to be examined and discussed. While the area's body of empirical research is growing prodigiously, the results do not coalesce beyond the general—but now hardly new—insight that good social relationships are related to good health. Social support research is becoming increasingly fragmented into separate areas, each with its own concepts, theories, and measurement instruments; and it is dominated by single studies dealing with ever more specific and narrow topics. This empirical fragmentation reflects a conceptual one: there seems to be no consensus about the definition, measurement, or even the concept of social support itself.

One of the symposium's goals was to provide a forum for a group of distinguished scientists to discuss what is meant by "social support" (or what *is* social support), how it is to be measured, and how matters of meaning and measurement bear on each other and on empirical issues. The second goal was the exchange of ideas across disciplinary and national boundaries. It turned out to be a very stimulating meeting, surpassing our high expectations, and we thank all participants for contributing to its success.

In this volume, the principal theses of the symposium are presented by their proponents. The original presentations were revised in the light of the discussions that followed them, and the volume is rounded off by two additional chapters on methodological issues. The overall emphasis is on concepts rather than empirical results. While each chapter stands on its own as an authoritative statement on its topic, in combination they present an overview of fundamental conceptual issues in social support research.

The editors are grateful for the assistance of many people who contributed to the success of the symposium; in particular, we recognize the support provided by the institutions that made it possible:

- The Werner Reimers Stiftung in Bad Homburg, Germany, on whose premises the meeting was held and which met lodging and travel expenses for the participants. The very pleasant setting and, above all, the staff's hospitality and administrative efficiency was greatly admired by all the participants.
- The German Research Association (Deutsche Forschungsgemeinschaft), which provided the funding for the overseas participants and for support staff.
- The Central Institute of Mental Health in Mannheim, Germany, which provided moral and administrative support during the preparatory phase.

The editors also would like to thank the publishers for their commitment early in the preparation of this volume. We also would like to thank Erika Feichtinger, Karin Lettner, and Elisabeth Reisenzein for their proofreading and editing assistance.

Hans O. F. Veiel
Urs Baumann

1

The Many Meanings of Social Support

Hans O. F. Veiel
Central Institute of Mental Health, Mannheim, Germany

Urs Baumann
Universität Salzburg, Austria

During the past two decades, the concept of social support has become immensely popular in mental health research. It seems as if every research project even remotely concerned with mental health today must include some measure or other of social support. Measured by both its impact on current thinking concerning the social etiology of mental and physical disorders, and by the sheer volume of publications, social support has joined stress and coping as one of the three most important constructs in current mental health research. While stress theory in its original form (Selye, 1950; Wolff, 1953) regarded the individual as a passive organism reacting to adverse environmental conditions, the introduction of social support complements this view by postulating beneficial environmental (social) conditions that may modulate and even compensate for the effects of environmental stress.

The notion of specific environmental factors promoting mental health is not a new one. All nonbiological theories of psychopathology—psychodynamic, behavioristic, or humanistic—posit certain psychosocial conditions as pathogenic, and other conditions as protective (cf. Rychlak, 1973). However, the beneficial conditions postulated by complex established theories (such as mature defense mechanisms or the availability of competent role models) are usually of rather circumscribed usefulness, and explanations of their effects draw heavily on theory-specific assumptions. In contrast, social support is understood as a general and directly beneficial, perhaps intrinsic, quality of social relationships.

The philosophical roots of the concept of social support can be found in postulates about basic human requirements (Bowlby, 1969; cf. Weiss, 1974). This makes it a largely atheoretical concept, since etiological models based on it do not need to refer to elaborate theories to explain empirical associations. In this way the support concept promised an enormous conceptual and empirical simplification: no intricate pathogenic mechanisms and processes, just a count of supportive elements or an assessment of the extent of existing "support," perhaps to be related to an equally global stress score. This conceptual simplification, without doubt, was mainly responsible for its basic appeal to policymakers (cf. Kiesler, 1985) and for its enthusiastic acceptance as a research paradigm in psychology, sociology, and psychiatry.

As tends to happen when ideas and concepts turn into scientific paradigms, the support paradigm has ceased to be seen as needing justification, and support measures are now routinely included in assessment batteries for no other reason than to "cover" it.

THE CHANGING MEANING OF SOCIAL SUPPORT

To better understand this development and its implications, we must look more closely at some changes in the concept of social support itself and in its applications. Two decades ago, social support was rarely used in a research context. The seminal paper by Nuckolls, Cassel, and Kaplan (1972), for example, did not use the term at all.

Before the mid-1970s, social support was primarily used in a concrete sense to denote a person, relationship, or transaction (Lowenthal & Haven, 1968), and even more recent authors use the generic plural "social supports" for a class of functionally comparable, concrete social interchanges or resources (Dohrenwend, Dohrenwend, Dodson, & Shrout, 1984). But in the 1970s, social support underwent an insidious conceptual transformation from a concrete term to an abstract construct, referring to an inferred characteristic or function of social relationships or transactions, rather than to the observable relationships or transactions themselves. (This is reflected in the abstract German nouns "soziale Unterstützung" and "sozialer Rückhalt," adopted in the late 1970s and early 1980s as translations for social support.)

More recently, social support has been said to represent a metaconcept (Vaux, Phillips, Holly, Thomson, & Stewart, 1986) lacking specificity and definition (Barrera, 1986), rather than a definable and measurable entity. This parallels some current views of the stress concept (Lazarus, DeLongis, Folkman, & Gruen, 1985). Nonetheless, the notion of a supportive quality, which can be abstracted from particular relationships and transactions and can be used to characterize them, has taken root in the backs of most researchers' minds.

As it is currently used in social and scientific parlance, the term "social support" commonly implies an abstract characteristic of persons, behaviors, relationships, or social systems. The evident diversity of what is subsumed under it is usually accounted for by postulating different kinds (e.g., emotional vs. instrumental), sources (e.g., spouses vs. family vs. friends), or other facets, forms, or expressions of the phenomenon "support." This view is best exemplified by multidimensional conceptual models, such as those proposed by House (1981).

DIVERGENT STRANDS OF EMPIRICAL RESEARCH

The empirical research on social support and health during the last two decades mirrored conceptual changes. Studies of specific relationships, whose characteristics were summarized as supportive or were called "supports," since this term seemed to capture their synthetic, health-promoting quality (Lowenthal & Haven, 1968), gave way to studies that explicitly examined social support as a kind of abstract commodity stored in certain individuals or social structures and traded in social transactions (Gore, 1978).

More recently, empirical research in the social support area seems to have split into several different strands with different agendas and with increasingly divergent operationalizations, concepts, and measures (Baumann, 1987). Among these strands are: (a) process-oriented research trying to detect supportive elements in microlevel social transactions, using diaries or even sophisticated electronic notebooks (Perrez & Reicherts, 1989); (b) research on the global subjective perception of being supported (Turner, Frankel, & Levin, 1983), and on its relationship to personality characteristics (Sarason & Sarason, 1982); (c) research on "confidants" and other support factors protecting against deleterious health consequences of severe stressful situations (Brown, Andrews, Harris, Adler, & Bridge, 1986); (d) research on the relationship between structural aspects of the social network and perceptions of support (as advocated by Gottlieb, 1985a) or the actual flow of support resources (Wellman, 1981); and (e) intervention-oriented research (Gottlieb, 1985b).

THE NEED FOR CONCEPTUAL CLARIFICATION

In the late 1970s and early 1980s, numerous definitions of social support were proposed. These ranged from the cognitive, as knowledge about one's position in the immediate social environment (Cobb, 1976), through the affective, as emotional states (Kaplan, Cassel, & Gore, 1977), and the behavioral, as a transaction (House, 1981), to the structural, as the presence of a particular kind of social relationship (Cohen & Syme, 1985; Pearlin, 1985). However, in recent years, attempts at definition have become considerably less frequent.

The declining emphasis on conceptual issues reflects the difficulty in formulating a definition of social support that encompasses all or even most uses of the term, and one that is not circular (cf. Wilcox & Vernberg, 1985). Of course, if asked, almost every researcher in the field will present a more or less precise definition of support, but, more than likely, it will be different from that of his or her colleagues.

The lack of a commonly accepted notion of to which social support refers, beyond the vague idea of a positive influence on health, makes it difficult to integrate the results obtained in different areas that differ in their agendas and their methods. As House and Kahn (1985) stated, it may be that "the term connotes enough that it has proved fruitful even in the absence of denotation" (p. 84), but connotations alone are not sufficient anymore when diverse findings, instruments, and concepts have to be integrated into a coherent conceptual edifice. To do so is particularly important now that the interests of many workers have shifted to building models of support effects (Sarason, Sarason, & Pierce, 1990). To prevent these efforts from leading to further and permanent fragmentation of the field, a widely shared notion of what is meant by "social support" is necessary. Such a notion should be more specific than the vague idea of positive influences of the social environment, but also encompass the diverse group of phenomena labeled social support. However, considering the various interests, agendas, and backgrounds of current empirical work, it is doubtful whether a single, unitary concept could fulfill these requirements. Alternatively, a group of related concepts may be as useful, but in this case their relationship to each other has to be made explicit.

SOCIAL SUPPORT AS AN INDIVIDUAL VERSUS A SOCIAL CHARACTERISTIC

A comprehensive support concept must take into account the many existing uses of the term. Several times in the past 15 years, disputes arose concerning what essentially constitutes effective support, thus introducing an interactive perspective with an emphasis on characteristics of the individual rather than his or her environment. For example, Henderson, Byrne, and Duncan-Jones (1981) claimed that a large part of the association of social support measures with health results from their reflecting personality traits. Wethington and Kessler (1986) argued that "received support" affects health only insofar as it changes a person's (global) perceptions of being supported. Gottlieb (1985a) and Lieberman (1986), on the other hand, decried the psychologization of the support concept, implying that social support should be primarily regarded as a characteristic of social networks and interaction patterns.

These conceptual disputes sometimes arose in the guise of disputes over measurement issues. However, the basic conceptual question to be dealt with is: How much of a social variable is social support supposed to be? Basically, social support can represent a characteristic of the recipient, of his or her environment, or of a social system including both the recipient and his or her environment. Within each of these domains, relevant characteristics may differ in their degree of stability over time.

Social Support as an Individual Characteristic

Support may be regarded as a relatively stable personal feature of the recipient (i.e., as an enduring individual trait or as several traits). For example, this is implied when Henderson et al. (1981) suspect neuroticism to be responsible for the association of support and health, rather than it being a genuine causal effect. Similarly, the notion of social support as an individual difference variable (Sarason & Sarason, 1982) explicitly focuses on this aspect.

Social support may denote a more transient individual state of mind, namely the perception or conviction of being cared for and loved (Cobb, 1976). This state may rapidly change upon receiving new information (or it may not, in which case it is better considered a trait), and it may or may not be a faithful reflection of the actual state of affairs.

A trait or state concept of support is quite removed from actual social structures and transactions. It is possible that the adjective "social" is not justified here, because it is the individual (a) who influences the size and composition of the social network, and hence its capacity to provide support; (b) who seeks or does not seek support; (c) who does or does not accept it; (d) who evaluates it; and (e) who integrates this evaluation into a relatively enduring and encompassing cognitive—emotional representation of the social world (cf. Gottlieb, 1985a; Lieberman, 1986).

Social Support as a Characteristic of the Social Environment

Social support may denote a behavior regarded as supportive because of its obvious helping or comforting nature (e.g., the behaviors targeted by some assessment instruments; e.g., Vaux, Riedel, & Stewart, 1987; Barrera, Sandler, & Ramsey, 1981). Conversely, behaviors are sometimes more generally (and tautologically) defined as supportive because they lead to subjective convictions (states) of being loved, esteemed, and so forth (cf. Hobfoll, 1988).

Social support may refer to a particular attitude of members of the social network, whether expressed in specific behaviors, nonverbal clues, or otherwise. This aspect has received comparatively little attention in the social support literature, but the Rogerian notion of "unconditional regard" (Truax & Carkhuff, 1967; cf. Hobfoll, 1988) comes to mind here. Conversely, the support value of particular behaviors often depends on real or perceived attitudes of the provider; seemingly supportive behaviors may be invalidated because accompanying attitudes and intentions are perceived to be less than sincere (cf. Hobfoll & Stokes, in press, cited in Hobfoll, 1988).

Social support may denote a synthetic characteristic of a person (social network member) who, by virtue of a specific, perhaps idiosyncratic combination of personality features, attitudes, and behaviors, represents a support. (This is how earlier researchers used the term.) For example, someone attempting to listen sympathetically when a friend tells of life problems (probably counted as support by most researchers in the field) may appear phony, or well-intended but incongruent, and therefore rather unhelpful, whereas the same attitude and behavior shown by someone else is believed to be genuine and is extremely helpful. In other words, it may not be the behavior or attitude itself, but the combination of a particular person and a particular behavior that makes for support.

Social Support as a Characteristic of the Interactional Context

Rather than characterizing individuals or their environments, support may be essentially a function of the dynamic system that encompasses both.

The more transient end of this category may be thought of as behavior in context. Situational requirements determine the supportive quality of behaviors, especially if they concern material provisions (cf. Cohen & McKay, 1984). Alternatively, a particular relationship may provide a context in which specific and otherwise trivial transactions, gestures, or utterances attain great support value, whereas others are inadmissible. Conversely, a person's reaction to receiving support may influence further provisions, either by affecting the provider's willingness, or by signaling the transition to a different stage in the sequence of support needs (Jacobson, 1986).

Social support may be intrinsically linked to the overall role relationship that exists between the provider and the recipient. The relevance of functional and narrow helping roles (e.g., therapist, nurse, priest, etc.) is obvious here, but the context of more encompassing role relationships (e.g., parent, spouse, friend) may also significantly determine the legitimacy, and hence the support value, of specific transactions or attitudes. For example, this is indicated when a close and confiding relationship with one's spouse has greater stress-protecting effects than the same relationship with a friend (cf. Brown et al., 1986), or when family and friends with seemingly similar support functions are differentially associated with health outcomes (Veiel, Brill, Haefner, & Welz, 1988). The cultural determination of the norms and expectations governing role relationships would seem to make the support value of specific supportive provisions by spouses, friends, or relatives rather culture specific. However, cultural determinants of social support have received very little research attention (Jacobson, 1986).[1]

Support may be regarded as a characteristic of the total social network that happens to include the individual in question (cf. Hall & Wellman, 1985). Thus, when "social integration," or "embeddedness" (Barrera, 1986), is regarded as a major component or aspect of support, reference is made to the position an individual occupies in a social network, which is a function of both the individual and the network.

THE PRESENT VOLUME

If social support can refer to a person, social structure, role, transaction, attitude, perception, or other state of mind, then the common feature of these structures, transactions, perceptions, and so forth, which warrants lumping them into one category, must be determined. Is it that they all tend to be related to health or, conversely, that examining their effect on health is the only way to establish their supportive character (Wilcox & Vernberg, 1985)? Such a notion is implied in much of the current empirical research in this area (e.g., House & Kahn, 1985, proposed health outcomes as a criterion for validating measurement instruments). However, from a research point of view this is not sufficient. Whenever the health effects of support are the topic of interest it leads into logical circles and becomes patently unsuitable for causal investigations.

The apparent heuristic usefulness of defining "social support" by its effect on health does not relieve the researcher from the obligation to specify what social support means in the context of his or her research, and to connect it to the wider "nomological networks" (Cronbach & Meehl, 1955) of psychological and sociological knowledge. This suggests the question: What distinguishes a "supportive" transaction from just any transaction, or a "supportive" person or relationship from other persons and relationships? What, in other words, makes support supportive?

The present volume addresses these issues by discussing a number of basic aspects of support research.

Part I addresses the phenomenological and conceptual context of social support. Argyle (Chapter 2) examines supportive transactions within a variety of interpersonal relationships, which are primarily defined by social roles. Laireiter and Baumann (Chapter 3) explore the conceptual space spanned by the related concepts of social support, social networks, and social integration, which is also discussed in Chapter 4 (Thoits).

In Part II, Schwarzer and Leppin (Chapter 5) summarize the evidence regarding the association of social support with mortality and physical illnesses, and Henderson (Chapter 6) does the same with respect to depression. Although, as these authors show, the presence of such associations can hardly be doubted in either

[1]Social roles shape specific interpersonal relationships, which in turn determine the significance of particular transactions. Speaking of the roles, rather than of specific interpersonal relationships as determinants of support, shifts the perspective of the observer but does not change the phenomenon in question.

case, they seem to be considerably stronger with regard to depression. Monroe and Johnson (Chapter 7) discuss the problems that arise when empirical associations between mental health and social support are to be interpreted in terms of causal effects.

As mentioned earlier, social support research is greatly in need of integrative theoretical perspectives. Such perspectives are most readily available in the area of stress research and are presented in Part III. Chapters 8 (Cohen) and 9 (Hobfoll, Lilly, & Jackson) represent two different ways of integrating the stress and support concepts. They demonstrate that dynamic models of support processes can be formulated that at the same time are elaborate and empirically testable. On the other hand, Sarason, Sarason, and Pierce (Chapter 10) stress the necessity of linking support research more closely to experimental personality research, both methodologically and conceptually.

The very notion of social support implies a positive experience. Part IV examines the opposite, namely nonsupportive and plainly destructive interactions. Rook (Chapter 11) reviews the considerable evidence regarding the effects of negative interpersonal experiences on health and demonstrates the importance of such a complementary perspective when discussing social support. Harris (Chapter 12) examines the circumstances under which usually supportive transactions fail to have the intended effect.

As necessary as theoretical elaborations of the support concept are, they have to be translated into empirical research to be useful. Part V addresses methodological questions that arise when differentiated hypotheses about support are empirically examined. Vaux (Chapter 13) examines the assessment options currently available, and Turner (Chapter 14) presents in detail two methods for subjectively assessing perceived support. In contrast, Brown (Chapter 15) argues for investigator-based assessment strategies designed to avoid the respondents' subjective biases. Critical design and analytical issues are discussed by Kessler (Chapter 16) and Veiel (Chapter 17).

In Part VI, Gottlieb (Chapter 18) deals with the problems posed by the application of the support concept and related findings to intervention.

Although it may seem preposterous to attempt to integrate the mainly conceptual and empirical layers of social support research in a single chapter, there are a number of basic themes underlying many of the problems discussed in Chapters 2 through 18. These are summarized and discussed in our final chapter in Part VII by Veiel and Baumann (Chapter 19).

The reader will find more questions posed than answered in this volume. However, their formulation, clarification, and discussion are necessary for the further development of the field.

REFERENCES

Barrera, M. (1986). Distinctions between social support concepts, measures, and models. *American Journal of Community Psychology, 14,* 413–445.

Barrera, M., Sandler, I. N., & Ramsey, T. B. (1981). Preliminary development of a scale of social support: Studies on college students. *American Journal of Community Psychology, 9,* 435–447.

Baumann, U. (Ed.). (1987). Soziales Netzwerk, Soziale Unterstützung (Special Issue). *Zeitschrift für Klinische Psychologie, 16* (4).

Bowlby, J. (1969). *Attachment and loss.* Volume I: Attachment. London: Hogarth Press.

Brown, G. W., Andrews, B., Harris, T., Adler, Z., & Bridge, L. (1986). Social support, self-esteem and depression. *Psychological Medicine, 16,* 813-831.

Cobb, S. (1976). Social support as a moderator of life-stress. *Psychosomatic Medicine, 38,* 300–314.

Cohen, S., & McKay, G. (1984). Social support, stress and the buffering hypothesis: A theoretical analysis. In A. Baum & S. E. Taylor (Eds.), *Handbook of psychology and health.* Hillsdale, NJ: Lawrence Erlbaum.

Cohen, S., & Syme, S. L. (1985). Issues in the study and application of social support. In S. Cohen & S. L. Syme (Eds.), *Social support and health.* Orlando, FL: Academic Press.

Cronbach, L. J., & Meehl, P. E. (1955). Construct validity in psychological tests. *Psychological Bulletin, 52,* 281-302.

Dohrenwend, B. S., Dohrenwend, B. P., Dodson, M., & Shrout, P. E. (1984). Symptoms, hassles, social supports, and life events: Problems of confounded measures. *Journal of Abnormal Psychology, 93,* 222–230.

Gore, S. (1978). The effect of social support in moderating the health consequences of unemployment. *Journal of Health and Social Behavior, 19,* 157–165.

Gottlieb, B. H. (1985a). Social support and the study of personal relationships. *Journal of Social and Personal Relationships, 2,* 351–375.

Gottlieb, B. H. (1985b). Social support and community mental health. In S. Cohen & S. L. Syme (Eds.), *Social support and health.* Orlando, FL: Academic Press.

Hall, A., & Wellman, B. (1985). Social networks and social support. In S. Cohen & S. L. Syme (Eds.), *Social support and health.* Orlando, FL: Academic Press.

Henderson, S., Byrne, D. G., & Duncan-Jones, P. (1981). *Neurosis and the social environment.* Sydney: Academic Press.

Hobfoll, S. E. (1988). *The ecology of stress.* New York: Hemisphere.

House, J. S. (1981). *Work stress and social support.* Reading, MA: Addison-Wesley.

House, J. S., & Kahn, R. L. (1985). Measures and concepts of social support. In S. Cohen & S. L. Syme (Eds.), *Social support and health.* Orlando, FL: Academic Press.

Jacobson, D. E. (1986). Types and timing of social support. *Journal of Health and Social Behavior, 27,* 250–264.

Kaplan, B. H., Cassel, J. C., & Gore, S. (1977). Social support and health. *Medical Care, 15,* 47–58.

Kiesler, C. A. (1985). Policy implications of research on social support and health. In S. Cohen & S. L. Syme (Eds.), *Social support and health.* Orlando, FL: Academic Press.

Lazarus, R. S., DeLongis, A., Folkman, S., & Gruen, R. (1985). Stress and adaptional outcomes. The problem of confounded measures. *American Psychologist, 7,* 770–779.

Lieberman, M. A. (1986). Social supports—The consequences of psychologizing: A commentary. *Journal of Consulting and Clinical Psychology, 54,* 461–465.

Lowenthal, M. F., & Haven, C. (1968). Interaction and adaptation: Intimacy as a critical variable. *American Sociological Review, 33,* 20–30.

Nuckolls, K. B., Cassel, J., & Kaplan, B. H. (1972). Psychosocial assets, life crisis and the prognosis of pregnancy. *American Journal of Epidemiology, 95,* 431–441.

Pearlin, L. I. (1985). Social structure and processes of social support. In S. Cohen & S. L. Syme (Eds.), *Social support and health.* Orlando, FL: Academic Press.

Perrez, M., & Reicherts, M. (1989). Belastungsverarbeitung: Computerunterstuetzte selbstbeobachtung im feld. *Zeitschrift fuer Differentielle und Diagnostische Psychologie, 10,* 129–139.

Rychlak, J. F. (1973). *Introduction to personality and psychotherapy.* Boston: Houghton Mifflin.

Sarason, B. R., Sarason, I. G., & Pierce, G. R. (1990). Traditional views of social support and their impact on assessment. In B. R. Sarason & I. G. Sarason (Eds.), *Social support: An interactional view.* New York: Wiley.

Sarason, I. G., & Sarason, B. R. (1982). Concomitants of social support: Attitudes, personality characteristics, and life experience. *Journal of Personality, 50,* 331–344.

Selye, H. (1950). *Stress.* Montreal: Acta.

Truax, C. B., & Carkhuff, R. R. (1967). *Toward effective counseling and psychotherapy: Training and practice.* Chicago: Aldine.

Turner, R. J., Frankel, B. G., & Levin, D. M. (1983). Social support: Conceptualization, measurement, and implications for mental health. *Research in Community and Mental Health, 3,* 67–111.

Vaux, A., Phillips, J., Holly, L., Thomson, B., Williams, D., & Stewart, D. (1986). The Social Support Appraisals (SS-A) scale: Studies of reliability and validity. *American Journal of Community Psychology, 14,* 195–218.

Vaux, A., Riedel, S., & Stewart, D. (1987). Modes of social support: The Social Support Behaviors (SS-B) scale. *American Journal of Community Psychology, 15,* 209–237.

Veiel, H. O. F., Brill, G., Häfner, H., & Welz, R. (1988). The social supports of suicide attempters: The different roles of family and of friends. *American Journal of Community Psychology, 16,* 839–861.

Weiss, R. S. (1974). The provisions of social relationships. In Z. Rubin (Ed.), *Doing unto others.* Englewood Cliffs, NJ: Prentice-Hall.

Wellman, B. (1981). Applying network analysis to the study of support. In B. H. Gottlieb (Ed.), *Social networks and social support.* Beverly Hills: Sage Publications.

Wethington, E., & Kessler, R. C. (1986). Perceived support, received support, and adjustment to stressful life events. *Journal of Health and Social Behavior, 27,* 78–89.

Wilcox, B. L., & Vernberg, E. M. (1985). Conceptual and theoretical dilemmas facing social support research. In I. G. Sarason & B. R. Sarason (Eds.), *Social support: Theory, research, and application.* The Hague: Martinus Nijhoff.

Wolff, H. G. (1953). *Stress and disease.* Springfield, IL: Thomas.

I

SUPPORT AND NETWORK CONCEPTS IN CONTEXT

2

Benefits Produced by Supportive Social Relationships

Michael Argyle
Oxford University, United Kingdom

The most important thing about relationships is that they are good for us. Berkman and Syme (1979) showed the benefits of social support for health and mortality, and this was confirmed by many later studies, as the meta-analysis by Schwarzer and Leppin (1989; Chapter 5) shows. Brown and Harris (1978) found intimate relationships to have a powerful buffering effect on depression, and the mental health benefits of close relationships have also been widely replicated. Many studies have shown that friendships and other relationships are important for happiness (Argyle, 1987). But what are the psychological processes that are responsible for these effects?

Different relationships work in different ways. For example, close relationships have a buffering effect, but networks of friends have a main effect—that is, they work whether stress is present or not (Cohen & Wills, 1985). To explain such differences we need to draw on research about the nature of different relationships. This chapter looks at three of the main ones—marriage, friendship, and work relations. We found considerable differences between relationships. Figure 1 shows a cluster analysis of relationships in terms of the rules that are thought to apply. There are two main clusters: in the intimate cluster, there are rules for keeping intimacy; in the other cluster, there are rules for avoiding it—that is, some of the opposite rules apply. Figure 1 shows the relationships that were most similar to each other, in that the same rules were thought to apply.

Some people benefit much less than others from social support. To explain this phenomenon we must draw on research about individual differences in personality and social skills.

THE EVOLUTIONARY AND HISTORICAL BASIS OF RELATIONSHIPS

Animals have complex sets of relationships, which are mainly unlearned. An important evolutionary model here is Hamilton's (1964) "inclusive fitness" theory, which states that the fundamental biological urge is for the welfare of genes, not individuals. This is supported by studies of a number of species, which found that help and cooperation between animals is proportional to the degree of genetic resemblance and can also explain other aspects of animal relationships. However, there is also help and cooperation between nonrelations, so a second evolutionary principle is needed. For example, pairs of mice lick and groom each others' heads, which are out of the owner's reach. It has been suggested that the inheritance of reciprocal altruism can explain such relationships (Trivers, 1971).

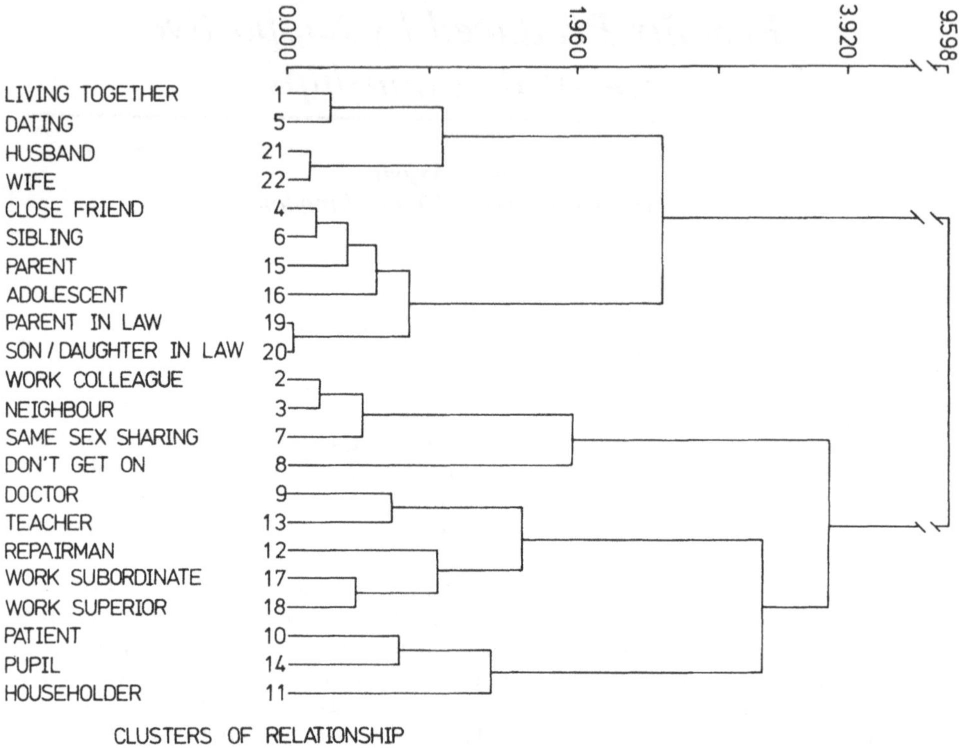

Figure 1 Clusters of relationships that have similar rules. (From Argyle, Henderson, & Furnham, 1985; reprinted with permission.)

It is not generally agreed how far such principles of sociobiology apply to humans, but there is evidence that they do apply. For example, human infants are able to interact and communicate at a very early age. Trevarthen (1980) found that 8-week-old infants could interact with their mothers over Closed Circuit Television (C.C.T.V.), and were frustrated by just seeing old tapes, which did not allow any interaction. It appears that this relationship does not have to be learned. Daly and Wilson (1988) found that there is very little neglect or abuse of biological children, but rather of step or adopted children. I shall use another evolutionary principle later to explain some of the findings; in short, where there is an important long-term goal, immediate rewards develop to reward and motivate individuals accordingly. An example is sex: the long-term goal of continuing the species is motivated by the joys of sex.

The same set of social relationships is found in all human societies—different family relationships, friendships, work relationships. However, these relationships take different forms in different cultures and historical periods. For example, work relationships were totally different in the Roman empire, the feudal system, and the Industrial Revolution compared with modern relationships. All had work groups with supervisors, but the relationships involved were quite different (Argyle, 1989). Some cultures are more cooperative, or collectivist, and provide more social support within the immediate group of family and friends than is found in Europe or North America (Triandis et al., 1988). We found that relationship rules in Japan and Hong Kong place much more emphasis on harmony in groups and obedience in hierarchies (Argyle et al., 1986) than in the West. Children are socialized into local types of relationships—an example being the Russian collective boarding schools described by Bronfenbrenner (1970).

MARRIAGE

Health

Marriage is good for physical health. Happy marriages are better still, but just being married makes a big difference. Married people have lower rates of heart attacks, strokes, lung cancer, tuberculosis, and cirrhosis. What is the explanation? First, spouses look after each other, including when they have serious illnesses like strokes and cancer. Spouses help with the treatment and make it more likely that the doctor's instructions will be carried out. Second, married people display better health behavior—less drink, drugs, smoking, and risky behavior, and better diet (Feist & Brannon, 1988). Third, the immune systems of the married are more active, especially for the happily married, compared with the divorced, single, and lonely, even when health behavior is held constant.

Mental Health

Marriage has a powerful effect on mental health. The number of married people who become mental hospital inmates in England per annum is 260 per 100,000, compared with 770 for the single, 980 for the widowed, and 1,437 for the divorced (Cochrane, 1988). Again, the marriage doesn't have to be happy; just being married helps. The quality of marriage is also important—having what is experienced as an intimate relationship with someone who "you can talk to about yourself and your problems." Brown and Harris (1978) found having such a confidant to have a strong buffering effect. For women who had experienced stressful life events, 41% were depressed if they did not have close social support at home, 10% if they did (Brown & Harris, 1978).

In the presence of serious stress, an intimate relationship inhibits or prevents the onset of depression or other mental disorders. Why is the buffering effect particularly a result of this kind of relationship? When people are in real trouble, with serious illness, money, or the law, they need real help, and usually it is only families that are prepared to offer this. When a person is in serious emotional trouble, he or she turns to family to confide problems. Another theory is that simply being loved is key, derived from the early and innate dependence of infants on their mothers' love and protection. In both cases, there is attachment or bonding; if the relationship is broken, great distress results.

Happiness

Married people are also happier. Veroff, Douva, and Kulka (1981) found that 41.5% of married women (35% of men) said that they were "very happy," compared with 25.5% single women (18.5% of men) and 15.5% divorced women

(18.5% of men). We carried out a factor analysis of 15 kinds of satisfaction in relationships and found three factors—instrumental help, emotional support, and companionship in shared interests and activities. The spouse was the greatest source of satisfaction for all three (Argyle & Furnham, 1983) (Figure 2).

Factor I here corresponds to instrumental help, Factor II to emotional support, and Factor III to companionship. Emotional support can be seen as one of three components of social support. The spouse is particularly strong as a source of instrumental satisfaction, as was also found by Rook (1987).

We can take the explanation of the benefits of marriage further by considering the nature of the family. The family is universal to all human societies. The distinctive characteristic of family life, I suggest, is cooperation over intimate domestic activities—over the basic biological processes of procreation and childrearing, eating, and mutual care, and with strong attachments to other members. The widespread phenomenon of mutual help in families and between kin is usually explained by the "inclusive fitness" theory.

Cooperation is needed for the production and rearing of children. Mothers feed babies, and families share food, home, and property. All these forms of cooperation are essential for long-term goals, such as continuing the species and maintaining health. Cooperation is also reinforced by more immediate rewards, such as sex, and various other forms of satisfaction from family life. It is not surprising that the spouse is the greatest source of satisfaction, compared with all other relationships.

The cooperative family system can be seen in characteristic marital activities, which are shown in Table 1. The data here show that distinctive marital activities consist of cooperation over intimate domestic affairs. Another is sex, which was not asked about in this study. Family relationships are intimate and major sources of emotional support.

Family life is not easy, however, and there are often conflicts that arise from the need to agree and coordinate over many issues. The solution is to follow the rules for family life, which are rather different from those for friends (Argyle & Henderson, 1985). Also, some special social skills are needed, and these are often incorporated in marital therapy—skills such as being rewarding and being able to negotiate and compromise when there is disagreement.

FRIENDSHIP

Health

Friends are less important than family and do not help much with serious illness, but do have some effect on health, as the Schwarzer and Leppin (1989) meta-analysis found. The explanation may be found in other benefits of friendship. For example, social activities and joy strengthen the immune system, and happy people live longer (Deeg & Zonneveld, 1989).

Mental Health

A number of studies found substantial main (i.e., not buffered) effects of networks of friends and neighbors. For example, a careful study of 2,234 people in Seattle, Washington, by Williams, Ware, and Donald (1981), found substantial

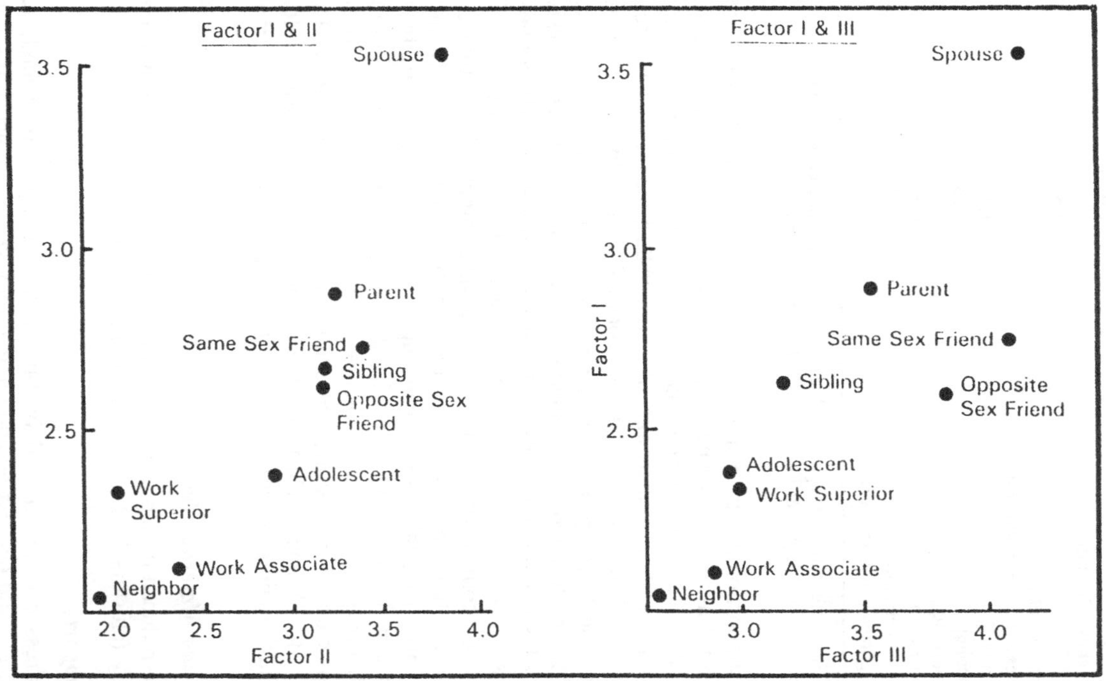

Figure 2 Relationships plotted on the satisfaction dimensions; I, instrumental satisfaction; II, emotional support; III, shared activities. (From Argyle & Furnham, 1983. Copyrighted by the National Council on Family Relations, 3989 Central Ave., NE, Suite 550, Minneapolis, MN 55421; reprinted with permission.)

Table 1 Distinctive activities shared with spouse

Spouse	
Mean ratio	1.64:1
Activities above this ratio	
Watch TV	2.61
Do domestic jobs	2.48
Play chess or other indoor games	2.31
Go for a walk	2.28
Go shopping	2.15
Play tennis, squash	2.03
Informal meal together	1.93
Intimate conversation	1.92
Have argument, disagreement	1.84

Note. These are ratios: frequency of activity with spouse/frequency in 8 relationships. (From Argyle & Furnham, 1982; reprinted with permission.)

effects of social support on mental health at all levels of stress. Another study was done by Lin, Edsel, Simeone, and Kuo (1979) of a Chinese-American community in Washington state. The benefits of social support from friends and neighbors here were as great as those from marriage, and greater than the (adverse) effects of stress. How does social support from friends work? The main focus of friendship is enjoying each other's company, in conversation and joint leisure (Argyle & Henderson, 1985). The forms of social support are shown in a cluster analysis by Wellman (1985) of support from friends, family, and neighbors. He found the following clusters: (a) information (e.g., job contacts); (b) services (e.g., minor household help); (c) companionship (e.g., discussing things, doing things together); (d) emotional (e.g., emotional support, family advice); and (e) financial.

This can help us to explain how social support from friends contributes to mental health. It can be taken together with the study by Argyle and Furnham (1983), in which three factors of satisfaction from relationships were found—instrumental help, emotional support, and shared interests and activities. These correspond closely to Wellman's clusters, except that three of his clusters refer to help. There are three main processes whereby friends produce social support (see Figure 1).

Instrumental and Material Help

Stresses can be reduced if help is given with problems—by information, domestic help, or money (clusters 1, 2, and 5 in Wellman, 1985).

Emotional Support

Emotional distress can be relieved by talking to a sympathetic friend; self-esteem can be raised, and depression and anxiety removed by an accepting confidant. Again, emotional support can be looked at as one component of social support, one of five components in this case.

However, there is a problem with "negative buffering." Nolen-Hoeksema (1987) asked subjects, "What do you do when you feel depressed?" Women were more likely than men to think about why they were depressed, talk to a friend about it, or cry, all of which would be likely to amplify their depression. Men were more likely to avoid thinking about it, or engage in vigorous exercise, which would have the effect of providing other rewards and increased feelings of control.

Ross and Mirowsky (1989) found that although social support was correlated with psychological well-being, talking to others when faced with a problem was correlated with depression, and they concluded that talking about problems makes thing worse and makes people less likely to solve their problems. This explains why women are twice as likely to be depressed as men, though they have more social support.

How should social support be given? Instrumental help is often needed, but giving it can have negative consequences, especially if the other loses autonomy (La Gaipa, 1990), is made to feel inadequate, or is unable to reciprocate. It is better if there is an ongoing relationship based on cooperation and mutual help (Argyle, 1991).

How can emotional support be given? The aforementioned results suggest that emotional support is often unsuccessful, at least in relieving depression. However, the generally positive results of psychotherapy show that some kinds of emotional support can work. Barbee (1990) found that subjects who were in a good mood were able to make considerable efforts to cheer another person up, and did so with problem-solving methods, like giving suggestions, or emotion-focused methods, like giving a hug. Burleson (1990) studied a range of comforting skills and found that those rated as most useful were "message acknowledging, elaborating, and legitimizing the feelings of distressed others."

We conducted a mood induction experiment (Figure 3), in which subjects were asked either to think by themselves about recent unhappy events, or to talk to

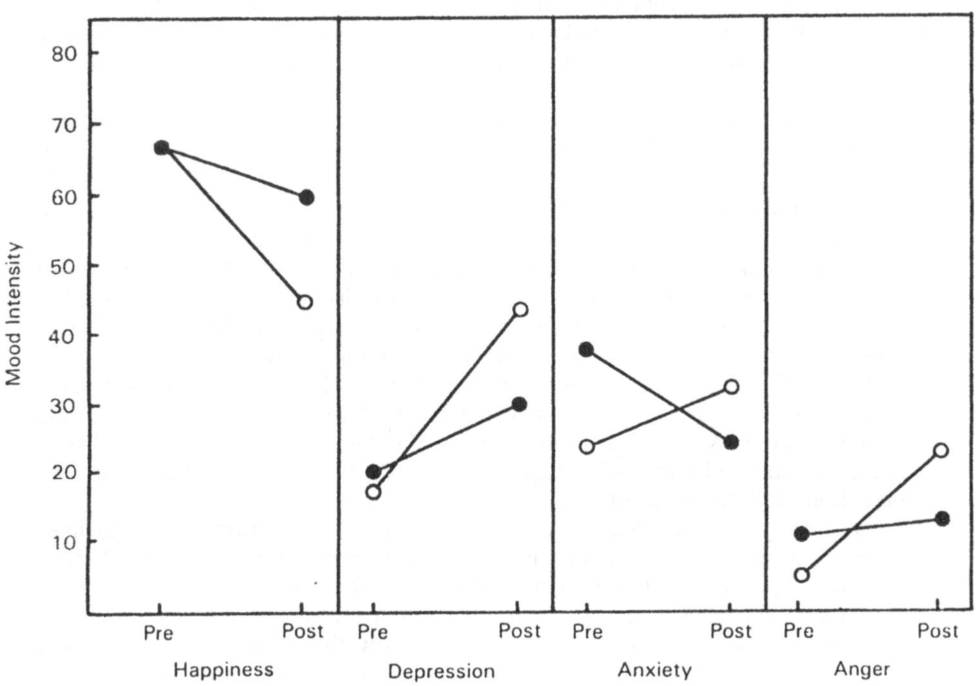

Figure 3 Mood levels for depressed induction. (From Argyle, Martin, & Crossland, 1989; reprinted with permission.) ●, social condition; ○, solitary condition.

another subject about such events. In both conditions, subjects became less happy and more depressed, but the effect was halved in the social condition. However, it was still better to do neither.

This suggests that emotional support has to be given very carefully—or not at all. What does work is constructive problem solving and integration into cheerful leisure activities, as described next.

Social Integration

Taking part in shared, cooperative leisure activities and being accepted into a social group removes loneliness, produces feelings of well-being, and strengthens social bonds.

The first factor is about help, and three of Wellman's factors were about help. However, there are grounds for thinking that other aspects of social support are even more important. Research on helping behavior finds that people often react negatively to being helped, and that cooperation produces more positive reactions (Worchel, 1979). An important part of social support is cooperating in joint activities and being embedded in the activities of a social group. Examples are dancing, music, games, and other leisure activities, and also, we shall suggest, conversation. This is supported by Rook (1987), who found that companionship had a greater effect on reducing loneliness and enhancing psychological well-being than emotional or instrumental support.

Friends affect happiness and mental health, and the processes are a little different. The most obvious effect is on positive emotion—joy. In a bleeping study, where subjects were bleeped on many random occasions to record their mood, it was found that being with friends was the most joyful, more so than being with family, or being alone. The effect was greatest for the young and the old (Larson, 1984).

Why do friends make us so cheerful? It may be because friends do enjoyable things together. Table 2 shows the results of a factor analysis of 39 leisure activities.

We report later a multiple regression analysis showing that factors 3 (teams and clubs) and 4 (parties, dances, debates) were predictors of happiness.

In earlier studies, we examined the activities that were most characteristic of friends: the ratios are frequencies of doing each activity with friends, compared to a range of relationships (Table 3). This gives some support to the hypothesis that friends enjoy each others' company because of the enjoyable activities.

What is the biological purpose of friendships? Nonhuman primates have "friends," who cooperate with gathering food, defense, finding a mate, and grooming—activities that are biologically useful but mainly offer sociability. I suggest that the biological advantages that friends provide are mutual help and cooperation, and the integration of the social group.

When we apply evolutionary ideas we see that if cooperation and social integration are a biological goal, then joy is the immediate short-term reward. It is mediated by special signals—the nonverbal signals for friendship. Eibl-Eibesfeldt (1989) argues that these signals evolved with the evolution of parental care, and were then used for friendship. Many studies show that when one person likes another he or she smiles more, looks more, moves closer, uses more head nods and other lively movements, offers an open posture, touches, and uses a special tone of voice. All of this is readily decoded as liking, and it is reciprocated

Table 2 Factor analysis on "participation" scale for 39 leisure studies

	Items	1	2	3	4	5
28	Gardening	.75				
34	Sleeping	−.72				
32	Dressmaking/knitting	.65				
7	Card games	.63				
1	Chat with friend	−.62				
16	Reading detective story	.61				
4	Country walk	.56				
31	DIY	.56				
22	Puttering about house	.52				
21	Exercise	.51				
30	Driving	.30				
9	Quiet family evening		.56			
26	Reading newspaper		.53			
35	Walking by yourself		.51			
29	Traveling		.51			
27	Reading magazines		.48			
17	Reading nonfiction		.47			
19	Pop music		.47			
18	Music (classical/jazz)		.47			
13	Soap opera		.30			
24	Film and video			.69		
36	Social club			.55		
3	Pubs			.52		
12	Other sports			.46		
11	Team sports			.44		
15	Reading novel				.65	
14	TV				.58	
2	Noisy party				−.55	
37	Long bath				.48	
10	Debates				−.47	
20	Dancing				−.46	
5	Meeting new people				−.40	
6	Party games					.68
8	Jokes/funny stories					.61
25	Cinema					.59
33	Sunbathing					.43
23	Writing letters					.31
	Reliability alpha	.80	.64	.60	.60	.57
	Variance explained	14.2	9.5	7.7	6.5	6.3

(Reprinted with permission from Argyle & Lu, 1990. The happiness of extraverts. *Personality and Individual Differences, 11,* 1014, Table 2.)

(Argyle, 1988). When engaged in leisure pursuits, these signals are frequently sent by friends, as was found by Kraut and Johnston (1979) in a study at a bowling alley; the players rarely smiled at the pins, but often smiled at each other. Being smiled at is a source of joy. Smiling also does the smiler some good, via the process of "facial feedback" (Laird, 1984).

A popular interpretation of friendship exists through reinforcement, as in exchange theory. However, there is now a lot of evidence that close friends especially are more concerned with the other's needs than with their own rewards and costs (Clark & Reis, 1988). Hays (1985) found that the best predictor of the survival of early student friendships was the sum of rewards *plus* costs. The motivation for

Table 3 Distinctive activities shared with friends

Friends, similar age	
Mean ratio	1.26:1
Activities above this ratio	
Dancing	2.00
Tennis	1.67
Sherry party	1.63
Joint leisure	1.63
Pub	1.60
Intimate conversation	1.52
Walk	1.50

(From Argyle & Furnham, 1982; reprinted with permission.)

friendship is more basic than seeking instrumental help; it is better conceptualized in McAdam's need for intimacy (1988).

Friends also exchange positive verbal signals. They take an interest in each other by asking questions, seeking things they have in common, agreeing, complimenting, using self-disclosure, using first names, making jokes, and talking about pleasant events. Conversational skills require a high degree of coordination and synchrony, including skills such as turn taking, using words that will make sense to listeners, responding to back-channel signals, following Grice's cooperative rules of relevance and helpfulness, and adhering to the rules of politeness (Argyle, 1991).

As mentioned earlier, the activities that make people happiest are various kinds of joint leisure (Tables 2 and 3). Another hypothesis is that the experience of coordination and synchrony, verbal or nonverbal, is a primitive source of joy, as well as social integration. An anthropological study of a Sudanese tribe, the Miri, found that the tribe members were very cooperative and helpful, and this appeared to be sustained by festivals of singing and dancing, in which all members of the village took part (Baumann, 1987). There is a lot of cooperation between friends; for example, most of the shared leisure activities listed earlier could not be carried out alone.

To sustain social integration and cooperation between friends, informal rules must develop. An example of such a rule is keeping to one side of the road. We found that certain rules, if broken, often lead to loss of friendship (Table 4). It is interesting that third-party rules (keeping confidences, etc.) are so important; they evidently keep social networks intact.

WORK RELATIONSHIPS

Health and Mental Health

Work relationships have often been found to buffer the effects of work stress on physical and mental health, as found by House (1981). In one study, we found that the effects of stress at work were less if people had at least one friend in the workplace (Henderson & Argyle, 1985). One way in which social support works is that stresses seem less stressful if a person knows he or she has a mate on which to rely. Brand and Hirsch (1990) found that, for married nurses on night shifts or other irregular hours, psychological well-being was very dependent on social sup-

Table 4 Friendship rules and break-up of friendships (Argyle & Henderson, 1984)

	Moderately or very important in breaking up friendship (%)	Slightly important in breaking up friendship (%)
Being jealous or critical of your other relationships	57	22
Discussing with others what was said in confidence with him or her	56	19
Not volunteering help in time of need	44	23
Not trusting or confiding in you	44	22
Criticizing you in public	44	21
Not showing positive regard for you	42	34
Not standing up for you in your absence	39	28
Not being tolerant of your other friends	38	30
Not showing emotional support	37	25
Nagging you	30	25

port at work, including support from supervisors. The nurses were not able to spend as much time with their families.

However, work is better for most people than unemployment. Banks and Jackson (1982) studied a large sample of English school drop-outs before and after they left school. Scores on the General Health Questionnaire increased for those who did not find jobs (i.e., their mental health deteriorated), but fell for those who did find jobs (Table 5).

Job Satisfaction

Some studies found that belonging to small and cohesive work groups provides an important source of job satisfaction. Other investigations found that work relationships are very superficial, and offer very minor sources of satisfaction or support. Our own study (Figure 2) is an example. However, some of these researchers used students or other people with little experience of long-term work relationships, or studied people on assembly lines (Goldthorpe, Lockwood, Berkovec, & Platt, 1968).

We thought that there would be differences between work relationships of different kinds. We compared work relationships of four levels of closeness. The closest level was of people who became friends in the usual sense (e.g., asking each other home and meeting outside work). These people helped each other a lot at work. They also engaged in a lot of nonwork activities—gossip, games, discuss-

Table 5 The effects of unemployment on the General Health Questionnaire (GHQ) (Banks & Jackson, 1982)

	Before leaving school	6–15 months after leaving school	16–23 months after leaving school
Unemployed	11.4	13.6	
	11.2		13.4
Employed	10.6	8.4	
	10.5		7.7

Table 6 Percentage of workers engaged in work and social activities more than several times a day at work

	With			
	Social friend (%)	Friend at work (%)	Work colleague (%)	Disliked colleague (%)
Helping other with work	52	32	18	8
Discussing work	49	52	32	17
Chatting casually	72	63	26	15
Joking with the other	72	54	24	13
Teasing the other person	46	32	18	20
Discussing personal life	30	19	13	11
Discussing personal feelings	26	10	5	5
Asking for or giving personal advice	33	19	8	6

(From Argyle & Henderson, 1985; reprinted with permission of William Heinemann Limited.)

ing personal life, having coffee or meals together, joking, and teasing. Then there are workmates who often get together for coffee or lunch at work but not outside; those who are often seen together at work but who do not get together for coffee; and those who one would rather not see at all. The rates of engaging in various activities with each level of workmates are shown in Table 6.

The essential feature of work relationships is that they arise out of doing work together, such as cooperating between equals and supervising. However, there is both sociability and work.

Table 6 shows that there are two main kinds of work activities—helping and cooperating with the work, and purely sociable, nonwork activities. Cooperation with work is essential for all but the smallest jobs, and is a reason that work is often done in groups. It is impossible to say how far any innate processes are involved. Ants are famous for their work; in an anthill one million ants may cooperate in elaborate ways, especially the worker ants; these are sexless females who share three quarters of their genes—a clear example of the inclusive fitness model. Coming nearer in the evolutionary scale, nonhuman primates do very little work, because food is readily available, waiting to be picked off trees, and they spend more time sleeping, grooming, and for the young, playing. In all primitive societies, even those otherwise very individualistic or competitive, there is cooperation with large tasks, like catching whales or hippos or building homes (Mead, 1937). However, this could be simply because cooperation is the universal solution to the same problems.

Let us, however, apply the evolutionary model. The biological purpose of work relationships is cooperation and help with important tasks. In cooperative groups, jobs can be done that could not be done alone; there is more help; there is division of labor so that individuals can specialize. The result is greater productivity and effectiveness (Argyle, 1991). It would be expected, from evolutionary principles, that such cooperation should be rewarding. It was found that job satisfaction is much greater for members of small, cooperative, or cohesive groups, especially when they are popular (Argyle, 1989). Job satisfaction is probably partly a result of working together in a synchronized manner. It is also generated by the social side of life at work, consisting of gossip, games, and jokes. This not only increases job satisfaction, but it also increases the bonds between people and provides the basis for cooperation and social support (Homans, 1950).

However, there is more conflict and friction at work than with friends, because it is more difficult to leave. Again, informal rules develop to encourage and enforce help and cooperation at work. Table 7 illustrates the rules we found for workmates (Argyle & Henderson, 1985).

So far we have dealt with workmates (i.e., equals). Supervisors raise another set of issues. Supervision is often seen as a difficult relationship with a lot of conflict. However, supervisors can also provide a great deal of support. They are able to solve real problems for subordinates, since they often have the power to do so. They can also be emotionally supportive; they recognize this, and may receive training in listening skills, and may have a good example from their own superiors (House, 1981). Certain supervisory styles are best for both the productivity and job satisfaction of subordinates. The use of participation and democratic persuasion methods are excellent examples of effective cooperative social styles (Argyle, 1991).

INDIVIDUAL DIFFERENCES IN ACCESS TO SOCIAL SUPPORT

There has been a lot of research on "hardiness"—the properties of personality that make individuals resistant to stress, or the reverse of vulnerability (Kobasa, 1982). This is partly because some people have more access to social support. Sarason and Sarason (1985) found that people who rated themselves low on social support also had higher scores for hostility and neuroticism and lower scores for extraversion. Type A personalities put less effort into social relationships with family and friends and have a cynical, mistrusting attitude toward others, thus producing social isolation.

Recent research on positive well-being has shown how some personalities regularly experience positive life events while others experience negative life events. Headey and Wearing (1989), in a four-phase panel study, found that extraversion predicts positive life events, especially in the spheres of friendship and work; and

Table 7 Rules for co-workers

Accept one's fair share of the work load.
Respect other's privacy.
Be cooperative with regard to shared physical working conditions (e.g., light, temperature, noise).
Be willing to help when requested.
Keep confidences.
Work cooperatively despite feelings of dislike.
Don't denigrate to superiors.
Address the co-worker by first name.
Ask for help and advice when necessary.
Look the co-worker in the eye during conversations.
Don't be overinquisitive about each others' private lives.
Repay debts, favors, and compliments no matter how small.
Don't engage in sexual activity with the co-worker.
Stand up for the co-worker in his/her absence.
Don't criticize the co-worker publicly.

(From Argyle & Henderson, 1985; reprinted with permission of William Heinemann Limited.)

neuroticism predicts negative life events, especially in the areas of work and money.

We pursued this direction of research in studying individual differences in happiness. The contribution of three aspects of personality in relation to social support will be described here.

Extraversion

We and others have found strong correlations between happiness and extraversion; this correlation was .39–.48 in our studies. What is the explanation? In this research, happiness was measured by the Oxford Happiness Inventory—a 29-item scale, modeled on the Beck Depression Inventory in reverse, with additional items—which has been found to correlate .43 with ratings by friends (Argyle, Martin, & Crossland, 1989).

Are extraverts happier because they engage in enjoyable activities more often? Using the list of activities shown in Table 2, we carried out a cross-sectional study with multiple regression, and this showed that factors 3 and 4 correlated with happiness, and partly explained the effects of extraversion. The happiness-extraversion correlation fell from .46–.25 when these two participation factors were taken into account. We concluded that extraverts are happy partly because they engage in factor 3 activities (clubs and teams) and factor 4 activities (parties and dances) (Argyle & Lu, 1990a).

Do extraverts have better social skills? A study discussed later shows that they are more assertive, and that this partly explains their happiness. Thorne (1987) conducted an experiment in which pairs of extraverts and pairs of introverts were put together. Thorne found that the extraverts talked more about pleasant events and leisure activities, agreed more, paid more compliments, and spoke less about their problems. The extraverts were rated as more cheerful, enthusiastic, outgoing, talkative, and sociable, and less shy, reserved, and serious. We replicated these findings, and confirm that extraverts seem to approach an unstructured social situation in a very positive way, as if they assume that it is going to be enjoyable, and have confidence that they can cope with it. Extraverts certainly enjoy a range of social activities more than introverts. In laboratory mood induction experiments, it was found that extraverts are made most happy by social encounters, whereas introverts prefer solitary activities, such as listening to music, reading, and thinking about recent pleasant events. If introverts and extraverts are asked to think or talk about recent enjoyable events, they choose quite different ones. As Figure 4 shows, extraverts think of social events and, to some extent, physical activities, whereas introverts think of solitary and parasocial ones.

Social Skills

Research on loneliness found that lonely people have poor social skills—they are shy, less assertive, suffer from social anxiety, have low self-esteem, have negative and distrusting attitudes about relationships, and feel alienated (Jones, 1985). We developed a social skills model, and proposed that a lack of social skills is a major factor of mental disorders, especially in neurotic disorders (Trower, Bryant, & Argyle, 1978).

As part of our extraversion research, we conducted a longitudinal study using

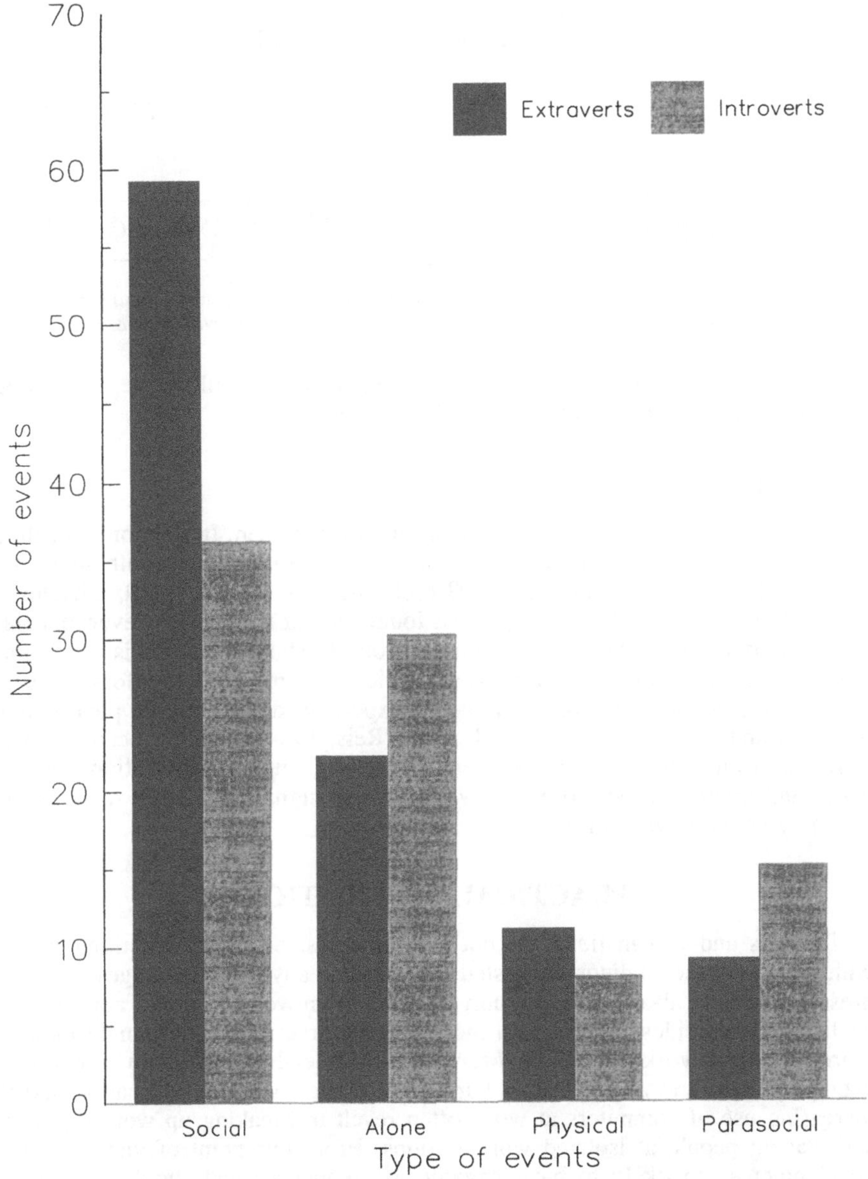

Figure 4 Recall of happy events by extraverts and introverts; all the differences are significant.

assertiveness as one of the predictors. When assertiveness was included in the regression, the happiness-extraversion correlation fell from .39–.28, showing that extraverts are happy partly because of their assertiveness (see Figure 5) (Argyle & Lu, 1990b).

We also expected that cooperative social skills are relevant to social support, for

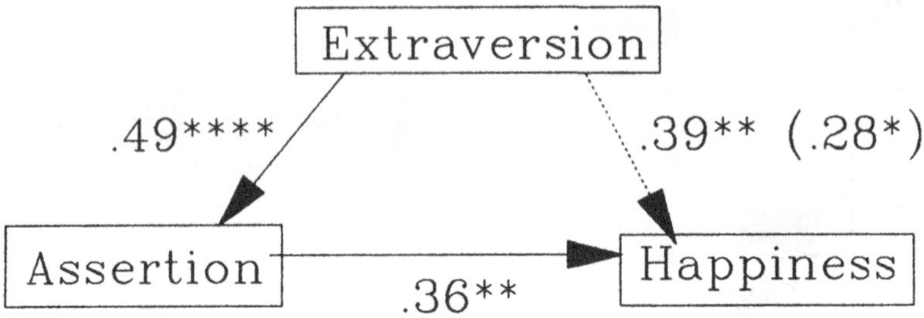

Figure 5 Assertion as a mediator of extraversion–happiness relation; the figure in brackets was the reduced coefficient when the mediator was present.

reasons explained earlier. We developed a cooperativeness skills scale, and a longitudinal study is in progress to test this hypothesis.

Women

Overall women gain more from social support than men. In relation to health, a recent meta-analysis found that for women there is a correlation with social support of .20, whereas for men it is .08 (Schwarzer & Leppin, 1989; Chapter 5). Research on mental health and happiness found similar results. However, marriage is an important exception—men gain more from it. The explanation is that women are better providers of social support, as confidants in marriage (Vanfossen, 1981), whereas interaction with women friends is experienced as higher on pleasantness, intimacy, and self-disclosure for both sexes (Reis, 1984). Female social styles are different from those of men. Women seek close, supportive relationships, are warm and trusting, send more positive nonverbal signals and other rewards, and are more cooperative than men.

PRACTICAL APPLICATIONS

Theories and explanations are not very impressive unless something is done with them. Do the findings suggested here lead to any specific suggestions? The pressing problem about social support in the modern would is that it appears to be declining on all sides. There is an increasing divorce rate, more single mothers, more women at work (though they receive more social support from work), more unemployment, and an increasing number of homeworkers. Automation and the increasing use of computers at work often result in breaking up working groups and placing people at isolated work stations. From our point of view, all these developments are likely to have negative consequences and should be opposed where possible.

Marriage

Marriage is doing very well as the major source of social support. Marital skills training is usually directed to save marriages and reduce marital conflict. There could also be marital skills training with the aim of improving the quality of marriage and increasing the level and effectiveness of social support. Because wives provide more social support than husbands (Vanfossen, 1981), such training should be directed primarily to the latter.

Friendship

Most people have friends, but there are many who are lonely and who would like more. We could help by educating them in what friendship is all about. We could tell them about the rules of friendship, which if broken often lead to loss of a friendship. Some of these rules are "keep confidences" and "don't criticize in public." Evidently, these need to be more widely known.

For those who have difficulty in finding friends, there is a simple piece of advice—join a club, class, or other leisure group in your neighborhood. This doesn't work for everyone, because not everyone has the social skills. Training for this is discussed later.

Working Arrangements

Social support from workmates is greater in small, cooperative work teams, where people both talk and work together. (Volvo's replacement of assembly lines by autonomous work teams is a good example.) Occupational psychologists should be alive to this issue and try to influence the design of working systems so that workers are not physically isolated. Supervisory training should include training in supportive skills.

Additional Sources of Social Support

Self-Help Groups

Self-help groups include organizations such as Alcoholics Anonymous. It is reported that 6 1/4 million Americans (3.7% of the adult population) belong to such groups, which now rival psychotherapy because they are less expensive (Jacobs & Goodman, 1989).

Social Workers' Groups

Groups of eight to ten members along similar lines are now being organized by social workers (Gottlieb, Chapter 18).

Provision of Companions

British social workers are providing volunteer companions, who can engage isolated clients in joint leisure activities.

The Provision of Leisure Facilities

Leisure activities, in the form of clubs, classes, sports, churches, and so forth, are a major source of social support, and an important source of happiness (Table 8). A surprising number of people belong to clubs; in a London survey, 53% belonged to clubs, and 16% were officers (Young & Wilmott, 1973). A British national survey found that many of the people who are known best come from such clubs (Table 9).

In my own college in Oxford, there are no fewer than 37 societies, all initiated,

Table 8 Predicting happiness from personality and social activities

Sources	R^2	R^2change	df	Beta	Final model
Sex	.00	.00	78	.02	
Extraversion	.19	$.19^d$	77	$.25^a$	
Factor 1 (PAR)	.23	.04	76	$.23^a$	
Factor 2 (PAR)	.23	.00	75	$-.11$	
Factor 3 (PAR)	.28	$.05^a$	74	$.22^a$	
Factor 4 (PAR)	.39	$.11^c$	73	$-.38^c$	$F = 6.64$
Factor 5 (PAR)	.39	.00	72	$-.02$	$p < .0001$

Beta values are derived from the final model whereas a particular variable was corrected by all the others entered into the equation in the order indicated in the table. (Reprinted with permission from Argyle & Lu, 1990. The happiness of extraverts. *Personality and Individual Differences, 11,* 1016, Table 5.)

$^a p < .05$
$^b p < .01$
$^c p < .001$
$^d p < .0001$

financed, and run by students. From the research that we have reported on leisure and happiness, it seems that doing enjoyable things together leads to increased happiness. These clubs usually also look after their members when they are in need or distress.

Although the growth of clubs can be spontaneous, it can be helped by environmental provision of facilities for meetings. In Britain, church halls, schools, and community centers are the usual locations.

However, there are some people who do not join the clubs. Some find that certain clubs are easier to join than others. For those still left out, there is social skills training.

Social Skills Training (SST)

SST is well established for neurotic outpatients and others, and for those training to be managers, teachers, doctors, nurses, police officers, and so forth. However, SST is not readily available for other people—those who are isolated or lonely and not receiving any social support but who are not patients. How could they be trained to establish and maintain supportive relationships? Some of the skills that might be incorporated have been offered here: extraversion, assertiveness, cooperativeness, and conversational skills (Argyle & Henderson, 1985).

Table 9 Percentage of people "known best" in Britain coming from clubs

	Men	Women
People at local pub or club	23	10
Members of church	7	12
Members of sporting club	11	5
Members of club associated with hobby or interest	10	7
Members of a voluntary association	2	3

REFERENCES

Argyle, M. (1987). *The psychology of happiness.* London: Methuen.

Argyle, M. (1988). *Bodily communication* (2nd ed.). London: Metheun.

Argyle, M. (1989). *The social psychology of work* (2nd ed.). Harmondsworth: Penguin.

Argyle, M. (1991). *Cooperation: The basis of sociability.* London: Routledge.

Argyle, M., & Furnham, A. (1982). The ecology of relationships: Choice of situation as a function of relationship. *British Journal of Social Psychology, 21,* 259–262.

Argyle, M., & Furnham, A. (1983). Sources of satisfaction and conflict in long-term relationships. *Journal of Marriage and the Family, 45,* 481–493.

Argyle, M., & Henderson, M. (1984). The rules of friendship. *Journal of Social and Personal Relationships, 1,* 211–237.

Argyle, M., & Henderson, M. (1985). *The anatomy of relationships.* London: Heinemann and Harmondsworth: Penguin.

Argyle, M., Henderson, M., Bond, M., Contarello, A., & Iizuka, Y. (1986). Cross-cultural variations in relationship rules. *International Journal of Psychology, 21,* 287–315.

Argyle, M., Henderson, M., & Furnham, A. (1985). The rules of social relationships. *British Journal of Social Psychology, 24,* 125–139.

Argyle, M., & Lu, L. (1990a). The happiness of extraverts. *Personality and Individual Differences, 11,* 1011–1017.

Argyle, M., & Lu, L. (1990b). Happiness and social skills. *Personality and Individual Differences, 11,* 1255–1261.

Argyle, M., Martin, M., & Crossland, J. (1989). Happiness as a function of personality and social encounters. In J. P. Forgas & J. M. Innes (Eds.), *Recent advances in social psychology: An international perspective.* North Holland: Elsevier.

Banks, M. H., & Jackson, P. R. (1982). Unemployment and risk of minor psychiatric disorder in young people: Cross sectional and longitudinal evidence. *Psychological Medicine, 12,* 789–798.

Barbee, A. P. (1990). Interaction coping: The cheering-up process in close relationships. In S. Duck (Ed.) *Personal relationships and social support.* London: Sage.

Baumann, G. (1987). *National integration and local integrity.* Oxford: Clarendon Press.

Berkman, L. F., & Syme, S. L. (1979). Social networks, host resistance, and mortality: A nine year follow-up study of Alameda county residents. *American Journal of Epidemiology, 109,* 186–204.

Brand, S., & Hirsch, B. J. (1990). The contribution of social networks, work-shift schedules, and the family life cycle to women's well-being. In S. Duck (Ed.), *Personal relationships and social support.* London: Sage.

Bronfenbrenner, U. (1970). *Two worlds of childhood.* New York: Sage.

Brown, G. W., & Harris, T. (1978). *Social origins of depression.* London: Tavistock.

Burleson, B. R. (1990). Comforting as social support: Relational consequences of supportive behaviors. In S. Duck (Ed.), *Personal relationships and social support.* London: Sage.

Clark, M. S., & Reis, H. T. (1988). Interpersonal processes of close relationships. *Annual Review of Psychology, 39,* 609–672.

Cochrane, R. (1988). Marriage, separation and divorce. In S. Fisher & J. Reason (Eds.), *Handbook of life stress, cognition and health.* Chichester: Wiley.

Cohen, S., & Wills, T. A. (1985). Stress, social support, and the buffering hypothesis. *Psychological Bulletin, 98,* 310–357.

Daly, M., & Wilson, M. (1988). Evolutionary social psychology and family homicide. *Science, 242,* 519–524.

Deeg, D., & van Zonneveld, R. (1989). Does happiness lengthen life? In R. Veenhoven (Ed.), *How harmful is happiness?* Rotterdam: Universitaire Press.

Eibl-Eibesfeldt, I. (1989). *Human ethology.* New York: Aldine de Gruyter.

Feist, J., & Brannon, L. (1988). *Health psychology.* Belmont, CA: Wadsworth.

Goldthorpe, J. H., Lockwood, D., Berkovec, F., & Platt, J. (1968). *The affluent worker: Industrial attitudes and behavior.* Cambridge: Cambridge University Press.

Hamilton, W. D. (1964). The evolution of social behavior. *Journal of Theoretical Biology, 7,* 1–52.

Hays, R. B. (1985). A longitudinal study of friendship development. *Journal of Personality and Social Psychology, 48,* 909–924.

Headey, B., & Wearing, A. (1989). Personality, life events, and subjective well-being: Toward a dynamic equilibrium model. *Journal of Personality and Social Psychology, 57,* 731–739.

Henderson, M., & Argyle, M. (1985). Social support by four categories of work colleagues: Relationships between activities, stress and satisfaction. *Journal of Occupational Behavior, 6,* 229–239.
Homans, G. C. (1950). *The human group.* London: Routledge and Kegan Paul.
House, J. S. (1981). *Work Stress and Social Support.* Reading, MA: Addison-Wesley.
Jacobs, M. K., & Goodman, G. (1989). Psychology and self-help groups. *American Psychologist, 44,* 536–545.
Jones, W. H. (1985). The psychology of loneliness: Some personality issues in the study of social support. In I. G. Sarason & B. R. Sarason (Eds.), *Social Support: Theory, research and application.* Dordrecht: Nijhoff.
Kobasa, S. C. (1982). The hardy personality: Toward a social psychology of stress and health. In G. S. Sanders & J. Suls (Eds.), *Social psychology of health and illness.* Hillsdale, NJ: Erlbaum.
Kraut, R. E., & Johnston, R. E. (1979). Social and emotional messages of smiling: An ethological approach. *Journal of Personality and Social Psychology, 37,* 1539–1553.
La Gaipa, J. (1990). The negative effects of informal support systems. In S. Duck (Ed.), *Personal relationships and social support.* London: Sage.
Laird, J. D. (1984). The real role of facial response in the experience of emotion: A reply to Tourangeau and Ellsworth, and others. *Journal of Personality and Social Psychology, 47,* 909–917.
Larson, R. W. (1984). States of consciousness in personal relationships: A life span perspective. Paper at International Conference on Personal Relationships, Madison.
Lin, N., Edsel, W. M., Simeone, R. S., & Kuo, W. (1979). Social support, stressful life events, and illness: A model and empirical test. *Journal of Health and Social Behavior, 20,* 108–119.
McAdams, D. P. (1988). Personal needs and personal relationships. In S. Duck (Ed.), *Handbook of personal relationships.* Chichester: Wiley.
Mead, M. (Ed.). (1937). *Cooperation and competition among primitive peoples.* New York: McGraw-Hill.
Nolen-Hoeksema, S. (1987). Sex differences in unipolar depression: Evidence and theory. *Psychological Bulletin, 101,* 259–282.
Reis, H. T. (1984). Social interaction and well-being. In S. Duck (Ed.), *Personal relationships, 5: Repairing personal relationships.* London: Academic Press.
Rook, K. S. (1987). Social support versus companionship: Effects on life stress, loneliness, and evaluations by others. *Journal of Personality and Social Psychology, 52,* 1132–1147.
Ross, L. E., & Mirowsky, J. (1989). Explaining the social patterns of depression: Control and problem-solving—or support and talking. *Journal of Health and Social Behavior, 30,* 206–219.
Sarason, I. G., & Sarason, B. R. (Eds.). (1985). *Social support: Theory, research and applications.* Dordrecht: Nijhoff.
Schwarzer, R., & Leppin, A. (1989). Social support and health: A meta-analysis. *Psychology and Health, 3,* 1–15.
Thorne, A. (1987). The press of personality: A study of conversation between introverts and extraverts. *Journal of Personality and Social Psychology, 53,* 718–726.
Trevarthen, C. (1980). The foundations of intersubjectivity: Development of interpersonal and cooperative understanding in infants. In D. R. Olson (Ed.), *The social foundations of language and thought.* New York: Norton.
Triandis, H., Bontempo, R., Villareal, M. J., Asia, M., & Lucca, N. (1988). Individualism and collectivism: Cross-cultural perspectives on self-group relationships. *Journal of Personality and Social Psychology, 54,* 323–328.
Trivers, R. L. (1971). The evolution of reciprocal altruism. *Quarterly Review of Biology, 46,* 35–57.
Trower, P., Bryant, B., & Argyle, M. (1978). *Social skills and mental health.* London: Methuen.
Vanfossen, B. E. (1981). Sex differences in the mental health effects of spouse support. *Journal of Health and Social Behavior, 22,* 130–143.
Veroff, J., Douva, E., & Kulka, R. A. (1981). *The inner American.* New York: Basic Books.
Wellman, B. (1985). From social support to social network. In I. G. Sarason & B. R. Sarason (Eds.), *Social support: Theory, research and applications.* Dordrecht: Nijhoff.
Williams, A. W., Ware, J. E., & Donald, C. A. (1981). A model of mental health life events, and social supports applicable to general population. *Journal of Health and Social Behaviour, 22,* 324–336.
Worchel, S. (1979). Cooperation and the reduction of intergroup conflict: Some determining factors. In W. G. Austin & S. Worchel (Eds.), *The social psychology of intergroup relations.* Monterey, CA: Brooks/Cole.
Young, M., & Wilmott, P. (1973). *The symmetrical family.* London: Routledge and Kegan Paul.

3

Network Structures and Support Functions—Theoretical and Empirical Analyses

Anton Laireiter and Urs Baumann
Universität Salzburg, Austria

Since the early 1960s, clinical researchers have developed a strong interest in social variables, especially in their function as etiological agents. The best examples are constructs like "social integration," "social assets," "social resources," "social adjustment," "social isolation," and "social alienation" (Laireiter & Baumann, 1988). Most of these constructs refer to having or not having social ties. Since the mid-1970s, research has concentrated on two major social variables: "social networks" and "social support." Despite much research in these areas, many important questions remain unanswered, especially those concerning precise terminology (see Vaux, Chapter 14), theoretical foundation, and, most importantly, the relationship between them.

This chapter examines the relationship between the two constructs through theoretical and empirical perspectives. The relationship between two constructs can also be determined by definition and through methodological confounding. Therefore, it is also necessary to perform conceptual and methodological analyses. These analyses consider all constructs elaborated on within the broader terms of "social networks" and "social support." The theoretical and empirical analyses concentrate on the association between network roles (kind of relationship—e.g., friend, neighbor, etc.) and network resources, supportive climates, and received and perceived social support. These are the main concepts elaborated on within this field of research. The major reason for the limitation of our paper on network roles and network resources is that research has not elaborated on the theoretical and the empirical relations between these constructs. Additionally, knowledge about the relation between network structures and support functions is very important for theory construction as well as practical applications in the current stage of research (Blöschel, 1987), especially for network interventions (Gottlieb, Chapter 18).

Preparation of this chapter and the studies reported within was supported partially by the "Fonds zur Förderung der wissenschaftlichen Forschung," Vienna, Austria. Grant nos. P5676, P5676S, and P6378S, dedicated to the second author. We would like to thank Elisabeth Reisenzein and Beth Chandler for translating this chapter into English.

CONCEPTUAL ANALYSES

Conceptual analyses need preparatory work because there is no consensus on the definition of social support (Veiel, 1987). A variety of components of social support are discussed, such as "network resources," "perceived support," "support appraisal," "received support," and so forth (Barrera, 1986; Vaux, 1988; Veiel, 1987). With these problems in mind, various authors attempted to precisely define the term "social support" by differentiating construct components (cf. Barrera, 1986; Sarason, Sarason, & Pierce, 1990; Veiel, 1987).

On the basis of the literature and our own conceptual considerations, only a multidimensional taxonomy seems adequate for solving the conceptual problems of social support. Such a taxonomy should comprise at least five components: (a) social integration (social embeddedness); (b) potential and actual supporters (support network, network resources); (c) support as a characteristic of the climate of social aggregates and social environments (supportive climate, supportive environment); (d) received and enacted support; and (e) the perception of being supported. The relationship between social network and social support must be formed, with consideration given to the aforementioned components.

Social Integration/Social Embeddedness

The construct of social integration refers to the "participation and involvement of a person in his or her social life in the community and in society. It also examines the goods and values of the community and society, as well as access to resources and support systems" (Laireiter & Baumann, 1988, p. 199). Criteria for defining a person's social integration inter alia are: "being in regular contact with neighbors," "having friends or relatives in the neighborhood," "memberships in social groups," "having good friends," "perceiving and/or receiving help and support from family and neighbors," and so forth (Table 1). It is important to stress that not every definition nor every method of measuring a person's integration considers all of these criteria. Some definitions and measures are rather complex, whereas others are simple. The construct is very complex. This complexity, combined with the different criteria used to define it, could cause the concepts of social integration, social networks, network resources, supportive climates, and perceived and received support to overlap with one another.

Social Network

The term "network" is used as a metaphor to describe points and their mutual ties. From both a social- and a clinical-psychological perspective, the term describes people and their relationships with each other (Boissevain, 1977). It is best understood as a highly differentiated and complex system of interpersonal relationships.

Conceptually, the network concept covers various structures, interactional features, and functions. For a first step, however, it is important to differentiate total and partial networks from each other (Boissevain, 1977). Total networks refer to social aggregations as a whole, and partial networks describe parts of aggregations—especially networks of singular individuals (person or egocentered networks; Boissevain, 1977).

Table 1 Empirical criteria for measurement of social networks and social support

Social integration (social embeddedness)
Marital status
Membership in clubs, associations, churches, and so forth
Church attendance and religious activities
Neighborhood contacts and interaction
Living conditions (alone, with partner, with family)
Length of stay in a certain area
Network characteristics (number of friends, relatives, co-workers, children, etc.)
Number of good friends, relatives, and acquaintances in the neighborhood
Social support resources (number of potentially supporting people, in general; in the neighborhood)
Frequency of contact with friends, relatives, and neighbors
Amount of support perceived and received (in general, from neighbors, and relatives)
Acceptance of social norms and values
Social network
Marital status
Family members and relatives
People with special social roles: neighbors, workmates, supervisors, club or leisure-time acquaintances, professional helpers, and so forth
People known by ego (superficial contacts)
People of emotional significance (friends, good friends, best friends, significant others, confidants)
People of negative emotional significance (conflictful relationships, ambivalent, etc.)
Social network resources (support network)
People, potentially supporting
People, actually supporting
People of emotional significance (significant others)
Social integration
Supportive climate (supportive environments)
Relationship cohesion, supportive attitudes
Involvement
Conflict (negative)
Perceived support in that area
Perceived support (cognition)
General perception of support
Specific perception of support from friends, partner, relatives, and so forth
Perceived support (evaluation)
Generalized evaluation of support (adequacy, satisfaction, need, etc.)
Specific evaluation of persons (friends) and received support
Enacted/received support
Amount of supportive behaviors received during a certain period of time (unspecific)
Amount of supportive behaviors received during a special situation or crisis
Supportive behaviors, received from certain persons (supporters) in everyday life or during a crisis or stressful episode

The structure of a network is categorized by various parameters such as size, density, number of clusters, centrality, and so forth (Hall & Wellman, 1985). Interactional parameters describe the singular relationship between "ego" and the members of its network (e.g., frequency of contact, multiplexity, reciprocity, emotional closeness, and kind of relationship). The concept of emotional closeness differentiates various zones (personal, intimate, effective, nominal, and causal zone; see Pattison & Pattison, 1981). Social networks have a variety of functions (e.g., contact, development of identity, regulation and control of behavior, distress, burden, etc.). One main function is to provide social support. It is important to emphasize this point because the term social support is often considered synonymous with social network. This is incorrect. The term "social network" describes the structure of social relationships, whereas the term "social support" describes specific functions of a network.

Network Resources/Support Network

To define a person's support network, one must examine a person's potential or actual supporters. These are also defined as "network resources" (Vaux, 1988). According to Vaux (1988, p. 28), network resources are the part of a social network to which the person routinely turns to or would turn to for support and help. Help and support also can be given spontaneously. Network resources, therefore, describe the social network from a functional perspective. However, it is not identical with it conceptually because supporters are not necessarily network members, and not all network members are supporters (Hall & Wellman, 1985). Comparing the term "social integration" with "support network" shows definition overlap because integration holds support resources as a criteria for definition. Therefore, support networks or network resources are intensionally distinct from the network and integration concepts. However, extensionally, the three concepts may overlap.

Supportive Climates/Supportive Environments

There has been scant research on the concept of social climates or environments, particularly the supportive climate. Moos (1984) introduced this term into his concept of stress and coping under a socioecological perspective. According to Moos, a supportive climate or environment refers to the quality of social relationships and systems: the family, the working place, hospital wards, groups, and so forth. Often these terms are defined by a high degree of interpersonal cohesion, involvement, and expressiveness, and a low degree of conflict. "Cohesion" means the degree of mutual help and support in that system; "involvement" characterizes the degree of concern and commitment in that system; "expressiveness" refers to the degree of mutual encouragement for an open expression of wishes, feelings, and needs; and "conflict" means the degree of stressful interactions and aggressive arguments. Supportive family climates are also defined as having a high degree of perceived support from the family (Procidano & Heller, 1983).

Within an intensional perspective, the construct of a supportive climate appears to be an aspect of network resources. Extensionally, however, it seems to be related to "perceived support." Because of its specificity, it cannot be characterized as a network resource or as a perceived support. It must be defined independently from these constructs.

Enacted and Received Support

The terms "enacted support" and "received support" refer to real interactions between people who exchange support. Sarason et al. (1990) use "enacted support" to describe the side of the provider and "received support" to describe that of the recipient. The concordance between both is usually not very high (Antonucci & Jackson, 1990). Conceptually, these terms are independent from the ones previously stated (integration, social networks, support networks, supportive climate) and from "perceived support."

Perceived Support

The concept of perceived support is not precisely defined for two reasons: (a) a lack of adequate theoretical integration, and (b) different authors use the term in different ways (cf. Barrera, 1986; Sarason et al., 1990; Vaux, 1988). Conceptual analyses and earlier works suggest that one should differentiate between two distinct phenomena: cognition of support and evaluation of support. Under a cognitive label, "perceived support" is best thought of as the "generalized experience of being supported from the social environment," and the "general perception of availability of supporting persons and actions" (general feelings and perceptions of being supported). More specific perceptions should be mentioned through specific terminology (e.g., perceived support from friends, or from partner/spouse, children, etc.) (see Procidano & Heller, 1983). The evaluative side examines the adequacy of and the satisfaction with supporters and received support.

The distinction between cognition and evaluation is based on theoretical considerations (Fiske & Taylor, 1984) and empirical results (Vaux & Harrison, 1985; Weinert, 1984). Most correlations are around .35, which is not strong enough for construct identity. For conceptual clarification, we shall use (cognition) and (evaluation) in parentheses in the following sections.

Comparing the term "perceived support" with others (e.g., integration, social network, support network, supportive climate, received support) hardly shows definition overlap. However, the cognitive part may relate to supportive climates if the latter is defined as "perceived support from the family," because both concepts contain cognitions that concern a person's own feelings of being supported.

Conceptual Comparisons

In summary, the terms "social network" and "social support" describe a complex system of social phenomena, which represents part of the "sozialen Lebensraum" (social world, Lewin) of a person and its functions. Each construct reveals a different aspect of this social world. To best understand how these constructs relate, one can order them in a logical-hierarchical manner (Figure 1). In this figure, relationships by definition are marked by lines through the related constructs.

Within this order, social integration represents the broadest construct and includes all others. Therefore, it stands at the top of the hierarchy. This phenomenon can be seen as a precondition for social networks, support networks, perceived support, and supportive behaviors. Although social integration may have these conceptions as criteria for definition, the terms are not synonymous. The same is true for supportive climate and perceived support, because, in some cases, the perception of support from the family is a criteria for the definition of a supportive family climate.

The social network characterizes one major aspect of the social integration, the structures, relational characteristics, and functions of the social relationships of a person.

Network resources are an extension of social networks under a specific perspec-

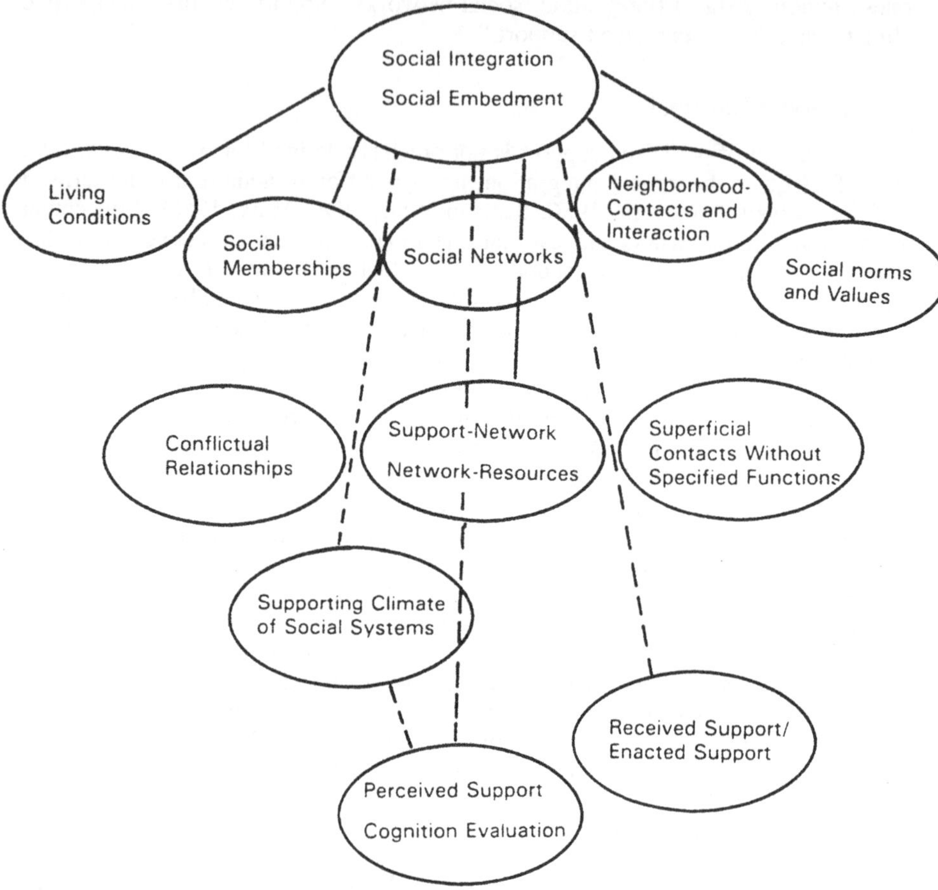

Figure 1 Hierarchy of the terminological field "social networks/social support." ________, relationship by definition (partially; totally); -------------, probable relationship by definition.

tive. Therefore, the first variable is a subordinate of the second one. Intensionally, however, they are independent; therefore, there is no line between them in Figure 1. The supportive climate subordinates the concept of network resources and social networks because of theoretical reasons. As mentioned before, some redundancy in defining a supportive climate could be assumed with perceived support (depending on the definition of the climate).

Supportive behaviors (received/enacted support) are a subordinate of the availability of supporting persons and aggregates. The perception and evaluation of support describes the personality side of the individual and the representation of support within its cognitive system.

To a small degree, all the aforementioned concepts are related to each other by definition (see the lines between the constructs). These relationships are not strong enough, however, to completely explain the amount of empirical associations found between them.

Relatedness by definition is not the only way in which constructs are associated with each other. There are also relationships on a measurement level, which are of great importance for empirical research. Therefore, it is important to look at these before analyzing theoretical relations.

METHODOLOGICAL ANALYSES

Concerning the measurement level, different problems can influence the association between constructs. The two most important problems are measurement redundancy or empirical confounding (Monroe & Steiner, 1986) and theoretical redundancy or theoretical confounding. Both problems become obvious through the analysis of methods, especially their operational criteria, and the analysis of the theoretical status of the constructs, especially under a "multimodal" point of view.

Operational Criteria

In the search for a clear picture of relationships between two constructs, one must look at the operational criteria established for measurement, because such an analysis makes obvious associations at a measurement level (Monroe & Steiner, 1986).

The literature developed various measures for every component of social networks and social support (cf. Vaux, Chapter 13), but not all of them measure distinct constructs at the level of item-criteria. Table 1 shows that some constructs have very similar operational criteria. Therefore, some of them are almost completely confounded with each other and some partially. This is especially true for integration, network, and support resource measures, but also for supportive climates and perceived support (cognition).

Partial measurement redundancy between resource, network, and integration measures mainly arises out of the criteria "emotionally significant persons" used for measuring all of these constructs. Broader confounding is possible between integration and network measures, because "neighbors," "relatives," "marital status," "children," "household members," "co-workers," and "acquaintances from club and religious affiliations" are used for measuring social integration and social networks (Sosna, 1983; Baumann, Laireiter, Pfingstmann, & Schwarzenbacher, 1987). Supportive climates are often measured through indices for "perceived support from special areas." Similar criteria are also used for measuring perceived support from friends, family, or workmates (e.g., Procidano & Heller, 1983). This is especially true for the "supportive family climate," which is usually operationalized as "perceived support from the family" (e.g., Sarason, Shearin, Pierce, & Sarason, 1987; Vaux et al., 1986). There is a lack of criteria for the "quality of interpersonal relationships" or the "quality of the environment and the climate of the family," which is the conceptual meaning of the construct. Therefore, adequate measurement of this construct is still lacking.

No confounding could be detected between measures for perceived and received support and between the two aspects of perceived support (cognition vs. evaluation). These constructs are separated very well at a measurement level.

Only some of the constructs are distinct from each other on a measurement level. Therefore, the prevention of confounding must be a major goal in analyzing empirical associations between the constructs just discussed. Prevention of confounding forces one to look at the items in use, especially at those for the structural variables (social integration, social networks, and network resources), but also at those for perceived support (cognition) and supportive climates.

Social Networks and Social Support as Multimodal Constructs

Measurement redundancy is not the only way that different constructs can be confounded with each other. Another major problem is theoretical confounding resulting from the fact that most of the constructs discussed here contain variables from the same psychological or subjective data level. This level also contains other variables, such as cognitive and emotional personality variables, mood, and coping styles, which can influence perception, information processing, and verbal report (Monroe & Steiner, 1986). Theoretical confounding, therefore, arises primarily out of the conceptual and theoretical relatedness of variables at the psychological data level.

Authors from different research areas in psychology (cf. Seidenstücker & Baumann, 1978, for a review) noticed this problem and established the so-called "multimodal perspective" as a methodological and theoretical way to precisely analyze the multiple relations of different constructs.

The multimodal perspective assumes methods, data level, data source, and construct taxonomies as the main sources of variance within and between constructs (Seidenstücker & Baumann, 1978). Table 2 shows a comprehensive view of social network and social support under a multimodal perspective.

The taxonomies of the constructs and the criteria for their definition and measurement are quoted on the left side of the table, followed by "data level," "data source," and "methods." Taxonomies of the constructs are discussed under conceptual analyses. As a science, psychology usually differs between social, psychological, biological, and ecological data levels, because each contains different groups of variables (e.g., psychological level: subjective experience vs. observable behavior; biological level: grades of neurobiological organization, such as cell, organ, systems, etc.). The borderline (i.e., the transition from one level to the other) is not clearly defined in most cases. This is also true for the constructs of network and support. Some phenomena contain both psychological and social data. An example is the term "friend." A friend is a social object (person), but also a psychological phenomenon, containing attitudes, emotional significance, subjective meanings, and so forth.

Constructs can be portrayed through three sources of data, self-reports, reports from others, and "objective data." Objective data are facts, obvious through objective examinations (e.g., marital status, sex, living area, age, etc.). There is a correspondence between data level and data source. Social and behavioral data can be registered through all three data sources, but subjective data (psychological level) can only be adequately measured through self-reports (Seidenstücker & Baumann, 1978).

Psychological research has elaborated many different methods for measuring constructs. Networks and support are primarily measured through self-report scales (e.g., interviews, questionnaires). The social integration, social networks,

Table 2 Social network and social support as multimodal constructs: Specification according taxonomies, empirical criteria, data level, data source, and methods

Constructs/criteria	Data level	Data source	Methods
	Social integration (selected criteria)		
Marital status	Social	Self, other Objective datum	Objective examination, questionnaire, observation
Memberships	Social	Self, other	Questionnaire, observation, objective examination
Living conditions	Social	Self, other	Questionnaire, observation, objective examination
Number of friends	Psychol/social	Self	Questionnaire
Number of relatives	Social	Self/other	Questionnaire, observation, objective examination
Frequency of contact	Social	Self, other	Questionnaire, observation
	Social network		
Family members and relatives	Social	Self, other	Questionnaire, observation, objective examination
People in social roles	Social	Self, other	Questionnaire, observation
People with regular contacts to	Social	Self, other	Observation, questionnaire
People, known by "ego"	Social	Self, other	Questionnaire, observation
People of emotional significance	Psychol/social	Self	Questionnaire
	Social network resources		
Potentially supportive persons			
Psychological	Psychol/social	Self	Questionnaire
Instrumental	Social	Self, other	Questionnaire, observation
Actually supportive persons			
Psychological	Psychol/social	Self, other	Questionnaire, observation
Instrumental	Social	Self, other	Questionnaire, observation
People of emotional significance	Psychol/social	Self	Questionnaire
	Supporting climate		
Cohesion/perceived supportedness	Psychol/social	Self, other	Questionnaire, observation
Conflict	Psychol/social	Self, other	Questionnaire, observation
	Perceived support		
Perception or evaluation of support	Psychol	Self	Questionnaire, projective tests
	Enacted/received support		
Everyday or crisis-support			
Psychological	Psychol/social	Self	Questionnaire
Instrumental	Social	Self, other	Questionnaire, observation

support networks, and supportive climates can also be examined through questionnaires for reports from others (e.g., interviewer, relatives, spouse, etc.). Some indicators can also be measured through objective tests and through observation (e.g., by self and others). Perceived support (cognition) can also be measured through projective tests (e.g., Kaplan Scale; Turner, Frankel, & Levin, 1983).

Applying the multimodal perspective to the constructs of network and support, as in Table 2, shows social integration, social networks, and support networks as really multimodal and multidimensional in nature. They not only represent data from the social and psychological levels, but they can also be portrayed through all sources of data (e.g., the self, others, and objective data in some cases), selectively using all methods just mentioned. A little less complex, but also multidimensional in nature, are supportive climates and received and enacted support. They mainly represent data from the psychological and social levels and can be recorded via self-reports and partly through reports from others, using questionnaires and observation methods. Table 2 shows "received instrumental support" and "received psychological support" as well as "actual instrumental supporters" and "actual psychological supporters" as theoretically distinct constructs under a multimodal point of view. The first (i.e., actual instrumental supporters and received instrumental support) are social phenomena. The second (i.e., actual psychological supports and received psychological support) are psychological and social phenomena that need actual exchange and subjective meaning for definition. These differences in the theoretical status have consequences for adequate data sources and methods (see Table 2).

Perceived support (i.e., cognition and evaluation) is clearly unidimensional, because it is a subjective psychological phenomenon that can only be examined through self-reports via self-observation or questionnaires and partially through projective tests.

The multimodal perspective makes two predictions concerning empirical associations of the constructs. First, it assumes a higher degree of correspondence between data from the same source (e.g., self) because of individual-specific patterns of self-presentation and self-report. Second, it assumes higher levels of correlation between measures of the same data level because of theoretical confounding mentioned earlier. Both problems, the "same data source" and the "same data level," lead to artificial homogenization of variance—raising empirical correlations between the measures. Two consequences arise out of these problems. First, one must test the criterion-validity of self-reports. Second, one must consider the aforementioned problems when interpreting empirical data. Empirical analyses must be careful not to use highly confounded measures and should remove items susceptible to this problem (cf. Cohen & Wills, 1985, for a related view in the support and life-event research). In principle, however, research should not only use self-report measures, but also should use objective tests and observation methods when applicable.

The constructs of social integration, social networks, network resources, supportive climates, and received and perceived support show a complex system of conceptual and methodological relationships between each other. It is important to pay great attention to them in empirical analyses because they can confound the results. However, conceptual and methodological relationships do not exist between all components and parameters of these constructs. Additionally, they are not strong enough to determine the whole association between them. Therefore, one can also assume theoretical (functional) relationships. We shall concentrate on such relationships in the next section.

THEORETICAL ANALYSES

Looking at the literature, one finds scant systematic work on the theoretical relationships between the constructs of social integration, social networks, network resources, supportive climates, and received and perceived social support. Additionally, the relationships between the constructs of social integration, social network, and network resources are mainly by definition (see earlier discussion). Depending on how broad the definition of social integration is, it is also true in some cases for supportive climates, received support, and perceived support (Sosna, 1983). Therefore, general relationships between the amount of integration, the size of a social network, and the number of supporters are in danger of being highly confounded by definition as well as measurement redundancy. Additionally, they are less interesting. More interesting for theory construction and practical application at the current stage of research are specific relationships between singular components of a person's social integration, social networks, support resources, and received and perceived social support.

The theoretical analysis of all the associations between the components of all constructs would be a longlasting work needing a broad elaboration and a research program over many years. Therefore, it is necessary to concentrate on some main topics. One topic of interest at the current stage of research is the relationship between network roles and the different components of support (e.g., resources, behaviors, cognition, and evaluation) (see Vaux, 1988). Two main questions shall be treated. First, which kinds of relationships (network roles) represent the most important supporters? Second, which roles are associated with highly supportive social climates and environments, high degrees of perceived and received support, and satisfaction with support? When answering these questions, one has to consider that the relationships between network structures and these support components are quite complex, because they are not fixed and depend on several margin conditions: (a) the focus of the problem (everyday problems vs. crises); (b) the degree of realization of support (actually applied vs. potentially available); (c) mode of support (appraisal, socializing, instrumental, etc.); (d) the special support component (resources, environments, behaviors, cognitions, and evaluations); and (e) outcome variables (well-being, psychopathology, social functioning, etc.). Depending on conditions (a) through (e), different people (sources) and structures of social networks may be addressed. Because there is a lack of knowledge, we shall concentrate on everyday problems and stressful experiences.

Network Roles and Support Resources

In the beginning, support research was characterized by a pretty clear relationship between network roles and support resources. For most authors, the term "support resource" was synonymous with the availability of very close and confidential persons (e.g., spouse, close friends, etc.) (Lowenthal & Haven, 1968; Cohen & Wills, 1985). This clear association also represents the theoretical assumption of these authors that very close persons are also the main supporters.

Contrary to these early notions, later formulations brought in some differentiations; Cobb (1976) associated three types of psychological support with three sources: (a) emotional support (information that one is loved and cared for) from close and intimate relationships; (b) information concerning self-esteem and value to public relationships and a person's social status; and (c) belonging-support and socializing to social networks. Weiss (1974) introduced a more complex system. He distinguished six basic social needs attachable to different sources: (a) attachment (close relationships); (b) social integration (friends, acquaintances, members of groups); (c) opportunity for nurturance (family, children, close friends); (d) reassurance of worth (network members); (e) sense of reliable alliance (closest people, children, spouse/partner); and (f) obtaining of guidance (people accepted as authorities).

These theoretical preconsiderations, therefore, see support functions distributed differently; some functions are related to a broad variety of people, some to a narrower variety, and some to the narrowest part of the social network. How a special kind of support is related to each kind of relationship depends mainly on two factors: (a) the kind of support on one side, and (b) the ego-involvement'' of that special function on the other.

The first condition means that not every person can satisfy every support need. On the contrary, theoretical notions suggest specific associations between support function and support resource (see earlier discussion). Under this heading, support functions can be classified into a logical-hierarchical order by degree of difficulty. There are easily satisfiable functions, such as "giving feedback," "socializing," and "giving information," that can be enacted through a broad range of interactions and persons. It is more difficult to fulfill one's need to express negative feelings, to rely on someone, and so forth. For these, one needs close friends and intimate relationships (e.g., spouse/partner, close relatives, children, etc.).

The second point maintains that the degree of difficulty mentioned earlier depends on the ego-closeness or ego-involvement associated with that special function and the degree of ego-threat, followed by a certain support need (Cohen & McKay, 1984; Thoits, 1986). It is expected that more ego-close and ego-threatening support needs can only be adequately satisfied through people with whom one feels very close, confident, and secure. More ego-distant needs can be met by people with whom one does not feel so intimate. Psychological support needs are usually more ego-close than instrumental and material needs. Therefore, it is expected that demands for instrumental and material support are satisfied by a greater number of persons and by those who do not have close personal contact.

The problem of the association between network roles and support resources can be approached from a different perspective, one that considers social-psychological analyses of functions and roles and rules of interpersonal relationships. Using this approach, two important results are uncovered: (a) a concentration of support functions on close and closely related persons, and (b) an indication of highly differentiated functions for single roles (e.g., neighbors, confidants, partners, working colleagues, etc.) (Argyle & Henderson, 1985). Social-psychological analyses of functions and rules also show that close and closely related people play an important role as supporters in crises and times of stress.

Theoretical considerations can conclude with the notion that a person will have a great range of potential supporters for all different kinds of everyday support needs. The core support network, however, will consist of close and very close persons, because these persons are able to satisfy a broad range of support needs, especially ego-close and ego-threatening ones. More distant persons enact a smaller range of support functions, which are probably very specific, depending on the special kind of relationship or role.

This general association for everyday conditions becomes more complex when demands of support in crises are considered (Cohen & McKay, 1984; Thoits, 1986). The kind of burden/distress and the resulting needs for support must be considered. Stressful events represent a class of situations or experiences whose main consequences are ego-involvement and ego-threat. They are mostly determined through threat to self-esteem, personal security, and the frustration of strong personal needs. As noted earlier, support and coping needs of this sort are primarily satisfied through very close and intimate persons without further threat to self-esteem within the relationship. Therefore, one has to conclude that closely related people also play important roles in fulfilling crisis- and stress-related support needs (Brown & Harris, 1978).

For providing satisfying support in crises, specific supporters, who have experience with and have mastered that special problem, are increasingly more significant because they can give adequate validation of feelings, good comprehension and insight into the stressful situation, and do not further threaten the self-esteem of the distressed person. Additionally, they can restore motivation and a positive view of the future (see Cohen & McKay, 1984; Thoits, 1986 for further arguments).

The core of a personal network (i.e., the intimate and personal zone) (Boissevain, 1977) represents the core of the support network of a person for everyday problems as well as for crises and stressful experiences. These people fulfill multiple and especially ego-close support functions, contrary to more uniplex and ego-distant functions of emotionally less significant persons.

Network Roles, Climates, and Received and Perceived Support

If the main supporters are very close, intimate members of a personal network, one can conclude that a person also receives a lot of support from these persons. Therefore, the availability of many very close persons should be associated with a high degree of received support. This is true for everyday conditions as well as for crises and stressful situations.

The relationship between perceived support and network roles is mediated through received support. Theoretically, a cognitive concept or schema of being supported (perceived support) emerges out of the repeated experience of receiving support from different people in different situations. As Sarason and Sarason (1985) pointed out, early experiences in childhood are of great importance for the establishment of generalized cognitive schemata of being supported. Because we assume that close and intimate members of a network enact the greatest amount of support, it is also easy to predict a strong association between these persons and the perception of being supported (perceived support). Less close persons enact a smaller amount of support; therefore, a smaller association between perceived support and these network persons must be assumed.

The relations between network roles and the evaluation of the adequacy of and the satisfaction with support should not be as strong with the perceptive construct for three reasons. First, perceiving a certain behavior as supportive is not the same as evaluating it as satisfying or adequate. Evaluations are partially independent from perceptions (Zajonc, 1980) because they depend on motivational and emotional systems and need an additional step in information processing. Therefore, the perception of support can only be a precondition for a positive evaluation of it. Second, evaluation needs a special quality of a supportive behavior, not the behavior per se. Third, empirical results (see Wortman & Lehman, 1985, for a review) show that not every supportive behavior is experienced as helpful and need-satisfying. The probability that one's need for support is frustrated is relatively high. Therefore, one can conclude that only special supporters and the support received from them will be evaluated as satisfying.

Who are these supporters? It can be predicted that these are again very close and intimate network members, because they usually know the person very well and for a long time. Both are good conditions for enacting need satisfying support. The satisfaction of needs is one precondition for evaluating a behavior as adequate or satisfying. Therefore, we can predict a high empirical association between satisfaction with support and close and confident network members.

The association between network roles and supportive social climates is less obvious, because the relationship between network roles and the quality of the relationships within a special social area needs several mediating steps. As far as perceived support from this special area is concerned, one can predict a relationship between the amount of close and supporting persons and the perception of that environment as supportive. There is a high probability that close persons also enact a great amount of support in that special social area. As predicted earlier, receiving much support goes along with a high amount of perceived support. Therefore, an association between the number of close persons in a special area and a perceived supportive climate in this area is to be predicted. Similar arguments can be found for the criteria "expressiveness" and "low conflict."

We can also predict a close relationship between the availability of close network members and receiving a high amount of support, and perceiving oneself as supported and being satisfied with the support received. If one has a lot of supporters and close persons in a certain social environment, one also should perceive that environment as supportive.

EMPIRICAL ASSOCIATIONS

Although it is important to know much about the relationships between network structures and support functions, no systematic research has been done on this topic. Our research group has tried to fill this gap, especially for network resources, and under everyday conditions. Work on perceived and received support is in preparation. Therefore, we want to present some data that were recorded with the "Interview on Social Networks and Social Support" (SONET; Baumann, Laireiter, Pfingstmann, & Schwarzenbacher, 1987). Some other workers explored the relationships between network roles, received and perceived support, and supportive family climates (also under everyday conditions). We shall concentrate here on everyday problems. For an example of the associations between network roles, support resources, and received support under conditions of stress, we shall cite one further study from our own research group.

Network Roles and Everyday Support Resources

SONET is a multidimensional, network-analytical interview measuring ego-centered social networks registered on the basis of two criteria: (a) regular frequency of contact, and (b) personal significance. Under the first criterion, all persons from defined social fields (e.g., household; relatives; neighborhood, workplace; club, church, and association memberships; leisure-time activities; and professional helping system) and with regular, field-specific contact with the individual in the last 6 months are listed (e.g., twice a month for neighbors and relatives; almost daily for household members and workplace contacts). The second criterion covers persons of personal significance under two headings: (a) valence (positive/negative) and closeness to the individual, including spouse/partner, children, close friends/confidants, friends, and acquaintances on the positive side; and (b) ambivalent, purely conflicting, threatening, and uneasy relationships on the negative side.

Persons categorized within these criteria constitute the personal network. The structure of it is described through the total size of the network, and the partial sizes of the sectors (e.g., relatives, neighborhood, close friends, etc.). The following interactional parameters are used: frequency of contact, length of relationship, geographical distance, and main mode of contact (face to face, by phone, by letter). Network resources are estimated through the question for the perceived availability of support for everyday problems from each network member. We distinguish two kinds of support: psychological (acceptance, great liking, reliable alliance, and venting of negative feelings) and instrumental (information and advice, money, and work).

In accordance with the literature (e.g., Angermeyer, 1989; Pattison & Pattison, 1981), we found that a social network, measured in this broad manner, contains a mean number of 28 persons, 12 of whom have personal significance. The sizes of the different sectors are as follows (overlapping): relatives 8, workplace 5, neighborhood 4, close friends/confidants 5, friends 6, acquaintances 5. Two thirds, or 21 persons, are perceived as potentially supportive (support network: acceptance 15, great liking 12, reliable alliance 10, venting 9, work-support 15, money 13, information and advice 12). Three persons are seen as negative (ambivalent, conflictful, threatening, and uneasy).

To test the main hypotheses of this chapter, different analyses were carried out (intercorrelations, principal component analyses, conditional probabilities). Table 3 shows the intercorrelations between the number of persons in each network sector and the number of persons in each support function.

Two theoretically predicted results are evident. First, correlations between the number of persons in each sector and the number of potential supporters are significant only for emotionally important persons (because of restricted variance,

Table 3 Intercorrelations between parameters of "social network" and "social support resources" (potentially supporting, for everyday problems) ($N = 114$; SONET)

	Person (ego)						
	Feels accepted	Feels liked	Can rely on	Can vent negative feelings	Can get information	Can borrow money	Receives help doing work
Relative	.44**	.45**	.44**	.28*	.37**	.32**	.41**
Neighbor	.20	.16	.13	.00	.06	.12	.18
Co-worker	.19	.05	.11	−.06	.13	.11	.18
Club acquaintance	.16	.08	.24	.21	.20	.18	.22
Leisure acquaintance	.12	.08	.03	.04	.03	.12	.14
Significant other	.50**	.63**	.70**	.57**	.63**	.45**	.52**
Confidant	.36**	.41**	.41**	.35**	.34**	.43**	.34**
Friend	.31**	.37**	.35**	.19	.44**	.44**	.41**
Acquaintance	.28*	.36**	.40**	.28*	.33**	.40**	.37**

*$p \leq .05$
**$p \leq .01$

spouse/partner, children, and professional helpers are not included). The correlations are not significant for persons from social roles alone (i.e., persons without subjective significance). Second, support resources are distributed differently over and within persons of emotional significance. Two trends are perceptible: the strength of the association increases with emotional closeness and decreases with emotional distance, and certain kinds of support seem specific to certain structures or roles (e.g., friends are very important for instrumental support, but less vital for venting negative feelings; significant others are important for all kinds of support; relatives primarily for psychological support, except venting negative experience).

The association between the availability of close network members and supporters within the intercorrelation matrix should result in a close relationship between them in principal component analyses. Our data confirm this assumption. Factorial analyses (Varimax, principal components-analysis) yield one main factor consisting of all supporters, close friends, and significant others. These results confirm that network members of emotional significance are highly associated with supporting functions. In other words: The core of a personal network consists of very close friends and emotionally significant persons, who, at the same time, are the main supporters. This conclusion is strongly confirmed by calculating conditional probabilities. This method computes the probability of a certain network structure or role having supportive functions (Table 4). This table also contains spouse/partner, children, and professional helpers, who were excluded in the previous analysis because of too little variance.

Emotionally significant network members show a higher probability of being perceived as potentially supportive, whereas neighbors, co-workers, and club and leisure-time acquaintances are perceived much less. Professional helpers, who produce only small amounts of supportive power, appear less important for community samples, contrary to clinical populations (Angermeyer, 1989). Children offer only moderate support.

The previously stated differential patterns of association between network roles

Table 4 Probability that a certain role (spouse/partner, child, etc.) has a certain supporting function (perceived by ego) P (support/role) ($N = 114$; SONET)

	Person (ego)						
	Feels accepted	Feels liked	Can rely on	Can vent negative feelings	Can get information	Can borrow money	Receives help doing work
Partner/spouse	.71	.73	.70	.70	.59	.60	.67
Child	.41	.49	.34	.25	.13	.22	.35
Relative	.56	.56	.46	.42	.48	.68	.59
Neighbor	.35	.21	.20	.17	.22	.28	.37
Co-worker	.33	.18	.17	.14	.21	.25	.30
Club acquaintance	.19	.11	.12	.11	.16	.13	.17
Leisure acquaintance	.30	.22	.20	.19	.20	.23	.28
Significant other	.71	.70	.63	.60	.60	.61	.68
Confidant	.80	.79	.72	.79	.67	.73	.78
Friend	.61	.52	.44	.45	.51	.51	.57
Acquaintance	.34	.21	.18	.15	.25	.28	.35
Professional helper	.14	.06	.12	.20	.19	.03	.07

Support

and support functions can also be found on this level of analysis; partner/spouse, significant others, and close friends/confidants are the main supporters, especially for psychological functions. Venting and reliable alliance seem to be very selective kinds of support, because only very close persons (e.g., close friends/confidants, partners, significant others, relatives) are perceived as supporters for these functions. Acceptance and the feeling of being liked are more easily perceived (higher levels of probability from more network sectors). The patterns of different distributions are also visible within instrumental functions of support.

Our results are confirmed by several workers, using both broad and narrow network analytical measures. Griffith (1985) and Weinert (1984), using broader network measures, and Norbeck, Lindsey, and Carrieri (1981), using a narrower one (the Norbeck Social Support Questionnaire, NSSQ, which collects only the partial network of "significant others"), found the central core of a support network consisting of family members (partner/spouse; children, only when confidants), close relatives, very close friends, and confidants. Other roles (workmates; acquaintances from churches, clubs, and associations; neighbors) were of minimal importance (cf. Vaux & Harrison, 1985, for similar results).

Empirical results, which confirm theoretical predictions, show very consistent patterns of association between network roles and support resources. As predicted, a broad range of the personal network is perceived as potentially supportive. However, the main supporters for everyday needs come from very selected social roles: the core family (especially partner/spouse, to a lesser degree children), relatives, very close friends/confidants, and very important persons. These persons, at the same time, are the main supporters for ego-close support needs. Easier, applicable kinds of psychological and instrumental support are perceived from a broader range of persons (acceptance, work support). One may conclude that the central emotional core of a network, the personal and intimate zone (Boissevain, 1977), represents the main support resources, in both quality (mode of support) and quantity (number of different support modes).

Network Roles, Climates, and Received and Perceived Support

Confirming predicted notions, Sarason et al. (1987) and Hobfoll, Nadler, and Leiberman (1986) did not find a significant association between the number of significant others, measured by the "Social Network List" (SNL; Stokes, 1983) and perceived family cohesion (Family Environment Scale, FES; Moos & Moos, 1981). The relation reached the significance level only for the relative number of family members and confidants within this partial network and for its density (Sarason et al., 1987). Persons from cohesive families live mostly in dense networks that consist of many close confidants and relatives.

Results are a bit complex concerning received/enacted support. All workers used the "Inventory of Socially Supportive Behaviors" (ISSB; Barrera, 1981; Vaux, Chapter 14). This scale measures the amount of received supportive behaviors in the last 4 weeks. It showed only moderate correlations with the number of important persons (SNL; Sarason et al., 1987; Stokes & Wilson, 1984). These results hold for the scale as a whole, but they differ for singular components of the ISSB. Both Sarason and Stokes report significant correlations for received information support. The other components of ISSB (emotional support, tangible assistance, directive guidance) show no consistent results in both studies. Density, as well as the proportion of relatives within the partial network of important others, did not correlate with either general or specified amounts of received support. The association between the number of confidants and the amount of received support was statistically significant (Stokes & Wilson, 1984: whole scale; Sarason et al., 1987: emotional support subscale), confirming the important role of close relationships for perceiving and receiving support.

The results concerning the relationships between network structures and perceived support are very consistent. With only one exception in the work of Hobfoll et al. (1986), no study found a relationship between perceived support (cognition) and the number of significant others (Blazer & Kaplan, 1983; Hobfoll, Nadler, & Leiberman, 1986; Norbeck et al., 1981). As in the case of received support, the association reached statistical significance for the number of very close and confident persons (close friends and relatives, confidants; Cohen, Mermelstein, Kamarck, & Hoberman, 1985; Turner et al., 1983; Vaux & Harrison, 1985; Vaux et al., 1986). Vaux and Harrison (1985), computing multiple regression analyses, confirmed these results. They found a significant positive and linear association between the degree of closeness of a relationship and perceived support and a negative association for distant and superficial contacts.

The results for the evaluation of support are very similar. Satisfaction with support was regularly associated with a great number of close friends, confidants, or very close relatives. No association, or a negative one, was found for emotionally more distant persons (neighbors, workmates, friends, etc.) (Hobfoll et al., 1986; Sarason et al., 1987; Stokes, 1983; Vaux & Harrison, 1985).

The association between the density of the network of significant others and satisfaction with support is less clear. Sarason et al. (1987) report a positive association, whereas Hobfoll et al. (1986) and Stokes (1983) found no relation. These contradictory results are hard to interpret. Measurement and sample differences between the studies could have been at work.

Despite the complexities with received support, the picture concerning the relationships of network roles, structures, supportive environments, behaviors, and the perception and evaluation of support is rather consistent. The core support system, which consists of very close and emotionally significant network members, enacts many supportive (psychological and instrumental) behaviors, which are also perceived as supportive and as satisfying most of the time.

Network structures, like the density of important others or the relative amount of relatives within the significant others, do not seem to be important for the reception and perception of support from the social environment. The critical structure is the intimate zone of a personal network. This appears responsible for regulating people's everyday needs for support. The amount of relatives within the partial network of significant others becomes important only when one looks at the perceived support from the family. People with a high number of relatives and confidants within this part of their network also perceive a high amount of cohesion and support from the family. Such a system can surely give much support for everyday problems.

However, Hirsch (1980) and Wilcox (1981) found that this pattern of support may have some faults, especially in certain crises (e.g., divorce, separation, leaving the family, bereavement, etc.), leading to negative consequences and a heightened susceptibility to emotional problems and diseases (see also Vaux, 1988). Under an adaptional point of view, one must conclude that the core support system should also include close friends, confidants, and emotional significant persons from outside the family.

Network Structures and Crisis Support

We conducted one study, which gives some evidence on the relationships between network roles and support resources, and received support under crisis. In this work (Mitteregger, Baumann, Pichler, & Teske, 1990), patients with a first coronary infarct were interviewed 6 months after the event (during the rehabilitation phase). The interview dealt with potential and actual supporters during this phase. Members of a control group—comparable in sex, age, marital status, and socioeconomic status, and consisting of healthy individuals—were asked who would support them in such a crisis (potential supporters for this event). Therefore, we can make statements on potential and actual supporters and received support during a crisis.

The authors found two important trends. First, patients more often considered health professionals and nurses as important actual supporters for psychological needs (venting of emotions, informations, cognitive feedback, self-esteem buffering) as well as instrumental needs (informations concerning the health security system, rehabilitation, prognosis of the disease, etc.). The healthy comparison group in contrast did not stress any health professional as a potential supporter. Second, patients actually received support more often from workmates, whereas the healthy comparison group did not believe support was available from these persons in the quantity that the patients received. On the other hand, the healthy group believed to have the most support available from spouse/partner, family members and relatives, close friends, and friends. Contrary to this, patients actually did not receive as much support as the healthy believed available from these groups.

The following conclusions can be drawn. Available crisis support is primarily perceived from the core zone of the personal network. Actual crisis support is also mostly enacted from the core zone of the network. More distant persons, like coworkers and friends, are also important as actual supporters as well as stress-related persons. Healthy people do not estimate the last category as important and overestimate the importance of the closest network persons as actual supporters. In summary, the results confirm the relative importance of different groups of persons as actual supporters: the core network, more distant people, and stressor-specific persons.

The difference in the estimation of potential and actual supporters at the same time gives insight into the complex work of the different phenomena of social support. When anticipating a harmful experience, a person expects the most support to come from the core network and estimates these persons as most important. In this phase (anticipatory), obviously the cognition of very close people as being available for support could be the main shield against the negative consequences of stress. Coping with a stressful experience and working it through leads to a shift in the need for support resources. Other persons, especially those out of the area of distress, become important. Therefore, in this phase, persons having experience with the special stressor and the support received from these persons seem to produce buffering functions (Cohen & McKay, 1984; Thoits, 1986).

CONCLUSION

Starting our work, we noticed that the relationships between social networks and social support were not yet clear. To clarify these relationships we took several approaches. The first was to show why it was necessary to differentiate the concept of social support, which resulted in five distinct concepts: social integration, network resources, supportive climates, received and enacted support, and perceived support (cognition and evaluation). Analyses of definition and methodology, including social networks, showed that these concepts construct a field of terminology and a structure of interrelations. These analyses also found that the relations between the constructs can be explained, to a small extent, by overlapping definitions, measurement redundancy, and theoretical confounding. This is higher for the structural conceptions integration, network, and network resources, and is slightly lower for supporting climates and perceived support (cognition). An adequate analysis of the relationships needs theoretical considerations and functional models that have to be empirically tested.

Theoretical analyses resulted in functional hypotheses involving relationships between network roles and support resources for everyday needs. These were also empirically explored with the use of our own data and results from the literature. The results confirm, with some minor exceptions, the theoretical notion that the most important supporting persons for everyday needs consist of emotionally close family members, relatives, and friends. These persons also seem to regulate emotional needs for support, venting negative feelings, and bolstering self-esteem. Data show a high correlation between the availability of these persons and perceived support, and satisfaction with received support in general, and specifically from these persons (see also Brown, Brady, Lent, Wolfert, & Hall, 1987). If these persons belong to the family or are relatives, a supporting and cohesive family climate is associated.

Emotionally more distant social roles, such as neighbors, co-workers, acquaintances from clubs and leisure-time activities, and professional helpers, do not seem to perform the critical role of regulating needs and providing satisfactory support. Therefore, a big network alone, without its close core, cannot guarantee satisfactory provision of support. Empirical correlations between the size of a network, well-being, and perceived health could be spurious, confounded with emotionally close members of the network. Threshold effects, discussed in the literature (Hobfoll, 1985), could thus be at work in these associations.

Special network structures, such as density, play a less clear-cut role as determinants of support resources, received and perceived support, and its evaluation as satisfying. Because of a very selective review on crisis support, this chapter only allows tentative conclusions. The study cited confirms the prediction that the availability of crisis support is mainly seen from intimate and very close relationships. For people undergoing a harmful experience of stress, other persons, especially stress-related ones, become of major significance. The main conclusion drawn from these results is that the availability of emotionally significant persons is of major importance in anticipatory coping. Actually coping with and mastering a stressful experience need other supporters, too—those having experience with the stress, and also persons from work, leisure time, and organizations.

Empirical research has drawn a differentiated and complex picture about the associations between network roles and support functions. Despite this, much work remains to be done. On the basis of the multitrait-multimethod matrix, one has to conclude that many cells of this matrix still remain blank. To counteract theoretical and methodological confounding, it would be necessary to vary data sources and the methods used. Not only should self-reports and questionnaires be used, but also observatory methods and objective examinations when applicable.

In some cases, methodological problems must be noted. This applies to the measurement of social networks and received support. In the first case, there is a lack of methodologically acceptable measures. Additionally, only a few measures consider a social network in the broad sense of its meaning. In the second case, there is a lack of a broader measurement of the construct, especially under conditions of stress and crisis. Until now, research on "supportive climates" only dealt with the family and its cohesion. It is now time to concentrate on other social systems and on measures adequate for the construct.

The authors hope that the present work sparks further theoretical and empirical work on this interesting and important field of network and support research.

REFERENCES

Angermeyer, M. C. (1989). Soziales Netzwerk und Schizophrenie: Eine Übersicht. In M. C. Angermeyer & D. Klusmann (Eds.), *Soziales Netzwerk—Ein neues Konzept für die Psychiatrie* (pp. 188–206). Berlin: Springer.

Antonucci, T. C., & Jackson, J. S. (1990). The role of reciprocity in social support. In B. R. Sarason, I. G. Sarason, & G. R. Pierce (Eds.), *Social support: An interactional view* (pp. 173–198). New York: John Wiley & Sons.

Argyle, M., & Henderson, M. (1985). *The anatomy of relationships.* London: Heinemann.

Barrera, M., Jr. (1981). Social support in the adjustment of pregnant adolescents: Assessment issues. In B. H. Gottlieb (Ed.), *Social networks and social support* (pp. 69-96). Beverly Hills: Sage Publications.

Barrera, M., Jr. (1986). Distinctions between social support concepts, measures, and models. *American Journal of Community Psychology, 14,* 413–445.

Baumann, U., Laireiter, A., Pfingstmann, G., & Schwarzenbacher, K. (1987). Fragebogen zum Sozialen Netzwerk und zur Sozialen Unterstützung (SONET), Kurzbericht. *Zeitschrift für Klinische Psychologie, 16,* 429–431.

Blazer, D. G., & Kaplan, B. H. (1983). The assessment of social support in an elderly community population. *The American Journal of Social Psychiatry, 3,* 29–36.

Blöschl, L. (1987). Soziales Netzwerk/Soziale Unterstützung, Lebensbelastung und Befindlichkeit. *Zeitschrift für Klinische Psychologie, 16,* 311–320.

Boissevain, J. (1977). *Friends of friends.* Oxford: Basil Blackwell.

Brown, G., & Harris, T. (1978). *Social origins of depression. A study of psychiatric disorder in women.* New York: The Free Press.

Brown, S. D., Brady, T., Lent, R. W., Wolfert, J., & Hall, S. (1987). Perceived social support among college students: Three studies of the psychometric characteristics and counseling uses of the Social Support Inventory. *Journal of Counseling Psychology, 34,* 337–354.

Cobb, S. (1976). Social support as a moderator of life stress. *Psychosomatic Medicine, 38,* 300–314.

Cohen, S., & McKay, G. (1984). Social support, stress and the buffering hypothesis: A theoretical analysis. In J. Baum, E. Singer, & S. E. Taylor (Eds.), *Handbook of psychology and health* (Vol. 4, pp. 253-267). Hillsdale, NJ: Erlbaum.

Cohen, S., Mermelstein, R., Kamarck, T., & Hoberman, H. M. (1985). Measuring the functional components of social support. In I. G. Sarason & B. R. Sarason (Eds.), *Social support: Theory, research and applications* (pp. 73–94). Dordrecht: Martinus Nijhoff.

Cohen, S., & Wills, T. A. (1985). Stress, social support, and the buffering hypothesis. *Psychological Bulletin, 98,* 310–357.

Fiske, S. T., & Taylor, S. E. (1984). *Social cognition.* New York: Random House.

Griffith, J. (1985). Social support providers: Who are they? Where are they met? and the relationship of network characteristics to psychological distress. *Basic and Applied Social Psychology, 6,* 41–60.

Hall, A., & Wellman, B. (1985). Social networks and social support. In S. Cohen & S. L. Syme (Eds.), *Social support and health* (pp. 23–41). Orlando, FL: Academic Press.

Hirsch, B. J. (1980). Natural support systems and coping with major life changes. *American Journal of Community Psychology, 8,* 159–172.

Hobfoll, S. E. (1985). Limitations of social support in the stress process. In I. G. Sarason & B. R. Sarason (Eds.), *Social support: Theory, research, and applications* (pp. 391–415). Dordrecht: Martinus Nijhoff.

Hobfoll, S. E., Nadler, A., & Leiberman, J. (1986). Satisfaction with social support during crisis: Intimacy and self-esteem as critical determinants. *Journal of Personality and Social Psychology, 51,* 296–304.

Laireiter, A., & Baumann, U. (1988). Klinisch-psychologische Soziodiagnostik: Protektive Variablen und Soziale Anpassung. *Diagnostica, 34,* 190–226.

Lowenthal, M. F., & Haven, C. (1968). Interaction and adaptation: Intimacy as a critical variable. *American Sociological Review, 33,* 20–30.

Mitteregger, G., Baumann, U., Pichler, M., & Teske, W. (1990). Zur Validität potentieller Unterstützung—Eine Pilotstudie bei Herzinfarktpatienten. *Zeitschrift für Klinische Psychologie, Psychopathologie und Psychotherapie, 38,* 123–134.

Monroe, S. M., & Steiner, S. C. (1986). Social support and psychopathology: Interrelations with preexisting disorder, stress, and personality. *Journal of Abnormal Psychology, 95,* 29–39.

Moos, R. H. (1984). Context and coping: Toward a unifying conceptual framework. *American Journal of Community Psychology, 12,* 5–36.

Moos, R. H., & Moos, B. S. (1981). *Family Environment Scale Manual.* Palo Alto, CA: Consulting Psychologists Press.

Norbeck, J. S., Lindsey, A. M., & Carrieri, V. L. (1981). The development of an instrument to measure social support. *Nursing Research, 30,* 264–269.

Pattison, E. M., & Pattison, M. L. (1981). Analysis of a schizophrenic psychosocial network. *Schizophrenia Bulletin, 7,* 135–143.

Procidano, M. E., & Heller, K. (1983). Measures of perceived social support from friends and from family: Three validation studies. *American Journal of Community Psychology, 11,* 1–24.

Sarason, B. R., Sarason, I. G., & Pierce, G. R. (1990). Traditional views of social support and their impact on assessment. In B. R. Sarason, I. G. Sarason, & G. R. Pierce (Eds.), *Social support: An interactional view* (pp. 9–25). New York: John Wiley & Sons.

Sarason, B. R., Shearin, E. N., Pierce, G. R., & Sarason, I. G. (1987). Interrelations of social support measures: Theoretical and practical implications. *Journal of Personality and Social Psychology, 52,* 813–832.

Sarason, I. G., & Sarason, B. R. (1985). Social support—insights from assessment and experimentation. In I. G. Sarason & B. R. Sarason (Eds.), *Social support: Theory, research, and applications* (pp. 39–50). Dordrecht: Martinus Nijhoff.

Seidenstücker, G., & Baumann, U. (1978). Multimethodale Diagnostik. In U. Baumann, H. Berbalk, & G. Seidenstücker (Eds.), *Klinische Psychologie: Trends in Forschung und Praxis* (Vol. 1, pp. 134–182). Bern: Huber.

Sosna, U. (1983). *Soziale Isolation und psychische Erkrankung im Alter. Eine medizinsoziologische Felduntersuchung.* Frankfurt am Main: Campus.

Stokes, J. P. (1983). Predicting satisfaction with social support from social network structure. *American Journal of Community Psychology, 11,* 141–152.

Stokes, J. P., & Wilson, D. G. (1984). The inventory of socially supportive behaviors: Dimensionality, prediction, and gender differences. *American Journal of Community Psychology, 12,* 53–69.

Thoits, P. A. (1986). Social support as coping assistance. *Journal of Consulting and Clinical Psychology, 54,* 416–423.

Turner, R. J., Frankel, B. G., & Levin, D. M. (1983). Social support: Conceptualization, measurement, and implications for mental health. In J. R. Greenley & R. G. Simmons (Eds.), *Research in community and mental health* (Vol. 3, pp. 67–111). Greenwich: Jai Press.

Vaux, A. (1988). *Social support: Theory, research, and intervention.* New York: Praeger.

Vaux, A., & Harrison, D. (1985). Support network characteristics associated with support satisfaction and perceived support. *American Journal of Community Psychology, 13,* 245–268.

Vaux, A., Phillips, J., Holly, L., Thomson, B., Williams, D., & Steward, D. (1986). The Social Support Appraisals (SS-A) scale: Studies of reliability and validity. *American Journal of Community Psychology, 14,* 195–219.

Veiel, H. O. F. (1987). Soziale Unterstützung gibt es nicht: Zur Strukturierung eines Konzepts. In M. Amelang (Ed.), *Bericht über den 35. Kongreß der Deutschen Gesellschaft für Psychologie in Heidelberg 1986* (Vol. 2, pp. 545–556). Göttingen: Hogrefe.

Weinert, C. (1984). Evaluation of the Personal Resource Questionnaire: A social support measure. In B. S. Raff & P. Carroll (Eds.), *Social support and families of vulnerable infants* (pp. 59–78). New York: March of Dimes Birth Defects Foundation.

Weiss, R. S. (1974). The provisions of social relationships. In Z. Rubin (Ed.), *Doing unto others* (pp. 17–26). Englewood Cliffs, NJ: Prentice-Hall.

Wilcox, B. L. (1981). Social support in adjusting to marital disruption: A network analysis. In B. H. Gottlieb (Ed.), *Social networks and social support* (pp. 97–115). Beverly Hills: Sage Publications.

Wortman, C. B., & Lehman, D. R. (1985). Reactions to victims of life crisis: Support attempts that fail. In I. G. Sarason & B. R. Sarason (Eds.), *Social support: Theory, research and applications* (pp. 463–490). Dordrecht: Martinus Nijhoff.

Zajonc, R. B. (1980). Feeling and thinking: Preferences need no inferences. *American Psychologist, 35,* 151–175.

4

Social Support Functions and Network Structures: A Supplemental View

Peggy A. Thoits
Vanderbilt University, Tennessee, USA

This commentary focuses first on the problematic relationship between perceived social support and social network structure, and then on the differing relationships of these distinct phenomena with health and mental health outcomes. These issues have been relatively neglected in social support research to date.

Most theorists and investigators agree that social networks and social support are conceptually different phenomena and should be treated as such (Laireiter & Baumann, Chapter 3; House & Kahn, 1985). Social support generally refers to the perception that assistance is or could be available from significant others (perceived support), or to reports of actual transactions that typically do occur or have occurred between people in times of trouble (received support). Social networks generally refer to people's ties to one another, in particular to the structure of those ties (e.g., the number of ties a person has, the frequency of his or her contact with various network members, the density and multiplexity of relationships among network members, the role relationship of each member to the target respondent, etc.). Of special interest to social support researchers have been respondents' "personal support structures"—the subset of others upon whom respondents rely for assistance when facing stressful circumstances.

Generally, we have lacked valid or reliable measures of social support and social networks, with some notable exceptions being perceived support measures developed by Sarason, Levine, and Basham (1983), Cohen, Mermelstein, Kamarck, & Hoberman (1985), Procidano and Heller (1983), Turner (1981), and Barrera, Sandler, and Ramsey (1981) (e.g., see House and Kahn, 1985; Vaux, Chapter 13). Interestingly, within the stress literature, social network measures have not been the focus of as much psychometric attention as perceived support measures. Although reliability and validity are key psychometric issues to be addressed for both conceptual variables, other measurement problems still need to be solved. For example, the fact that most conceptions of networks and social support are multidimensional in nature adds practical methodological issues. How do we summarize or aggregate across dimensions appropriately, for both network measures and support measures? Or should we aggregate across dimensions? Some of the most basic psychometric and exploratory empirical work has been neglected by many researchers working in this substantive area, primarily because many have been using limited indicators available in secondary data rather than attempting primary data collection.

THE RELATIONSHIP BETWEEN NETWORK STRUCTURES AND PERCEIVED SUPPORT

Beyond measurement problems are substantive problems. Given that perceived support and social networks are (or should be) conceptually distinct phenomena, what is the relationship between the two? We have failed to look closely at the relationships of larger social network structures and smaller personal support structures with perceived support and received support (see also Laireiter & Baumann, Chapter 3). In particular, we prefer to treat perceived or received social support as independent, intervening, or moderating variables in our research, but not as dependent variables in their own right (for an exception, see Wethington & Kessler, 1986).

Presumably, the existence of network ties precedes perceptions and receipt of support. Thus, one question that needs serious study is the degree to which perceptions and receipt of support depend on the structure of a person's social network (Laireiter & Baumann, Chapter 3). Another question, important to sociologists, is this: To what degree do both the network structure and perceived/received support depend on individuals' sociodemographic characteristics, or their location in the social structure? One recent study examined these issues, with a focus on the sociodemographic and network determinants of perceived support availability in a stratified random community sample of married and divorced adults (Demerath, 1990). Demerath reports only very weak positive correlations between structural variables—such as the number of network ties, the frequency of contacts with those ties, or the types of ties possessed (e.g., spouse, relative, friend, neighbor)—and the amount of support a person perceives to be available. Furthermore, although sociodemographic differences in network ties and perceived support are generally small, some telling systematic differences in this study still emerge. For example, married men and women differ very little in the degree of support they perceive to be available, but the source of those perceptions for men is primarily the spouse, while for women it is the spouse and friends.

Differing structural sources of perceived support, as well as the generally weak associations between network variables and perceived support, raise a more general question: What are the origins of social support perceptions, if not in the social network? One possibility is that we have been looking at or within the wrong parts of the network. When we examine structural variables, we typically focus only on that subset of people upon whom our respondents say they rely— the personal support network. Yet Granovetter's (1974) work on "the strength of weak ties" suggests that a very important source of informational and/or instrumental support (especially received support) may be social ties that are not part of our personal support networks. In fact, our respondents may not even be aware of such ties as supportive ones, if they take informational exchange as a normal, accepted part of social life (Pearlin & Schooler, 1978; see also Pearlin & McCall, 1990). These observations suggest that the associations among structural variables, support perceptions, and support transactions deserve much more serious attention than we have given to date. We tend to assume that grafting a support provider or a support group to a person's social network is an appropriate way to intervene in people's lives. However, this intervention strategy only makes sense if perceived or received support in fact covaries strongly and systematically with network structure (see Turner, Chapter 14).

NETWORKS, SUPPORT, AND HEALTH OUTCOMES

That network structure and perceived/received social support are (and should be kept) conceptually and empirically distinct also is reflected in the fact that these variables operate in different ways with respect to health and mental health outcomes. The weight of the evidence indicates that network variables have direct or "main" effects on health and mental health outcomes and do not buffer stress. In contrast, perceived support is typically found to interact with, or buffer, the effects of stress exposure on health and mental health outcomes (Cohen & Wills, 1985; Kessler & McLeod, 1985).[1] These differing processes (direct effects vs. buffering effects) reinforce the observation that social networks and social support must be different phenomena. And these differing relationships with outcome variables need further explanation by support researchers.

The following discussion offers some thoughts on why structural and support variables seem to operate in different ways with respect to mental health outcomes. The discussion considers only mental health outcomes here, because this is the area that this author knows best.

Network factors and support factors may operate differently with respect to psychological well-being, in part, because they are related in different ways (both conceptually and operationally) to problems in people's lives. Network ties are a potential *source* of problems and thus can have direct effects on well-being, whereas perceived or received support is *contingent* on problems, and thus additionally can have stress-buffering effects on well-being.

Elsewhere I have argued that network variables partially tap a more abstract concept, that of social integration-isolation (Thoits, 1982, 1983b, 1985). In one sense, social integration can be seen as a relatively stable, enduring characteristic of people's social lives. In this sense, integration is an aggregate or summary variable indicating a level or degree of contact with others (e.g., summarized as the total number of social relationships, or the total number of ties weighted by frequency of contact). Individuals can derive relatively stable benefits from high numbers of ties and/or high levels of regular and sustained contacts with others: a sense of belonging or security, a sense of purpose and behavioral guidance, and, perhaps, a global sense that support is available, should they need it (Thoits, 1985). In short, our social ties, in the aggregate, are a source of psychological "sustenance." Thus a lack of overall integration—or social isolation—can be a problem or stressor in itself, directly increasing psychological symptoms. Furthermore, to the degree that perceived support (along with a sense of belonging, security, purpose, and guidance) depends on an aggregate level of ongoing social interaction, perceived support should help explain the direct effect of social integration-isolation variables on psychological well-being. Social isolation is a stressor in itself, which reduces the benefits typically derived from ongoing interaction (such as perceived support availability), which in turn should directly increase psychological symptoms.

But social ties are potential sources of stress in other ways. Not all of our relationships are positive ones; we can have ongoing and bitter conflicts with spouses, friends, relatives, or co-workers. Thus the *quality* of various social ties

[1]The direct and buffering effects of received support have been little studied (Wethington & Kessler, 1986).

is an issue. When the overall level of social integration-isolation is disaggregated into its component relationships, and the quality of each of those relationships is assessed, we should see positive relationships directly increasing perceived support and thus psychological well-being, and negative relationships—stressors in themselves—reducing perceived support and psychological well-being. One reason why social network variables are only weakly related to perceived support and well-being may be because researchers rarely disaggregate network ties into those that are positive and unproblematic and those that are problematic or strained (e.g., Berbrier, 1990).

Changes in social integration, such as becoming divorced or widowed, losing one's job, having friends and relatives move away or die, and so forth, are also stressors in themselves, familiar to us in the guise of major life events. Such events certainly increase symptoms of psychological distress (see review in Thoits, 1983a). They may do so, in part, through reducing the perceived availability of social support.

In short, *levels* of integration, *components* of integration, and *changes* in integration are themselves the stuff of potential problems. Thus, we should expect direct or main effects of social network measures on mental health. If perceived support is one intervening, explanatory mechanism for this effect, then we should expect levels, components, and changes in integration to have influences on mental health *through* perceived support. We should expect few, if any, stress-buffering effects of network ties, because many, if not most, of the stressors to be buffered (social isolation, relationship strains, and major changes in social relationships) consist of problems or changes in those ties.

Why then do most studies find a stress-buffering effect with perceived support? A sense of support is not only a factor that is a global or generalized benefit derived from social integration, but it can more easily change with stress exposure, or depend on stress exposure, as the previous commentary suggests. We conceive of perceived support (and especially support transactions) as responsive to problems in people's lives. Support is typically defined as the functions performed for someone by their significant others—specifically, the provision of instrumental, informational, and/or emotional assistance (House & Kahn, 1985). Although these functions may be performed on an ongoing basis (as with the daily exchange of affection between spouses or esteem between co-workers), the usual connotation of "social support" is the provision of assistance *when needed.* Conceptually and operationally, we tie potential support or perceived support to problems. For example, "If you needed a loan, would you have someone to turn to?" Or, less obviously, "My spouse is someone I can rely on for understanding and advice." The implicit question here is a contingent one: "[When you need it] is your spouse someone you can rely on for understanding and advice?" The greater one's social network, or the more positive the marital relationship, the higher the probability that the answers to such questions would be "yes." But integration and support should (and empirically do) operate in different ways because they are differentially related to problems in people's lives. Network variables or integration variables are themselves potential sources of stress or benefit. Support variables, implicitly or explicitly, are contingency variables—responsive to or dependent on the occurrence of stress, by usual definition and by typical operational measurement. Consequently, we should not expect integration and support variables to operate in the same ways with respect to mental health outcomes, and we probably should not expect extremely strong positive relationships between the two kinds of variables, either.

CONCLUSION

The aim of the preceding commentary is to underscore Laireiter and Baumann's (Chapter 3) plea for conceptual clarity and distinctiveness, and to add a plea that in future work we try to elaborate our understanding of how social networks and social integration directly affect well-being, and how social support operates, effectively or ineffectively, to buffer the consequences of particular life problems. These are different issues, requiring different theoretical mechanisms, at different levels of data and analytical specificity. In particular, to understand network or integration effects on mental health more thoroughly, we need to disaggregate structural measures, assess the quality of relationship ties, and examine the influences of qualitative ties on perceived support and well-being. To understand buffering effects more thoroughly, we need to examine specific kinds of problems experienced by individuals and the match or mismatch between those problems and the assistance perceived to be available from or actually offered by providers (Cohen & Wills, 1985). It seems that social network and social support research has come to a recent standstill—with some of the most basic and key questions about what these phenomena are, how they are related to one another, and how and why they work to sustain health and well-being still awaiting answers.

REFERENCES

Barrera, M., Sandler, I., & Ramsay, T. (1981). Preliminary development of a scale of social support: Studies on college students. *American Journal of Community Psychology, 9,* 434–447.

Berbrier, M. (1990). *Disaggregating the main effect of social integration on psychological distress: Relational costs and rewards.* Unpublished master's thesis, Department of Sociology, Indiana University, Bloomington, Indiana.

Cohen, S., Mermelstein, R., Kamarck, T., & Hoberman, H. M. (1985). Measuring the functional components of social support. In I. G. Sarason & B. R. Sarason (Eds.), *Social support: Theory, research and applications.* Dordrecht, The Netherlands: Martinus Nijhoff.

Cohen, S., & Wills, T. A. (1985). Stress, social support, and the buffering hypothesis. *Psychological Bulletin, 98,* 310–357.

Demerath, L. (1990). *Sociodemographic differences in social networks and social support.* Unpublished master's thesis, Department of Sociology, Indiana University, Bloomington, Indiana.

Granovetter, M. S. (1974). *Getting a job: A study of contacts and careers.* Cambridge, MA: Harvard University Press.

House, J. S., & Kahn, R. L. (1985). Measures and concepts of social support. In S. Cohen & S. L. Syme (Eds.), *Social support and health.* Orlando, FL: Academic Press.

Kessler, R. C., & McLeod, J. D. (1985). Social support and mental health in community samples. In S. Cohen & S. L. Syme (Eds.), *Social support and health.* Orlando, FL: Academic Press.

Pearlin, L. I., & McCall, M. E. (1990). Occupational stress and marital support: A description of microprocesses. In J. Eckenrode & S. Gore (Eds.), *Stress between work and family.* New York: Plenum.

Pearlin, L. I., & Schooler, C. (1978). The structure of coping. *Journal of Health and Social Behavior, 19,* 2–21.

Procidano, M. E., & Heller, K. (1983). Measures of perceived social support from friends and from family: Three validation studies. *American Journal of Community Psychology, 11,* 1–24.

Sarason, I. G., Levine, H. M., Basham, R. B., & Sarason, B. R. (1983). Assessing social support: The Social Support Questionnaire. *Journal of Personality and Social Psychology, 14,* 127–139.

Thoits, P. A. (1982). Conceptual, methodological, and theoretical problems in studying social support as a buffer against stress. *Journal of Health and Social Behavior, 23,* 145–159.

Thoits, P. A . (1983a). Dimensions of life events that influence psychological distress: An evaluation and synthesis of the literature. In H. B. Kaplan (Ed.), *Psychosocial stress: Trends in theory and research.* New York: Academic.

Thoits, P. A. (1983b). Multiple identities and psychological well-being: A reformulation and test of the social isolation hypothesis. *American Sociological Review, 48,* 174–187.

Thoits, P. A. (1985). Social support and psychological well-being: Theoretical possibilities. In I. G. Sarason & B. R. Sarason (Eds.), *Social support: Theory, research and applications.* Dordrecht, The Netherlands: Martinus Nijhoff.

Turner, R. J. (1981). Social support as a contingency in psychological well-being. *Journal of Health and Social Behavior, 22,* 357–367.

Wethington, E., & Kessler, R. C. (1986). Perceived support, received support, and adjustment to stressful life events. *Journal of Health and Social Behavior, 27,* 78–89.

II

SUPPORT AND HEALTH: THE EVIDENCE

5

Possible Impact of Social Ties and Support on Morbidity and Mortality

Ralf Schwarzer and Anja Leppin
Freie Universität Berlin, Germany

EMPIRICAL RESEARCH ON SOCIAL RELATIONSHIPS

According to recent reviews of empirical evidence compiled within the last two decades, social relationships appear to have inconsistent effects on physical health—if any effects at all (Cohen, 1988; Ferraro, 1989; Ganster & Victor, 1988; Israel & Rounds, 1987; Leppin & Schwarzer, 1990; House, Umberson, & Landis, 1988; Rodin & Salovey, 1989; Schwarzer & Leppin, 1989a, 1989b, 1991). Many researchers have strongly emphasized the necessity to assess various types of support (Barrera, 1981; Baumann, 1987; Cohen & Hoberman, 1983; Cohen & McKay, 1984; Cutrona & Russell, 1988; Dunkel-Schetter, Feinstein, & Call, 1987; Heitzmann & Kaplan, 1988; House & Kahn, 1985; Vaux, 1988; Veiel, 1987; Wills, 1985).

House et al. (1988) argue for a theoretical subdivision of social relationships into social integration, social networks, and relational content. *Social integration,* referring to the mere existence of a quantity of social relationships, comprises the size of a network, such as number of relatives or friends, and the frequency of contact. The term has also been conceptualized as the number of important roles a person holds, such as being a friend or a boss, or being married (Thoits, 1983). *Social network structure* has been defined as a set of relational properties, such as density, reciprocity, sex composition, durability, or homogeneity of one's network. The assessment of social networks has been discussed by Mueller (1980), Pilisuk and Froland (1978), Vaux and Harrison (1985), Walker, MacBride, and Vachon (1977), and recently by Laireiter and Baumann (1988). *Relational content* comprises social support as well as social regulation and control, and social demands and conflicts.

The distinctions by House et al. (1988) represent a more sociological view, whereas the psychological perspective mainly deals with positive relational content (i.e., the function and quality of beneficial social relationships). One can make a further subdivision of function and quality into categories such as emotional support, instrumental support, informational support, tangible support, esteem support, and appraisal support. From this functional viewpoint, the subjective interpretation of expected or enacted support plays a crucial role (Cobb, 1976; Hobfoll, 1988; Vaux, 1988).

However, within a functional perspective, perceived availability of support has yet to be distinguished from received support (i.e., the activation of support when needed) (Dunkel-Schetter, 1984; Dunkel-Schetter, Folkman, & Lazarus, 1987; McCormick, Siegert, & Walkey, 1987; Newcomb, 1990). *Perceived support* has also been called "cognitive support," whereas received support has been called "behavioral support" (Dunkel-Schetter & Bennett, 1990). Sarason, Pierce, and Sarason (1990) write that perceived support is " . . . best defined as a sense of acceptance, an inherently stable personality characteristic that contributes to the perception of social support separately from what the environment actually offers at any particular point in time" (p. 110). *Received support* is the concept that deals with beneficial behaviors by others. Although it also may concern subjective perceptions of the recipient, these do not pertain to hypothetical situations or general impressions but to behaviors that have been perceived as having actually occurred (Cutrona, 1986a, 1986b, 1989).

Most authors today agree that social integration, perceived social support, and received social support represent distinct concepts that operate in different ways and that have to be measured separately. Vaux (Chapter 13) even abandons the term social support completely in favor of the tripartite approach. He labels the three constructs "network resources," "social support appraisal," and "social support behavior."

Social Factors in Morbidity: Possible Causal Mechanisms

The following section concerns possible mechanisms through which social relationships may influence the development of physical illness. Some research has concentrated on *main effects* of social support (Barrera, 1986; Thoits, 1985) (i.e., effects that come about independent of whether or not the individual finds him- or herself in a stressful situation). Social support, according to this model, would either prevent the event altogether (stress prevention model) or would affect well-being independently of this event (additive model). The *buffer model,* on the contrary, states that social support plays a role especially under stressful circumstances (Cohen & Wills, 1985). Only when something important is at stake for the individual does the presence or absence of social support make a difference. That is, only then can it buffer the deleterious impact of the event by reducing stress appraisal or by giving coping assistance. Some authors attempt to go beyond the simple dichotomy of main effects versus buffer effects by specifying more complex causal models (Barrera, 1988; Cohen, 1988; Schwarzer & Leppin, 1989a, 1990, 1991).

Attempts to deal with the complex causality problem in this field have not been very convincing for further discussion because of conceptual deficits in the support construct itself: Support has mainly been used as a single predictor instead of a set of orthogonal factors (see Barrera, 1986; Cohen & Wills, 1985). Cohen (1988), who modeled the possible influence of social support on the etiology of disease, distinguished generic, stress-centered, and psychosocial process models. This distinction may be helpful in emphasizing the actual difference between various social support processes. Generic models simply refer to the assumption that the beneficial effect of support is mediated either by behavior, biological responses, or both. Stress-centered models pertain to the buffer effects that social support is assumed to have. Support may have either a benign effect on health in the normal population, thus appearing as a statistical main effect, or it may alleviate stress and its consequences. In the stress-buffering model, support may be influential at two points in time: when stressful demands are cognitively appraised, and by dampening health-damaging physiological processes. The stress-centered models are refined in the psychosocial process models.

For both the main effect and the buffer effect hypotheses, Cohen (1988, p. 280) postulates separate types of content-specific models. Thus, the information-based model refers to the fact that wide networks might also provide a wider range of information pertaining to health-relevant behaviors, which ease the access to medical services or help avoid exposure to infectious agents. Identity and self-esteem models, on the other hand, refer to the general self-worth improving effect of social support, which is supposed to contribute to less psychological despair, a greater motivation for self-care, or—more directly health-related—to suppressed neuroendocrine response. Social influence models again maintain that social integration entails controls and pressures by close others that might either promote or discourage certain health-relevant behaviors. Finally, tangible resource models focus on the beneficial effects of aid and material resources provided by others that offer a healthier environment for the individual.

When exposed to prolonged stress, additional lack of social support might lead to a chronically elevated neuroendocrine response and an immune suppression, which in the long run would impair bodily resistance toward illness. Social support, on the other hand, is expected to suppress neuroendocrine reactivity and to enhance immune functioning (Cohen, 1988). Combined with the impairment of health behaviors, the genesis and progression of illness would be negatively affected by lack of support. These processes represent a "missing link" in social support research, insofar as only few empirical studies have tried to investigate these theoretical assumptions. Although these mediating processes are underresearched, there is, on the other hand, an abundance of theoretical and empirical literature on the mere relationship between social support and physical health outcomes (cf. Badura, 1981; Berkman, 1985, 1986; Cohen, 1988, 1989; Cohen & Syme, 1985).

Some empirical studies have dealt with the question of how social integration and social support relate to disease onset (Berkman & Syme, 1979; House, Robbins, & Metzner, 1982; Reed, McGee, Yano, & Feinleib, 1983; Siegrist, 1986). Others have studied the role of social support in coping with chronic illnesses, such as AIDS (Namir, Alumbaugh, Fawzy, & Wolcott, 1989), cancer (cf. Dunkel-Schetter, 1984; Filipp, Ferring, & Klauer, 1986), or coronary heart disease (Badura, Kaufhold, Lehmann, Pfaff, Schott, & Waltz, 1987; Dehnen, Fydrich, & Sommer, 1987; Fontana, Kerns, Rosenberg, & Colonese, 1989; Kulik & Mahler, 1989; Ruberman, Weinblatt, Goldberg, & Chaudhary, 1984). Many studies have

	Psychosocial Functioning Health Behavior / Well-being/ Depression	Morbidity Onset / Recovery	Mortality
Social Integration			
Perceived Support			
Received Support			

Figure 1 A heuristic matrix of social factors and health outcomes.

reported a significant impact of social support on health-related variables, although more empirical evidence exists for mental than for physical health changes (Blöschl, 1987; Brown, Andrews, Harris, Adler, & Bridge, 1986). There is no agreement, however, on the actual effect size in the population as correlations differ in degree and even in direction. The present chapter, therefore, aims to estimate effect sizes for the associations between social factors and morbidity and social factors and mortality.

Multiple Predictors and Multiple Outcomes

As described earlier, social integration has to be distinguished from functional social support, and the latter is made up by two components: perceived (cognitive) and received (behavioral) support. For analytical purposes, Figure 1 displays a matrix made up of the three social variables on the left side and three health outcome variables on the top.

The most typical health outcomes discussed in the literature on social support are (a) psychosocial functioning, including depression and subjective well-being; (b) health behavior; (c) morbidity, including various illness indicators and disease stages; and (d) mortality. This matrix may be useful in the research on social factors and health, with nine resulting cells for different sets of empirical findings. This chapter will not deal with psychosocial functioning but will restrict itself to morbidity and mortality. Most of the evidence has been obtained by the method of meta-analysis, and therefore this approach is described first.

META-ANALYSIS: METHOD, DATA BASE, AND OVERALL RESULTS

The Rationale of Meta-Analysis

The aim of meta-analysis is to integrate a multitude of effect sizes, for instance correlations, that can be found in original empirical studies (Hedges & Olkin, 1985). There is a variety of different meta-analytical techniques, whose common purpose is to integrate information provided by the original studies on a higher statistical level. The present study is based on the Schmidt-Hunter method (Hunter, Schmidt, & Jackson, 1982). This technique makes use of correlations without being restricted to purely correlational studies. Other statistical values (such as *t*, *F*, or *p* values) can be transformed into the "effect size *r*." All sample effect sizes are weighted by the corresponding sample size *N*. Thus the population effect size is defined as the weighted average of all *r* values.

The chosen strategy aims to determine a population effect size for a homogeneous data set of effect sizes. This is achieved by decomposing the observed variance of effect sizes into variance resulting from artifacts and variance resulting from systematic factors (i.e, moderators). Most important for the majority of applications is the determination of this unexplained population variance s^2_{rho} by subtracting the sampling error s^2_e from the observed variance s^2_r.

$$s^2_{rho} = s^2_r - s^2_e$$

The population variance s^2_{rho} is also called the residual variance, and its square root is called residual standard deviation (res_{SD}). An approximation for the sampling error is obtained by

$$s^2_e = ((1 - \bar{r}^2_w)^2 * k)/N$$

where $\bar{r}^2_w$ is the squared weighted mean of the effect sizes, *k* the number of studies, and *N* the total sample size (Hunter et al., 1982).

It is desired that all the observed variance s^2_r be made up by the sampling error s^2_e, making the residual variance s^2_{rho} equal to zero. In that case the percentage of observed variance accounted for by sampling error would be 100% as an indication of homogeneity. Very often, however, only a small percentage can be explained by artifacts, leaving a state of heterogeneity that requires further searches for moderator variables. A total of 100% is usually very difficult to achieve, so that the rule of thumb suggested by Hunter et al. (1982) is a level of at least 75% of variance explained by artifacts to evaluate a data set as being sufficiently homogeneous. The computations were performed with meta-analysis programs designed for personal computers (Schwarzer, 1989).

Data Base

Eighty studies were compiled that yielded a total of 110 effect sizes.[1] Sample sizes ranged from $n = 17$ to $n = 6,534$ with an overall size of $N = 60,936$, a mean of $N_M = 553$, and a median of $N_{Md} = 134$.

The unit of analysis was the subject sample. Some studies were based on more than one independent sample, for instance, in those cases where men and women were dealt with separately. In these cases, each sample was represented by one effect size. A total of 110 samples (= 110 correlations), derived from the 80 studies, were used in this meta-analysis. When the authors did not report any correlations, other statistical values were transformed into effect sizes, or the available material was reanalyzed, wherever possible. Many studies dealing with the given topic did not publish any effect sizes but, rather, risk ratios or exact probabilities. Further information on the data base can be found in Schwarzer and Leppin (1989a, 1989b).

Overall Results

All 110 effect sizes were combined to obtain a first estimate to be used later as a yardstick for comparison. These 110 correlations varied from $r = -.43$ to $r = +.17$. The majority of coefficients was located near zero (Figure 2). The population effect size was $\bar{r}_w = -.07$. The magnitude of such a correlation might seem small, but is not negligible (see discussion section). As expected, the large data set, on which this result was based, was not homogeneous (38%).

MORTALITY AND SOCIAL INTEGRATION

Within studies on mortality, a distinction can be made between large-scale epidemiological studies, where social integration (e.g., marital status) has been related to longevity, and life event studies, where the breakdown of a social network (e.g., loss of a spouse) was related to premature death. We will briefly comment on both lines of research.

Some prospective studies of community populations have repeatedly found that the relative risk to die within a certain time period is higher for the less socially integrated (for a review, see House et al., 1988). The well-known Alameda county study by Berkman and Syme (1979), for instance, states that the mortality risk of weakly integrated persons is about two times higher than that of socially well-integrated men and women. Although the study is based on data from a random sample of 2,229 men and 2,496 women, only extremely small subgroups with high or low social network scores have been selected to compute the relative risk ratios. This implies an overestimation of the true effect size in the population. In contrast, we have estimated an affect size of only $\bar{r}_w = -.07$ for this risk ratio based on the complete Alameda county data set as published by the authors (a more extensive elaboration on this point can be found in Schwarzer & Leppin, 1989a, pp. 209–213). Such a transformation reveals that: (a) effect sizes are less spectacular than some other statistics, at least in those cases where large samples or extreme groups

[1]A list of the studies can be obtained from the authors.

are involved; and (b) small effect sizes can nevertheless be important if serious consequences are at stake.

Another line of research on social integration and mortality is devoted to widowhood (Bowling, 1987; Stroebe & Stroebe, 1983; Walker et al., 1977). In general, marriage is regarded as being beneficial to human functioning (Depner & Intersoll-Dayton, 1985), and, therefore, loss of a spouse represents a breakdown of one's social network with serious health consequences. Can the life event of losing a spouse be so detrimental that it results in the premature death of the

```
-.9 I
-.8 I
-.7 I
-.6 I
-.5 I
-.4 I 003
-.3 I 0014577
-.2 I 01123456777
-.1 I 0011222233344444455555667889
-.0 I 0000111222333344445555666666688888888999999
+.0 I 000123346667
+.1 I 012257
+.2 I
+.3 I
+.4 I
+.5 I
+.6 I
+.7 I
+.8 I
+.9 I
```

Figure 2 Stem-and-leaf display of all 110 effect sizes.

Table 1 Studies on mortality risk after conjugal bereavement (based on Ferraro, 1989)

Study	Mortality risk, (x) months after bereavement
Young et al., 1963	Higher (6)
Cox & Ford, 1964	Higher (24)
Rees & Lutkins, 1967	Higher (24), higher for men (12)
Parkes et al., 1969	Higher (6)
Ward, 1976	Higher for men (6)
Helsing & Szklo, 1981	Higher for men (12)
Helsing et al., 1981	Higher for men (12) who did not remarry
Jones, 1987	Higher (12), esp. for women

survivor? Many studies addressed this question and came to inconsistent results (Dimond, Lund, & Caserta, 1987; Ferraro, Mutran, & Barresi, 1984; for reviews, see Bowling, 1987; Ferraro, 1989). The mortality risk for widows/widowers seems to be increased compared to married people. It is greatest for men during the first 6 months of bereavement. Eight studies of the mortality risk after bereavement are summarized in Table 1. All studies found an increased risk of the survivor also passing away, especially in the first 6 months after the loss of a spouse, and especially for widowers as compared to widows.

There may be two reasons for the gender difference: (a) the social network for men is on the average smaller than that for women, and (b) widowhood seems to occur at an older age for men than for women. To explain the latter point, because of the typical age difference in couples and the biological gender differences in longevity, men die earlier than their spouses. As a result, the death of a wife leaves a widower who, on the average, is considerably older and lacks a supportive network. Men usually confide in their spouse as their most intimate and reliable, if not only, network member. In contrast, women cultivate a somewhat larger network of family members and friends until they die. Their higher level of social integration may buffer the stressful experience of the loss of their husbands (Haas-Hawkings, Sangster, Ziegler, & Reid, 1985; McGloshen & O'Bryant, 1988; Wister & Strain, 1986).

There may be several reasons why widowers have a slightly increased risk of dying within the first half year of bereavement. One reason among others may be the lack of coping assistance by close network members (Figure 3). When men feel socially isolated during the grieving process, they may develop severe loneliness and depression, which in turn may lead to further consequences. First, they might be at greater risk for committing suicide and, second, on a more long-term perspective, their immune systems or cardiovascular health may be affected, resulting in illness and, eventually, death. The latter pathway may represent one possible explanation for the association between social isolation and morbidity.

In the present meta-analysis, we identified 18 data sets based on 10,735 subjects, arriving at a weighted average of $\bar{r}_w = -.07$. This gives the best estimate to date of the association between mortality and social integration. This is a homogeneous and therefore reliable set of effect sizes (98% of the observed effect size variance is explained by sampling error alone). These were studies typically of the same kind as the Alameda county study, which alone provided 6 of the 18 effect sizes in this analysis (because of gender and age different samples). It is very unlikely that further studies will deviate from this mean except if they use different populations, methods, or definitions. A second look at the data revealed a slight trend in gender differences, with men having closer relationships between social integration and mortality, based on a perfectly homogeneous data set of nine effect sizes (Table 2). The effect for males would have been stronger without the six effect sizes taken from the Alameda county study.

The studies cited so far have investigated death from all causes. There seem to be some differences, however, with respect to specific causes of death (see Lynch & Convey, 1979). Litwak and Messeri (1988) report on national mortality statistics and conclude that (a) singles are at higher risk than married persons, (b) for some causes (such as suicide) this single-to-married ratio is higher than for others (such as cancer), and (c) for males this ratio is higher than for females (Figure 4). We mention in passing that studies have explored the role of social networks and supports in suicide attempters (e.g., Veiel, Brill, Häfner, & Welz, 1988). This means, for example, that almost twice as many single as married individuals die from coronary heart disease, and that about three times as many single as married men die from pulmonary diseases, whereas only twice as many single as married women die from this disease.

MORBIDITY AND SOCIAL INTEGRATION OR SOCIAL SUPPORT

There is empirical evidence that bereaved persons experience an immediate health decline after the loss of a spouse (Ferraro, 1985), but the results are incon-

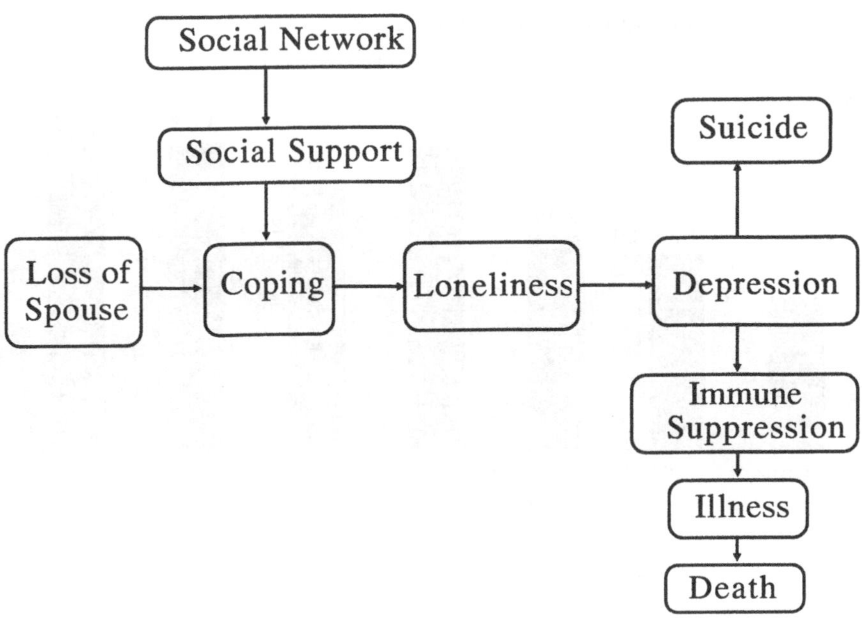

Figure 3 Causal pathways to death after loss of a spouse.

Table 2 Relationships between social integration and mortality

Variable	k	N	$\bar{r}_w$	% homogeneity
Women	9	5,293	−.06	59
Men	9	5,442	−.08	100

k, number of studies; N, total sample size; $\bar{r}_w$, population effect size; % homogeneity, percentage of observed variance accounted for by sampling error.

sistent and have to be discussed with respect to different health indicators and to length of time anticipating the death.

Widowed people show impaired psychological and social functioning, including depression, but only few studies demonstrate a significant decline in physical health. Perceived health seems to decline in the short run, especially for men (Hyman, 1983; Wan, 1984), and disability seems to increase (Wan, 1982). Frequency of sick days, use of ambulatory physician services, and onset of illness according to medical exams seem to be the same for the widowed and for controls (see review by Ferraro, 1989). There is no evidence that the onset of specific diseases such as cancer or coronary heart disease is triggered by the loss of a spouse or by any other kind of bereavement.

Length of time anticipating the death of a spouse seems to be related in a curvilinear way to perceived health. "Sudden and unexpected loss of a spouse creates special problems, but so may attempting to provide care for a spouse over several years. Death stings in most cases, but the former resembles a sharp pain

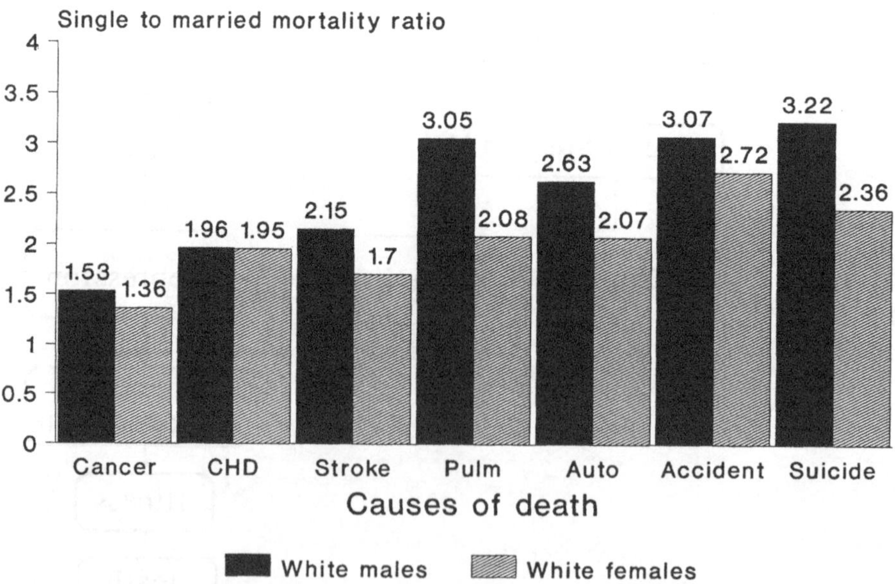

Figure 4 Benefits from marriage, especially for men (based on 1981 data of NCHS, cited after Litwak & Messeri, 1988).

demanding reorganization while the latter is a dull, chronic pain that delays life reorganization" (Ferraro, 1989, p. 76).

In the present meta-analysis, a population effect size of −.07 was computed for the relationship between social integration/social support with morbidity as well as with mortality. A distinction between social integration, functional support, and support satisfaction as related to illness brought about more revealing results. For social integration we determined a population effect size of −.07, for functional social support −.08, and for satisfaction with support −.25 (for details see Leppin & Schwarzer, 1990).

Relationships Between Social Support/Social Integration and Different Operationalizations of Illness

It was necessary to have a look at how different indicators of health and illness were affected by social embeddedness, hence several indicator subgroups were formed. These included general health ratings, where persons were asked to rate their health on an "excellent/good/fair/poor" scale, and symptom indices, where persons were requested to fill in lists of symptoms such as headache, stomach pains, fever, and so forth. Chronic diseases such as angina pectoris or arthritis comprised another group. This group was further split into one subgroup containing only cardiovascular diseases and another subgroup dealing with all other chronic illnesses. Another subcategory was severity of disease (i.e., progress and/or recovery) and, finally, mortality. Table 3 contains the meta-analytic results for each of these categories.

Population effect sizes ranged from $\bar{r}_w = -.03$ to $\bar{r}_w = -.13$. Obviously, social support yielded higher correlations with the more subjective indicators, such as general health ratings ($\bar{r}_w = -10$) and symptoms indices ($\bar{r}_w = -.11$), than with the more objective criteria such as chronic disease ($\bar{r}_w = -.04$). Only two of these effect sizes were reliable: for illness severity, and for chronic illness when cardiovascular diseases were excluded. The more social support, the less severe the respective illnesses, and the less prevalence and incidence of chronic disease. However, relationships were only weak to moderate. Interesting to note is the subset of data dealing with chronic disease. It was possible to split up data pertaining exclusively to cardiovascular diseases and contrast them to all other types of chronic disease (which in the majority of cases meant summary indices of chronic

Table 3 Relationships between social support/social integration and different operationalizations of illness

Variable	*k*	*N*	$\bar{r}_w$	% homogeneity
Health rating	10	10,714	−.10	43
Symptom indices	45	16,536	−.11	37
Diseases (all)	19	22,787	−.04	31
Diseases (without CHD)	8	3,172	−.13	100
CHD	12	19,684	−.03	34
Severity of disease	7	1,316	−.08	83

k, number of studies; *N*, total sample size; $\bar{r}_w$, population effect size; % homogeneity, percentage of observed variance accounted for by sampling error.

diseases). The effect size for cardiovascular diseases was very small ($k = 12$; $N = 19{,}684$; $\bar{r}_w = -.03$), however this subset was not homogeneous (34%). In comparison, for the subject of "all other illnesses" a considerably higher population effect size was yielded ($k = 8$; $N = 3{,}172$; $\bar{r}_w = -.13$), which was based on a totally homogeneous data set.

For the purpose of the present discussion, only some aspects of the findings are important. We therefore turn to those subanalyses in which specific kinds of social relationships have been related to physical symptoms, thereby excluding results on illness incidence, blood pressure, time of recovery, and other illness indicators. The majority of studies used symptoms such as headache, fever, and stomach pains as a cumulative index. Social integration was only slightly associated with reports of physical symptoms (−.07), whereas functional support was more closely connected, especially in the case of instrumental support (−.18). The highest correlation was obtained for the evaluative component (i.e., satisfaction with support [−.25]). This points to the fact that the quality of support that is subjectively experienced is most crucial for physical symptoms—at least as far as self-reports of such symptoms are concerned.

Another question answered by this meta-analysis was whether cognitive (perceived) and behavioral (received) support would relate to symptom reporting to a similar degree, or whether there would be large differences. It turned out that perceived availability of support was correlated with physical symptoms in the expected way (−.11). However, received support had a surprising positive correlation with symptoms (+.12). A striking result such as this one was found nowhere else in the entire data set, which is based on seven studies with 451 subjects and can be considered reliable because the observed effect size variance was almost completely explained by sampling error (97%).

Why should more symptom complaints be associated with more support? There may be different reasons, but one seems to be particularly salient. Behavioral social support refers to seeking, receiving, and evaluating tangible aid, care, and emotional attachment. In times of prolonged stress, physical symptoms may develop, and simultaneously one's social network may be activated for assistance. A positive correlation between poor health and social support can thus be a result of such a mobilization effect, with the prior stress episode being the eliciting cause of both support and complaints. This possibility is discussed in more detail elsewhere (Schwarzer & Leppin, 1991).

Gender Differences

Another step focused on the analysis of specific kinds of social support broken down by gender (Table 4). Note that for three of the results in Table 4, the 75% level of homogeneity was passed. Because of the absence of substantial systematic factors, valid conclusions can be drawn in these cases. Above and beyond the overall gender gap that became apparent again, the kind of predictor (i.e., network or functional support) made a difference for women but not for men. For women the relationship with health was considerably stronger for functional support ($\bar{r}_w = -.14$), including perceived support ($\bar{r}_w = -.16$) and emotional support ($\bar{r}_w = -.13$), than for social integration ($\bar{r}_w = -.06$). In contrast, for the male subgroup, effect sizes were quite consistent across types of support measured ($\bar{r}_w = -.04$ for network, $\bar{r}_w = -.04$ for functional and perceived support, and $\bar{r}_w = -.02$ for

Table 4 Relationships between social integration/social support, different types of social support and illness for female and male samples

Variable	k	N	$\bar{r}_w$	% homogeneity
Network/women	21	6,735	−.06	76
Network/men	17	14,561	−.04	77
Support/women	20	2,024	−.14	53
Support/men	19	15,606	−.04	34
Perceived support/women	16	1,786	−.16	56
Perceived support/men	17	15,502	−.04	35
Emotional support/women	8	634	−.13	100
Emotional support/men	6	8,048	−.02	44

k, number of studies; N, total sample size; $\bar{r}_w$, population effect size; % homogeneity, percentage of observed variance accounted for by sampling error.

emotional support). However, restrictions apply to this interpretation because only the marginal gender difference in terms of social integration was based on reliable data subsets. An interesting finding was that, for the female sample, satisfaction with support yielded the highest effect size overall ($k = 6$; $N = 463$; $\bar{r}_w = -.26$; 38% explained by sampling error). Unfortunately, there were not enough effect sizes on this dimension for men, so comparisons could not be made.

Recovery from a Disease or Medical Treatment

When relating social factors to illness, it is important to distinguish between the onset of a disease, its severity, and the process of recovery (Cohen, 1988, 1989; Wallston, Whitcher Alagna, De Vellis, & De Vellis, 1983). There is not yet convincing evidence that social integration or social support has considerable effects on the onset of specific diseases, but there is evidence that the severity of a chronic disease can be favorably affected by social support. In a review on social factors and breast cancer, for example, Vernon and Jackson (1989) concluded that the evidence is conflicting. Some studies found that married cases had longer survival than unmarried cases, but one study reported the opposite finding, and others have found no association between either social integration or social support with survival or time to recurrence of the cancer.

Kulik and Mahler (1989) studied the effect of natural social support on recovery from surgery. They measured time spent in a surgical intensive care unit as well as time spent in the hospital for 56 married male coronary-bypass patients, half of them with low support and half of them with high support. Behavioral support was assessed unobtrusively by observing the actual number of spouse visits in the hospital. In addition, 16 unmarried fellow patients were studied. Highly supported married males were released 1.26 days sooner on the average than their low-supported counterparts. The effect size is $r = -.31$ (converted by us from $F[1,52] = 5.44$). The unmarried men fell in between. Unmarried patients who are used to coping with everyday life in the absence of a significant other are apt to be more self-reliant. Married patients, however, are accustomed to someone being around and usually expect their spouses to be supportive in times of crisis. Therefore, they might be worse off when expectations are not met. The authors discuss several causal pathways that may have produced gains in recovery. First, it is possible that spouse support improved the emotional states of patients (e.g., by holding their hands, cheering them up, being understanding and compassionate). Second, spouses may have directly encouraged recommended recovery behaviors such as deep-breathing exercises, ambulation, eating the right diet, or getting sufficient rest, combined with an expression of confidence in the patient's skill to recover. This excellent study is noteworthy in particular because (a) it assessed behavioral support in terms of observed sections (visits), and (b) it used an objective outcome measure (recovery time), thus going beyond most other studies where predictor and outcome variables tend to be more or less confounded.

CONCLUSION

The present meta-analysis reflects the current empirical evidence about the linear statistical relationship between social integration/social support and mortality or physical illness. It has been revealed that the relation between these variables is a negative, if moderate-sized, one. Another recent meta-analysis established that social support is much more closely linked to depression than to physical health (Schwarzer & Leppin, 1989a)—a result that does not come as a surprise considering the conceptual closeness of many definitions of support on the one hand, and psychological well-being on the other. Although moderate and small effect sizes like those found here might seem somewhat disappointing at first sight, a closer look at the practical relevance of these results might change one's perspective. If we take, for instance, the population effect size of $\bar{r}_w = -.07$, found for the relationship between social embeddedness and mortality, this might seem a negligible correlation. Rosenthal's (1984) binomial effect size display, however, demonstrates that such a correlation of $-.07$ can be interpreted in a different manner: If there were 100 persons with weak social embeddedness, 53.5% of whom die, in another group of 100 persons with strong social embeddedness, only 46.5% would die during the same time range. This example may show that small correlations may well be of importance where matters of life and death exist.

There is good reason to believe that the social support and health relationship might be empirically underestimated. First, negative and positive correlations are counterbalanced when averaged. Although in the majority of cases more support is associated with less illness, there may be substantial positive correlations under specific conditions. More illness may be associated with more support, for example when accidents or sudden diseases occur, resulting in the mobilization of one's network. At a later point in time, this spurious correlation may disappear. Unfortunately, most studies do not control for changes over time. It may be that the onset of an illness initially mobilizes a network until caregiver burnout or other factors once more reduce the amount of support. If all positive correlations would result from such a mobilization effect, then they would represent a category of their own and should not be collapsed with negative correlations from studies where different causal mechanisms are at work. Second, the relationship between support and health is underestimated in studies that fail to specify an appropriate causal model or where health behaviors are held constant. Social support operates partly through other variables and exerts indirect effects on health that may even exceed the straightforward direct effect. Social support can prompt health behavior, such as adherence to medical regimens. The same applies when the effect of social isolation on illness is determined after partialling out all other risk factors, such as smoking, lack of exercise, or substance use. The latter risk factors may be mediators, thus contributing to the total effect of social isolation on illness. Partialling out risk factors may at least obscure the causal relationship between social resource factors and health outcomes.

Illness Indicators and Mortality

Interpreting the meta-analytic results for different illness indicators suggests that support and social integration might be more important for the subjective illness indicators, such as general health ratings and symptom indices (often in terms of psychosomatic symptoms), than for chronic disease or disease severity (i.e., progression or recovery) and mortality. Although it is not surprising that a psychological construct such as social support should be more strongly related to subjective indicators of health than objective ones, questions still remain for the majority of these issues. Only the effect sizes for illness severity, mortality, and chronic diseases minus cardiovascular conditions were based on homogeneous data. Data for mortality all came from longitudinal studies and therefore carry considerably more weight than, for instance, those for physical symptoms where a majority of studies were of a cross-sectional nature.

Even though the issue of social integration and mortality might be settled, the topic of social support and mortality has not even been tackled yet. In fact, all effect sizes in this meta-analysis for the mortality data were based on measures of social integration only. Also, chronic disease deserves a lot more attention than it has received to date. The very low rate of homogeneity suggests that this general category might yet be much too broad. Until now, however, any subgroupings along these lines were difficult because of the lack of a sufficient number of studies within such subsamples.

Limitations

There are a number of limitations in this study, some of which pertain to the meta-analytic method and some of which reflect the current empirical status within the field of support research. For instance, it is unknown whether the compiled 80 studies are representative of research done in this field. Retrieval, publication, and reporting bias may all have contributed to an unknown number of studies remaining in "file drawers." Although Rosenthal (1984) developed a method for developing some rough estimate of this bias, this "fail safe *N*-formula" is not yet applicable to effect sizes *r*.

Yet another meta-analytic deficiency contributes to the problem of representativeness. Although methodologically poor studies often can be used in meta-analysis by transforming *p* values, cell frequencies, or percentage tables to effect sizes *r*, methodologically sophisticated studies using multiple regressions, structural modeling, or log-linear analysis often fail to provide the reader with elementary statistics (such as correlation tables), and thus have to be excluded from meta-analytic computations. The same restriction applies for curvilinear relationships. A further shortcoming of this study pertains to the fact that some advanced options available to meta-analysts could not be employed because of limitations inherent in the empirical material. Meta-analytic techniques nowadays permit researchers to consider the unreliability of the measures employed, and to compute a population effect size that is not biased by this kind of artifact. However, only a minority of the studies on social support and health reported reliability coefficients, and it did not seem appropriate to provide results for unbiased effect sizes.

Also, the currently available empirical material lacks in specificity (i.e, studies do not separate their samples on the basis of different characteristics, or use very general measures for support or illness). This deficiency makes it difficult to break down large samples into smaller, more specific subsamples.

In the future, controlled longitudinal studies are needed that will not deal with any general effect of social support or social integration on any kind of illness indicator, but very specific research into the effects of different types of support on very specific outcome indicators for different people under different circumstances. Subjective measures of support should be enriched by behavioral indicators (Cutrona, 1986a, 1986b, 1989; Kulik & Mahler, 1989; Vaux, 1988), experimental manipulations (Sarason, 1986), or systematic support interventions in natural settings (Gottlieb, 1988). Also, the onset of a disease, its severity, and the recovery from it should be analyzed separately, because social factors may operate in different ways at various stages of the pathogenic process.

REFERENCES

Badura, B. (Ed.). (1981). *Soziale Unterstützung und chronische Krankheit. Zum Stand sozial-epidemiologischer Forschung.* Frankfurt: Suhrkamp.

Badura, B., Kaufhold, G., Lehmann, H., Pfaff, H., Schott, T., & Waltz, M. (1987). *Leben mit dem Herzinfarkt.* Berlin: Springer.

Barrera, M. (1981). Social support in the adjustment of pregnant adolescents. In D. Gottlieb (Ed.), *Social support networks* (pp. 69–96). San Francisco, CA: Jossey-Bass.

Barrera, M. (1986). Distinctions between social support concepts, measures, and models. *American Journal of Community Psychology, 14,* 413–445.

Barrera, M. (1988). Models of social support and life stress: Beyond the buffering hypothesis. In L. H. Cohen (Ed.), *Life events and psychosocial functioning* (pp. 211–236). London: Sage.

Baumann, U. (1987). Zur Konstruktvalidität der Konstrukte Soziales Netzwerk und Soziale Unterstützung. *Zeitschrift für Klinische Psychologie, 16,* 305–310.

Berkman, L. F. (1985). The relationship of social networks and social support to morbidity and mortality. In S. Cohen & S. L. Syme (Eds.), *Social support and health* (pp. 141–160). Orlando, FL: Academic Press.

Berkman, L. F. (1986). Social networks, support, and health. Taking the next step forward. *American Journal of Epidemiology, 123,* 559–562.

Berkman, L. F., & Syme, S. L. (1979). Social networks, host resistance, and mortality: A nine-year follow-up study of Alameda county residents. *American Journal of Epidemiology, 109,* 186–204.

Blöschl, L. (1987). Soziales Netzwerk/Soziale Unterstützung, Lebensbelastung und befindlichkeit. Eine Standortbestimmung aus psychologischer Sicht. *Zeitschrift für Klinische Psychologie, 16,* 311–320.

Bowling, A. (1987). Mortality after bereavement: A review of the literature on survival periods and factors affecting survival. *Social Science and Medicine, 24,* 24–117.

Brown, G. W., Andrews, B., Harris, T., Adler, Z., & Bridge, L. (1986). Social support, self-esteem, and depression. *Psychological Medicine, 16,* 813–831.

Cobb, S. (1976). Social support as a moderator of life stress. *Psychosomatic Medicine, 38,* 300–314.

Cohen, S. (1988). Psychosocial models of the role of social support in the etiology of physical disease. *Health Psychology, 7*(3), 269–297.

Cohen, S. (1989). Social support and physical health: Symptoms, health behaviors and infectious disease. In M. Cummings, A. L. Greene, & K. H. Karraker (Eds.), *Lifespan developmental psychology: Perspective on stress and coping.* Hillsdale, NJ: Erlbaum.

Cohen, S., & Hoberman, H. M. (1983). Positive events and social support as buffers of life change stress. *Journal of Applied Psychology, 13,* 99–125.

Cohen, S., & McKay, G. (1984). Social support, stress, and the buffering hypothesis: A theoretical analysis. In A. Baum, S. E. Taylor, & J. E. Singer (Eds.), *Handbook of psychology and health* (Vol. 4, pp. 253-267). Hillsdale, NJ: Erlbaum.

Cohen, S., & Syme, S. L. (1985). *Social support and health.* New York: Academic Press.

Cohen, S., & Wills, T. A. (1985). Stress, social support, and the buffering hypothesis. *Psychological Bulletin, 98,* 310-357.

Cox, P. R., & Ford, J. R. (1964). The mortality of widows shortly after widowhood. *Lancet, 1,* 163-164.

Cutrona, C. E. (1986a). Behavioral manifestations of social support: A microanalytic investigation. *Journal of Personality and Social Psychology, 51,* 201-208.

Cutrona, C. E. (1986b). Objective determinants of perceived social support. *Journal of Personality and Social Psychology, 50,* 349-355.

Cutrona, C. E. (1989). Ratings of social support by adolescents and adult informants: Degree of correspondence and prediction of depressive symptoms. *Journal of Personality and Social Psychology, 57*(4), 723-730.

Cutrona, C. E., & Russell, D. W. (1988). The provisions of social relationships and adaptation to stress. In W. H. Jones & D. Perlman (Eds.), *Perspectives on interpersonal behavior and relationships.* Greenwich, CT: JAI Press.

Dehnen, D., Fydrich, T., & Sommer, G. (1987). Soziale Unterstützung und soziale Belastung bei Patienten mit Herzinfarkt [Social support and social burden with coronary patients]. *Zeitschrift für Klinische Psychologie, 16,* 414-419.

Depner, C. E., & Intersoll-Dayton, B. (1985). Conjugal social support: Patterns in later life. *Journal of Gerontology, 40*(6), 761-766.

Dimond, M., Lund, D. A., & Caserta, M. S. (1987). The role of social support in the first two years of bereavement in an elderly sample. *Gerontologist, 27*(5), 599-604.

Dunkel-Schetter, C. (1984). Social support and cancer: Findings based on patient interviews and their implications. *Journal of Social Issues, 40,* 77-98.

Dunkel-Schetter, C., & Bennett, T. L. (1990). The availability of social support and its activation in times of stress. In I. G. Sarason, B. R. Sarason, & G. R. Pierce (Eds.), *Social support: An interactional view* (pp. 267-296). New York: Wiley.

Dunkel-Schetter, C., Feinstein, L., & Call, J. (1987). *A self-report inventory for the measurement of social support.* Unpublished manuscript, Los Angeles, UCLA, Department of Psychology.

Dunkel-Schetter, C., Folkman, S., & Lazarus, R. S. (1987). Correlates of social support receipt. *Journal of Personality and Social Psychology, 53,* 71-80.

Ferraro, K. F. (1985). The effect of widowhood on the health status of older persons. *International Journal of Aging and Human Development, 21,* 9-25.

Ferraro, K. F. (1989). Widowhood and health. In K. S. Markides & C. L. Cooper (Eds.), *Aging, stress and health* (pp. 69-90). Chichester: Wiley.

Ferraro, K. F., Mutran, E., & Barrersi, C. M. (1989). Health and friendship support in later life. *Health and Social Behavior, 25,* 245-259.

Filipp, S. H., Ferring, D., & Klauer, T. (1986). *Deskription und Effektanalyse von Formen der Krankheitsbewältigung bei Tumorpatienten (Forschungsbericht Nr. 8).* Trier: Universität Trier, Fachbereich I Psychologie.

Fontana, A. F., Kerns, R. D., Rosenberg, R. L., & Colonese, K. L. (1989). Support, stress, and recovery from coronary heart disease: A longitudinal model. *Health Psychology, 8,* 175-193.

Ganster, D. C., & Victor, B. (1988). The impact of social support on mental and physical health. *British Journal of Medical Psychology, 61,* 17-36.

Gottlieb, B. H. (1988). *Marshaling social support. Formats, processes, and effects.* Beverly Hills, CA: Sage.

Haas-Hawkings, G., Sangster, S., Ziegler, M., & Reid, D. (1985). A study of relatively immediate adjustment to widowhood in later life. Special issue II: Feminist psychology: Single life and married life: Women's sexuality. *International Journal of Women's Studies, 8*(2), 158-166.

Hedges, L. V., & Olkin, I. (1985). *Statistical methods for meta-analysis.* New York: Academic Press.

Heitzmann, C. A., & Kaplan, R. M. (1988). Assessment of methods for measuring social support. *Health Psychology, 7*(1), 75-109.

Helsing, K. J., & Szklo, M. (1981). Mortality after bereavement. *American Journal of Epidemiology, 114,* 41-52.

Helsing, K. J., Szklo, M., & Comstock, G. W. (1981). Factors associated with mortality after widowhood. *American Journal of Public Health, 71,* 802-809.

Hobfoll, S. E. (1988). *The ecology of stress.* Washington, DC: Hemisphere.

House, J. S., & Kahn, R. L. (1985). Measures and concepts of social support. In S. Cohen & S. L. Syme (Eds.), *Social support and health* (pp. 83–108). New York: Academic Press.

House, J. S., Robbins, C., & Metzner, H. L. (1982). The association of social relationships and activities with mortality: Prospective evidence from the Tecumseh Community Health Study. *American Journal of Epidemiology, 116,* 123–140.

House, J. S., Umberson, D., & Landis, K. R. (1988). Structures and processes of social support. In W. R. Scott & J. Blake (Eds.), *Annual review of sociology* (Vol. 14, pp. 293–318). Palo Alto, CA: Annual Reviews.

Hunter, J. E., Schmidt, F. L., & Jackson, G. B. (1982). *Meta-analysis: Cumulating research findings across studies.* Beverly Hill, CA: Sage.

Hyman, H. H. (1983). *Of time and widowhood.* Durham, NC: Duke University.

Israel, B. A., & Rounds, K. A. (1987). Social networks and social support: A synthesis for health educators. In W. B. Ward (Ed.), *Advances in health education and promotion* (Vol. 2, pp. 311–351). Greenwich, CT: JAI Press.

Jones, D. R. (1987). Heart disease mortality following widowhood: Some results from the OPCS longitudinal study. *Journal of Psychosomatic Research, 31,* 325–333.

Kulik, J. A., & Mahler, H. I. M. (1989). Social support and recovery from surgery. *Health Psychology, 8,* 221–238.

Laireiter, A., & Baumann, U. (1988). Klinisch-psychologische Soziodiagnostik: Protektive Variablen und soziale Anpassung. *Diagnostika, 34,* 190–226.

Leppin, A., & Schwarzer, R. (1990). Social support and physical health: An updated meta-analysis. In L. R. Schmidt, P. Schwenkmezger, J. Weinman, & S. Maes (Eds.), *Health psychology: Theoretical and applied aspects* (pp. 185–202). London: Harwood.

Litwak, E., & Messeri, P. (1988). Social supports and mortality rates: A disease specific formulation. In S. K. Steinmetz (Ed.), *Family and support systems across the life span* (pp. 257–282). New York: Plenum.

Lynch, J. J., & Convey, W. H. (1979). Loneliness, disease, and death: Alternative approaches. *Psychosomatics, 20,* 702–708.

McCormick, I. A., Siegert, R. J., & Walkey, F. H. (1987). Dimensions of social support: A factorial confirmation. *American Journal of Community Psychology, 15,* 73–77.

McGloshen, T. H., & O'Bryant, S. L. (1988). The psychological well-being of older, recent widows. *Psychology of Women Quarterly, 12*(1), 99–116.

Mueller, D. P. (1980). Social networks: A promising direction for research on the relationship of the social environment to psychiatric disorder. *Social Science and Medicine, 14,* 147–161.

Namir, S., Alumbaugh, M. J., Fawzy, F. I., & Wolcott, D. L. (1989). The relationship of social support to physical and psychological aspects of AIDS. *Psychology and Health, 3,* 77–86.

Newcomb, M. D. (1990). What structural equation modeling can tell us about social support. In B. R. Sarason, I. G. Sarason, & G. R. Pierce (Eds.), *Social support: An interactional view* (pp. 26–63). New York: Wiley.

Parkes, C. M., Benjamin, B., & Fitzgerald, R. G. (1969). Broken heart: A statistical study of increased mortality among widowers. *British Medical Journal, 1,* 740–743.

Pilisuk, M., & Froland, C. (1978). Kinship, social networks, social support and health. *Social Science and Medicine, 12B,* 273–280.

Reed, D., McGee, D., Yano, K., & Feinleib, M. (1983). Social networks and coronary heart disease among Japanese men in Hawaii. *American Journal of Epidemiology, 117,* 384–396.

Rees, W. D., & Lutkins, S. G. (1967). Mortality of bereavement. *British Medical Journal, 4,* 13–16.

Rodin, J., & Salovey, P. (1989). Health psychology. *Annual Review of Psychology, 40,* 533–579.

Rosenthal, R. (1984). *Meta-analytic procedures for social research.* Beverly Hills, CA: Sage.

Ruberman, W., Weinblatt, E., Goldberg, J. D., & Chaudhary, B. S. (1984). Psychological influences on mortality after myocardial infarction. *New England Journal of Medicine, 311,* 552–559.

Sarason, B. R. (1986). Social support, social behavior, and cognitive processes. In R. Schwarzer (Ed.), *Self-related cognitions in anxiety and motivation* (pp. 77–86). Hillsdale, NJ: Erlbaum.

Sarason, B. R., Pierce, G. R., & Sarason, I. G. (1990). Social support: The sense of acceptance and the role of relationships. In B. R. Sarason, I. G. Sarason, & G. R. Pierce (Eds.), *Social support: An interactional view* (pp. 97–128). New York: Wiley.

Schwarzer, R. (1989). *Meta-analysis programs. Version 4.0.* Raleigh, NC: National Collegiate Software Clearinghouse.

Schwarzer, R., & Leppin, A. (1989a). Social support and health: A meta-analysis. *Psychology and Health: An International Journal, 3,* 1–15.

Schwarzer, R., & Leppin, A. (1989b). *Sozialer Rückhalt und Gesundheit: Eine Meta-Analyse* [Social support and health: A meta-analysis]. Göttingen: Hogrefe.
Schwarzer, R., & Leppin, A. (1990). Social support, health, and health behavior. In K. Hurrelmann & F. Lösel (Eds.), *Health Hazards in Adolescence* (pp. 363-384). Berlin/New York: Walter de Gruyter.
Schwarzer, R., & Leppin, A. (1991). Social support and health. A theoretical and empirical overview. *Journal of Social and Personal Relationships, 8,* 99–127.
Siegrist, K. (1986). *Sozialer Rückhalt und kardiovaskuläres Risiko.* München: Minerva.
Stroebe, M. S., & Stroebe, W. (1983). Who suffers more? Sex differences in health risks of the widowed. *Psychological Bulletin, 93,* 279–301.
Thoits, P. A. (1983). Dimension of life events as influences upon the genesis of psychological distress and associated conditions: An evaluation and synthesis. In H. B. Kaplan (Ed.), *Psychosocial stress: Trends in theory and research* (pp. 33–103). New York: Academic Press.
Thoits, P. A. (1985). Social support processes and psychological well-being: Theoretical possibilities. In I. G. Sarason & B. R. Sarason (Eds.), *Social support: Theory, research and applications* (pp. 51–72). Dordrecht, The Netherlands: Martinus Nijhoff.
Vaux, A. (1988). *Social support: Theory, research, and intervention.* New York: Praeger.
Vaux, A., & Harrison, D. (1985). Support network characteristics associated with support satisfaction and perceived support. *American Journal of Community Psychology, 13,* 245–268.
Veiel, H. O. F. (1987). Einige kritische Anmerkungen zum Unterstützungskonzept [Some critical remarks on the concept of support]. *Zeitschrift für Klinische Psychologie, 16,* 397–399.
Veiel, H. O. F., Brill, G., Häfner, H., & Welz, R. (1988). The social supports of suicide attempters: The different roles of family and friends. *American Journal of Community Psychology, 16,* 839–861.
Vernon, S. W., & Jackson, G. L. (1989). Social support, prognosis and adjustment to breast cancer. In K. S. Markides & C. L. Cooper (Eds.), *Aging, stress and health* (pp. 165–198). Chichester: Wiley.
Walker, K. N., MacBride, A., & Vachon, M. L. S. (1977). Social support networks and the crisis of bereavement. *Social Science and Medicine, 11,* 35–41.
Wallston, B. S., Whitcher Alagna, S. W., De Vellis, B. M., & De Vellis, R. F. (1983). Social support and physical health. *Health Psychology, 2,* 367–391.
Wan, T. T. H. (1982). *Stressful life events, social-support networks, and gerontological health.* Lexington, MA: Lexington.
Wan, T. T. H. (1984). The health consequences of major role losses in later life: A panel study. *Research on Aging, 6,* 469–489.
Ward, A. W. M. (1976). Mortality of bereavement. *British Medical Journal, 1,* 700–702.
Wills, T. A. (1985). Supportive functions of interpersonal relationships. In S. Cohen & S. L. Syme (Eds.), *Social support and health* (pp. 61–82). New York: Academic Press.
Wister, A. V., & Strain, L. (1986). Social support and well-being: A comparison of older widows and widowers. *Canadian Journal on Aging, 5*(3), 205–220.
Young, M., Benjamin, B., & Wallis, C. (1963). The mortality of widowers. *Lancet, 2,* 454–456.

6

Social Support and Depression

A. S. Henderson
The Australian National University, Canberra, Australia

The environment is the source of most human stresses and noxious influences. After two decades of enthusiastic research on the health consequences of adverse life events, with only a modest yield in useful knowledge, attention has now turned to the intuitively appealing notion that the social environment may contain some beneficial elements. The manner in which the social support hypothesis seems to have come about has been described elsewhere (Henderson, Byrne, & Duncan-Jones, 1981; Henderson, 1988, p. 98). In his essay, "On Friendship," sixteenth century English writer Francis Bacon captured the issue with remarkable clarity, distinguishing between social interaction in the relief of distress and in the promotion of well-being. Bacon said:

> "... *this communicating of a man's self to his friend works two contrary effects; for it redoubleth joys, and cutteth griefs in halfs. For there is no man that imparteth his joys to his friends, but he joyeth the more; and no man that imparteth his griefs to his friends, but he grieveth the less.*"

For present purposes, we start with the proposition that supportive social relationships confer some degree of protection against depressive symptoms, depressive disorder, and anxiety. A separate proposition is that they may promote well-being or positive mental health. This author is not aware of hypotheses relating to the onset of schizophrenia, bipolar affective disorder, substance abuse, dementia, or other major categories of psychiatric morbidity. There is, though, the remarkable finding of a possible link between social support and lower mortality (House, Landis, & Omberson, 1988; Schwarzer & Leppin, Chapter 5). The broad hypothesis currently under investigation is that social support protects against both symptoms of anxiety or depression and an unspecified range of physical disorders contributing to mortality in later life. This implies an unusually broad spectrum of effects. Furthermore, there is at present no biologically plausible explanation for the reduction in mortality that is claimed. By contrast, the hypothesis for depression and anxiety does have a plausible theoretical basis.

SOCIAL SUPPORT AND DEPRESSION

This discussion first examines the hypothesis that the probability of developing depressive symptoms is higher in persons who are conspicuously deficient in social support. It is this hypothesis that has attracted by far the most research effort in the social support area. The hypothesis can be further specified according to whether a direct or a buffering effect is proposed, whether only intimate ties or more diffuse relationships are effective, whether the effect is looked for at all levels of morbidity (or only for cases of depression), and whether it is to be observed in both untreated and treated samples. There is one further hypothesis that deserves as much attention, but which has been relatively neglected: that social support has a *therapeutic* effect on depressive symptoms that are already established.

THE EVIDENCE

We have carried out a search of the English-language literature, selecting only those publications that addressed social support and depression, and that were conducted on community or other untreated samples. The latter restriction carries the advantage of not having the study variables confounded by help-seeking. There is good reason for this. Both Henderson, Byrne, Duncan-Jones, Adcock, and Scott (1978) and Brugha et al. (1982), using almost the same methodology with neurotic outpatients, found a strong association between symptoms and the lack of social support. The strength of this association was much greater than is typically reported in cross-sectional community studies, suggesting that it is more apparent in those who have reached not just general practice but specialist services. In such persons, the level of social support may be confounded by help-seeking or some selection effect akin to Berkson's bias (Berkson, 1946). On the other hand, the possible disadvantage of a community sample is that the severity of the disorder, or the attendant social and occupational disability, may be less than in a treated series. This is a problem that is commonly encountered in psychiatric epidemiology.

Thirty-five studies were identified. Our intention was to conduct a meta-analysis on the data. This proved to be impracticable because of the considerable variability in the characteristics of the sample, the measures of social support and stressors, and, above all, of depression as the dependent variable. The only alternative is to critically examine the studies reported and the significance of their findings.

Of the 35 studies, 9 were longitudinal in design, and thereby offered some advantage in investigating causal effects. Sample sizes ranged from 70 to 2,234. The measure of social support was of highly variable quality, ranging from the theoretically sophisticated, interviewer-based Bedford College method (Brown & Harris, 1978) or the systematic Interview Schedule for Social Interaction (Henderson et al., 1981), to brief postal questionnaires (e.g., Holohan & Moos, 1981), or even a single item on the presence or absence of a confidant (O'Neill, Lance, & Freeman, 1986). This is emphasized to illustrate the range in the quality of the data that have been gathered on the social environment of respondents. In a similar way, the measure of depression varied from very brief, self-completed inventories to well-established, standardized psychiatric interviews based on specified diagnostic criteria.

Across this mélange of study characteristics, two findings emerge with remarkable consistency: (a) there is an inverse association between social support and affective symptoms, and (b) there is a buffering effect in the presence of severe stressors. Indeed, only four studies found no evidence for this protective effect (Andrews, Tennant, Hewson, & Vaillant, 1978; Aneshensel & Stone, 1982; Parry & Shapiro, 1986; O'Neill et al., 1986). Contrary to the expectation of many investigators, a direct effect was found in several studies, where the lack of social support seemed to have contributed to depression whether or not severe life events had also taken place.

Particularly noteworthy is the unexpected finding of Husaini, Newbrough, Neff, and Moore (1982) that support from relatives and friends, in the presence of adverse life events, was directly associated with *higher* levels of symptoms. Seven of the nine longitudinal studies reported a buffering effect, and four found a direct effect; none found no buffering effect, and only one reported no direct effect. There was one additional feature of these findings: the association or effect was usually not a strong one. Regrettably, it was not possible to quantify this, expressed as an effect size, because of the reasons given earlier.

INTERPRETATION

On the basis of the studies listed in Table 1, a case can be made that the hypothesis about depression should be accepted—that is, that deficient social support increases the risk of developing depressive symptoms. The direction of the findings points to such an association; and the longitudinal studies give at least some confidence that support influences mood, and not the reverse. What is remarkable is the consistency of findings from studies that vary so greatly in the quality of their method. Although most are based on community samples, some have used special populations, such as general practice lists, postpartum women, and working-class women. The subjects' gender, which is a potentially important variable, has been mainly both men and women, or only women, and the sample sizes have varied from just more than 100 to more than 2,000.

The difference that one would expect to most influence the results is in how depressive symptoms and social support were measured. For both domains, the range in Table 1 is considerable. Social support was determined by an extensive interview in some studies, but in others by only a few items in a self-completed questionnaire. All assessments were by self-report. Support was usually taken to be based on more diffuse social interaction or engagement, but in some studies special attention was also accorded to intimate ties and the relationship with confidants. Depressive states were determined mainly by self-completion inventories, requiring endorsement of items concerning depressive symptoms. In a few studies, there was a clinical interview leading to a diagnosis.

What is notable is that the more brief instruments, for either support or depression, seem to show the association just as strongly as the more elaborate methods. Either there is indeed an association that is strong enough to show up even when measurement error is marked, or there is confounding between the two variables, whereby the one contains elements of the other, at least as they are measured in these studies. It would help to have some validation of self-reported data on social support.

If a causal effect is accepted, whereby deficient social support contributes to the onset of depressive states, the next step is to consider how this might come about. In the studies listed here, social support consisted of very diverse elements, from intimate ties to involvement with neighborhood activities. We have to ask, therefore, what is common to such diverse representations of social support? In this author's opinion, this is not yet known. The crucial issue is whether this unknown is a core element of the social environment that affords support, or whether it is a

Table 1 Social support and depression

Year	Author	Design	Sample	Size	Gender	SS measure	Depression measure (Dp)	Finding direct (D) buffer (B)
1975	Brown et al.	c/s	Community	220	F	Bedford interview	PSE	B^+
1976	Miller & Ingham	c/s	GP lists	337	M&F	Interview	Symptom list in interview	D^+ B^+
1978	Andrews et al.	c/s	Community	863	M&F	16 items, self-comp.	GHQ-20	D^+ B^0
	Brown & Harris	c/s	Community	458	F	Interview	PSE	B^+
	Eaton	L (2 yr)	Community	720	M&F	Interview (soc. role perf.)	20-item Gurin	B^+
1980	La Rocco et al.	c/s	Diverse	636	M	12 items (supervisor, co-workers, and family, 4 each)	Langner, 6 items Dp	D^+ B^+
	Paykel et al.	c/s	Postpartum women	120	F	5-pt. rating for confidant, etc.	Raskin Scale	B^+
	Henderson et al.	c/s	Community	756	M&F	ISSI	GHQ-30 PSE Zung	D^+ B^+ (B^0 in men)
1981	Holohan & Moos	L (1 yr)	Community	493	M&F	Mailed, self-comp. interview (work and family)	7-item interview	D^+ (weak)
	Henderson et al.	L	Community	231	M&F	Interview	GHQ	B^+ D^0
	Williams et al.	L (1 yr)	Community	2,234	M&F	9 items, contacts and resources	38 items; anx, anxiety, and Dp	D^+ + B^+
1982	Aneshensel & Stone	c/s	Community	1,003	M&F	2 measures by interview; no. of close rels.; perceived soc. supp.	CES-D	D^+ B^0
	Bell et al.	c/s	Community	2,029	M&F	8 pt. SS index	Dp invent.	D^+ B^+
	Costello	c/s	Community	449	F	Rating	PSE	D^+; intimacy only
	Husaini et al.	c/s	Community	965	M&F	Questionnaire, 8 items	CES-D	D^+ B^+
	Murphy	c/s	Community and patients (elderly)	200 + 100	M&F	Intimacy rating	PSE	B^+

	Fleming	c/s	Special pop (TMI)	109	M&F	6 items	SCL-90 Beck	B^+
	Solomon & Bromet	c/s	Community	435	F	Interview confidant	SADS-L (last 2/52)	D^+ B^+
	Campbell	c/s	Selected soc. classes iv and v	110	F	Bedford College method	PSE (1 yr)	B^+
	Cohen & Hoberman	c/s	Students	70	M&F	Questionnaire available and perceived	CES-D	D^+ B^+
	Turner & Noh	c/s	Parturient women	312	F	Questionnaire	19 sys (6 Dp)	B^+ (qual)
1984	Eisemann	c/s	Depressed patients	111	M&F	Interview	Clinical diagnosis	+
	Bebbington	c/s	Community	310	M&F	Bedford	PSE	B^-
	Surtees	c/s L	Community	576	F	Interview	PAS	D^+
	D'Arcy & Siddique	c/s	Community	417	F	Questionnaire: spouse and community	GHQ	D^+
1985	Dressler	c/s	Black community	285	M&F	Detailed interview	HSCL-Dp subscale	B^+ (only in males)
	Lin & Dean	L	Community	696 (for 3 years)	M&F	Interview	CES-D	D^+ B^+
1986	Hallstrom	c/s	Community	800	F	Intimacy	DSM-III interview	D^+
	Brown et al.	L	Selected community	400	F	SIS and interview	PSE	B^+ (& let down)
	Henderson et al.	c/s	Community elderly	274	M&F	ISSI	GMS	D^+
	Parry & Shapiro	c/s	Working-class mothers	193	F	Interview	PSE	D^+ B^0
	O'Neill et al.	c/s	Students	206	M&F	Interview: one item on confid.	Beck	D^+ B^0
1987	Bolton & Oatley	L	Unemployed vs. employed	94	M	Interview	Beck	B^+
	Harris et al.	c/s	Community	225	F	Bedford	PSE	B^+
1988	Andrews & Brown	L	Working-class women	150	F	Bedford	PSE	B^+

third variable residing in the individual's capacity to establish and maintain mutually satisfying personal relationships. The study by Sarason and Sarason (1982) suggests such a link between support and personality. There are, then, three major questions that remain unclear or unknown about social support and depression. First, what components of the social environment, when lacking, increase the risk of onset of depression? Second, are these components specific in their effect for particular age groups or gender? Third, what is the relevance of personality as a third variable, influencing both social relationships and vulnerability to depression?

CONCLUSION

It seems reasonable to conclude that the evidence, and particularly the epidemiological evidence, is in favor of the social support hypothesis. But the contribution seems to be quite modest compared to factors such as a family history of depression. Indeed, it is notable that not one of the studies reviewed here included family history of affective disorder in the data, presumably because that belongs to a different paradigm. Very few studies offered data on previous history of depression. Where an association is demonstrated between low social support and an increased incidence of depression, it is hard to know what this means. Actual events and interactions between participants are apparently impossible to separate from the attitudes and behavior of the subject.

The choice for future work lies between (a) refining the original hypothesis with particular attention to the problem of personality, or (b) turning our attention to the therapeutic hypothesis concerning the effects of support on persons who are already depressed, or at risk of relapse. The first choice has the attraction of being highly relevant to the related hypothesis about differential mortality. It would clearly be an advance to know what elements in the social environment are beneficial for physical and mental health. To achieve this would require methods and instruments capable of dissecting the many facets of social relationships that seem to be candidates (Henderson et al., 1981). The second choice is an entirely different strategy, but it might contribute to the management of patients and their aftercare, and thereby have an applied value. What is clear is that it is not satisfactory to study the social or interpersonal environment without simultaneously bearing in mind the contribution made by that individual to the manner in which that environment operates.

A therapeutic or preventive trial would have the advantage of being able to control for personality factors, provided the size and design of the study were appropriate. What is not clear is how the findings in Table 1 could be translated into a social treatment. Here there is scope for some innovative designs in which samples of persons with longstanding or recurrent depressive symptoms would undergo a controlled trial consisting of augmentation in selected components of their social environment. As with research on expressed emotion, this work would need to examine the effect of interaction with medication. Little is known about the acceptability of such a social treatment, nor about the duration over which it would have to be maintained. Another appropriate group for a preventive trial would be groups who are conspicuously deficient in social support and who are believed to have an increased incidence of depression. But without efforts to find some application for social support research, the knowledge now available will offer little contribution to public health.

REFERENCES

Andrews, B., & Brown, G. W. (1988). Social support, onset of depression and personality: An exploratory analysis. *Social Psychiatry, 23*, 99–108.

Andrews, G., Tennant, C., Hewson, D. M., & Vaillant, G. E. (1978). Life event stress, social support, coping style, and risk of psychological impairment. *Journal of Nervous and Mental Disease, 166*(5), 307-316.

Aneshensel, C. S., & Stone, J. D. (1982). Stress and depression. *Archives of General Psychiatry, 39*, 392-396.

Bebbington, P. E., Sturt, E., Tennant, C., & Hurry, J. (1984). Misfortune and resilience: A community study of women. *Psychological Medicine, 14*(2), 347-363.

Bell, R. A., LeRoy, J. B., & Stephenson, J. J. (1982). Evaluating the mediating effects of social support upon life events and depressive symptoms. *Journal of Community Psychology, 10*, 325–340.

Berkson, J. (1946). Limitations of the application of fourfold table analysis to hospital data. *Biometrics Bulletin, 2*, 47–53.

Bolton, W., & Oatley, K. (1987). A longitudinal study of social support and depression in unemployed men. *Psychological Medicine, 17*(2), 453–460.

Brown, G. W., Andrews, B., Harris, T., Adler, Z., & Bridge, L. (1986). Social support, self-esteem and depression. *Psychological Medicine, 16*, 813–831.

Brown, G. W., Bhrolchain, M. N., & Harris, T. (1975). Social class and psychiatric disturbance among women in an urban population. *Sociology, 9*(2), 225–254.

Brown, G. W., & Harris, T. (1978). *Social origins of depression: A study of psychiatric disorder in women*. London: Tavistock.

Brugha, T., Conroy, R., Walsh, N., Delaney, W., O'Hanlon, J., Dondero, B., Daly, L., Hickey, N., & Burke, G. (1982). Social networks, attachments and support in minor affective disorders: A replication. *British Journal of Psychiatry, 141*, 249–255.

Campbell, E. A., Cope, S. J., & Teasdale, J. D. (1983). Social factors and affective disorder: An investigation of Brown and Harris' model. *British Journal of Psychiatry, 143*, 548–553.

Cohen, S., & Hoberman, H. (1983). Positive events and social supports as buffers of life change stress. *Journal of Applied Social Sciences, 13*, 99–125.

Costello, C. G. (1982). Social factors associated with depression: A retrospective community study. *Psychological Medicine, 12*(2), 329–339.

D'Arcy, C., & Siddique, C. M. (1984). Social support and mental health among mothers of pre-school and school age children. *Social Psychiatry, 19*, 155–162.

Dressler, W. W. (1985). Extended family relationships, social support, and mental health in a southern black community. *Journal of Health and Social Behavior, 26*(1), 39–48.

Eaton, W. W. (1978). Life events, social supports and psychiatric symptoms: A re-analysis of the New Haven data. *Journal of Health and Social Behavior, 19*, 230–234.

Eisemann, M. (1984). Depressed patients and non-psychiatric controls: Discriminant analysis on social environment variables. *Acta Psychiatrica Scandinavica, 71*, 495–498.

Fleming, R., Baum, A., Gisriel, M. M., & Gatchel, R. J. (1982). Mediating influences of social support on stress at Three Mile Island. *Journal of Human Stress, 8*, 14–22.

Hallstrom, T. (1986). Social origins of major depression: The role of provoking agents and vulnerability factors. *Acta Psychiatrica Scandinavica, 73*, 383–389.

Harris, T., Brown, G. W., & Bifulco, A. (1987). Loss of parent in childhood and adult psychiatric disorder: The role of social class position and premarital pregnancy. *Psychological Medicine, 17*, 163–183.

Henderson, A. S. (1988). *An introduction to social psychiatry.* Oxford: Oxford University Press.

Henderson, S., Byrne, D. G., Duncan-Jones, P., Adcock, S., Scott, R., & Steele, G. P. (1978). Social bonds in the epidemiology of neurosis: A preliminary communication. *British Journal of Psychiatry, 132*, 463–466.

Henderson, S., Byrne, D. G., Duncan-Jones, P., Scott, R., & Adcock, S. (1980). Social relationships, adversity and neurosis: A study of associations in a general population sample. *British Journal of Psychiatry, 136*, 574–583.

Henderson, S., Grayson, D. A., Scott, R., Wilson, J., Rickwood, D., & Kay, D. W. K. (1986). Social support, dementia and depression among the elderly living in the Hobart community. *Psychological Medicine, 16*, 379–390.

Henderson, S., Byrne, D. G., & Duncan-Jones, P. (1981). *Neurosis and the social environment.* Sydney: Academic Press.

Holohan, C. J., & Moos, R. H. (1981). Social support and psychological distress: A longitudinal analysis. *Journal of Abnormal Psychology, 90*(4), 365–370.

House, J. S., Landis, K. R., & Omberson, D. (1988). Social relationships and health. *Science, 241,* 540–545.

Husaini, B. A., Newbrough, J. R., Neff, J. A., & Moore, M. C. (1982). The stress-buffering role of social support and personal competence among the rural married. *Journal of Community Psychology, 10,* 409–426.

La Rocco, J. M., House, J. S., & French, J. R. P. (1980). Social support, occupational stress, and health. *Journal of Health and Social Behavior, 21,* 202–218.

Lin, N., & Dean, A. (1985). Social support in the etiology of depression: A panel study. In P. Pichot, P. Berner, R. Wolf, & K. Thau (Eds.), *Psychiatry: The state of the art.* Epidemiology and Community Psychiatry (Vol. 7, pp. 123–128). New York: Plenum Press.

Miller, P. M., & Ingham, J. G. (1976). Friends, confidants, and symptoms. *Social Psychiatry, 11,* 51–58.

Murphy, E. (1982). Social origins of depression in old age. *British Journal of Psychiatry, 141,* 135–142.

O'Neill, M. K., Lancee, W. J., & Freeman, S. J. J. (1986). Psychosocial factors and depressive symptoms. *Journal of Nervous and Mental Disease, 174,* 15–23.

Parry, G., & Shapiro, D. A. (1986). Social support and life events in working class women. *Archives of General Psychiatry, 43*(4), 315–323.

Paykel, E. S., Emms, E. M., Fletcher, J., & Rassaby, E. S. (1980). Life events and social support in puerperal depression. *British Journal of Psychiatry, 136,* 339–346.

Sarason, I. G., & Sarason, B. R. (1982). Concomitants of social support: Attitudes, personality characteristics, and life experiences. *Journal of Personality, 50*(3), 331–344.

Solomon, Z., & Bromet, E. (1982). The role of social factors in affective disorders: An assessment of the vulnerability model of Brown and his colleagues. *Psychological Medicine, 12*(1), 123–130.

Surtees, P. (1984). Kith, kin and psychiatric health: A Scottish survey. *Social Psychiatry, 19,* 63–67.

Turner, R. J., & Noh, S. (1983). Class and psychological vulnerability among women: The significance of social support and personal control. *Journal of Health and Social Behavior, 24,* 2–15.

Williams, A. W., Ware, J. E., & Donald, C. A. (1981). A model of mental health, life events, and social supports applicable to general populations. *Journal of Health and Social Behavior, 22,* 324–336.

7

Social Support, Depression, and Other Mental Disorders: In Retrospect and Toward Future Prospects

Scott M. Monroe and Sheri L. Johnson
University of Oregon, USA

Twenty years after interest in social support began to take strong theoretical and empirical form, the topic now finds itself in what perhaps can be described as the awkward state of late adolescence. Although there has been much development, growth alone does not define maturity, and the present state of knowledge is not without its infelicities and blemishes. This is not to say that thinking on social support has not progressed along a number of lines. We clearly have more differentiated conceptualizations of the component dimensions of the idea, more refined methods for measuring individual differences along such dimensions, better research designs for studying the effects of support, and a wealth of empirical reports from which to draw inferences about our ideas and with which to guide future inquiry. Yet the gangly literature lacks an overriding sense of coordination and coherence. It is time to highlight areas in which understanding has not progressed so smoothly and in which immaturities may hinder further developments.

The theme of the present chapter is that social support concepts should become more closely tied to relatively specific psychological states and processes. Turning our attention from social support per se and enlarging our attention to include specific forms and facets of psychopathology forces us to confront many shortcomings of prior research. By this we mean that support may be related to different forms of psychological disturbances on the one hand, and that social support may be related to the development and variable course of different disorders on the other. This suggests that a more differentiated perspective on the dimensions and characteristics of psychopathology may help to clarify what elements of social support, and under what psychological conditions, are of importance for modifying symptomatology. By expanding our concepts and research to address such considerations, we may find better pathways to lead us to a more cogent theory about social factors and psychological functioning. Our discussion of these issues is confined to primarily mental disorders, especially depression, although the

This work was sponsored in part by National Institute of Mental Health Research Grant MH39139.
The authors wish to thank Anne D. Simons and Hans O. F. Veiel for their helpful comments on previous drafts of the chapter.

points raised are applicable across a wide range of outcomes of interest to social support investigators.

The first objective of the chapter is to evaluate the research evidence on social support and psychological distress. From this exercise we conclude that the bulk of existing work is far too general in its approach to the issues, and in fact may be very misleading. Drawing from this analysis, the second objective is to provide a preliminary framework for how investigators might go about attaining a better understanding of social support influences in psychopathology. Specifically, we use depression as an example to outline how support might be more closely examined with reference to specific aspects of the disorder over time. This includes not only the onset of disorder, but also the exacerbation and remission of existing conditions, as well as the future susceptibility to relapse and recurrence over an individual's lifetime. Overall, we raise issues that have not already received widespread attention yet may be influential for rethinking the nature of social support in psychopathology. Consequently, we forego many of the more well-trodden topics of discussion (several of which are still timely), as well as intricate issues involving measurement and modeling associations of support with stress in the study of these disorders, to highlight a particular vantage point on this large amount of research literature.

SOCIAL SUPPORT AND GENERAL PSYCHOLOGICAL FUNCTIONING IN RETROSPECT

Unlike many topics of isolated academic interest, social support research has captured the interests of scientists and nonscientists alike. Although few without specific training attempt to conduct research on the molecular genetics of psychopathology, many people—by virtue of common grounding in a social world—feel qualified to comment on, if not actively investigate, the role of social support and its influences on such disturbances. The intuitive appeal and attraction of social support ideas underlies the research areas' explosive popularity and has resulted in the proliferation of research on the topic over the past two decades.

Probably the majority of studies have employed either nonclinical groups of convenience or general population samples. At the most general level of association, these studies have consistently linked aspects of social support with general measures of psychological functioning (Barrera, 1986; Cohen & Wills, 1985; Kessler, Price, & Wortman, 1985). Beyond the consistency in the overall association, though, myriad findings paint an often confusing and contradictory picture of the more specific processes and possible mechanisms that may be involved. Separating the meaningful from the mundane under such circumstances becomes an arduous undertaking. Thus, although there is a wealth of information on the association between social support (variously defined and measured) and psychological functioning (variously defined and measured), there is little consensus in the research literature on what it might all collectively mean.

One way around this impasse might be to focus in greater detail on the nature of the symptoms typically found in such samples. Does such an intensified focus on the characteristics of such symptomatology yield insights compatible with prevailing opinions? Put differently, if we closely examine the characteristics of the psychological problems typical in such research, do we arrive at similar beliefs as those that currently typify thinking on the topic? Our conclusion is "no." In particular, we discuss: (a) the nature of changes in symptoms over time, and (b) the specific psychological states associated with such symptoms. This analysis places us in a better position to then clarify under what conditions and how social support might influence psychological functioning.

The Nature of Change in Psychological Functioning

As just noted, social support has repeatedly been found to predict subsequent psychological functioning. It is commonly inferred from this that deficiencies in support predict subsequent onset of, or increases in, psychological distress. Is this inference tenable from the existing research?

In the majority of longitudinal investigations on community or nonpatient samples that measure psychological symptoms, mean levels of psychological symptoms do not change appreciably over time. Indeed, follow-up measures often indicate minor to significant decreases in symptomatology (Henderson, Byrne, & Duncan-Jones, 1981; Lin, Ensel, & Dean, 1986). What do associations between social support and subsequent changes in symptoms indicate in the context of an overall decreasing level of symptoms? This clearly places a very different theoretical tone on the findings. Several interpretations can be offered (e.g., test-retest artifact; Ormel, Koeter, & van den Brink, 1989). Overall, though, such findings suggest that it may not be justified to infer onset of symptomatology, or exacerbation of existing symptomatology, from such research. In other words, given decreasing symptoms over time, research on social support findings may more appropriately be characterized as favoring a "symptom reduction effect" (i.e., greater levels of social support predict fewer symptoms over time) rather than a "symptom onset effect" (i.e., lower levels of social support predict an increase in symptoms over time). Thus much of the evidence from this work might be interpreted with the idea that social support is most relevant for helping people better their psychological condition, rather than for helping them to prevent the onset of, or increase in, distress (Henderson et al., 1981).

Although overall levels of symptoms do not appear to markedly change over time in the samples studied (and indeed may decrease), we might also ask on a more individual basis about the frequency and degree of changes in psychological functioning over time. That is, could there be subgroups of people who make large shifts into and out of different psychological states that tend to cancel each other out in terms of mean scores over time? It does not appear so. People tend to maintain a high degree of stability in their symptomatic profiles (Depue & Monroe, 1986). Indeed, invariably the largest predictor of subsequent psychological functioning is simply previous psychological functioning. For example, up to 30%–40% of the variance in symptoms over a one-year period is accounted for by prior symptoms (Depue & Monroe, 1986). This suggests something quite important about the waxing and waning of such psychological states over time. The majority of people maintain their relative ranking. They "drift" about a personally characteristic mean level, rather than "shift" into qualitatively different psychobiological states. This literature, then, indicates that major changes in psychological symptoms are relatively infrequent, and that most changes in psychological symptoms are of relatively minor magnitude. Coupled with the point previously raised about mean levels of symptom scores decreasing over time, this suggests that what is being modeled by social support research in such studies is relatively small scale shifts for the better in psychological status.

This interpretation is at odds with the typical view of such research, yet it forces investigators to consider three points. First, although social support seems to influence people's mood states for the better, this can mean either not becoming symptomatic or becoming less symptomatic. Second, it is clear that such research is clumsy. Existing approaches are not well designed to detect the phenomena of ostensible primary interest—major shifts in psychological functioning over time. Such shifts are overwhelmed by the more common, lower-level fluctuations in psychological status. Yet this raises a final, equally important issue: These lower-level movements in emotional status, too, may have interesting—but potentially different—relations to social support.[1]

The Nonspecificity of Symptoms and Distinctive Psychological States

The measures of psychological symptoms typically employed in the research we have been discussing are very nonspecific with regard to the psychological conditions that contribute to the final score (Depue & Monroe, 1986). It is likely that there are qualitatively distinct psychological states that are indiscriminately merged within the final summary index. Indeed, this is one of the major reasons psychopathologists have adopted formal definitions and operational criteria in psychiatric diagnosis and classification. In essence, we suggest that investigators may look for common effects of support across very different conditions or mood states, whereas the underlying situation may be one wherein there are many subtle interactions between social support and qualitatively different psychological states.

Social support, or particular components of support, that influence one psychological state simply may not be relevant for the others. Although people vary in the degree to which they may be characterized as suffering from psychological distress, they may also vary in the degree to which they may be characterized as being satisfied with their lives, or as having positive affect (Watson, Clark, & Cary, 1988). Recent research on the structure of mood states might be interpreted to suggest that casual social interactions are influential in regulating satisfaction and well-being (e.g., positive affect), yet it does not directly follow that such processes are operative in buffering severe stress and preventing depression. In the latter case, it may be only the availability of a confidant, or the confidant "coming through" in the hours of need, that are effective (Brown & Harris, 1986). Thus while certain features of social support may be inherent in the regulation of normal day-to-day mood and cognition, other features of social relations may be more influential for the more extreme degrees of emotional turmoil. There may be more

[1]We are not implying that research does not exist to substantiate that social support is related to onset of clinical cases of psychological distress. Such research does exist as we shall soon discuss. Unfortunately, though, these latter studies are in a distinct minority and are far outnumbered by these nonspecific correlational protocols. As opinions are often swayed more by quantitative rather than qualitative considerations, the clinical studies are not accorded an influence commensurate to their caliber. What we are suggesting, though, is that the implications of the studies that form the largest base for existing reviews and opinions derived thereof may be quite different than is commonly believed.

relevant partitions in the "extreme degrees of emotional turmoil"—or specific classes of psychopathology—that extend this idea further. Given the likely influence of social processes and support concepts across a wide range of psychological phenomena, there is no reason to assume a priori that the nature of such associations is the same across these levels of emotional functioning. Indeed, it is scientifically imprudent to do so at this stage of knowledge.

Finally, the principle of specificity—that support may be differentially related to different psychological conditions or states—is applicable "within" as well as "between" different psychological conditions. Thus social support (or different features of support) may be relevant for certain stages in the course of a psychological disorder (e.g., onset vs. remission), but not for others. Note, too, that this premise incorporates the idea that support may both prevent increases and/or promote decreases in symptoms.

A selective overview of past research on the general associations between social support and psychological symptoms raises the concern at several levels for greater specificity in modeling aspects of support in relation to specific features of psychopathology. It seems more prudent at the present stage of knowledge to disaggregate conceptualizations of both social support and psychological disorders and to study in a more refined manner the range of support-affect interactions that may be involved. This will provide a more discriminating approach for clarifying under what conditions and how social support might influence particular aspects of psychological functioning. We attempt to illustrate how these concerns may be addressed next with specific reference to social support and the depressive disorders.

SOCIAL SUPPORT AND SPECIFIC PSYCHOLOGICAL STATES: FUTURE PROSPECTS

The next generation of studies on social support and psychopathology needs to be more detailed with respect to where in the nosology and clinical course of these disorders social support concepts might have impact. Although inroads have been made by several investigators already, a large research agenda remains. We next attempt to outline these considerations and thereby provide the framework for investigating where in the clinical and lifetime course of depression social support may be of importance. With our focus on specificity involving psychological states, though, the following discussion foregoes the many equally vital considerations involving the specification and measurement of social support. This is not to indicate that such matters are not of equal importance, but rather their neglect is a result of the relative emphasis placed on the two topics in past research. Indeed, the logical extension of our theme is to apply specific qualities of social support to specific dimensions and processes involving psychopathology. Nonetheless, in bringing this neglected side of social support research into greater focus we do not want the reader to lose sight of the many issues that remain concerning specificity in the conceptualization and measurement of social support.

The Nature of Change in Psychological Functioning: The Onset and Course of Depression

It is perhaps most useful to think of depression in terms of a process with relatively distinctive stages over time. This includes not just onset of the disorder, but the exacerbation or mitigation of symptoms over time, including formal remission, relapse, and recurrence. Social support may have relevance not only for the initiation of the disorder, but also for the transitions between the different phases of the process (Monroe & Depue, 1991). Furthermore, there may be relevant subcategories of depression that deserve separate attention (e.g., endogenous vs. nonendogenous). Each of these issues requires relatively specific research considerations with respect to the possible role(s) of support.

Acute "Episodic" Disorders and Chronic Depressions

Many individuals exhibit the classical picture of an episode of depression: They move from relatively normal mood states into more profoundly disabling conditions. Much of what is known about depression comes from such investigations of onset, and suggests that such features as having a confidant, perceiving the availability of support, and receiving crisis support may decrease the likelihood of developing depression of such clinical proportions (Brown & Harris, 1978, 1986; Henderson et al., 1981).

There is a significant degree of variability in the course of these episodes once they have begun. The major dimensions involve the possible exacerbation (or mitigation) of symptoms on the one hand, and the possible protraction (or termination) of symptoms on the other (Brown, Adler, & Bifulco, 1988; Monroe, 1982). Qualities of support transactions may play a role in either of these two important arenas. Does the nature of the supportive relationship change under stress, or in reaction to the depressed person, in ways that herald a different course or outcome? For instance, do support systems that solidify around the person and remain intact under the strain of a depressed person's behavior promote recovery? Do support systems that fall apart under the strain of the pathology—either through magnifying previous problem areas or through introducing new hardships into the relationship—exacerbate the condition or hinder recovery? Such thinking suggests that it may be changes in support, under particular challenge conditions, that are most predictive of the longitudinal course, as opposed to the nature of support evident before the incidence of stress or before the onset of the disorder (Brown, Andrews, Adler, & Bridges, 1986).

How social support concepts may influence the longitudinal course of depression constitutes largely uncharted territory for this area of research. In terms of the available information, the work of Brown and Harris (1986) has shown that crisis support—receiving support from a confidant at the time of an actual crisis and need for such support—is crucial in preventing the onset of depression in response to severe life stress. One wonders if similar processes apply to staving off exacerbations of an ongoing episode, or if other support provisions might help to bring the episode to a more rapid or complete ending. Interestingly, Veiel and Kühner (in press) found that attributes of the social support network, which are traditionally viewed as positive (e.g., satisfaction), may actually be detrimental and predict increased symptomatology 7 months following inpatient treatment for depression. There have been other recent preliminary reports on the course and outcome of depression in relation to social support (e.g., Brugha, Bebbington, MacCarthy, Potter, Sturt, & Wykes, 1987; Brugha, Bebbington, MacCarthy, Sturt, Wykes, & Potter, 1990; George, Blazer, Hughes, & Fowler, 1989). Unfortunately, there is little standardization for such matters as defining outcome or developing common time frames over which these processes are studied. It is noteworthy, though, that the literature on psychotherapy efficacy is quite compatible with the notion of supportive interventions alleviating depression (Elkin et al., 1989). Future research explicitly investigating social support needs to develop more explicit criteria for (a) defining change points in psychological functioning over time, and (b) defining good and poor outcomes (e.g., specifying symptoms and duration criteria).[2]

Research on the outcome of depression eventually shades into research on the chronicity of depression. A disconcertingly large number of individuals do not remit from their depressions for a distressingly long period of time. For instance, Scott (1988) recently indicated a prevalence of 12%–15% for depressions of 2 or more years duration. The course of such chronic problems, too, may be punctuated by fluctuations in severity, and again presents an opportunity to investigate other potentially important avenues of support effects (Depue & Monroe, 1986).

Research on such issues presents many challenges, particularly with respect to determining cause-and-effect sequences (Monroe, 1983; Monroe & Steiner, 1986). One criticism of such work has been that there is an inherent confound: The association between symptoms and support is simply an artifact of the severity of disturbance, and not a "legitimate" influence in and of itself. In groups of individuals with chronic psychological problems, one might well expect support to have been molded over time in characteristic ways. Indeed, some of the ideas about support maintenance under stress or in the face of active distress suggest that it may be the characteristics of support under such duress that distinguish its subsequent utility. Although investigators need to be mindful of such possibilities, at the present state of knowledge it would seem narrow-minded to categorically exclude these areas of research. It is clear, though, that responsibility must be borne by the investigator to limit as best as possible the viability of such alternative interpretations. For example, research might be designed to stratify along severity levels of the disorder.

Subsyndromal Forms of Disorder

Portraying people as either depressed or nondepressed is a convenience that simplifies the complexity of the gray zones between the two psychological states. Many recent studies indicate a large number of individuals who do not meet criteria for full syndromal disorder exist, yet they have significant degrees of symptoms that lead to considerable distress and impairment (Brown & Harris, 1986; Depue, Slater, Wolfstetter-Kausch, Klein, Goplerud, & Farr, 1981; Keller, Lavori, Lewis, & Klerman, 1983). These people may represent either acute conditions that do not meet full syndromal criteria, or chronic subsyndromal conditions. It is also clear that such individuals, particularly those from the latter category, are likely to be the ones who give rise to the majority of clinical episodes in the population at large. Specifically, people with low-grade depression, or dysthymia, constitute a high-risk group for developing full syndromal forms of the disorder (Brown, Bifulco, Harris, & Bridge, 1986; Keller, Lavori, Endicott, Coryell, & Klerman, 1983).

[2]It is worth mentioning that these concerns for explicit criteria and definitions are equally applicable to the concepts and measures involving social support.

It is these gray areas of psychological functioning that perhaps simultaneously present investigators with the most potential for developing an understanding of social factors in depression, as well as with the most problems in clarifying such effects. Thus, although investigations of psychologically healthy individuals who make the transition to clinical states may be very informative for certain purposes (e.g., clarifying cause-and-effect relations), it may not represent the modal pathways through which most people attain such undesirable endpoints. (Such studies will also tend to be impractical, for the incidence of disorder will be low in such samples: a "low-risk" paradigm; Monroe & Peterman, 1988.) It may be that the very people who are most vulnerable to developing clinical degrees of disturbance are those who already evidence the disorder in milder forms. Thus whether couched in terms of prodromal symptoms, subsyndromal disorder, or personality, it is likely that the majority of clinical cases in the community and in the hospital derive from individuals who already lead troubled lives (Andrews & Brown, 1988; Heller, 1979; Rutter, 1986). Much as we argue that the course of disorder in relation to support may be a somewhat messy affair, so it will be with such subsyndromal problems. Yet the yield from well-designed work may offset the pains of such endeavors, and may help to unravel some of the subtle pathways through which such serious shifts in mental functioning take place.

We have no simple solutions to these dilemmas at present. However, if social support plays an obvious and specific role in the genesis or maintenance of depression, it has not been so obvious that investigators can readily verify it or agree upon it. We suspect that the influences of support may be important, but their detection may be difficult owing to the subtle interplay between conspiring forces that may, from alternative viewpoints, be interpreted as "confounding." We need to derive more productive ways—both in theory and in practice—to disentangle and understand the interrelations between such tightly meshed processes and their interactions over time.

The Lifetime Course of Depression

Individuals who have suffered from depression are at increased risk for subsequent episodes of the disorder. Estimates vary, but approximately 50% of individuals who recover from depression relapse in the following 2 years (Belsher & Costello, 1988; Keller, Lavori, Lewis, & Klerman, 1983), whereas 40%–50% of individuals who experience an episode of depression may experience one or more recurrences at some further point in their lifetime (Klerman, 1978).[3] Other forms of psychopathology, especially the neurotic disorders, are also characterized over time by such a repeatedly fluctuating course. The role of social support in either facet of the lifetime course of depression has received little, if any, systematic attention.

Could living through an episode of depression create social circumstances that heighten vulnerability to subsequent disorder? For example, could the propensity toward relapses or recurrences be attributed at least in part to the subsequent

[3]Relapse refers to the re-emergence of symptoms shortly following an episode of depression, and thereby is believed to be a continuation of the index disturbance. Recurrence, alternatively, refers to the initiation of a separate, but new, episode. More formal operational definitions of the two aspects of lifetime course are required to ensure standardization across studies (see Belsher & Costello, 1988).

fragility of social relations following prior disorder? As Coyne (1976) has pointed out, interactions with depressed persons can be aversive. Perhaps experiencing depression could weaken ties so that subsequent stressors either do not elicit the necessary support or, more perniciously, more minor stressors and their emotional consequences could serve to sever such relations. Or might repeated episodes, or chronic impairment, increase the likelihood of soliciting support from unreliable sources (Brown & Harris, 1986)? Or could such impairment increase the likelihood of alienating sources of social support? There are clearly social implications to having experienced depression, and it might be within the social network and instantiated within the social interactions that clues to the long-term vulnerability of such individuals at least partly resides.

The Nonspecificity and Specificity of Symptoms: Depression

It is possible to take the theme of symptom specificity yet further within depression. One way in which this might be done pertains to the specific symptoms constituting the syndrome. There are individual differences in the component symptoms that define the disorder, and different symptoms may have different implications for social support over the longitudinal course of depression. For example, one individual might report increased social withdrawal or anxiety, whereas another may not; irritability may be a very prominent feature for another depressed person, whereas much less so for a different individual. A finer analysis of the individual differences in symptoms constituting depressive profile may also be useful to undertake, particularly with respect to the potential social implications of the symptomatology.

Interestingly, there are at least two ways in which such associations between specific depressive symptoms and social support might be conceptualized. First, it could be that the form of symptoms derive in part from the ambient interpersonal network and relations available for supportive transactions. For example, a person with a demanding or intrusive social network may be more inclined to evidence social withdrawal during their depression. This example suggests a "symptom formation factor," such that the social environment accounts for variability in expression of the disorder (Brown & Harris, 1986). Particular interpersonal contexts might "pull for" such socially relevant behaviors as irritability and aggressive symptoms, whereas other contexts might elicit other social responses of passivity and withdrawal.

Second, irrespective of the origins of the differences in symptoms of depression, the interpersonal consequences of such symptoms also require study. Some depressive symptoms are likely to have very different social implications than others. For example, hostility, irritability, and suicidal gestures will likely tax supportive ties in ways that passivity and social withdrawal do not. Thus it may not be depression per se that strains interpersonal relations. Rather, certain components of the depressive picture may be more likely to pull for or impair potential support. Such individual differences in depressive symptoms may be especially important for studying the previously mentioned issues of clinical and lifetime course of the disorder.

CONCLUSION

In linking social support concepts to more specific psychological states and processes, the role of the construct expands considerably from its past legacy of general associations with nonspecific psychological symptomatology. Although this opens the area of inquiry to many new and potentially exciting avenues of study, which are beginning to appear in the research literature, there are many procedural requirements that are required to study such multifaceted and complex processes. In outlining the many ways in which social support may be related to depression, we hope to provide an overview of many of these concerns that may be generalizable to inquiry into other forms of mental disorder. In closing, we would like to further discuss the ways in which one might envision such generalization.

In accord with the principle of specificity, there may be unique properties of support that are relevant only for particular kinds of disorders. These specific effects may be operative only at relatively specific phases of the disorder's course. For instance, the nature of support benefits in schizophrenia may be very different than those for depression. This is likely to be true in terms of the factors contributing to onset, but perhaps especially true for the factors contributing to relapse. The extensive literature on expressed emotion, a notion possessing conceptual overlap with social support, appears to be particularly important for understanding the longitudinal course of schizophrenia (Hooley, 1985; Vaughn & Leff, 1976; see also Hooley, Orley, & Teasdale, 1986, for possible similarities with depression).

On the other hand, there may be commonalities that cut across diagnostically different groups. For example, a confidant may help protect an individual from anxiety disorder as well as depression in the face of severe life stress. Recent work indicated the high degree of overlap between depressive and anxiety symptoms, both at one point in time, as well as in interchangeable symptom profiles over time for afflicted individuals (Monroe, 1990). In other words, people who present with depression currently may well present with primary anxiety disorder in the future (and vice versa). Of course, such protean symptomatology has been at the heart of the concept of neurosis for decades (Tyrer, 1986), yet it also has potentially interesting implications for understanding the process of support. Congruent with the questions posed earlier for the differential formation of depressive symptoms and the consequences of different depressive symptoms, analyses of the anxiety symptoms and disorders and their comparison to depressive symptoms in relation to social support concepts may provide another arena for gaining greater insight into the role of social support. For example, could the changes over time in support availability and quality either be in part related to the types of symptoms expressed (e.g., a symptom formation factor), or could the changing nature of symptoms over time influence the structure and qualities of the support network? With the framework provided, emphasizing specificity in the nature of the disorder and the process of its course should help to systematize research efforts and organize findings along more meaningful lines.

Finally, a frequent topic often addressed in the literature, which we have not addressed here, concerns the type of effect of social support on psychological functioning. Is it a direct, main effect, or a buffering effect of stress? Our approach to the question emphasizes the need to entertain both types of influences in the context of the specificity of effects support might have. Both influences may hold under different conditions. For example, we have noted how particular types of social support might bolster the day-by-day feelings of life satisfaction and well-being, whereas other dimensions of support might mitigate the effects of severe stressors capable of bringing about depression. Further, there is often a good degree of overlap, if not outright confounding, between certain forms of stress and lack of social support (Monroe, Bromet, Connell, & Steiner, 1986; Thoits, 1982). Crises involving individuals in the support network may have direct effects on depression that require analysis independent of the possible buffering effects of support (Thoits, 1982). Thus there is some evidence to suggest that a subgroup of depressions resulting from termination of an important relationship (i.e., a support crisis) evidence at least partially some specificity of symptoms (e.g., loss of appetite and sleep problems), and have a better outcome (Parker & Blignault, 1985). Although such work requires replication, it suggests that there may be rather direct influences on social support losses that influence the onset, morphology, and outcome of depression (Matussek & Wiegand, 1985; Parker & Blignault, 1985). Such influences may hold independent of, or in interaction with, other influences that derive from different supportive provisions.

As we suggested in the beginning of the chapter, the promise of social support research has outgrown its early origins. Concepts and methods must move beyond the security of the proven associations with general psychological functioning and push toward the more complicated world of diverse and specific associations. Only with such advances will the extent and depth of social support influences on psychological functioning be revealed. We hope that with such progress we witness the emergence of a next generation of studies that produces long-lived benefits for understanding the onset and longitudinal course of depression and other forms of mental disorders.

REFERENCES

Andrews, B., & Brown, G. W. (1988). Social support, onset of depression and personality: An exploratory study. *Social Psychiatry and Psychiatric Epidemiology, 23,* 99–108.

Barrera, M., Jr. (1986). Distinctions between social support concepts, measures, and models. *American Journal of Community Psychology, 14,* 413–445.

Belsher, G., & Costello, C. G. (1988). Relapse and recovery from unipolar depression: A critical review. *Psychological Bulletin, 104,* 84–96.

Brown, G. W., Adler, Z., & Bifulco, A. (1988). Life events, difficulties and recovery from chronic depression. *British Journal of Psychiatry, 152,* 115–128.

Brown, G. W., Andrews, B., Adler, Z., & Bridge, L. (1986). Social support, self-esteem and depression. *Psychological Medicine, 16,* 813–831.

Brown, G. W., Bifulco, A., Harris, T. O., & Bridge, L. (1986). Life stress, chronic psychiatric symptoms and vulnerability to clinical depression. *Journal of Affective Disorders, 11,* 1–19.

Brown, G. W., & Harris, T. O. (1978). *Social origins of depression: A study of psychiatric disorder in women.* New York: The Free Press.

Brown, G. W., & Harris, T. O. (1986). Establishing causal links: The Bedford College studies of depression. H. Katschnig (Ed.), *Life events and psychiatric disorders: Controversial issues* (pp. 107–187). Cambridge, England: Cambridge University Press.

Brugha, T. S., Bebbington, P. E., MacCarthy, B., Sturt, E., Wykes, T., & Potter, J. (1990). Gender, social support and recovery from depressive disorders: A prospective clinical study. *Psychological Medicine, 20,* 147–156.

Brugha, T., Bebbington, P. E., MacCarthy, B., Potter, J., Sturt, E., & Wykes, T. (1987). Social networks, social support and the type of depressive illness. *Acta Psychiatrica Scandanavica, 76,* 664–673.

Cohen, S., & Wills, T. A. (1985). Stress, social support, and the buffering hypothesis. *Psychological Bulletin, 98,* 310–357.

Coyne, J. C. (1976). Depression and the response of others. *Journal of Abnormal Psychology, 85,* 186–193.

Depue, R. A., & Monroe, S. M. (1986). Conceptualization and measurement of human disorder in life stress research: The problem of chronic disturbance. *Psychological Bulletin, 99,* 36–51.

Depue, R. A., Slater, J., Wolfstetter-Kausch, H., Klein, D., Goplerud, E., & Farr, D. (1981). A behavioral paradigm for identifying persons at risk for bipolar depressive disorder: A conceptual framework and five validation studies (monograph). *Journal of Abnormal Psychology, 90,* 381–437.

Elkin, I., Shea, M. T., Watkins, J. T., Imber, S. D., Sotsky, S. M., Collins, J. F., Glass, D. R., Pilkonis, P. A., Leber, W. R., Docherty, J. P., Fiester, S. J., & Parloff, M. B. (1989). National Institute of Mental Health Treatment of Depression Collaborative Research Program: General effectiveness of treatments. *Archives of General Psychiatry, 46,* 971–982.

George, L. K., Blazer, D. G., Hughes, D. C., & Fowler, N. (1989). Social support and the outcome of major depression. *British Journal of Psychiatry, 154,* 478–485.

Heller, K. (1979). The effects of social support: Prevention and treatment implications. In A. P. Goldstein & F. H. Kanfer (Eds.), *Maximizing treatment gains: Transfer enhancement in psychotherapy.* New York: Academic Press.

Henderson, S., Byrne, D. G., & Duncan-Jones, P. (1981). *Neurosis and the social environment.* New York: Academic Press.

Hooley, J. M. (1985). Expressed emotion: A review of the critical literature. *Clinical Psychology Review, 5,* 119–139.

Hooley, J. M., Orley, J., & Teasdale, J. D. (1986). Levels of expressed emotion and relapse in depressed patients. *British Journal of Psychiatry, 148,* 642–647.

Keller, M. B., Lavori, P. W., Endicott, J., Coryell, W., & Klerman, G. L. (1983). Double depression: Two-year follow-up. *American Journal of Psychiatry, 140,* 689–694.

Keller, M. B., Lavori, P. W., Lewis, C. E., & Klerman, G. L. (1983). Predictors of relapse in major depressive disorder. *Journal of the American Medical Association, 250,* 3299–3304.

Kessler, R., Price, R. H., & Wortman, C. B. (1985). Social factors in psychopathology: Stress, social support, and coping processes. *Annual Review of Psychology, 36,* 531–572.

Klerman, G. L. (1978). Long-term maintenance of affective disorders. In M. A. Lipton, A. Dimascio, & K. F. Killam (Eds.), *Psychopharmacology: A generation of progress.* New York: Raven Press.

Lin, N., Dean, A., & Ensel, W. (1986). *Social support, life events, and depression.* New York: Academic Press.

Matussek, P., & Wiegand, M. (1985). Partnership problems as causes of endogenous and neurotic depressions. *Acta Psychiatrica Scandanavica, 71,* 95–104.

Monroe, S. M. (1982). Life events and disorder: Event-symptom associations and the course of disorder. *Journal of Abnormal Psychology, 91,* 14–24.

Monroe, S. M. (1983). Social support and disorder: Toward an untangling of cause and effect. *American Journal of Community Psychology, 11,* 81–97.

Monroe, S. M. (1990). Psychosocial factors in anxiety and depression. In J. D. Maser & C. R. Cloninger (Eds.), *Comorbidity in anxiety and mood disorders.* Washington, DC: American Psychiatric Press.

Monroe, S. M., Bromet, E. J., Connell, M. M., & Steiner, S. C. (1986). Social support, life events, and depressive symptoms: A one-year prospective study. *Journal of Consulting and Clinical Psychology, 54,* 424–431.

Monroe, S. M., & Depue, R. A. (1991). Life stress and depression. In J. Becker & A. Kleinman (Eds.), *Psychological aspects of depression* (pp. 101–130). New York: Erlbaum.

Monroe, S. M., & Peterman, A. M. (1988). Life stress and psychopathology. In L. Cohen (Ed.), *Research on stressful life events: Theoretical and methodological issues* (pp. 31–63). New York: Sage.

Monroe, S. M., & Steiner, S. C. (1986). Social support and psychopathology: Interrelations with preexisting disorder, stress, and personality. *Journal of Abnormal Psychology, 95,* 29–39.

Ormel, J., Koeter, M. W. J., & van den Brink, W. (1989). Measuring change with the General Health Questionnaire (GHQ): The problem of retest effects. *Social Psychiatry and Psychiatric Epidemiology, 24,* 227–232.

Parker, G., & Blignault, I. (1985). Psychosocial predictors of outcome in subjects with untreated depressive disorder. *Journal of Affective Disorders, 8,* 73–81.

Rutter, M. (1986). Meyerian psychobiology, personality development, and the role of life experiences. *American Journal of Psychiatry, 143,* 1077–1087.

Scott, J. (1988). Chronic depression. *British Journal of Psychiatry, 153,* 287–297.
Thoits, P. A. (1982). Conceptual, methodological, and theoretical problems in studying social support as a buffer against life stress. *Journal of Health and Social Behavior, 23,* 145–159.
Tyrer, P. (1986). New rows of neuroses—Are they an illusion? *Integrative Psychiatry, 4,* 25–31.
Vaughn, C. E., & Leff, J. P. (1976). The measurement of expressed emotion in the families of psychiatric patients. *British Journal of Social and Clinical Psychology, 15,* 157–165.
Veiel, H. O. F., & Kühner, C. (in press). Relatives and depressive relapse: The critical period after discharge from in-patient treatment. *Psychological Medicine.*
Watson, D., Clark, L. A., & Carey, G. (1988). Positive and negative affectivity and their relation to anxiety and depressive disorders. *Journal of Abnormal Psychology, 97,* 346–353.

III

MODELS OF THE SUPPORT PROCESS

8

Stress, Social Support, and Disorder

Sheldon Cohen
Carnegie Mellon University, Pennsylvania, USA

The concepts of social support and stress have been closely tied in both theoretical and empirical work on the influence of support on health and well-being (Cassell, 1976; Cobb, 1976; Cohen & Syme, 1985; House, 1981). Social supports are thought to contribute to the generation of stressful events, the avoidance of stressful events, the appraisal of events, and the ability to cope with events and their consequences. Conversely, stressful events and coping responses are thought to influence the stability of social networks as well as the availability and maintenance of social supports. This chapter provides an overview of the interrelations between stress and social support with implications for health outcomes.

SUPPORT CONCEPTS

There is little agreement among members of the scientific community in regard to a precise definition of social support (Cohen & Syme, 1985; Shumaker & Brownell, 1984; Wilcox & Vernberg, 1985). Moreover, existing studies apply the term to a broad range of social networks and functions that they provide (House, 1981; Turner, 1983). Rather than attempt an all-encompassing definition, I propose broad categorical classifications of the concepts commonly included under the social support rubric. Three classes of support concepts (measures) are proposed: social networks, perceived social support, and supportive behaviors.

Social networks refer to the structure of social relationships—the existence, quantity, and type of relationships. Perceived social support refers to the function of social relationships—the perception that social relationships will (if necessary) provide resources such as emotional support or information. Finally, supportive behaviors refer to the mobilization and receipt of behaviors intended to aid persons in the face of stressful events.

THE TRANSACTIONAL MODEL OF STRESS

Figure 1 depicts the major concepts and mechanisms involved in relations between stress and support in the prediction of disorder. Disorder is broadly used here to refer to both psychological and physiological symptoms and disease states. For the sake of simplicity and brevity, the figure does not include all possible relations between represented concepts.

The core of Figure 1 is the transactional model of stress and disorder (e.g., Lazarus & Folkman, 1984). (The "core" concepts key to the transactional model

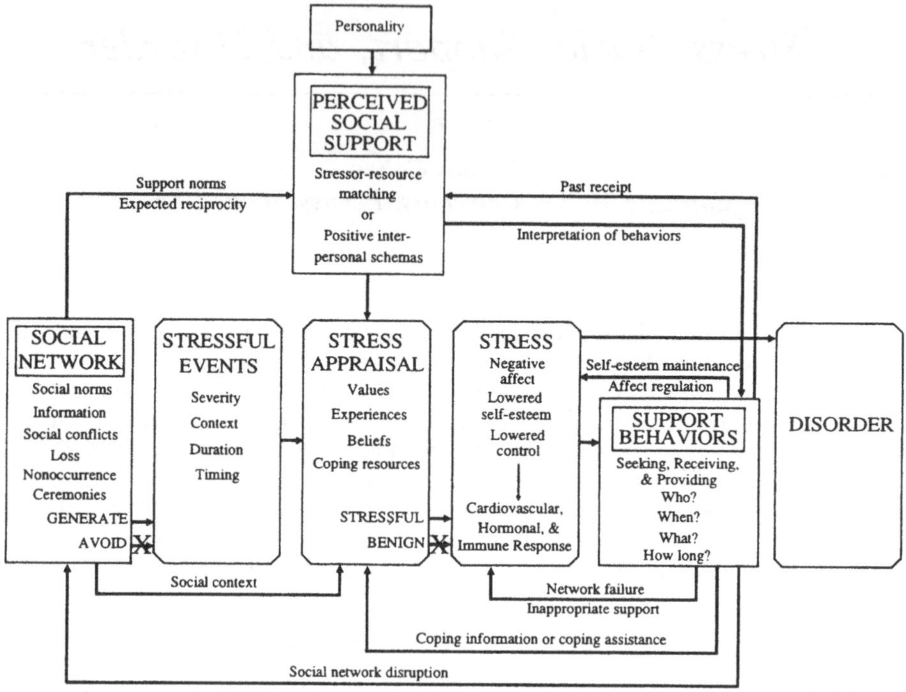

Figure 1 Major concepts and mechanisms involved in relations between stress and social support in the prediction of disorder.

are in the octagonal boxes.) In short, potentially stressful events are appraised as either stressful or benign in the context of an individual's own values, beliefs, experiences, and coping resources. The appraisal of events as stressful can result in a range of psychological and physiological changes that put a person at risk for disorder.

As apparent from the figure, there are a number of objective event characteristics that contribute to whether or not stressful events result in stress and disorder. These include severity, context in which they occur, duration, and timing of the events in relation to the life course. There is also evidence that specific types of events are risk factors for specific disorders. For example, depressive affect and clinical depression appear to be triggered by interpersonal events (e.g., Bolger, DeLongis, Kessler, & Schilling, 1989; Brown & Harris, 1989). Finally, the accumulation of multiple events may, within a specific category (e.g., interpersonal events, economic events) or across categories, create a greater risk than single events.

As noted earlier, stress appraisal occurs in the context of a person's values, beliefs, experiences, and coping resources. Appraisal represents the meaning of events to the individual—specifically, the extent to which the demands of situations are greater than the ability to cope.

In the current discussion, we use the term *stress* to refer to both the psychological and physiological effects of stress appraisal. Psychological effects of appraisal that are implicated in disorder include increased negative affect, lowered self-esteem, and lowered feelings of control. Physiological changes in response to stress appraisal are presumed to be mediated by these changes in affect, esteem, and control. Physiological stress effects implicated in physical disorder include changes in cardiovascular response, such as increased heart rate and blood pressure; secretion (into the bloodstream) of a range of hormones, including catecholamines, CRF, ACTH, cortisol, and growth hormone; and changes in immune function (Rabin, Cohen, Ganguli, Lysle, & Cunnick, 1989).

The remainder of Figure 1 depicts the interrelations of social networks, perceived support, and support behaviors within the transactional model. This includes their effects on the components of the core model and their effects on one another. The figure is intended as an organizational tool, not as the representation of a formal model. The following discussion reviews what is known about the interrelations represented in the figure and speculates about relations when data are insufficient. The reader may want to refer to Figure 1 as an organizational guide while reading this discussion.

SOCIAL NETWORKS, STRESS, AND DISORDER

Social networks can influence both the occurrence and appraisal of stressful life events. Event occurrence can be affected by social norms. For example, prohibitions of divorce, birth control, and abortion can operate to create and/or maintain acute and chronic stressors. Alternatively, norms supporting the use of birth control and "safe" sex practices could prevent unwanted pregnancies and sexually transmitted diseases (e.g., Fisher, 1988). Likewise, network availability of appropriate information can help people avoid certain stressful life events (e.g., unwanted pregnancies), whereas inappropriate information may facilitate their occurrence.

Network membership itself provides the possibility for stressful interpersonal events, such as social conflicts and losses, that are less likely for more isolated persons. However, networks also generate events, such as religious and ethnic ceremonies, whose occurrences mark different stages of the life cycle. These events contribute to the development of senses of self, predictability, and control that are essential for maintenance of psychological well-being. The nonoccurrence of these normative events among relatively isolated persons may also be stressful interpersonal events (Schulz & Rau, 1985; Rabkin & Struening, 1976). Interpersonal events (occurrence or nonoccurrence) may put people at greater risk for disorder than nonsocial events. Interpersonal events play primary roles as risk factors in psychological distress (e.g., Bolger et al., 1989; Monroe & Simons, in press; Fiore, Becker, & Coppel, 1983; Pagel, Erdly, & Becker, 1987; Thoits, 1985), clinical depression (e.g., Brown & Harris, 1989; Paykel, 1974), and physical illness (e.g., Graham, Douglas, & Ryan, 1986; Meyer & Haggerty, 1962).

Social networks can also influence the appraisal of stressful events (see path from social networks to stress appraisal in Figure 1). Social norms and information networks provide a social context in which events are appraised (Brown & Harris, 1978, 1989; Lazarus & Folkman, 1984; Monroe & Depue, 1991). For example, unwanted pregnancies, divorces, and abortions are considerably more stressful when network norms forbid or stigmatize them than when norms are accepting or even facilitating. Social networks also directly influence perceptions of support (see path from social networks to perceived social support in Figure 1). Support norms prescribe when support should be provided to other network members. Similarly, expected reciprocity norms prescribe supporting others who have provided support in the past.

PERCEIVED SOCIAL SUPPORT AND THE STRESS-BUFFERING MODELS

The stress-buffering hypothesis posits that support "buffers" (protects) persons from the potentially pathogenic influence of stressful events. The majority of research on this hypothesis tests what Wheaton (1985) refers to as the interactive model of buffering. In this model, support operates as a moderating variable—an existing condition (e.g., the perception of available support) under which stress has substantially less impact (see path from perceived social support to stress appraisal in Figure 1). This effect is statistically represented by a stress by social support interaction (House, 1981; Cohen & Wills, 1985; Veiel, Chapter 17; Wheaton, 1985). The following discussion addresses this model. Our later discussion on the effectiveness of support behaviors in coping with stressful events may in some cases reflect the interactive model but in many cases may reflect an additive model (Wheaton, 1985). In the additive model stressors result in the mobilization of support (supportive behaviors) that dampen the overall stressor impact (see path from stress to support behaviors in Figure 1).

Perceived availability of social support has been found to act as a stress buffer (stressful events by perceived support interaction) over a wide range of studies; hence I focus on perceived support as the source of stress buffering (Cohen & Wills, 1985; Kessler & McLeod, 1985; Schwarzer & Leppin, 1989; Wethington & Kessler, 1986). The two prominent theories of why perceived support operates as a stress buffer are discussed here.

Stressor-Resource Matching

The matching hypothesis proposes that stress buffering occurs only when there is a match between the needs elicited by the stressful event and the functions of support that are perceived to be available (Cohen & McKay, 1984; Cohen & Wills, 1985). For example, having someone who would loan you money may be useful in the face of a temporary job loss, but useless in the face of the death of a friend. Cohen and Wills (1985) also argue that certain types of support may be useful in coping with all or many stressors. Specifically, having people to talk to about problems (appraisal or informational support) and having people who make you feel better about yourself (self-esteem or esteem support) may be generally useful because these are coping requirements elicited by most stressors. A corollary of the globally useful resource argument is that confidants who tend to be good sources of appraisal and self-esteem support are universally effective support sources. Although existing research supports the effectiveness of confidants as stress buffers (see review by Cohen & Wills, 1985), there is a strong suggestion that women show more benefit from confidant support than men (Husaini, Newbrough, Neff, & Moore, 1982; Henderson, Byrne, & Duncan-Jones, 1981), indicating the possibility of sex differences in the effectiveness of "globally" useful resources.

Although literature reviews generally conclude that existing evidence is consistent with matching notions (Cohen & Wills, 1985; Cutrona & Russell, 1990), there are few studies designed to test specific hypothetical predictions. The lack of studies is to some degree attributable to the difficulty in providing an adequate test of the matching hypothesis. It requires the definition and measurement of distinct categories of stressors and of social support, relatively orthogonal measures of subtypes within each category, and a conceptual link between stress and support categorizations (Cohen & McKay, 1984; Tetzloff & Barrera, 1987).

An elaboration of the matching model proposed by Cutrona (1990; Cutrona & Russell, 1990) provides some of this specificity. Cutrona suggests that the controllability of a stressor is the primary dimension in terms of an appropriate match. Potentially controllable stressful events are presumed to elicit needs for problem-focused coping (informational and tangible support) to aid in preventing event occurrence or consequences. Uncontrollable events are presumed to elicit needs for emotion-focused coping (emotional support) to help persons recover from the negative emotions elicited by an event. Like Cohen (Cohen & McKay, 1984; Cohen & Wills, 1985), Cutrona also emphasizes matching support to the needs elicited by specific stressor domains. In her scheme, stressors are viewed as events that create deficits or losses (Hobfoll, 1989; Stroebe & Stroebe, 1985). The nature of the loss is presumed to affect the nature of the required replacement. For example, a loss of assets (tangible resources and physical capabilities) would be associated with a need for tangible support. Because stressors (by definition) create deficits, domain specific matching should apply to replacing a deficit whether it is controllable or not. However, Cutrona argues that it is especially important for long-term uncontrollable deficits such as those created by the loss of an intimate relationship. This conceptualization of the matching model is promising but awaits empirical verification.

Perceived Support as a Proxy for Positive Interpersonal Schemas

An alternative explanation for why perceived support acts as a stress buffer views support as a stable individual difference that generates changes in cognition or self-concept (Sarason, Sarason, & Pierce, 1990). The specific argument is that early experiences with attachment relationships (particularly parental attachments) have enduring effects on schemas about relationships (i.e., the meaning of relationships) and support expectancies (Sarason et al., 1990). In this approach, perceived support is a manifestation of a set of positive interpersonal schemas. Presumably, persons with positive expectancies about relationships feel less constrained in revealing needs to network members and in asking for help (Reis, 1990). Positive expectancies may also influence how supportive transactions are interpreted. For example, expectancies for support have been associated with responding more positively to supportive behaviors and viewing them as more helpful (Lakey & Cassady, 1990). Sarason et al. (1990) also argue that relationship schemas include a "sense of acceptance"—the belief that others accept us for who we are, including our best and worst points. This sense of acceptance is presumed to contribute to the development of competencies, which aid persons in dealing with stressful events.

Perceived Support as a Personality Measure

A striking difference between the need-matching and the positive interpersonal schema explanations of stress buffering is that the former suggests that perceived support measures reflect support provided from the social environment and the latter that perceived support reflects an enduring characteristic of personality. It is likely that both are partly correct. That is, some of the variance in perceived support measures is based in personality, whereas other variance is based on the availability of support in the environment. In support of the personality argument are data indicating that high levels of perceived support are related to a number of personality characteristics including social competence, internal locus of control, and low anxiety (Sarason et al., 1990; see also Lakey & Cassady, 1990). There are also data indicating relatively high test-retest correlations for perceived support over periods of several months.

In support of the argument that perceived support is environmentally based are data indicating that: (a) test-retest correlations over several months are much attenuated among persons adapting to a new social environment (Cohen, Sherrod, & Clark, 1986); (b) using factor analysis perceived support has been shown to be independent of self-esteem, control, depression, and anxiety (Lakey & Cassady, 1990); (c) stress-buffering effects remain after controlling for the possible role of social skills (Cohen et al., 1986); (d) existing studies do not indicate that related personality variables operate as stress buffers (Cohen & Edwards, 1989); and (e) perceived support is strongly associated with the nature and pattern of persons' social interactions (Cutrona, 1986; Reis, personal communication; Vinokur, Schul, & Caplan, 1987).

A recent proposal suggests an integration of the matching and sense of acceptance explanations. Sarason et al. (1990) argue that viewing social support in terms of disaggregated social needs and provision leads to a focus on short-term effects—for example, coping with particular setbacks or solving a current problem. On the other hand, viewing social support as a sense of acceptance leads to a focus on long-term effects, such as the development of feelings of personal control and self-efficacy that facilitate the ability to cope with stressful events. However, the distinction between short- and long-term stressor effects is probably too simple to provide a resolution of this problem. For example, how would this resolution treat the importance of matching needs (deficits) incurred when stressors have long-term implications—for example, the loss of a spouse or intimate friend (Cutrona, 1990)?

SUPPORT BEHAVIORS

The processes of support seeking, providing, and receiving have received little attention relative to their complexity and importance in understanding how others' behaviors may be helpful in confronting stress. The following discussion highlights some important issues about seeking, providing, and receiving aid in the face of stressful events. The concepts discussed in this section are represented in Figure 1 in the support behavior box and in the feedback loops connecting support behaviors to stress and stress appraisal.

Support behaviors may be helpful or harmful to persons who appraise a situation as stressful. An important factor in assessing the effectiveness of support is whether or not it is requested. Support is often made available naturally in the course of normal social interactions without specific requests for aid (Cohen & Wills, 1985; Pearlin & Schooler, 1978; Bolger, Kessler, & Schilling, unpublished manuscript; Coyne & Bolger, 1990). Asking for aid entails different interpersonal processes (e.g., Fisher, Nadler, & DePaulo, 1983) and often implies the lack of a relationship that is close enough that a request would not be required. In many cases, support provided without request may be more effective than that which one must request. The following discussion is not concerned with active seeking (asking for) aid but rather with receiving unsolicited support when the need arises. (See Wills & DePaulo, 1991, for a recent discussion of help seeking.)

Who provides social support? The provision of support is thought to vary with gender, relationship between the giver and receiver, social-cultural context, and personality characteristics of the giver. At least in regard to emotional support, it is generally thought that women are more likely to provide it to both men and women (e.g., Kessler, McLeod, & Wethington, 1985). This might occur because women take greater responsibility for members of their social networks, because they are more open in regard to discussing emotions, because they place a greater weight on the importance of relationships, or because they have better interpersonal skills than men.

Closer relations such as family members and close friends are more likely to provide support than acquaintances (e.g., Dakof & Taylor, 1990). This more obvious finding is probably attributable to normative support responsibilities, greater concern for a close relation, and reciprocity expectations. Support provision may also be influenced by group structure and social determinants such as community size and resources, SES, ethnic group customs, and cultural norms (Wortman & Conway, 1985).

The provision of support is to a great extent dependent on the appropriateness of specific sources. The appropriateness depends on the nature of the stressful event, its impact on the individual, and the source's relevance for an event. For example, emotional support for cancer patients may be best provided by close friends and relatives, whereas information support may be best provided by physicians and others with cancer (Dakof & Taylor, 1990). An acquaintance or work supervisor, however, may find it inappropriate to provide emotional or informational support to a cancer patient.

Who receives social support? Individual differences play a role in the receipt of support. For example, persons with high self-esteem (Newcomb, 1990) and with social skills such as sociability, assertiveness, comfort with intimacy, and ability to empathize with others are more able to maintain and draw upon support networks (Clark & Reis, 1988; Cohen et al., 1986; Heller & Swindle, 1983; Shumaker & Brownell, 1984). In research on a number of other individual differences, internal locus of control, positive beliefs in the benefits of help seeking, and higher levels of education were all found to be positively related to the number of persons who actually provided aid in the face of stressful events and to reported effectiveness of support under stress (e.g., Eckenrode, 1983; Riley & Eckenrode, 1986). Although some have postulated that females receive more support than males (Belle, 1989), gender differences in support receipt are not well documented. It is probable that if such differences exist, they are moderated by both the gender of the giver and type of support.

When (under what conditions) is support sought or desired? Social comparison models of support seeking argue that there are conditions under which support will be neither desired nor effective in reducing stress (Cohen & McKay, 1984). Particularly, support will only be sought (or have stress-reducing effects) when (a) the stressor is one that is socially acceptable and does not result in feelings of guilt and shame, (b) discussion of the stressor will not be detrimental to one's relationship with the supporter, (c) the support is provided by people who are perceived as providers of accurate information (e.g., others who have similar attitudes, personalities, and the like, or others who have experienced a similar stressor), and (d) the supporter communicates a relatively calm reaction to the potential stressor.

When (under what conditions) is support provided? Dunkel-Schetter and Skokan (1990) propose four classes of factors influencing the willingness to provide support: (a) stress appraisal factors, (b) recipient factors, (c) relationship factors (provider-recipient history), and (d) provider factors. Stress appraisal refers to whether the situation is perceived as stressful by the potential recipient. Support will be offered if it is. Recipient characteristics that are generally presumed to increase aid include increased distress (excepting severe distress; e.g., Coyne, 1976), active coping, and personality characteristics such as mastery and high self-esteem (e.g., Dunkel-Schetter, Folkman, & Lazarus, 1987). Support is more likely to be provided in intimate relationships, when persons are satisfied with their relationship, and when social norms indicate the appropriateness of aid. Other provider characteristics that may influence aid include affect, empathy regarding another's fate, altruistic motivation to help, guilt, and perception of responsibility for the other person.

What kinds of behaviors are supportive? Studies reporting interviews of cancer patients (Dakof & Taylor, 1990; Dunkel-Schetter, 1984) and the recently bereaved (Lehman, Ellard, & Wortman, 1986) indicate that victims generally perceive emotional support as most effective. These perceptions are consistent with evidence that emotional support from significant or primary others is the most powerful predictor of reduced psychological distress (Cohen & McKay, 1984; Heller, 1979; House, 1981; Turner, 1983; Thoits, 1985). They are also consistent with Cutrona's (1990) argument that uncontrollable events are best buffered by emotional support and Cohen and Wills' (1985) argument that emotional support is a globally useful support function.

Even in the context of traumatic and victimizing events like cancer, the perceived helpfulness of an act is partly dependent on the source. For example, Dakof and Taylor (1990) found that intimate others were most valued for the esteem/emotional support they provided, whereas information support and tangible aid were less frequently experienced as helpful. Other cancer patients and physicians, on the other hand, were most valued for information support.

There is also theoretical work suggesting some specific behaviors that are predicted to be inappropriate or ineffective. For example, Wortman and Dunkel-Schetter (1979, 1987) theorized that victimizing events (e.g., cancer) often elicit ineffective responses from the social network such as (a) physically avoiding the victim, (b) avoiding open communication about the victimizing event and its consequences, or (c) engaging in forced cheerfulness or minimizing of the victim's circumstances. Recent data, however, suggest that although these behaviors are usually perceived as unsupportive, primary supporters of cancer patients—spouse and close family members—seldom behave in this manner (Dakof & Taylor, 1990).

A series of studies of the effectiveness of spouse (living partner) support for quitting smoking indicates some rather clear classifications of behaviors that result in successful quitting. "Positive" behaviors (those expressing cooperation, participation, and reinforcement) increased probability of success and "negative" behaviors (nagging, shunning, and policing) decreased the probability of success (e.g., Coppotelli & Orleans, 1985; Mermelstein, Cohen, Lichtenstein, Baer, & Kamarck, 1986). Moreover, the effectiveness of these behaviors is dependent on the content and context of a relationship (Cohen & Lichtenstein, 1990). First, the effectiveness of positive and negative behaviors is dependent on the base rate of smoking relevant support behaviors that occur within the relationship. This is demonstrated by results indicating that higher positive to negative behavior ratios were better predictors of successful smoking cessation and maintenance of abstinence than either the frequencies of positive or negative behaviors (Cohen & Lichtenstein, 1990). Second, prequitting expectations of the frequency of supportive behaviors that a spouse or partner would provide moderated the effectiveness of the behaviors that were actually provided. Those receiving more positive to negative behaviors than they expected before they began the quitting process were most successful, those who received what they expected fell in the middle, and those who received less support than expected were the least successful (Cohen, in press).

How long will persons provide support? There is little theory (or data) on the dynamics of support giving. For the purpose of this discussion, however, we will make a number of assumptions about what determines the onset and offset of support: (a) the giver's perception that the receiver is under stress, (b) the nature of the relationship between giver and receiver, (c) the amount of time and effort required in providing support, (d) the duration of support needs, (e) the apparent effectiveness of support, and (f) the indication that the supportee appreciates the effort. Factors (d) through (f) are probably moderated by giver expectancies about what is appropriate or prescribed for specific stressors and relationships. In other words, to the extent that the need for support exceeds givers' expectancies of appropriate support, givers will be more likely to withdraw, induce conflict, or experience the support giving as a stressor (e.g., Schulz, Tompkins, & Rau, 1988). Discrepancies between supporter expectancies and supportee needs are probably common (see Melamed & Brenner, 1990). For example, in our own work on spousal support for quitting smoking, spouses often feel that their work is done a couple of weeks after cessation, but many former smokers continue to have strong cravings months later.

We have suggested a view of support maintenance as a balance between costs of giving and relationship with the person receiving support. However, for some relationships, even extreme costs are accepted without withdrawal. For example, caregiving for close others with terminal or progressively deteriorating diseases (e.g., cancer and Alzheimer's) can have uniquely high costs for the supporter. Because the act of support requires constant observation of and contact with a loved one who is suffering, a great deal of emotional pain can result for the supporter. Sometimes the support role can be transferred to (or shared with) another, either a professional or a member of the support system. However, often no alternative supporters are available and withdrawal from the relationship is normatively unthinkable.

How do social relationships influence adaptation? Social relationships probably influence both problem- and emotion-focused coping. Problem-focused coping refers to instrumental attempts to manipulate stressful events and persons' relations to events. Emotion-focused coping refers to adjustments to emotional and psychological (e.g., loss of self-esteem or control) responses to stressful events (Lazarus & Folkman, 1984). Discussions of support and problem-focused coping primarily focus on the social environment as a source of information or material-coping resources (Cohen, 1988; Thoits, 1986). These resources may assist persons to change a situation or the meaning of a situation and hence their stress appraisal. These processes are represented in Figure 1 as a feedback loop connecting support behaviors to stress appraisal. The availability of coping assistance and/or the coping success of that assistance has also been viewed as a contributor to feelings of specific control over a stressor as well as generalized expectancies of control (e.g., Cohen, 1988; Krause, 1987; Pearlin, Menaghan, Lieberman, & Mullan, 1981; Thoits, 1985).

Discussions of support and emotion-focused coping have centered on the regulation of self-esteem and/or affect. These processes are represented in Figure 1 as feedback loops connecting support behaviors to stress. Most theories of support effects on self-esteem postulate support contributions to esteem maintenance (Brown & Harris, 1978; Heller, Swindle, & Dusenbury, 1986; Kessler & Essex, 1982; Krause, 1987; Pearlin et al., 1981; Wills, 1985). For example, Thoits (1985) argues that emotional support from significant others may buffer or reduce distress by bolstering one or more aspects of self that have been threatened by objective difficulties (most often, negative role changes and role-related strains). However, some have argued that receiving (needing) support can undermine self-esteem (DiMatteo & Hays, 1981; Wortman & Conway, 1985). This would presumably occur when aid is provided in a domain in which the receiver perceives him or herself as competent or when the support comes from a person whose aid threatens perceptions of competence. This is represented in Figure 1 by the arrow labeled "inappropriate support."

Another of the feedback loops connecting support behaviors to stress in Figure 1 is network failure. Brown and Harris (1989) have insightfully suggested that psychological distress and disorder may be less a consequence of stressor exposure and appraisal and more a consequence of the network's failure to respond when a person is in need. Evidence consistent with the importance of network responsiveness is provided in a study of caregivers for Alzheimer's patients (Pagel, Erdly, & Becker, 1987). Caregivers' degree of upset with their networks was negatively associated with their satisfaction with their social networks and positively associated with depression.

Figure 1 also includes a feedback loop from supportive behaviors to perceived support. This loop represents the influence of previous experiences with support on expectations of future support. The final feedback loop connects supportive behaviors to the social network and represents network deterioration as a result of the support process (Schulz & Tompkins, 1990). This deterioration might occur because of prolonged demands on support exceeding the expectancies and/or norms of a network.

CONCLUSION

Given the myriad published research on stress and social support, our understanding of these processes is disappointing. This is because we: (a) tend to poorly conceptualize and operationalize stressors and supports, (b) have an insufficient understanding of how stressors influence various disorders, (c) have an insufficient understanding of how support concepts interact with the stress process, and (d) lack an integrated theoretical perspective to drive empirical research.

Conceptualization and Measurement of Stressors and Supports

The disagreements and problems in defining and measuring stress are well documented elsewhere and are beyond the scope of this chapter (e.g., Ostfield & Eaker, 1985). An elaborate interview methodology allowing for disaggregation of event categories and assessment of the meaning of events for the individual is available (Brown & Harris, 1989); however, good life event measures taking less time, and hence useful in a broader range of studies, are harder to come by. A focus on persons experiencing single traumatic events (e.g., bereavement or divorce) provides an alternative to the conceptual and methodological problems that are intrinsic to cumulative life event measurement (Cohen & Williamson, 1991). Measurement issues also plague assessment of other conceptions of stress such as perceived stress, psychological distress, and affect. However, because these concepts are "perceived" in nature, self-report instruments are presumed to be face valid.

The three categories of support discussed in this chapter represent a reasonable starting point, but more refined typologies of the social environment as it effects these processes would be welcome. Measures of social networks used in the stress and disorder literature generally suffer both conceptually and psychometrically. The great shame is the failure to use a formal social network theory to provide concepts and measures of social networks (Hall & Wellman, 1985; Hirsch, 1981). Several psychometrically valid perceived support measures are available (e.g., Cohen & Hoberman, 1983; Sarason, Levine, Basham, & Sarason, 1983; Prociadano & Heller, 1983), but there is still a major challenge in the measurement of supportive behaviors (see Cohen & Lichtenstein, 1990; Reis et al., 1985). There is too little theory and data on supportive behaviors themselves. We need to know the types of behaviors that are supportive and the social contexts under which the same behaviors are supportive or not. Additional microlevel analyses (e.g., daily diary data) of support content and context, and of perceptions of support by supporter and supportee, are imperative (e.g., Bolger, DeLongis, & Kessler, 1989; Cohen & Lichtenstein, 1990). There is also a need to develop psychometrically valid measurement instruments specific to a number of domains (e.g., support for persons with cancer, Alzheimer's, and AIDS, and for caregivers of the elderly and chronically ill).

How Stressors Influence Various Disorders

A major problem in studying the interrelations of stress and social support as applied to a disorder model is our poor understanding of the relations between stress and disorder. Although the hypothesis that stressful events result in both psychological and physiological disorder is generally accepted by the press and public, the evidence for such effects is less than impressive. Although a thorough discussion of this issue is not possible in this context, it is worth emphasizing some of the things that may result in a clearer understanding of the role of stressful life events in disorder: (a) a clearer theoretical distinction between events (severity, duration, controllability, event clusters, and categories, etc.) (Brown & Harris, 1989; Thoits, 1983), (b) identification of the role of specific stressful events (or event domains) in specific disease processes (diseases and disease stages) (Cohen, 1988; Cohen & Williamson, 1991; Harris, 1989), and (c) distinction between processes involved in stressor influences on illness behaviors (symptom and illness reporting and health utilization) and those involved in verified clinical disease (Cohen & Syme, 1985; Cohen, 1988; Cohen & Williamson, 1991).

How Support Concepts Interact with the Stress Process

We need more broadly conceived theories of social support. As a start, these theories need to recognize and incorporate the different conceptions of social support and their various implications for the pathways through which support may influence the relation between stress and disorder. New theories also need to recognize and identify differences in stressors. For example, interpersonal stressors present unique problems for stress-support models, because the stressors themselves may impact the nature of social networks, availability of support, and type and quality of support behaviors. At the same time, we know interpersonal stressors are important contributors to the development of disorder and disease, possibly because they are simultaneous indicators of both a stressor and the disruption of social networks and supports.

Another important issue is the relationship of support provision to the time course of stressor and disease processes (Jacobson, 1986). Support that is appropriate and effective at one point in the unfolding of a stressful event may be useless or harmful at another (Cohen & McKay, 1984). For example, emotional support may be most appropriate when a person loses a job and the offer of tangible aid may be inappropriate. Several months later, however, the offer of aid might be most appropriate.

Lack of an Integrated Theoretical Perspective

It is easy to criticize this area for lacking a broader-integrated theoretical perspective, but it is much more difficult to derive such an approach. This chapter contains a rough outline of the issue involved in such an endeavor. Hopefully, future work will build on an understanding of the concepts and mechanisms proposed, and will aid in the development of a truly integrated theory of the role of social networks, supports, and supportive behaviors in a stress and disorder model.

REFERENCES

Belle, D. (1989). Gender differences in children's social networks and supports. In D. Belle (Ed.), *Children's social networks and social supports* (pp. 173–188). New York: Wiley.

Bolger, N., DeLongis, A., Kessler, R. C. & Schilling, E. A. Effects of daily stress on negative mood. *Journal of Personality and Social Psychology, 57,* 808–817.

Bolger, N., Kessler, R. C., & Schilling, E. A. (1989). Visible support, invisible support, and adjustment to daily stress. Manuscript submitted for publication.
Brown, G. W., & Harris, T. O. (Eds.). (1978). *Social origins of depression: A study of psychiatric disorders in women.* London: Tavistock.
Brown, G. W., & Harris, T. O. (Eds.). (1989). *Life events and illness.* New York: Guilford Press.
Cassell, J. (1976). Social science in epidemiology: Psychosocial processes and stress theoretical formulation. In E. L. Struening & M. Guttentag (Eds.), *Handbook of evaluation research, vol. I* (pp. 537–549). London: Sage Publications.
Clark, M. S., & Reis, H. T. (1988). Interpersonal processes in close relationships. *Annual Review of Psychology, 39,* 609–672.
Cobb, S. (1976). Social support as a moderator of life stress. *Psychosomatic Medicine, 38,* 300–314.
Cohen, S. (1988). Psychosocial models of the role of social support in the etiology of physical disease. *Health Psychology, 7,* 269–297.
Cohen, S. (in press). The content and context of effective spousal support. In K. W. Schaie, J. S. House, & D. Blazer (Eds.), *Aging, health behaviors, and health outcomes.* Hillsdale, NJ: Erlbaum.
Cohen, S., & Edwards, J. R. (1989). Personality characteristics as moderators of the relationship between stress and disorder. In R. W. J. Neufeld (Ed.), *Advances in the investigation of psychological stress.* New York: Wiley.
Cohen, S., & Hoberman, H. (1983). Positive events and social supports as buffers of life change stress. *Journal of Applied Social Psychology, 13,* 99–125.
Cohen, S., & Lichtenstein, E. (1990). Partner behaviors that support quitting smoking. *Journal of Consulting and Clinical Psychology, 58*(3), 304–309.
Cohen, S., & McKay, G. (1984). Social support, stress, and the buffering hypothesis: A theoretical analysis. In A. Baum, J. E. Singer, & S. E. Taylor (Eds.), *Handbook of psychology and health, vol. 4.* Hillsdale, NJ: Erlbaum.
Cohen, S., Sherrod, D. R., & Clark, M. S. (1986). Social skills and the stress protective role of social support. *Journal of Personality and Social Psychology, 50,* 963–973.
Cohen, S., & Syme, S. L. (1985). Issues in the study and application of social support. In S. Cohen & S. L. Syme (Eds.), *Social support and health* (pp. 3–22). San Francisco: Academic Press.
Cohen, S., & Williamson, G. (1991). Stress and infectious disease in humans. *Psychological Bulletin, 109,* 5–24.
Cohen, S., & Wills, T. A. (1985). Stress, social support, and the buffering hypothesis. *Psychological Bulletin, 2,* 310–357.
Coppotelli, H. C., & Orleans, C. T. (1985). Partner support and other determinants of smoking cessation maintenance among women. *Journal of Consulting and Clinical Psychology, 53,* 455–460.
Coyne, J. C. (1976). Depression and the response of others. *Journal of Abnormal Psychology, 85,* 186–193.
Coyne, J. C., & Bolger, N. (1990). Doing without social support as an explanatory concept. *Journal of Social and Clinical Psychology, 9,* 148–158.
Cutrona, C. E. (1986). Behavioral manifestations of social support: A microanalytic investigation. *Journal of Personality and Social Psychology, 51,* 201–208.
Cutrona, C. E. (1990). Stress and social support: In search of optimal matching. *Journal of Social and Clinical Psychology, 9,* 3–14.
Cutrona, C. E., & Russell, D. (1990). Type of social support and specific stress: Toward a theory of optimal matching. In I. G. Sarason, B. R. Sarason, & G. R. Pierce (Eds.), *Social support: An interactional view* (pp. 319–366). New York: Wiley.
Dakof, G. A., & Taylor, S. E. (1990). Victims' perceptions of social support: What is helpful from whom? *Journal of Personality and Social Psychology, 58*(1), 80–89.
DiMatteo, M. R., & Hays, R. (1981). Social support and life stress. In B. H. Gottlieb (Ed.), *Social networks and social support* (pp. 117–148). Beverly Hills, CA: Sage.
Dunkel-Schetter, C. (1984). Social support and cancer. Findings based on patient interviews and their implications. *Journal of Social Issues, 40,* 77–98.
Dunkel-Schetter, C., Folkman, S., & Lazarus, R. S. (1987). Correlates of social support receipt. *Journal of Personality and Social Psychology, 53,* 71–80.
Dunkel-Schetter, C., & Skokan, L. A. (1990). Determinants of social support provision in personal relationships. *Journal of Social and Personal Relationships, 7,* 437–450.
Eckenrode, J. (1983). The mobilization of social supports: Some individual constraints. *American Journal of Community Psychology, 11,* 509–528.

Fiore, J., Becker, J., & Coppel, D. B. (1983). Social network interactions: A buffer or a stress? *American Journal of Community Psychology, 11,* 423–439.

Fisher, J. D. (1988). Possible effects of reference group-based social influence on AIDS-risk behavior and AIDS prevention. *American Psychologist, 43,* 921-927.

Fisher, J. D., Nadler, A., & DePaulo, B. M. (1983). *New directions in helping: vol. 1. Recipient reactions to aid.* New York: Academic Press.

Graham, N. M. H., Douglas, R. B., & Ryan, P. (1986). Stress and acute respiratory infection. *American Journal of Epidemiology, 124,* 389–401.

Hall, A., & Wellman, B. (1985). Social networks and social support. In S. Cohen & S. L. Syme (Eds.), *Social support and health* (pp. 23-41). Orlando, FL: Academic Press.

Harris, T. O. (1989). Physical illness: An introduction. In G. W. Brown & T. O. Harris (Eds.), *Life events and illness.* New York: Guilford Press.

Heller, K. (1979). The effects of social support: Prevention and treatment implications. In A. P. Goldstein & F. H. Kanfer (Eds.), *Maximizing treatment gains: Transfer enhancement in psychotherapy.* New York: Academic Press.

Heller, K., & Swindle, R. W. (1983). Social networks, perceived social support and coping with stress. In R. D. Felner, L. A. Jason, J. Moritsugu, & S. S. Farber (Eds.), *Preventive psychology, research and practice in community intervention* (pp. 87-103). New York: Pergamon.

Heller, K., Swindle, R. W., & Dusenbury, L. (1986). Component social support processes: Comments and integration. *Journal of Consulting and Clinical Psychology, 54,* 466–470.

Henderson, S., Byrne, D. G., & Duncan-Jones, P. (1981). *Neurosis and the social environment.* Sydney: Academic Press.

Hirsch, B. J. (1981). Social networks and the coping process: Creating personal communities. In B. H. Gottlieb (Ed.), *Social networks and social support.* Beverly Hills, CA: Sage.

Hobfoll, S. E. (1989). Conservation of resources: A new attempt at conceptualizing stress. *American Psychologist, 44,* 513-524.

House, J. S. (1981). *Work stress and social support.* Reading, MA: Addison-Wesley.

Husaini, B. A., Newbrough, J. R., Neff, J. A., & Moore, M. C. (1982). The stress-buffering role of social support and personal competence among the rural married. *Journal of Community Psychology, 10,* 409–426.

Jacobson, D. E. (1986). Types and timing of social support. *Journal of Health and Social Behavior, 27,* 250–264.

Kessler, R. C., & Essex, M. (1982). Marital status and depression: The role of coping resources. *Social Forces, 61,* 484-507.

Kessler, R. C., & McLeod, J. D. (1985). Social support and mental health in community samples. In S. Cohen & S. L. Syme (Eds.), *Social support and health* (pp. 219-240). New York: Academic Press.

Kessler, R. D., McLeod, J., & Wethington, E. (1985). The costs of caring: A perspective on the relationship between sex and psychological distress. In I. G. Sarason & B. R. Sarason (Eds.), *Social support: Theory, research and applications* (pp. 491-506). The Hague, the Netherlands: Martinus Nijhoff.

Krause, N. (1987). Life stress, social support, and self-esteem in an elderly population. *Psychology and Aging, 2,* 349-356.

Lakey, B., & Cassady, P. B. (1990). Cognitive processes in perceived social support. *Journal of Personality and Social Psychology, 59,* 337-343.

Lazarus, R. S., & Folkman, S. (1984). *Stress, appraisal, and coping.* New York: Springer Publishing.

Lehman, D. R., Ellard, J. H., & Wortman, C. B. (1986). Social support for the bereaved: Recipients' and providers' perspectives on what is helpful. *Journal of Consulting and Clinical Psychology, 54,* 438–446.

Melamed, B. G., & Brenner, G. F. (1990). Social support and chronic medical stress: An interaction based approach. *Journal of Social and Clinical Psychology, 9,* 104–117.

Mermelstein, R., Cohen, S., Lichtenstein, E., Baer, J. S., & Kamarck, T. (1986). Social support and smoking cessation and maintenance. *Journal of Consulting and Clinical Psychology, 54,* 447–453.

Meyer, R. J., & Haggerty, R. J. (1962). Streptococcal infections in families. *Pediatrics, 29,* 539-549.

Monroe, S. M., & Depue, R. A. (1991). Life stress and depression. In J. Becker & A. Kleinman, (Eds.), *Psychosocial aspects of depression* (pp. 101-130). New York: Erlbaum.

Monroe, S. M., & Simons, A. D. (in press). Diathesis-stress theories in the context of life stress research: Implications for the depressive disorders. *Psychological bulletin.*

Newcomb, M. D. (1990). Social support and personal characteristics: A developmental and interactional perspective. *Journal of Social and Clinical Psychology, 9,* 54–68.

Ostfield, A. M., & Eaker, E. B. (Eds.). (1985). *Measuring psychosocial variables in epidemiologic studies of cardiovascular disease.* (NIH Publication No. 85-2270). Washington, DC: U. S. Department of Health and Human Services.

Pagel, M. D., Erdly, W. W., & Becker, J. (1987). Social networks: We get by with (and in spite of) a little help from our friends. *Journal of Personality and Social Psychology, 53,* 793–804.

Paykel, E. S. (1974). Life stress and psychiatric disorder: Applications of the clinical approach. In B. S. Dohrenwend & B. P. Dohrenwend (Eds.), *Stressful life events: Their nature and effects* (pp. 135–149). New York: Wiley.

Pearlin, L. I., Menaghan, E. G., Lieberman, M. A., & Mullan, J. T. (1981). The stress process. *Journal of Health and Social Behavior, 22,* 337–356.

Pearlin, L. I., & Schooler, C. (1978). The structure of coping. *Journal of Health and Social Behavior, 19,* 2–21.

Procidano, M. E., & Heller, K. (1983). Measures of perceived social support from friends and family: Three validation studies. *American Journal of Community Psychology, 11,* 1–24.

Rabin, B. S., Cohen, S., Ganguli, R., Lysle, D. T., & Cunnick, J. E. (1989). Bidirectional interaction between the central nervous system and immune system. *Critical Reviews in Immunology, 9,* 279–312.

Rabkin, J. G., & Struening, E. L. (1976). Life events, stress, and illness. *Science, 194,* 1013–1020.

Reis, H. T. (1990). The role of intimacy in interpersonal relationships. *Journal of Social and Clinical Psychology, 9,* 15–30.

Reis, H. T., Wheeler, L., Kernis, M. H., Spiegel, N., & Nezlek, J. (1985). On specificity in the impact of social participation on physical and psychological health. *Journal of Personality and Social Psychology, 48,* 456–471.

Riley, D., & Eckenrode, J. (1986). Social ties: Subgroup differences in costs and benefits. *Journal of Personality and Social Psychology, 51,* 770–778.

Sarason, I. G., Levine, H. M., Basham, R. B., & Sarason, B. R. (1983). Assessing social support: The Social Support Questionnaire. *Journal of Personality and Social Psychology, 44,* 127–139.

Sarason, I. G., Sarason, B. R., & Pierce, G. R. (1990). Social support: The search for theory. *Journal of Social and Clinical Psychology, 9,* 133–147.

Schulz, R., & Rau, M. T. (1985). Social support through the life course. In S. Cohen & S. L. Syme (Eds.), *Social support and health.* New York: Academic Press.

Schulz, R., & Tompkins, C. A. (1990). Life events and changes in social relationships: Examples, mechanisms, and measurement. *Journal of Social and Clinical Psychology, 9,* 69–77.

Schultz, R., Tompkins, C. A., & Rau, M. T. (1988). A longitudinal study of the psychosocial impact of stroke on primary support persons. *Psychology and Aging, 3,* 131–141.

Schwarzer, R., & Leppin, A. (1989). Social support and health: A meta-analysis. *Psychology and Health, 3,* 1–15.

Shumaker, S. A., & Brownell, A. (1984). Toward a theory of social support: Closing conceptual gaps. *Journal of Social Issues, 40*(4), 11–36.

Stroebe, M. S., & Stroebe, W. (1985). Social support and the alleviation of loss. In I. G. Sarason & B. R. Sarason (Eds.), *Social Support: Theory, research and applications* (pp. 439–462). Boston: Martinus Nijhoff.

Tetzloff, C. E., & Barrera, M. J. (1987). Divorcing mothers and social support: Testing the specificity of buffering effects. *American Journal of Community Psychology, 15,* 419–434.

Thoits, P. A. (1985). Social support and psychological well-being: Theoretical possibilities. In I. G. Sarason & B. R. Sarason (Eds.), *Social support: Theory, research and applications* (pp. 51–72). The Hague, the Netherlands: Martinus Nijhoff.

Thoits, P. A. (1983). Dimensions of life events that influence psychological distress: An evaluation and synthesis of the literature. In H. B. Kaplan (Ed.), *Psychosocial stress: Trends in theory and research* (pp. 33–103). New York: Academic.

Thoits, P. A. (1986). Social support as coping assistance. *Journal of Consulting and Clinical Psychology, 54,* 416–423.

Turner, J. (1983). Direct, indirect, and moderating effects of social support on psychological distress and associated conditions. In H. B. Kaplan (Ed.), *Psychosocial stress: Trends in theory and research* (pp. 105–155). New York: Academic Press.

Vinokur, A., Schul, Y., & Caplan, R. D. (1987). Determinants of perceived social support: Interper-

sonal transactions, personal outlook, and transient affective states. *Journal of Personality and Social Psychology, 53,* 1137–1145.
Wethington, E., & Kessler, R. C. (1986). Perceived support, received support, and adjustment to stressful life events. *Journal of Health and Social Behavior, 27,* 78–89.
Wheaton, B. (1985). Models for the stress-buffering functions of coping resources. *Journal of Health and Social Behavior, 26,* 352–364.
Wilcox, B. L., & Vernberg, E. (1985). Conceptual and theoretical dilemmas facing research. In I. G. Sarason and B. R. Sarason (Eds.), *Social support: Theory, research, and application* (pp. 3–20). The Hague, The Netherlands: Martinus Nijhoff.
Wills, T. A. (1985). Supportive functions of interpersonal relationships. In S. Cohen and S. L. Syme (Eds.), *Social support and health.* Orlando, FL: Academic Press.
Wills, T. A., & DePaulo, B. M. (1991). Interpersonal analysis of the help-seeking process. In C. R. Snyder & D. R. Forsyth (Eds.), *Handbook of social and clinical psychology* (pp. 350–375). Elmford, NY: Pergamon
Wortman, C. B., & Conway, T. L. (1985). The role of social support in adaptation and recovery from physical illness. In S. Cohen, & S. L. Syme (Eds.), *Social support and health* (pp. 281–302). Orlando, FL: Academic Press.
Wortman, C. B., & Dunkel-Schetter, C. (1979). Interpersonal relationships and cancer: A theoretical analysis. *Journal of Social Issues, 35,* 120–155.
Wortman, C. B., & Dunkel-Schetter, C. (1987). Conceptual and methodological issues in the study of social support. In A. Baum & J. Singer (Eds.), *Handbook of psychology and health* (pp. 63–108). Hillsdale, NJ: Erlbaum.

9

Conservation of Social Resources and the Self

Steven E. Hobfoll, Roy S. Lilly, and Anita P. Jackson
Kent State University, Ohio, USA

Years of research have uncovered a great deal about the complexity of social support (Sarason & Sarason, 1985; Sarason, Sarason, & Pierce, 1990; Vaux, 1988). Overall, social support is depicted as a valuable commodity. Those who receive social support exhibit better physical health and emotional well-being than those who do not (Vaux, 1988). In addition, at times of high stress, those who experience greater social support are less likely to display the negative sequalae that otherwise accompanies stress. What remains to be determined is the process by which social support's benefits are derived, or a theory that might predict both the support process and the outcomes of social support transactions (Hobfoll, 1986).

This chapter examines the theory of Conservation of Resources (COR) (Hobfoll, 1988, 1989), as it applies to social support. COR theory is a general theory of human motivation that is especially relevant to the process of coping with stress. We suggest that this is an overarching theory of human behavior that provides a model for understanding and predicting the commerce of social support and the products of this commerce. It explains when social support will occur, when it will be most helpful, when it will have limited ramifications, and even when it is counterproductive. This approach can be contrasted to the atheoretical approach that is generally represented in the field today, which basically says social support is supportive because it helps people or gives them the feeling of being helped.

To develop our arguments, we will first present a brief review of Hobfoll's (1988, 1989) COR theory, along with some discussion of special corollaries of the model regarding social support. We will next present a method that we have been developing for examining COR theory, together with some preliminary data on the method's reliability and validity. We will then outline other findings from our research program and the work of others that explores COR theory. In discussing some of these new areas of social support research, we will also share new instruments that we have developed to explore what we see as one avenue for the next generation of social support investigations. Finally, we will explore applications of the theory to interventions involving social support.

CONSERVATION OF RESOURCES: A MOTIVATIONAL THEORY

COR begins with the basic motivational tenet that people strive to gain and protect that which they value and consequently to avoid loss of that which they value. It is further postulated that loss is more salient than gain. Thus, stress is defined as occurring when resources are either (a) threatened, (b) actually lost, or (c) invested without sufficient subsequent gain. Resources, in turn, are defined as those objects, conditions, personal characteristics, and energies that people value or that aid them in obtaining that which they value. Objects are characterized by their physical nature (e.g., a crystal goblet, basic transportation); conditions are states of being that have value (e.g., tenure, a good marriage); personal characteristics are aspects of the self that are valued or that aid achievement of goals (e.g., high self-esteem, social skillfulness); and energies are resources that have little or no innate value, but that may be used to obtain other resources (e.g., money, knowledge, favors).

An immediate question arises as to whether loss is central to stress, or whether it is more specifically related to depression. There is ample evidence that loss is related to depression (Lazarus, 1968), but this line of research did not carefully examine whether loss would also be related to other negative health or emotional sequalae. Analysis of all common loss event scales indicates that the most highly weighted events are all obvious loss events (e.g., death of a loved one, negative change in health, losing one's job). Experiencing these events has often been shown to predict a full spectrum of negative emotional and physical health outcomes, in no way limited to depression. More ambiguous events, such as change in job status, have only been found to be stressful to the extent that they indicate negative change (e.g., loss of job status) (Thoits, 1983). Experience of these events has also been found to relate to deleterious effects other than depression.

Likewise, transitions have been noted to be stressful and to be accompanied with negative consequences for the individual not limited to depression to the extent they follow or entail resource losses (cf., Wilcox, 1986). Research by our group has found that loss is related to anxiety, anger, depressive mood, and practical functioning (Hobfoll & Leiberman, 1989; Hobfoll, London, & Orr, 1988; Lane, 1990). Until further study, the most accurate depiction of the literature is that the notion that loss is solely linked with depression is based on psychodynamic theory, not empirical evidence. Although it is true that loss and depression are linked, depression is part of the more general effects of loss on negative physical and psychological outcomes.

COROLLARIES FOLLOWING FROM COR THEORY

A number of corollaries follow from the premises of COR theory. First, the theory implies that people are not passive reactors to outside stressors. Rather, people play an active role in creating their environment and the circumstances that are likely to result in loss or gain. On the other hand, resources are not distributed randomly and life circumstances often limit resource availability beyond the reach of individual control. Poverty, physical violence, racism, sexism, and ageism all infringe on the array of resources that might otherwise be at an individual's control. Furthermore, such circumstances may also detract from the belief that one possesses resources, even if one actually does. For example, scholarships for school may be available, but past experiences of racism may diminish the belief that one would really receive such aid. Overall then, it can be said that people play an active role in determining their resources and their use of these resources, but this picture must be tempered so as not to be interpreted in a way that blames the victim when environmental or social circumstances are dominant. This chapter will explore this issue further with the presentation of relevant research findings.

A second corollary of COR theory is that people use resources to conserve and protect other resources. Self-esteem is used both to meet a difficult challenge and to preserve self-esteem. Money may be used to protect other material investments by purchasing insurance. What follows from this corollary is that those who lack resources are more vulnerable to the deleterious effects of stressors. It also follows that those rich in resources may be able to withstand greater stressful circumstances and for a longer period of time than those who are not rich in resources (Pearlin, Leiberman, Menaghen, & Mullan, 1981). For example, a very recent study found that those with greater social and personal resources were more stable during a stressful period and even gained resources when confronted with a crisis (Holahan & Moos, 1990).

A third corollary follows from this second premise; specifically, that the process of coping incurs costs because resources must be invested in the act of coping. For example, when attempting a difficult task, people high in mastery tell themselves that they can tackle the problem successfully based on their belief that in the past they have been able to perform positively in similar circumstances. They are thereby investing this resource, because if they fail this may detract from their sense of mastery, and if they succeed their sense of mastery may be further enhanced. Even in love, people invest time, energy, trust, and affection, expecting that their contribution to the relationship will result in a response in kind.

A final corollary of COR theory is that resource loss and gain tend to produce negative and positive spirals, respectively. Because resources are invested when losses occur, and because those who already lack in resources are more vulnerable to loss following initial stressful events, a negative spiral is created. If initial attempts at coping are not successful—more likely for those unendowed with resources—the spiral is likely to accelerate. Successful coping, in contrast, can result in a building of resources because gains make further gains more likely and reduce vulnerability. Social support can be seen as especially important because it extends resources beyond those possessed within the self and helps prevent initial loss, halts or limits loss spirals, and increases the likelihood of further resource gain.

CONSERVATION OF RESOURCES AND SOCIAL SUPPORT

COR theory also lends itself to specific corollaries regarding social support. The first social support corollary related to COR is that social support is a major mechanism by which the availability of resources for the individual is widened beyond the level that is available to the self. A car may be loaned, knowledge may be shared, and insights into the self may be gained through the process of social support. There are two ways that this is made possible: (a) by outright giving of a resource by another, or (b) by providing the complement to what an individual already possesses, but cannot otherwise place into action. The first case is simple (e.g., a person provides another an apartment for 2 weeks in between moves). The second case is more complex, but much more common. Here, for instance, emotional support is provided, but it is only effective to the extent that it fuels the recipient's sense of self-esteem, which is temporarily lagging, perhaps owing to recent setbacks. For a concrete example, an individual may have the strength to carry a table, but may need another individual's support on the other end to balance it and turn corners to get it up stairs. The support made the individual's strength useful as it was otherwise of limited value.

COR theory relates to social support in a second key fashion. Because social attachments underlie social resources, social resources are linked to people's senses of identify. This depiction of identity is consistent with the views of many personality theorists, because identity consists, in part, of one's social self and sense of attachment (cf., Erikson, 1968; Maslow, 1968). Children, for example, do not clearly separate themselves from their parents. Likewise, adolescents and young adults see themselves in view of and at times inseparable from their peers and, later, intimate others. For adults, the attachment to children and partners produce similar vagaries in the boundary of the self. Indeed, when asked who we are, we often respond by saying father or mother, husband or wife.

The association of social relationships with identity leads to the second social support corollary of COR—specifically, that people strive to maintain social resources both to meet their need to preserve resources and to protect and maintain their identify. Hence, support resources are more vital to the individual than many other kinds of resources. Many resources are valued principally because of their contribution to the individual in preventing loss and obtaining gains, but social resources are valued beyond this for their intrinsic association with how individuals see themselves. Clearly, there is biological and social evidence for this as close attachments are common to all societies, but the level of these attachments differ between societies. Clan societies may, for example, have a broader web of primary attachments than nuclear family societies.

RESOURCE EVALUATION

To examine COR theory, an instrument was devised to measure people's resources and their loss and gain of these resources. Employing a group process, groups of varying composition nominated resources that they judged to be of primary importance. Groups added and removed resources from lists and shared their lists with parallel groups, until a single list was developed for which the group process did not select an additional resource that did not overlap with resources already nominated. This is not to say that the list was exhaustive; however, it was comprehensive. Recently, the same process was used on a group of some 30 researchers in the Netherlands, and few, if any, resources were nominated that were not on the list that was constructed by the original group process.

The resources named in the COR-Evaluation are presented in Table 1. As may be observed, the kinds of resources broadly represent the four resource domains originally defined (i.e., objects, conditions, personal characteristics, and energies). There were 74 resources named in all. Individuals reported their (a) recent losses, (b) losses during the past year, (c) recent gains, and (d) gains during the past year on scales ranging from 1 to 7, where 1 equals little loss or gain and 7 equals great loss or gain for that period. Respondents did not rate resources where there was no loss or gain.

We set out to begin evaluation of the COR-Evaluation as a resource tool using two different samples. The first validating sample of 74 people consisted of indi-

Table 1 Resources from COR-Evaluation

- Personal transportation (car, truck, etc.)
- Feeling that I am successful
- Time for adequate sleep
- Good marriage
- Adequate clothing
- Feeling valuable to others
- Family stability
- Intimacy with one or more family members
- Clothing that is more than what I need
- Sense of pride in myself
- Free time
- Time for work
- Feeling that I am accomplishing my goals
- Hope
- Good relationship with my children
- Time with loved ones
- Necessary tools for work
- Children's health
- Stamina/endurance
- Necessary appliances for home
- Personal health
- Feeling my future success depends on me
- Positively challenging routine
- Housing that suits my needs
- Sense of optimism
- Status/seniority at work
- Adequate food
- Home that is more than what I need
- Stable employment
- Intimacy with spouse or partner
- Adequate furnishings for home
- Feeling that I have control over my life
- Sense of humor
- Role as a leader
- Ability to communicate well
- Essentials for children
- Feeling that my life is peaceful
- Acknowledgment for accomplishment
- Ability to organize tasks
- "Extras" for children
- Sense of commitment
- Intimacy with at least one friend
- Money for "extras"
- Self-discipline
- Understanding from my employer/boss
- Companionship
- Savings or emergency money
- Motivation to get things done
- Spouse/partner's health
- Support from co-workers
- Adequate income
- Feeling that I know who I am
- Adequate credit (financial)
- Feeling independent
- Financial assets (stocks, property, etc.)
- Knowing where I am going with my life
- Affection from others
- Financial stability
- Feeling that my life has meaning or purpose
- Positive feelings about myself
- People I can learn from
- Money for transportation
- Help with tasks at work
- Medical insurance
- Involvement with church, synagogue, and so forth
- Retirement security (financial)
- Help with tasks at home
- Loyalty of friends
- Help with childcare
- Financial help if needed
- Health of family/close friends
- Involvement in organizations with others who have similar interests
- Money for advancement or self-improvement (education, starting a business)
- Advancement in my education or training

viduals from a church group and others attending an evening community college, whose student body represented a broad sampling of the local community. The second sample consisted of 255 undergraduate students who participated for class credit. Participants completed the COR-Evaluation and a battery of measures of emotional distress on two occasions over a 2-week period.

We did a number of checks on reliability. It was expected that test-retest reliability would be at moderately high levels. If reporting was influenced substantially by mood, then we expected low test-retest reliability. To the extent individuals are reporting actual losses and gains, however, then at least moderate test-retest reliability would be noted. If, on the other hand, people were reporting a traitlike representation of how they viewed their resources, we would expect exceedingly high correlations. Test-retest correlations for the two groups ranged from .55 to .64 for recent losses and losses during the past year, and from .64 to .67 ($p < .001$

for all correlations) for gains during the past year. As might be expected, recent losses were slightly lower in magnitude than losses during the past year, as these were more likely to change during the testing interval. These levels were consistent with our predictions that depict reporting of losses and gains as relatively free of influence of mood or trait characteristics.

A further test of the instrument concerned whether individuals were reporting a general sense of loss and gain as opposed to the more accurate depiction of particular losses and gains experienced. To examine this question, we investigated the factor structure of reported losses. If individuals were merely reporting a global sense of loss, then factor analysis would reveal one principal factor on which many items showed factor loading. If, however, individuals were reporting the more particular losses that the COR-Evaluation was designed to tap, then several factors would be revealed. Regarding the social support corollaries mentioned previously, we also expected that social support resources would be among the primary factors represented.

Exploratory principal components analyses were performed for each sample, using 74 × 74 correlation matrix among the average ratings (from the two separate administrations of the instrument) of recent losses. Based on parallel analyses of random data, five factors were extracted and rotated to simple structure using the varimax criterion for the community sample. Six factors emerged from the corresponding analysis of the student sample. Congruence coefficients (Gorsuch, 1983) were used to compare the similarity of the factors from the two samples. There appeared to be little congruence between any of the pairs of factors. The results of the varimax rotations are presented in Table 2. Only the highest loading items are given—those above .45 for the community sample and those above .40 for the student sample.

The results support the construct validity of the instrument. No global factor was found for either sample, indicating that participants did not view their loss globally. Rather, factors were distinguishable in discrete, reasonably clear categories. A personal resource factor was one of the strongest factors in both samples. Financial loss also played a key role. In the context of this chapter, it is most interesting to note that three of the factors in each of the samples had loadings for support resources. These were related to work and accomplishing work-related tasks, close personal ties, and marriage and children. The factors were clearly distinguishable in each case. The separation of social support into each of these other life domains suggests the pervasiveness and centrality of support in the coping process. It also is consistent with our conceptualization of social support as tied in with many aspects of the self.

We were also able to examine an important aspect of the COR-Evaluation's validity by observing whether developmental differences were found between the two samples. We expected the community sample to report losses more related to family and marriage than the students, whereas we expected the college sample to report more losses concerned with identity than the community sample. As noted in Table 2, the first factor for the student sample had strong loadings for accomplishment-related resources that are tied with identity. The first factor for the community sample was financial. Problems of health and family were represented on a stronger factor for the community sample than for the student sample. Again, these results represent a pattern consistent with COR theory and our expectations.

Table 2 Results of factor analysis

Adult sample—averaged ratings: Recent losses

	Factor 1 (Financial)
.88	Financial stability
.85	Savings or emergency money
.83	Money for transportation
.82	Adequate income
.79	Money for "extras"
.70	Money for advancement/self-improvement
.69	Financial assets (stocks, property, etc.)
.68	Financial help if needed
.66	Stable employment
.64	Adequate credit (financial)
.57	Help with tasks at home
.54	Personal transportation
	Factor 2 (Personal/support)
.68	Self-discipline
.68	Positive feelings about myself
.66	Ability to organize tasks
.65	Time for adequate sleep
.63	Feeling that my life has meaning/purpose
.61	Advancement in my education/training
.61	Stamina/endurance
.60	Free time
.60	Sense of optimism
.60	Help with tasks at work
.58	Motivation to get things done
.57	Feeling that I am successful
.55	People I can learn from
.53	Help with childcare
.70	Children's health
.69	Necessary appliances for home
.69	Adequate food
.68	Essentials for children
.67	Adequate furnishings for home
.67	Necessary tools for work
.65	Adequate clothing
.59	Retirement security (financial)
.57	Good relationship with my children
.50	Clothing that is more than what I need
.53	Housing that suits my needs
	Factor 4 (Personal/support)
.73	Good marriage
.71	Knowing where I am going with my life
.66	Feeling valuable to others
.65	Intimacy with spouse or partner
.63	Feeling that I have control over my life
.63	Ability to communicate well
.63	Feeling that my life is peaceful
.61	Necessary tools for work
.60	Hope
.60	Affection from others
.60	Feeling that I know who I am
.59	Sense of humor
.58	Feeling that I am accomplishing my goals
.58	Companionship
.52	Spouse/partner's health
.54	Sense of optimism
	Factor 5 (Work support/accomplishment)
.78	Understanding from my employer/boss

Student sample—averaged ratings: Recent losses

	Factor 1 (Personal/attainment)
.78	Feeling that I am accomplishing my goals
.75	Feeling that I have control over my life
.73	Positive feelings about myself
.72	Hope
.72	Feeling that I am successful
.70	Feeling my future success depends on me
.69	Sense of pride in myself
.68	Sense of optimism
.66	Feeling that my life has meaning/purpose
.65	Motivation to get things done
.63	Knowing where I am going with my life
.62	Feeling that my life is peaceful
.60	Self-discipline
.60	Feeling that I know who I am
.60	Ability to communicate well
.53	Stamina/endurance
.53	Clothing that is more than what I need
.53	Feeling valuable to others
.53	Advancement in my education or training
.50	Sense of humor
.49	Ability to organize tasks
.49	Feeling independent
.48	Acknowledgment for accomplishments
.46	Adequate clothing
.41	Positively challenging routine
.42	Sense of commitment
	Factor 2 (Financial)
.73	Adequate income
.70	Financial stability
.70	Money for advancement or self-improvement
.57	Savings or emergency money
.56	Understanding from my employer/boss
.54	Stable employment
.48	Support from co-workers
.48	Money for transportation
.47	Adequate credit (financial)
.47	Medical insurance

Table 2 Results of factor analysis (*Continued*)

Student sample—averaged ratings: Recent losses (*Continued*)	
.44	Financial help if needed
.48	Money for "extras"
	Factor 3 (Time/financial)
.57	Adequate food
.56	Time with loved ones
.56	Free time
.54	Housing that suits my needs
.54	Time for adequate sleep
.54	Personal transportation
.49	Money for "extras"
.45	Time for work
.44	Adequate furnishings for home
.48	Necessary appliances for home
.41	Home that is more than I need
	Factor 4 (Work support/financial)
.63	Adequate furnishings for home
.56	Necessary appliances for home
.54	Help with tasks at home
.54	Home that is more than I need
.51	Involvement with organizations with others who have similar interests
.48	Status/seniority at work
.44	Financial assets
.43	Help with tasks at work
.42	Role as a leader
.46	Support from co-workers
	Factor 5 (Intimacy)
.70	Affection from others
.67	Intimacy with at least one friend
.64	Companionship
.57	Loyalty of friends
.53	Intimacy with spouse or partner
.46	Sense of commitment
	Factor 6 (Marriage/children)
.83	Essentials for children
.75	Good relationship with my children
.68	Children's health
.62	Help with childcare
.58	Good marriage
.57	"Extras" for children
.42	Necessary tools for work

Clearly, individuals are reporting losses that are of a particular and not a global nature.

APPLICATIONS OF THE COR-EVALUATION

A first study tested some of the basic corollaries of COR theory; specifically, whether loss elicits a coping response and leads to psychological distress. Freedy, Resnick, & Kilpatrick (in press) investigated the role of loss on coping behavior and psychological distress in the aftermath of the 1989 hurricane Hugo in the city of Charleston, South Carolina. The hurricane was extremely destructive and left the city in ruins. Freedy adopted a 52-item version of the COR-Evaluation, trimming items that were not related to his sample's particular circumstances. The sample included 418 employees of the Medical University of South Carolina in Charleston. Faculty, medical staff, clerks, and support staff were included, and men and women were equally represented.

Following the principles of COR theory, it was predicted that greater loss would be related to greater coping efforts as the loss experience cues coping behavior to prevent further loss. It was also predicted that loss would be related to greater psychological distress. The Carver (1989) Coping Scale was used to measure coping behavior and the SCL-90 was used as a measure of psychological distress.

Loss was significantly correlated with emotion-focused coping ($r = .24$, $p < .01$), problem-focused coping ($r = .28, p < .01$), and disengagement coping ($r = .57, p < .001$). Loss was also significantly correlated to the general severity index score of the SCL-90 ($r = .64$, $p < .001$). Controlling for gender, marital status, and household income, resource loss had a greater contribution to the SCL-90 score than any of the three coping behaviors. Freedy and colleagues concluded that loss is a central component of the postdisaster experience and that those who undergo greater loss are more likely to respond with both positive (problem-focused coping) and negative (emotion-focused coping and disengagement) coping behaviors. These conclusions support the basic tenet of COR theory pertaining to the central nature of loss and provide evidence for the second corollary, regarding coping reactions in response to loss.

In another study based on the COR-Evaluation, Lane (1990) examined how loss impacted patients' anger, and how this anger might limit the availability of social resources. She administered the COR-Evaluation along with measures of anger, hostile behavior (obstreperousness), and physical symptoms to a group of patients suffering from dyspnea, a severe breathing disorder that results in loss of lung capacity and a feeling of suffocating. Both patients' responses and responses of a most-significant other elected by the patient were tapped. Patients and their significant others responded twice to questionnaires over a 3-month period.

Partialling out the contribution of symptoms, patients' reports of loss had an independent concurrent effect on their recent anger. In addition, loss had an independent prospective effect on patients' anger-out (expressed anger), controlling for prior anger-out and symptoms. These findings indicate that loss has a significant negative effect on anger, over and above the effect of losses that are directly related to symptoms (as this common variance is partialled out), indicating the importance of loss on psychological distress. Such loss is probably related to secondary losses that occur in the form of loss of feeling of identity, loss of self-esteem, loss of income, and other negative consequences of increasing physical illness.

It is also interesting to note how loss translates to the further diminishment of resources, as suggested by the third corollary regarding loss spirals. As patients felt more angry, they acted in a more obstreperous fashion. When supporters (i.e., significant others) were subjected to this hostile behavior, they, in turn, responded with greater anger. Thus, the experience of loss led to an alienation of the main potential provider of support in the patients' lives. We can imagine how this would contribute to a further cycle of loss that would result in subsequent increases in anger and so on.

RESOURCES AND SOCIAL SUPPORT: OTHER APPROACHES

Use of the COR-Evaluation is one approach to investigation of COR theory vis-a-vis social support. However, other methods are also available to researchers. These methods have included research studies focused on particular hypotheses that would be predicted by COR theory. In one such study, Hobfoll and Linetzy (1990) examined whether knowledge of what constitutes good support and support skills leads to greater intimacy between partners. COR theory suggests that resources are often interrelated and that possession of resources leads to other resources. Prior research had suggested that satisfaction with support and other perceptions of support were central to the support experience and perhaps the major active ingredient in support (Barrera, 1986; Heller & Lakey, 1985). COR theory, in contrast, puts greater weight on knowledge and skills as underlying resources in the support experience, although clearly these underlying strengths also would result in perceptions of support.

In evaluating these hypotheses, 48 couples from an Israeli kibbutz were asked to complete a series of questionnaires about themselves and their partners. This approach limited the problem of common method variance associated with self-report. In addition, individuals completed a test of their support knowledge and partners reported what their spouses actually did during a recent important problem situation. The extent that partners performed supportive and unsupportive behaviors from a list of 14 behaviors was rated by each spouse, and this instrument was scored based on whether, during prior research, each behavior was seen as positive or negative (e.g., emotional support would be evaluated positively; philosophizing would be evaluated negatively). The knowledge and skills method also avoids problems of self-report or of the couple presenting a believed model of themselves, as it would be difficult to "fake good" on either of these two instruments. These new approaches for studying social support are presented in Tables 3 and 4.

The dyadic data permitted two kinds of analyses. In the first instance, individuals' own support knowledge, support skills (rated by spouse), and their partners' satisfaction with the support they provided were used to predict their feelings of intimacy with their spouses. Employing a conservative regression approach (back-

Table 3 Social support knowledge

Imagine that you are with someone close to you (family member, friend) who is going through a difficult crisis (failure at work, marital difficulty, serious illness, etc.), and you wish to help him or her. The following items are a number of things a person might do to help or not help a person in distress. Indicate next to each item whether, in your opinion, in your first meeting the behavior would most likely be helpful (circle 1) or not helpful (circle 2) in most instances. (Scoring is provided before each item in brackets.)

[+]	1.	Show concern.
[+]	2.	Let them openly express their feelings (to cry, to be angry, to yell).
[−]	3.	Give advice about what they should do.
[−]	4.	Encourage them to stand up to the problem and "to pull themselves up by their own bootstraps." (In Hebrew the expression is literally "Take yourself in your own hands.")
[−]	5.	Tell them that you know exactly what they are feeling, "I know exactly what you're going through."
[−]	6.	Give them the message not to make such a big deal out of this, "It could be worse" or "It's not so bad."
[−]	7.	Act cheerful, even if you have to force it.
[−]	8.	Provide a philosophical reason or meaning to the event, "It's just fate."
[−]	9.	Provide religious meaning to the event, "It's God's will."
[+]	10.	Show interest.
[+]	11.	Show willingness to invest time and attention.
[−]	12.	Steer the conversation to a happier topic.
[+]	13.	Show that you understand their feelings, "I understand what you're feeling."
[+]	14.	Help them with practical tasks.
[+]	15.	Listen.
[+]	16.	Provide support by physical closeness.
[−]	17.	Share your experience (in a similar situation).
[−]	18.	Encourage them to forget and "open a new page in their life."
[+]	19.	Free up time for them.
[+]	20.	Show affection.

Table 4 Social support behavior questions

Listed below are some things a person can do to be helpful or not be helpful to someone in distress. Under each item are a few examples or an explanation. When you are in distress and need help (support), to what extent does your spouse/partner perform each behavior described (indicate from 1 - not to all, to 5 - a lot)? (Scoring direction is indicated before each item in brackets.)

[+]	1.	Shows concern. (Examples: shows interest, shows warmth, shows that they are also affected by the problem.)
[+]	2.	Provides you the chance to openly express your feelings. (Examples: listens, asks questions that don't close the topic of your expression of feelings, encourages expression of feelings, even painful feelings.)
[−]	3.	Gives advice. (Example: tells you what you should do.)
[−]	4.	Tells you that they know exactly how you feel. (Example: "I know exactly what you're going through.")
[−]	5.	Encourages you to simply overcome what has occurred to you. (Example: Tells you to "pick yourself up by your own bootstraps.")
[−]	6.	Communicates that you shouldn't make too big a thing out of the situation. (Examples: "It's not too bad," "Everything will be okay," "It could be a lot worse.")
[−]	7.	Tries to be cheerful despite the situation. (Examples: smiles despite the fact that it is not consistent with the situation, acts in a forced cheerful manner.)
[−]	8.	Gives a philosophical reason for the situation. (Examples: "To everything there is a reason," "Everything is decided in advance," "It was just written in fate that this should happen.")
[−]	9.	Gives a religious reason for the situation. (Examples: "It's God's will," "God has a reason for everything he does.")
[+]	10.	Supports you by their close physical presence. (Example: any display of physical closeness that displays affection and caring).
[−]	11.	Talks about themselves. (Example: steers attention to themselves; "Yes, I know what you're going through, one time I was in a similar situation and I . . . ")
[+]	12.	Stays with you when you need it. (Examples: invests time and attention in you, shows clear willingness to do so.)
[+]	13.	Shows that they understand your feelings. (Example: "I understand what you're feeling.")
[+]	14.	Gives help with tasks. (Examples: helps with housework, children, arrangements at work, errands, and other responsibilities.)

ward regression), each variable was entered last to derive its contribution independent of all other variables. All three predictors were significantly related to intimacy (borderline for skills, $p < .06$), and the combined model explained about 36% of the variance in intimacy ratings. In the second instance, partners' support knowledge, partners' support skills, and their satisfaction with support their partner provided were used to predict individuals' assessments of intimacy with their partners. In this case, all three variables were again significantly related to intimacy (borderline for knowledge, $p < .09$), and the combined model explained 31% of the variance in intimacy scores. Follow-up analysis further indicated that knowledge, skills, and satisfaction with support were not predictive of intimacy with friends or family, further suggesting that the resources were specifically related to intimacy with spouse as had been predicted. In this regard, some knowledge and skills might be general for different kinds of relationships, but what is expected in terms of support in the marital relationship is also quite different from what might be expected for family and friends.

Support in performing tasks during stressful circumstances is another important aspect of social support. Again applying COR theory, Hobfoll, Shoham, and Ritter (in press) predicted that, following delivery, women with greater relational and personal resources would be more likely to receive aid than those who lacked such resources. Greater aid with infant care and division of household labor were the particular outcome variables studied. It was predicted that women with greater intimacy with their partners would receive greater support under both moderate stress (i.e., normal vaginal delivery without complications) and stressful delivery (C-section). It was further predicted that possession of a strong resource—sense of mastery—would be especially linked to receipt of social support under high stress conditions, whereas women high in mastery would be more likely to rely on their self-resources under the more moderate stress conditions. This follows because, under more moderate stress, the high-mastery women would feel that their personal resources were adequate. In contrast, under high stress, (a) they would feel the need for social support, (b) they would have the resources to mobilize social support, and (c) because of their coping ability, they would attract support. This last, somewhat counterintuitive, hypothesis suggested by other research that indicates that people want to help those who are likely to be successful at coping (Dunkel-Schetter, Folkman, & Lazarus, 1987).

In contrast, possession of a weak resource was predicted to lead to greater aid only under lower stress conditions. This follows from the principle of COR theory that states that resources are expended during stressful circumstances. It follows that a weak resource would not be sufficient in the case of more major stressors, because it would be quickly expended. The weak resource chosen for study was low discomfort in seeking support. We had previously found discomfort in seeking support to be a common problem for most everyone we tested (Hobfoll & Lerman, 1989). Some, however, are less uncomfortable than others; hence, we envisioned feeling less uncomfortable seeking support as a weak resource, as it was not that these persons felt comfortable in this position of relative weakness and being a burden than others.

The findings from this study are presented in Figures 1 and 2. We did not find that greater intimacy was related to greater aid at tasks, nor did we find that greater mastery or less discomfort led to increases in men's contribution to the general load of household labor. However, for aid with the new infant we found that both our predictions were confirmed. In the first instance, greater mastery did not lead to greater support under more moderate stress conditions, but did lead to increased aid under the circumstances of higher stress C-section. As hypothesized, women high in mastery seemed to rely more on their own selves in the relatively lower stress normal birth circumstances. In the second case, women who were lower in discomfort seeking support did receive greater aid than women who felt more uncomfortable. However, as we predicted, their advantage was only evidenced in the lower stress situation. When confronted with greater stress, there was no advantage in being less uncomfortable seeking help. It would seem that this weak resource was taxed too greatly to serve women during this greater challenge.

A recent study not based on COR theory, reported by Holahan and Moos (1990), offers an exceptional confirmation of COR theory, because although COR was not considered by the authors, COR would predict each of their findings. Specifically, COR suggests that greater resources have a positive contribution under both high and low stress conditions. Further, under high stress, those possessing stronger resource reserves should display more positive coping behaviors (e.g., approach rather than avoidance) and that this, in turn, should lead to more

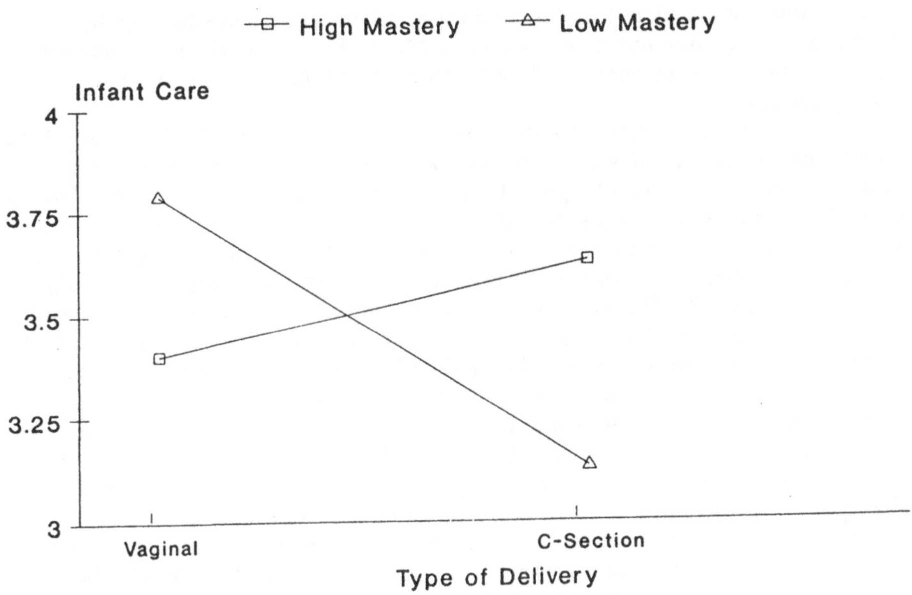

Figure 1 Effects of mastery and type of delivery on receipt of infant care.

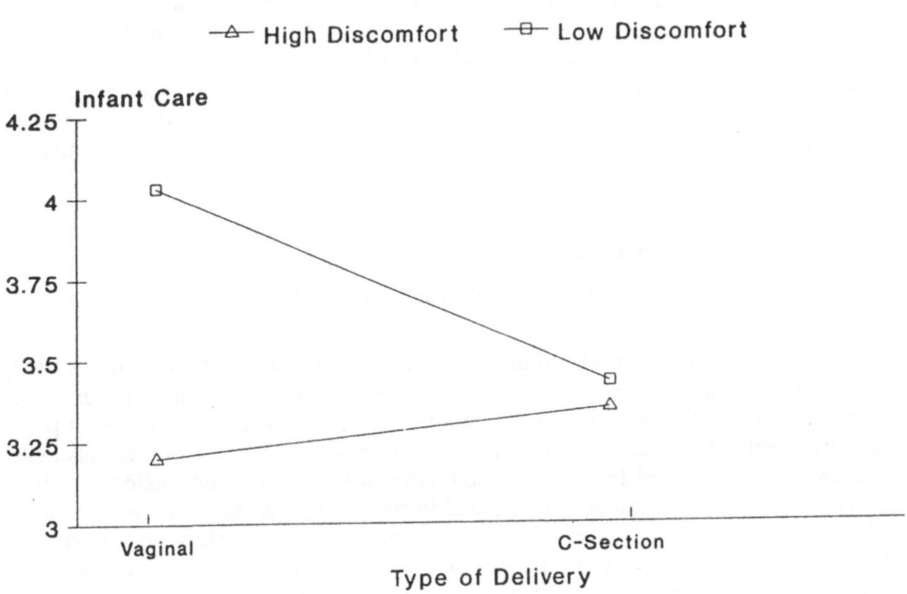

Figure 2 Effects of discomfort seeking support and type of delivery on receipt of infant care.

positive outcomes under stressful conditions. Moreover, successful coping should lead to resource enrichment. Holahan and Moos chose to study a combination of personal and social resources as they considered both domains to be critical to the coping process.

Studying 400 community residents over a 1-year period, Holahan and Moos found that greater social support resources and personal resources are related to better coping during stressful periods and better psychological outcomes. This is consistent with COR theory's depiction of resource investment in service of coping. The study also indicated that improved psychological functioning under low stress is predicted by resources themselves (i.e., not via coping), as would be consistent with the COR prediction that those high in resources are hardly taxed by low stress conditions. Further, Holahan and Moos noted that improved functioning results in increases in resources. This finding is clearly predicted in COR theory's depiction of positive spirals, whereby successful resource investment results in an increase in resources. COR would have also made a further prediction that poor psychological outcome would be related to depletion of resources (a negative spiral). Although this was not predicted by Holahan and Moos, careful reading of their paper indicates that this, in fact, was also a significant finding of the study.

The issue could be raised here, "Why call on a complex theory such as COR, when others predict similar outcomes without COR?" The study by Holahan and Moos answers this point. In their study, one of their predictions is theory-based, two of their predictions are atheoretical and based on prior empirical work, and one of their major findings was not predicted. In contrast, COR theory would predict each of their findings under one comprehensive model. Since it is the basis of all science to search for common overarching theories to explain otherwise piecemeal phenomena, it would seem that COR theory serves this purpose. Also, as Holahan and Moos write, it is critically important that we find theories that not only explain pathological outcomes, but that we explore theories that also explain adaptively oriented health frameworks. COR theory outlines processes that do both.

APPLICATIONS OF COR TO SOCIAL SUPPORT INTERVENTION

COR theory carries implications for social support interventions and the likely outcomes of such attempts. Freedy (1990) built a stress management program for nurses based on COR theory. Nurses either received a mastery enhancement package or a combined mastery enhancement and social support development package. Groups were controlled for time of total exposure to intervention using a waiting list control design. All nurses participated in five 75-minute sessions. According to COR theory, impacting a constellation of resources (e.g., mastery and social support) would be more effective than if only mastery was targeted. As predicted, nurses in the mastery–support intervention demonstrated enhanced social support at posttest and 5-week follow-up. Participants in the full intervention also achieved greatest gains in resource enhancement and stress reduction. Nurses in the mastery-only intervention experienced few gains. It is unlikely that gains resulted from the social support aspects alone, because mastery-related effects were especially noticeable. Nevertheless, future research might test this alternative explanation more directly.

In another study, Hobfoll, Jackson, and Lavin (1990) have applied COR theory to an intervention program concerning health promotion and AIDS prevention of inner-city women. Different groups of women will receive different levels of "intervention dose." Some women will participate in four skill and competency enhancement groups, others will participate in these groups and receive related health newsletters, whereas other women will receive group training, newsletters, and home visitors who will reinforce what they learn.

Based on COR theory, it is seen as paramount that women's personal and social resources are enhanced if they are to be able to cope with this new, ominous stress in their lives—the threat of AIDS. The interventions focus on enhancing these resources by increasing self-esteem, mastery, and social support. The theoretical background of the program is presented in Figure 3. As seen in this figure, the

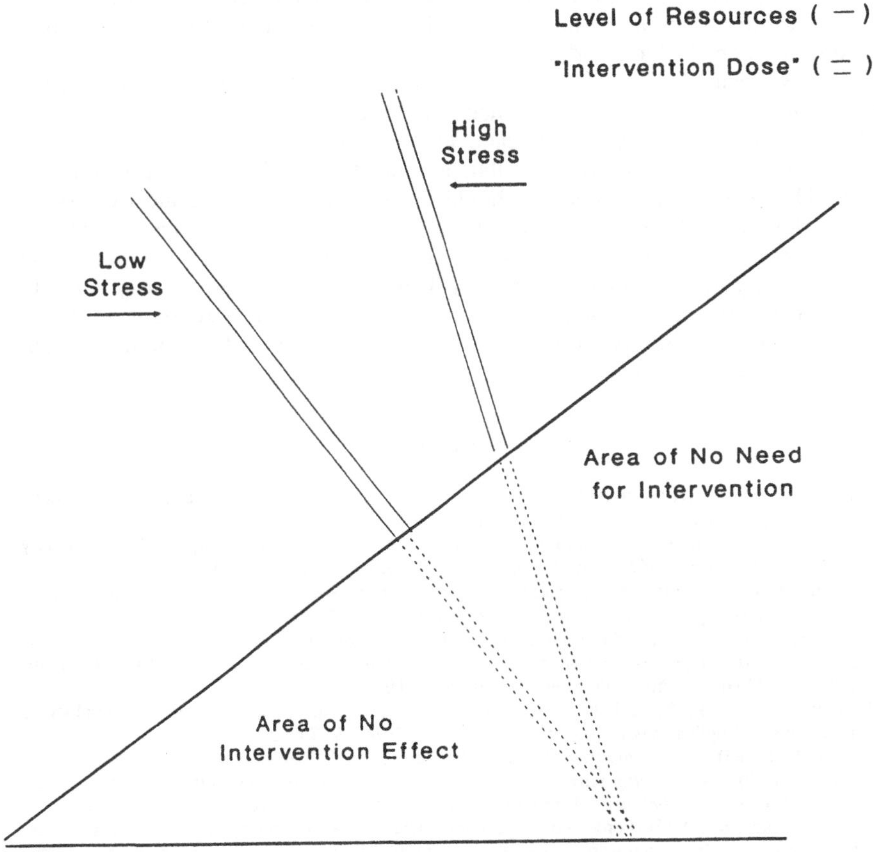

Figure 3 Interaction of intervention dose and resources under varying levels of stress. Note: To the right of the intersection, no intervention is required for the desired outcome, and, in fact, individuals may be able to withstand negative impact on their lives and still obtain the desired outcome; there is no range under high stress and very low resources where no level of intervention will produce the desired outcomes.

weaker the resources, the greater the intervention dose required. Those women with very high resources may even require no intervention and may be able to withstand considerable other stressors and still maintain positive health behavior. Women with very low resources, in contrast, may be incapable of sustaining positive health behavior because their resources are already expended in the coping process. Women who fall between these two extremes will require more or less intervention dose, depending on their resource endowment. These predictions are being studied at this time in a multiwave longitudinal study. Preliminary reports based on the model were encouraging, but indicated the need for more refined, long-term, intensive intervention (Gruber, 1990).

CONCLUSION

Reviewing the studies presented, there is accumulating evidence of the validity of COR theory. The COR-Evaluation is a beginning method for directly assessing arrays of resources. Initial examination of the instrument is promising. Still, it is in its developmental phase and, like the early life-event measures, much refinement will be necessary. It is hoped that, as in the case of life-event research, the COR-Evaluation also will serve as a heuristic tool.

Most germane to the current chapter, there is evidence supporting the central nature of social resources—in particular, among the broad array of potential resources. However, social resources should not be seen as so separate from other resource domains. Personal and social resources interact with one another. In addition, personal resources may lead to greater social resources, as well as an increased ability to use social resources. Likewise, social resources may serve to enhance such personal resources as optimism, self-esteem, and mastery. These interactions and complex pathways are the most fertile ground for future generations of social support research.

REFERENCES

Barrera, M., Jr. (1986). Distinctions between social support concepts, measures, and models. *American Journal of Community Psychology, 14,* 413–445.

Carver, C. S., Scheier, M. F., & Weintraub, J. K. (1989). Assessing coping strategies: A theoretically based approach. *Journal of Personality and Social Psychology, 56,* 267–283.

Dunkel-Schetter, C., Folkman, S., & Lazarus, R. S. (1987). Social support received in stressful situations. *Journal of Personality and Social Psychology, 53,* 71–80.

Erikson, E. H. (1968). *Identity: Youth and crisis.* New York: Norton.

Freedy, J. R. (1990). *Stress inoculation for prevention of burnout: A conservation of resources approach.* Unpublished doctoral dissertation, Kent State University.

Freedy, J. R., Resnick, H. S., & Kilpatrick, D. G. (in press). A conceptual framework for evaluating disaster impact: Implications for clinical intervention. *Tramatic Stress.*

Gorsuch, R. L. (1983). *Factor analysis* (2nd ed.). Hillsdale, NJ: Erlbaum.

Gruber, V. A. (1990). *Overcoming barriers to AIDS prevention: Risk underestimation and the psychological costs of low-risk behavior.* Unpublished doctoral dissertation, Kent State University.

Heller, K., & Lakey, B. (1985). Perceived support and social interaction among friends and confidants. In I. G. Sarason & B. R. Sarason (Eds.), *Social support: Theory, research, and applications* (pp. 287–300). The Hague, the Netherlands: Martinus Nijhoff.

Hobfoll, S. E. (1986). *Stress, social support, and women.* Washington, DC: Hemisphere.

Hobfoll, S. E. (1988). *The ecology of stress.* Washington, DC: Hemisphere.

Hobfoll, S. E. (1989). Conservation of resources: A new attempt at conceptualizing stress. *American Psychologist, 44,* 513–524.

Hobfoll, S. E., Jackson, A., & Lavin, J. (1990). *AIDS prevention among young inner-city women.* NIH/NICHD Grant # 1RO1MH 45669.

Hobfoll, S. E., & Leiberman, J. R. (1989). Effects of mastery and intimacy on anxiety following pregnancy: For whom is support supportive and from whom? *Anxiety Research, 1,* 327–341.

Hobfoll, S. E., & Lerman, M. (1989). Predicting receipt of social support: A longitudinal study of parents' reactions to their child's illness. *Health Psychology, 8,* 61–77.

Hobfoll, S. E., London, P., & Orr, E. (1988). Mastery, intimacy, and stress resistance during war. *Journal of Community Psychology, 16,* 317–331.

Hobfoll, S. E., Shoham, S. B., & Ritter (in press). Women's satisfaction with social support and receipt of aid following delivery. *Journal of Personality and Social Psychology.*

Hobfoll, S. E., & Zalcberg-Linetzy, A. (1990). How social support predicts relational intimacy: A dyadic study. Manuscript submitted for publication.

Holahan, C. J., & Moos, R. H. (1990). Life stressors, resistance factors, and improved psychological functioning: An extension of the stress resistance paradigm. *Journal of Personality and Social Psychology, 58,* 909–917.

Lane, C. D. (1990). *Anger, social support, and illness symptoms: Their interrelationships among persons with chronic obstructive pulmonary disease.* Unpublished doctoral dissertation, Kent State University.

Lazarus, A. A. (1968). Learning theory and the treatment of depression. *Behavior Research & Therapy, 6,* 83–89.

Maslow, A. H. (1968). *Toward a psychology of being.* New York: Van Nostrand Reinhold.

Pearlin, L. I., Leiberman, M. A., Menaghan, E. G., & Mullan, J. T. (1981). The stress process. *Journal of Health and Social Behavior, 22,* 337–356.

Sarason, I. G., & Sarason, B. R. (Eds.). (1985). *Social support: Theory, research and applications.* The Hague, the Netherlands: Martinus Nijhoff.

Sarason, B. R., Sarason, I. G., & Pierce, G. R. (Eds.). (1990). *Social support: An interactional view.* New York: Wiley.

Thoits, P. A. (1983). Dimensions of life events that influence psychological distress: An evaluation and synthesis of the literature. In H. B. Kaplan (Ed.), *Psychosocial stress: Trends in theory and research* (pp. 33–103). New York: Academic Press.

Vaux, A. (1988). *Social support: Theory, research, and intervention.* New York: Praeger.

Wilcox, B. L. (1986). Stress, coping, and the social milieu of divorced women. In S. E. Hobfoll (Ed.), *Stress, social support, and women* (pp. 115–133). Washington, DC: Hemisphere.

10

Three Contexts of Social Support

Irwin G. Sarason, Barbara R. Sarason, and Gregory R. Pierce
University of Washington, USA

This chapter focuses on a research program rooted in previous work on social support and organized around a recently developed theoretical perspective. The chapter has three aspects. First, we briefly review diverse approaches to the role of social support in physical and psychological health, focusing on several methodological and conceptual issues. (One important conclusion of this review is the need for an increased diversity of methodological approaches—especially experimental and observational studies—and clearly articulated theoretical frameworks.) Second, we describe the theoretical model that has guided much of our research—as it has considerable empirical and heuristic potential. The model focuses on interactions among a triad of variables in determining the impact of supportive efforts on important personal outcomes. Third, we illustrate the model with pertinent examples from our research.

RESEARCH ON SOCIAL SUPPORT

Over the years, epidemiological research has provided data from large population samples indicating that supportive relationships are associated with a lower probability of mortality (Berkman & Syme, 1979; Reed, McGee, Yano, & Feinlieb, 1983). Interest in the area of clinical medicine in social support grew out of intriguing findings indicating that the presence of social ties is negatively correlated with illness and positively correlated with speed of recovery (Kaplan & Toshima, 1990). In addition, there was also evidence that provision of emotional support by health-care personnel or others is beneficial to health (Auerbach & Kilmann, 1977; Gore, 1978; Nuckolls, Cassell, & Kaplan, 1972; Whitcher & Fisher, 1979). Despite this evidence, little is understood about the manner in which social support promotes health.

Two important papers by Cassell (1976) and Cobb (1976) helped launch the research domain of social support. From an epidemiological perspective, Cassell emphasizes the role of the social environment and the presence of other members of the same species as factors in susceptibility to disease. Both animal and human research have stimulated interest in the buffering effects of social support on stress, and the need to strengthen individuals' social support as a way to prevent disease. Cobb describes social support as a moderator of life stress. He defines it as information leading to one or more of three outcomes: (a) a feeling of being cared for; (b) the belief that one is loved, esteemed, and valued; and (c) the sense of belonging to a reciprocal network. He believes that social support provides protection from pathological states, accelerates recovery from illness, and enhances compliance with medically recommended regimens.

Another important influence in stimulating research on social support was work in the area of child development. Bowlby's (1969, 1980) writings on attachment were especially influential in providing a basis for thinking of social support as a personality variable rooted particularly in early close relationships. This conceptualization directed attention to the question of the stability of support over time, support as a perceptual product, and the nature of interpersonal relationships that provide support.

Two related issues pose current challenges to social support researchers. One is the need to broaden the range of methodological approaches to the topic and the other is the need for better articulated theories to guide empirical efforts. The restricted range of methodological approaches in research on social support has hampered the generalizability of available findings. For example, cross-sectional designs have been used in most studies of social support, although longitudinal or follow-up studies are often needed to evaluate certain hypotheses related to its antecedents and development. Many studies reported in the literature are either correlational or compare groups that may not be truly comparable in important respects. For instance, recently divorced couples have been compared with married couples with a frequent finding that the groups differ in availability of social support, social networks, and friendship patterns (Hughes, 1988). However, interpretation of these findings is clouded by the possibility that the differences obtained might be correlates of preexisting personality or social factors that are relevant to these variables as well as being basic to whether couples divorce and their subsequent adjustment to the divorce. In addition to methodological problems, most social support research has not flowed from a systematic theoretical position. This has posed problems in interpreting results (Sarason, Sarason, & Pierce, 1990).

Within any given definition of social support (e.g., presence of certain types of supportive others, satisfaction with one's social ties), there are differences, unrelated to theoretical formulations, concerning its operationalization. However, a theory-based approach to the assessment of social support focused on the individual's perceptions of available support is now gaining momentum. This momentum has grown out of the frequent finding that perceptions of available support are more likely to be related to criterion indices of interest than are measures of network characteristics or particular classes of supporter behavior (Sarason, Pierce, & Sarason, 1990). As a consequence, there has been increased emphasis on the distinction between perceived support and received support. Perceived support refers to how supported the person feels about potentially available support as contrasted with the enumeration of various specific types of support received from others.

Even when social interactions and potentially supportive behaviors occur, social support is not simply an objective property of these social behaviors. It is not possible to determine whether a specific social interaction constitutes social support without reference to the cognitive appraisals of that interaction. These appraisals occur in conjunction with one or more specific aspects of an observable interaction between two relationship participants in a particular situation. This implies that social support should be assessed by both objective observation of specific social interactions and determination of the perceptions of both participants. We are attempting to do just this in a series of studies in which dyads (e.g., a parent and child, friends) are videotaped while they are interacting, and their social perceptions of behaviors within the interaction are compared with each other and with those of disinterested observers (Sarason, Pierce, & Sarason, 1990; Sarason, Pierce, Sarason, & Rosenkranz, 1990).

This chapter presents a theoretical approach, together with empirical examples, that focuses on interactions among people's perceptions of support, their interpersonal relationships, and outcome variables. The approach views the perception of available support as a personality characteristic that plays an important role in how people view and draw inferences concerning the nature of interpersonal relationships. Perception of support availability can range from the general (how forthcoming people are likely to be in their contacts with other people) to the particular (how willing one's mother, spouse, or friend is to provide support). These perceptions are features of individuals' personal theories about themselves in relation to the social environment.

A TRIADIC HYPOTHESIS

We believe that a theory of social support requires attention to three interrelated classes of variables: personality characteristics, interpersonal relationships, and the situations that stimulate supportive efforts. These variables can be thought of as contexts of social support because the effects of supportive efforts depend on the interaction of the three contexts (person, interpersonal, and situational) with the supportive behavior. The impact of any particular supportive effort depends on the motivations and expectations of both provider and recipient, the nature of the relationship in which the supportive exchange occurs, and the problematic situation to which the supportive efforts are directed. From this perspective, perceived support is a product of interactions among these variables. There is an important link between potentially supportive transactions and the personal meanings people attach to them. Social support is not likely to be a straightforward, objective property of social interactions. Whether or not a specific social interaction constitutes social support must be approached within the context of the cognitive appraisals of the participants in that interaction.

Referring to a specific category of social interactions as social support does not imply that in every case these interactions will contribute positively in helping people cope with stressful situations. Under certain circumstances, behaviors intended as social support may even have a deleterious impact (Pagel, Erdly, & Becker, 1987; Hobfoll & London, 1986). An important research task is to determine the conditions under which efforts to be helpful either facilitate or impede the recipient's efforts to successfully cope with a challenging event. Important as that task is, the effort to more clearly understand the impact of each of the triad of factors mentioned above—personality characteristics, interpersonal relationships, and the nature of situations that stimulate supportive efforts—as they relate to adjustment and the coping process.

Personality Context

Although behavior is obviously influenced by situational factors, it is also influenced by stable patterns of perceiving oneself, important others, and the nature of interpersonal relationships. These patterns interact with situational factors to produce behavioral outcomes.

In our research, using the Social Support Questionnaire (SSQ), which assesses a person's perception of available support and satisfaction with the perceived support, we found that attributions and expectations concerning the general availability of social support reflect a stable personality characteristic, the sense of support, which influences behavior (Sarason, Levine, Basham, & Sarason, 1983; Sarason, Pierce, & Sarason, 1990). In one recent study, we found that people's expectations concerning the supportiveness of others' social networks are strongly related to their attributions about the supportiveness of their own networks (Sarason, Pierce, Shearin, Sarason, Waltz, & Poppe, 1991). The study also showed that the sense of support is related to the individual's self-concept. People who perceive others to be available to provide support also report greater self-esteem and believe others hold a similarly positive view of them. In addition, this study demonstrated an objective basis for these positive expectations regarding the views of others. Both views of self and anticipated views of others were consistent with the actual views of these others when they were asked to provide ratings of the subject.

The individual's sense of support may be related to an additional feature of personality, the sense of acceptance, which grows out of inferences about the self that are related to, but not necessarily implied in, the sense of support (Sarason et al., 1990; Sarason et al., 1991). The sense of acceptance is the belief that others love and care for us, and accept us for who we are, including our best and worst points. People who develop a positive sense of acceptance are able to confront stressful events without concern that failure will bring with it a loss of being loved, valued, and accepted by important others. The sense of acceptance may play a role in fostering the ability to take advantage of opportunities. Both the sense of support and the sense of acceptance are aspects of personality, products of the individual's history of social interactions in a variety of situations, and parts of personality.

Interpersonal Context

Each individual's interpersonal relationships have distinctive qualitative and quantitative features. Not only do the sizes of social networks differ, but the quality of relationships within them also vary widely. Many individuals identified as part of a person's network may be the source of both positive and negative interactions (Brenner, Norvell, & Limacher, 1989). For example, two sets of parents might provide financial assistance to their children who are in college. One set might constantly give their children reminders of all the sacrifices associated with the assistance, whereas the other might not seek a "thank you."

Close relationships are especially important interpersonal contexts because they are often characterized by strong emotions, ranging from love to jealousy to rage, and also by various levels of emotional experience. Both the range of emotions and their intensity need to be considered. Neither the type of emotion nor its intensity is an infallible predictor of the enduring quality or meaningfulness of the relationship to the participants. Although those who exhibit high levels of positive affect can probably be reliably classified as experiencing a close relationship, the other three quadrants composed of the remaining combinations of relationship intensity and positivity are less easy to categorize as close or not close.

People who experience a great deal of intense negative affect in a relationship pose particular problems when describing the degree of closeness. Many relationships that would be classified as close using nonaffective criteria (e.g., family membership) may sometimes be characterized by intense negative emotion. For instance, not only has the family been called the most physically violent group or institution a typical person is likely to encounter (Straus & Hotaling, 1980), but most of the anger that adults experience in their daily lives is also in a relationship with a blood relative or, to a slightly lesser degree, with a romantic partner (Fitz & Gerstenzang, 1978). In addition, the level of anger experienced in this sort of relationship tends to be higher than the level of anger resulting from interactions in other, less close relationships (Argyle & Furnham, 1983).

The literature on close relationships makes it clear that some are characterized by high levels of negative emotion and that for close relationships, as a whole, negative emotion is common. It seems evident that the quality of close relationships (their intensity, the degree to which they are marked by ambivalence, and the participants' positive and negative views of one another) provides an important context for social interactions in which efforts are made to provide support.

Situational Context

The situational context encompasses the event to which relationship participants respond. The aspect of the context that has received the most attention from researchers concerns whether or not a situation is stressful (challenging and anxiety provoking). According to the buffering hypothesis, social support is beneficial only during stressful situations. In the absence of stress, it is presumed to have no significant impact on health or well-being. From this point of view, social support is a moderator of stress associated with life events (Cohen & Wills, 1985). Although there is evidence that social support can function as a stress moderator, there is also evidence that it influences behavior in nonstressful situations. This suggests that the impact of the situational context is more complex than is implied in the buffering hypothesis. Social support may be an important aspect of the situational context for negative life events, but it may also play a role in the development of coping repertories and orientations of life. It has become increasingly clear that dichotomizing events as stressful or not stressful may be insufficient to account for the role of social support in health and well-being.

Cutrona and Russell (1990) have gone beyond the typical stressful-nonstressful distinction by emphasizing that, although situations may be equally stressful, they do not necessarily pose similar challenges or demands and the role of social support may vary as a function of the situational context (Hobfoll & Stephens, 1990). They hypothesize that social support is optimally beneficial when it meets the needs created by the particular stressful situation. For example, they argue that stress resulting from an event that poses a threat to self-esteem (e.g., loss of a job) is best buffered by support that bolsters the person's self-esteem. A jobless situation might be simple or complex. For example, the impact of losing a job involves a multitude of factors (e.g., how much money is in the bank account of the person who loses a job; whether the job loss resulted from poor performance, product phase-out, or company move; and the current state of the job market). A focal event (e.g., job loss) is usually the highlight of the situational context.

Another dimension of the situational context concerns the extent to which situations engender needs for support, not only for a focal person, but also for other members of that person's network. Events that primarily impact on a focal network member might only have an indirect impact on other network members. This happens when the only implications of a situation for other network members is that they may need to provide support to the focal person. An example is the breakup of a romance of a son or daughter. A direct impact results when an event poses demands on network members other than the need to provide support and requires that they also cope directly with the situation. An example is the support given by children to a divorcing parent when they, too, are experiencing the effects of their parents' marital breakup.

People experience the effects of a variety of life events, such as job loss and death of a loved one, within the context of their own personal characteristics and interpersonal networks. The impact of an event also depends on the situational context in which it is embedded.

RESEARCH BASED ON THE TRIADIC HYPOTHESIS

We mentioned that many studies have focused on measures of social support primarily as correlates or predictors of clinical and epidemiological indicators. Valuable as this correlational evidence has been, we need to go beyond it to a better understanding of social ties and interpersonal relationships so as to clarify the basis for the correlations and to enhance prediction. We would argue that efforts by one person to help another should not be looked on as isolated behaviors that can be easily categorized. Rather, they are features of a complex supportive process to which personal, relational, and situational factors also make contributions. We need a better understanding of this process and a wider range of constructs than are presently available. More empirical investigations are needed so as to encompass the complexity of interpersonal and intrapersonal factors that may contribute to individuals' perceptions regarding their relationships with people in general as well as with specific significant people in their lives. Studying social support as a process requires tapping into the diversity of cognitions, feelings, and behaviors associated with specific personal relationships.

We have conducted a series of research investigations that relate to social support conceived in triadic terms. The number and scope of these investigations are not sufficient for drawing final conclusions—but they do suggest aspects of the support process that merit further inquiry.

Perceived Social Support and Cognitive Models of Self and Others

Perceptions of social support are distinct from the observable features of potentially supportive transactions. The events that lead person A to feel supported might have no effect—or even a negative effect—on person B. Recognizing the important role of perceptions of support, we attempted to identify aspects of the person's perceptions of self and others that might be particularly associated with support perceptions. We carried out two studies of the relationship between level of perceived social support and perceptions of self and others.

The first study examined the association between perceived social support and cognitive or working models of generalized peers. The importance of this topic is made clear by research indicating that social comparisons, particularly between self and similar others, play an important role in the appraisal of and response to stressful events (Goethals, 1986; Taylor, 1985). Individuals who favorably compare themselves with others may accrue considerable benefits, including increased self-confidence, which may reduce stress produced by a challenging situation. This study explored the relations between college students' perceived social support and their perceptions or personal norms concerning typical, same sex college students. The second study investigated perceived social support and self-related cognitive models, including individuals' perceptions of themselves, their reflected appraisals of others (individuals' imagined views of how important others see them), and the actual views of these others. The second study was intended to provide relevant data and to establish links between individuals' perceptions of social support and other self-perceptions, and the views of important network members.

The first study was conducted with small groups of subjects who participated in two separate sessions, 1 week apart. In one session, in addition to the Social Support Questionnaire (SSQ), the subjects completed instruments intended to tap loneliness, shyness, social skills, and recollections of childhood experiences involving parents. In the other session, subjects were given specially devised typical student questionnaires. They were requested to fill out the SSQ, loneliness, and shyness measures as they thought a typical student of their age and sex would. The order of session was counterbalanced across subjects.

Most of the subjects tended to engage in downward social comparisons. That is, they tended to see themselves as more favorably adjusted than others with whom they might compare themselves. However, low SSQ scorers were not only the most negative in their evaluation of others, but their perceptions of the average person were most discrepant from reality defined as the average scores actually obtained on the self-related measures. Low SSQ scorers may have resorted to extreme downward social comparisons to bolster their self-esteem and to reassure themselves that they are worthy of affection and personal regard from individuals in their own social network. The result of the downward social comparisons made by low SSQ scorers was to estimate others to be similar to themselves, with a result that low perceived support individuals were, in effect, denying their relatively low standing in relation to others.

The effect of social comparisons made by high SSQ scorers was quite different. Their relative standing to others was accurate; these individuals accurately identified themselves as special and deserving of the attention and affection of others. However, their perceptions of the average person's characteristics indicated considerably more favorable adjustment than the actual group mean showed. For instance, high SSQ scorers not only believed others to have more available social support and to be more satisfied with support available to them than did low SSQ scorers, but they also viewed others as more socially embedded and satisfied with their ability to engage in social interaction than is actually the case. These perceptions of personal worth and the social characteristics of others may be an important ingredient in the ability of those high in perceived social support to negotiate social situations with greater effectiveness and less anxiety than others (Sarason, Sarason, Hacker, & Basham, 1985).

The second study moved from a focus on perceptions of hypothetical peers to an investigation of the relationship between availability of, and satisfaction with, perceived social support and (a) how people view themselves, (b) how they believe important others view them, and (c) how these others actually do view them. The study showed that individuals who perceive support to be available to them if needed and are satisfied with support also perceive themselves to have a variety of positive attributes and relatively few negative characteristics. Clear differences emerged in the self-perceptions of individuals who also differed in perceived social support. Those who were confident that others would be responsive to their needs when confronted with adversity also believed themselves to be competent and interpersonally successful. Lack of perceived social support was accompanied by feelings of personal inadequacy, anxiety, and social rejection. These findings are consistent with other research linking perceived social support to self-perception (Rosser, 1986).

We found that perceived social support is related to one's view of one's interpersonal relationships. Those high in social support believe others share a similarly positive view of them. There was also a substantial association between individuals' cognitive models of self and how they believed others view them. In addition, individuals' working models regarding the perceived views of others were distinct and specific to particular relationships. Perhaps current operationalizations of perceived social support that focus on general measures of the construct of social support (i.e., summed across individuals) may be inadequate for certain purposes. More information is needed concerning the concordance between general (across relationships) measures of social support and support associated with a particular relationship.

The results of these two studies are consistent with the idea that cognitive models of self and important relationships serve as a lens through which people view others' feelings and behavior, and the nature of supportive acts. This lens serves both to focus attention and to filter information in such a way that perceptions of others reflect the unique properties of these lenses. It becomes important to understand the characteristics of these lenses and their effects on self and other perceptions. Perceived social support may reflect important organizing principles of individuals' cognitive models of self-attributes, personal characteristics, and the nature of relationships of others.

The results of the studies we have described show that perceived social support is not simply a composite view of one's relationships. Instead, it represents an interaction between general cognitive sets that are part of an individual's personality and his or her view of particular relationships experienced in the course of social development. Perceived social support might be thought of as a cognitive adaptation that individuals make given the constraints and opportunities, both real and imagined, that are placed on them by a history of experiences resulting in cognitive models of self and others. These models incorporate self-identity and expectations about the nature of relationships, both in terms of what individuals have to offer others and what others have to offer them. Seen in this way, perceived social support is not an isolated perception relevant only when individuals are confronted by a stressful situation demanding coping behavior. It is part of a constellation of cognitions that drives social behavior and accounts for differences in interpretations regarding the behavior and motivation of others and what others are "really like."

General and Relationship-Based Perceptions of Social Support

Although there is some evidence suggesting that general perceptions of available support reflect stable cognitive models concerning the self, important others, and the nature of supportive relationships, there is a much smaller body of literature that emphasizes perceptions of available support stemming from specific relationships (B. Sarason et al., 1990; I. Sarason et al., 1990). We have approached the topic of general and relationship-based measures of perceived available support by comparing the SSQ with measures of specific relationships (e.g., mother, father, close friend). In a recent study (Pierce, Sarason, & Sarason, 1990), we tested the hypothesis that both general perceptions of available support and perceptions of available support from specific relationships make independent (rather than shared) contributions to personal adjustment.

For this study a special instrument, the Quality of Relationships Inventory (QRI), was developed to assess specific current relationships. The QRI was developed by writing items to assess the perceived availability of social support from specific relationships (e.g., "To what extent can you turn to this person for advice about problems?") (Pierce, 1990). Items were also developed to assess two other dimensions of specific relationships: the extent to which the relationship is perceived as positive, important, and secure (e.g., "How significant is this relationship in your life?"), and the extent to which the relationship is a source of conflict and ambivalence (e.g., "How often does this person make you feel angry?"). Each subject was asked to complete a 39-item QRI for each of the following persons: mother, father, and up to four other relationships that the subject regarded as important. In addition, subjects completed the SSQ, and measures of loneliness, social skills, and perceived parental relationships.

We found that correlations between measures of support in these specific relationships (QRI) and the general perceived available support measures (SSQ) were only moderate. This suggests that the two types of measures reflect differentiated constructs. Most important for our hypothesis, general perceptions of available support and perceptions of available support from several specific categories of relationship, each made a significant, unique contribution to the prediction of loneliness. All of the results were consistent with the conclusion that beliefs concerning the availability of social support as a general perception and as an attribute of specific social ties play unique roles in personal adjustment.

It may be possible that our understanding of the contribution to personal adjustment made by social support can be increased by distinguishing between these aspects of perceived available support. Just as no two people are alike, neither can any two relationships be expected to be supportive in precisely the same way. Each individual has not only a personal theory of what can be expected from other people generally, but also theories about certain specific people in their lives. Our results underline the importance of the need to operationalize perceptions of available support both as a general attribute and as a property of specific relationships. With measures of these personal theories, future research can now be directed toward determining the pathways through which general perceptions of available support and relationship-based attributions concerning support exert their influences.

Predicting Perceptions of Social Support

Experimental manipulations have rarely been incorporated into research on social support. This is surprising because the idea that experimentation is the hallmark of scientific inquiry is by now a cliché. Implicit in the triadic hypothesis is the need to identify the elements of situations that interact with the intrapersonal and interpersonal contexts of situations. Although experimentation on stable personal attributes and relationships with one's mother and father may not be amenable to experimental influence, the situations in which personal attributes and relationships play roles can and should be manipulated in experimental studies.

In an experimental study, people's perceptions of supportive transactions, the interpersonal context in which supportive transactions occur, and individuals' cognitive models of their relationships with other people were all assessed (Pierce, 1990). The subjects, undergraduate college students and their mothers, were studied in three laboratory situations. In one, the student was asked to prepare and give a speech under experimental conditions intended to be either high or low in stress. At two different times before they gave the speech, the students received supportive, reassuring notes in their mothers' handwriting concerning the speech task on which they were working. These notes, purportedly from the mother, were actually copied by her from a prepared text and were the same for all students. In another situation, the students and their mothers discussed a current source of conflict in their relationship. In the third situation, the students and their mothers role-played how they would each like the other to respond to the conflict situation they had discussed together earlier.

We found that students' perceptions of their mothers' notes were positively related to students' general perceptions of social support and their perceptions of support and conflict in the mother-child relationship. The study demonstrated that, although general perceptions of support were related to students' perceptions of their mothers' notes, the relationship was much stronger for students' appraisals of their mothers' notes and students' expectations for support that were specific to the relationships with their mothers.

The major finding of the study was that both global and relationship-based assessment aspects of social support are important and make valuable contributions to prediction. We now have evidence that people's cognitive models of specific individuals and their network are quite distinct. The expectations and assumptions that form the basis of each of these cognitive models play an important role in both perceptions of social support and in adjustment.

CONCLUSION

The sense of social support is a joint product of personality and experience that, in turn, influences how people cope with various types of situations. Our work reflects developments in the area that are leading in the direction of theories that reflect the complex phenomena involved in the subtle and obvious dimensions of social interaction. To the extent that social support is linked to close interpersonal relationships, we need to study behavior and cognitions within these relationships—and to do it experimentally when it is appropriate and possible to do so. Such an approach may lead to both an increased ability to predict those at risk and also to shed some light on how social support promotes health.

This chapter has described a theoretical orientation focusing on interactions among personality, relationships, and situational factors in determining the complex processes linking social behavior to important personal outcomes such as health and psychological well-being. We believe that research on social support will benefit greatly from the development of interactional theories that do justice to the wide range of cognitive, affective, and behavioral elements involved in the giving and getting of social support. We illustrated our model by reviewing recent research guided by this theoretical orientation. Although further research is needed to evaluate and refine this model, we believe it provides one example of the value of continued interplay between theory development and empirical hypothesis testing.

REFERENCES

Argyle, M., & Furnham, A. (1983). Sources of satisfaction and conflict in long-term relationships. *Journal of Marriage and the Family, 45,* 481–493.

Auerbach, S. M., & Kilmann, P. R. (1977). Crisis intervention: A review of outcome research. *Psychological Bulletin, 84,* 1189–1217.

Berkman, L. F., & Syme, S. L. (1979). Social networks, host resistance, and mortality: A nine-year follow-up study of Alameda County residents. *American Journal of Epidemiology, 109,* 186–204.

Bowlby, J. (1969). *Attachment and loss: Vol. 1. Attachment.* New York: Basic Books.

Bowlby, J. (1980). *Attachment and loss: Vol. 3. Loss: Sadness and depression.* New York: Basic Books.

Brenner, G. F., Norvell, N. K., & Limacher, M. (1989). Supportive and problematic social interactions: A social network analysis. *American Journal of Community Psychology, 17,* 831–836.

Cassel, J. (1976). The contribution of the social environment to host resistance. *American Journal of Epidemiology, 104,* 107–123.

Cobb, S. (1976). Social support as a moderator of life stress. *Psychosomatic Medicine, 38,* 300–314.

Cohen, S., & Wills, T. A. (1985). Stress, social support, and the buffering hypothesis. *Psychological Bulletin, 98,* 310–357.

Cutrona, C. E., & Russell, D. W. (1990). Type of social support and specific stress: Toward a theory of optimal matching. In B. R. Sarason, I. G. Sarason, & G. R. Pierce (Eds.), *Social support: An interactional view.* New York: Wiley.

Fitz, D., & Gerstenzang, S. (1978). Anger in everyday life: When, where and with whom? St. Louis: University of Missouri (ERIC Document Reproduction Service No. ED 160966).

Goethals, G. R. (1986). Social comparison theory: Psychology from the lost and found. *Personality and Social Psychology Bulletin, 12,* 261–278.

Gore, S. (1978). Effects of social support in moderating health consequences of unemployment. *Journal of Health and Social Behavior, 19,* 157–165.

Hobfoll, S. E., & London, P. (1986). The relationship of self-concept and social support to emotional distress among women during war. *Journal of Social and Clinical Psychology, 12,* 87–100.

Hobfoll, S. E., & Stephens, M. A. P. (1990). Social support during extreme stress: Consequences and intervention. In B. R. Sarason, I. G. Sarason, & G. R. Pierce (Eds.), *Social support: An interactional view.* New York: Wiley.

Hughes, R., Jr. (1988). Divorce and social support: A review. *Journal of Divorce, 11,* 112–145.

Kaplan, R. M., & Toshima, M. T. (1990). The functional effects of social relationships on chronic illnesses and disability. In B. R. Sarason, I. G. Sarason, & G. R. Pierce (Eds.), *Social support: An interactional view.* New York: Wiley.

Nuckolls, K. B., Cassel, J., & Kaplan, B. H. (1972). Psychosocial assets, life crisis and the prognosis of pregnancy. *American Journal of Epidemiology, 95,* 431–441.

Pagel, M. D., Erdly, W. W., & Becker, J. (1987). Social networks: We get by with (and in spite of) a little help from our friends. *Journal of Personality and Social Psychology, 53,* 793–804.

Pierce, G. R. (1990). *Predicting perceptions of social support: An experimental study of behavioral, personality, relationship, and situation variables.* Unpublished thesis, University of Washington, Seattle, WA.

Pierce, G. R., Sarason, I. G., & Sarason, B. R. (in press). General and relationship-based perceptions of social support: Are two constructs better than one? *Journal of Personality and Social Psychology.*

Reed, D., McGee, D., Yano, K., & Feinleib, M. (1983). Social networks and CHD among Japanese men in Hawaii. *American Journal of Epidemiology, 117,* 384–396.

Rosser, C. (1986). *Self-concept, personal disclosure, and social support.* Unpublished data, University of Washington, Seattle, WA.

Sarason, B. R., Pierce, G. R., & Sarason, I. G. (1990). Social support: The sense of acceptance and the role of relationships. In B. R. Sarason, I. G. Sarason, & G. R. Pierce (Eds.), *Social support: An interactional view* (pp. 97–128). New York: Wiley.

Sarason, B. R., Pierce, G. R., Sarason, I. G., & Rosenkranz, S. L. (1990). *Parent-child interactions: Personality and personal relationships.* Manuscript in preparation.

Sarason, B. R., Pierce, G. R., Shearin, E. N., Sarason, I. G., Waltz, J. A., & Poppe, L. (1991). Perceived social support and working models of self and actual others. *Journal of Personality and Social Psychology, 60,* 273–287.

Sarason, B. R., Sarason, I. G., Hacker, T. A., & Basham, R. B. (1985). Concomitants of social support: Social skills, physical attractiveness, and gender. *Journal of Personality and Social Psychology, 49,* 469–480.

Sarason, I. G., Levine, H. M., Basham, R. B., & Sarason, B. R. (1983). Assessing social support: The Social Support Questionnaire. *Journal of Personality and Social Psychology, 44,* 127–139.

Sarason, I. G., Pierce, G. R., & Sarason, B. R. (1990). Social support and interactional processes: A triadic hypothesis. *Journal of Social and Personal Relationships, 2,* 495–506.

Sarason, I. G., Sarason, B. R., & Pierce, G. R. (1990). Social support: The search for theory. *Journal of Social and Clinical Psychology, 9,* 133–147.

Straus, M. A., & Hotaling, G. T. (Eds.). (1980). *The social causes of husband-wife violence.* Minneapolis: University of Minnesota Press.

Taylor, S. E. (1985). Adjustments to threatening events: A theory of cognitive adaptation. *American Psychologist, 38,* 1161–1173.

Whitcher, S. J., & Fisher, J. D. (1979). Multidimensional reaction to therapeutic touch in a hospital setting. *Journal of Personality and Social Psychology, 36,* 87–96.

IV

NONSUPPORT

11

Detrimental Aspects of Social Relationships: Taking Stock of an Emerging Literature

Karen S. Rook
University of California–Irvine, USA

In a seminal paper published over a decade ago, Heller (1979) observed that social scientists' conceptions of how social relationships affect health and well-being have been characterized by major swings, shifting from a preoccupation with the pathological effects of social bonds in one historical era to a preoccupation with the restorative effects of social bonds in another era. Heller (1979) lamented the lack of more balanced approaches to the study of social relationships and adaptation, and noted, as others have (e.g., Coyne, 1990; Eckenrode & Gore, 1981; House, Landis, & Umberson, 1988; Rook & Pietromonaco, 1987), that contemporary work has been dominated by nearly unwavering enthusiasm for the construct of social support. That is, most contemporary work on the adaptive significance of social ties has been guided by the assumption that the availability of support through one's exchanges with others is what matters most for emotional and physical health. More recently, researchers have challenged this assumption and have urged greater attention to the problematic as well as the supportive aspects of social bonds. The purpose of this chapter is to take stock of an emerging literature on the troublesome interactions that occur with informal social networks.

Researchers have pursued three general strategies in studying the effects of negative social exchanges. This chapter illustrates each strategy and summarizes the major findings that have emerged thus far from research published in the United States. It also discusses several conceptual and methodological parallels that characterize work on supportive and problematic social ties. Recognition of these parallels helps to highlight gaps in our existing knowledge base regarding negative social exchanges and suggests an agenda for further work. Beyond these parallels, unique questions arise in seeking to investigate the joint (rather than the separate) effects of social support and social strain, and several of these questions also receive attention in the chapter. The chapter concludes with an argument for a balanced perspective on the dual aspects of social relationships—one that exaggerates neither their beneficial nor their detrimental aspects.

It is important at the outset to clarify what I mean by negative, or problematic, exchanges. In this chapter, I will emphasize actions by a member of a person's social network that cause the person to experience psychological distress (e.g., resentment, shame, sadness) and at least some reservations about the relationship itself (cf. Rook, 1989). This emphasis excludes many of the conventional costs of social relationships that have been discussed by social exchange theorists (Homans, 1974; Thibaut & Kelley, 1959), such as the time, money, and material goods that may be required to maintain a relationship or the displacement of opportunities to engage in other kinds of activities. This emphasis also excludes actions by network members that may be irritating but that do not cause lingering distress because they can be attributed to good intentions. Instead, I will concentrate on actions that people perceive as misdeeds or transgressions and that cause distress. This includes both acts of omission and acts of commission. This admittedly broad definition subsumes some instances of clumsy or "miscarried" support (Coyne, Ellard, & Smith, 1990; Coyne, Wortman, & Lehman, 1988; Wortman & Lehman, 1985), but also encompasses other kinds of troublesome social exchanges.

My focus on actions by social network members that people regard as misdeeds precludes consideration of actions that detract from emotional or physical health but that go unnoticed or that, if noticed, do not evoke resentment or suspicion. For example, ample evidence indicates that people can unintentionally undermine the health practices of family members and friends in a variety of ways (Kaplan & Toshima, 1990; Suls, 1982), such as inadvertently interfering with prescribed medical regimens, modeling unhealthy behaviors, or being overprotective following a serious illness or injury.

Despite their unfortunate consequences, such actions are not always recognized or viewed as illegitimate by the individuals involved. Consider another example: intimate relationships increase vulnerability to stressful life events by exposing individuals to misfortunes that befall their loved ones. Research on "stress transmission" has demonstrated that such events can cause considerable emotional distress, even though they are experienced indirectly rather than directly (e.g., Riley & Eckenrode, 1986; Rook, Dooley, & Catalano, 1991). Similarly, providing crisis support to family members and close friends can take a substantial toll on the caregiver's psychological health, particularly if the caregiver is a woman (Kessler, McLeod, & Wethington, 1985). This emotional strain may occur even when the support is provided on an entirely voluntary basis and when all parties involved view the support as an appropriate and affirming expression of relational commitments.

The "hazards" presented by social relationships should not be overstated, but these examples illustrate that relationships can adversely affect health and well-being even when criticism, exploitation, betrayal, and other social wounds are not implicated. Although a comprehensive analysis of the detrimental aspects of social bonds would require attention to unintentional and unnoticed forms of harm, my goal is to consider social behaviors that fall into the category of perceived affronts.

This chapter is also necessarily limited in other respects. It focuses on the consequences of problematic social exchanges in nonpsychiatric populations, despite the existence of an important body of research that has examined pathological interaction patterns in seriously disturbed marital relationships (e.g., Gottman, 1979) and dysfunctional families (e.g., Jacob, 1975; Leff & Vaughn, 1981; Veiel & Kühner, 1990). The interpersonal dynamics that have been identified in clinical populations may well have relevance to analyses of nonclinical populations, but a serious consideration of such links is beyond the scope of this chapter.

PREVIOUS RESEARCH ON NEGATIVE SOCIAL EXCHANGES

Although the literature on negative social exchanges in informal social networks is not large, researchers generally have pursued three different strategies in their efforts to understand how such exchanges affect psychological well-being. One strategy has involved explicitly contrasting the effects of positive and negative exchanges on various aspects of emotional health and functioning (Brenner, Norvell, & Limacher, 1989; Finch, Okun, Barrera, Zautra, & Reich, 1989; Fiore, Becker, & Coppel, 1983; Pagel, Erdly, & Becker, 1987; Rook, 1984; Stephens, Kinney, Norris, & Ritchie, 1987). A less common strategy has involved conceptualizing such negative exchanges as stressors (Eckenrode & Gore, 1981; Shinn, Lehmann, & Wong, 1984) and comparing the impact of interpersonal versus noninterpersonal stressors (Bolger, DeLongis, Kessler, & Schilling, 1989). A third approach to gauging the effects of negative social exchanges has been to contrast the stress-alleviating effects of social support with the stress-exacerbating (or stress-amplifying) effects of social conflict (cf. Shinn et al., 1984).

Comparisons of the Effects of Positive and Negative Exchanges

A study by Pagel et al. (1987) typifies the first strategy, which involves contrasting the effects of positive and negative social exchanges on emotional health. In this study, 68 spouse caregivers of individuals with Alzheimer's disease rated both how helpful and how upsetting members of their social network had been in various contexts, such as socializing, offering emotional support, or providing tangible assistance. Analyses that controlled for the caregiver's age and sex indicated that the upset ratings were strongly related to greater depression, whereas the helpfulness ratings were unrelated to depression.

Several studies that have sampled different populations and that have used different measures of supportive and problematic exchanges have yielded similar evidence of such a "negativity effect" (see reviews by Rook, 1990a; Rook & Pietromonaco, 1987; see Gottman, 1979, for a discussion of the impact of negative interaction on marital satisfaction). That is, the results of these studies all suggest that the detrimental effect of negative social exchanges exceeds the beneficial effect of positive social exchanges. Indeed, in several studies, positive social exchanges have been found to make weak or nonsignificant contributions to the emotional health of the individuals studied (e.g., Barrera, 1981; Norris, Stephens, & Kinney, 1990; Pagel et al., 1987; Rook, 1984).

Other investigators have found that positive interactions and negative interactions have comparable effects when gauged with reference to a single dimension of psychological health, but negative interactions have more pervasive effects when evaluated with reference to multiple dimensions of psychological health. In a sample of 246 older adults, Finch et al. (1989) assessed positive social ties, negative social ties, and two aspects of adjustment—psychological well-being and psychological distress. Drawing on Zautra and Reich's (1983) two-factor model of adjustment, the researchers expected positive social ties to be related primarily to psychological well-being and negative social ties to be related primarily to psychological distress. The results only partially confirmed their expectations:

Positive ties were related solely to psychological well-being, but negative ties were related both to well-being and to distress. Finch et al. (1989) concluded that negative interactions may be so salient to an individual that their effects spill across various affective domains.

A different pattern of outcome-specific results emerged in a study of 48 older adults who were recovering from a stroke (Stephens et al., 1987). In this study, both positive and negative exchanges experienced in the recovery period proved consequential but for distinctly different aspects of respondents' adjustment. Controlling for respondents' health status on discharge from the hospital, analyses indicate that negative exchanges were associated with lower morale and more psychiatric symptoms, whereas positive exchanges were unrelated to these two outcomes. In contrast, positive exchanges were related to better cognitive functioning (e.g., fewer memory problems, less disorientation and confusion), but negative exchanges were unrelated to cognitive functioning. These results suggest that the relative importance of negative interaction versus positive interaction depends on the outcome examined.

This study and several others (e.g., Brenner et al., 1989) do not indicate that negative social exchanges consistently have more powerful effects than do positive social exchanges, but it is important to note that negative exchanges rarely fail to exhibit a strong relationship with emotional health. That is, the effects of problematic exchanges generally have been quite robust across studies, whereas the effects of supportive exchanges have proven more elusive. Although it appears premature to conclude that negative social interactions outweigh positive interactions in significance, a growing body of evidence clearly indicates that negative interactions can have quite potent effects on emotional health.

Of course, the possibility exists that the adverse impact of negative exchanges documented in these studies represents a mere artifact of respondents' states of psychological adjustment. Pagel et al. (1987) pursued this possibility in the study that was described earlier. The researchers analyzed data collected at a 10-month follow-up to determine whether changes in negative social exchanges predicted changes in participants' depression levels. Controlling for initial depression levels and age, sex, and health status, they found that participants who reported an increase in problematic exchanges over the 10-month period also reported increased depression. Further analyses indicated that participants' initial depression levels did not predict their later exposure to problematic exchanges. Finch et al. (1989) similarly found that negative exchanges significantly affected older adults' psychological health *after* controlling for neuroticism and extraversion. Thus preliminary evidence casts doubt on the notion that the adverse effects of negative exchanges can be attributed simply to personality factors or psychological adjustment.

Comparisons of Social and Nonsocial Stressors

Another approach to studying problematic social exchanges has been to conceptualize such exchanges as stressors and to contrast the effects of social and nonsocial stressors. Although relatively few studies have explicitly undertaken such comparisons, those that have testify to the uniquely distressing effects of interpersonal stressors (Thoits, 1982). For example, Bolger et al. (1989) examined 10 different categories of daily stress in a sample of 166 married couples, including several kinds of stressful interpersonal experiences (family demands, demands from other individuals, and interpersonal conflicts or tensions with one's spouse, child, another person, or multiple persons at the same time). Respondents kept daily diaries for 6 weeks in which they recorded the occurrence of these stressors and their moods. Regression analyses were designed to analyze within-person covariation in daily stressors and mood.

These analyses clearly revealed that interpersonal conflicts had the most serious consequences for emotional health. In fact, interpersonal conflicts accounted for over 80% of the explained variance in respondents' moods. Additional analyses of multiday stress episodes indicated that the adverse effects of interpersonal stressors tended to persist over several days, whereas the effects of noninterpersonal stressors dissipated more quickly.

Although these data did not address the relative impact of negative and positive social events in people's everyday experiences, they do suggest that, among daily stressors, those of an interpersonal nature have the greatest significance for psychological well-being. Bolger et al. (1989) concluded from their research that future investigations of daily stressors should concentrate intensively on the interpersonal domain.

The reasons why social stressors disrupt everyday functioning to a greater degree than do nonsocial stressors await identification in future research. However, theoretical perspectives on life stress suggest several possibilities. Theorists have argued than stressors that threaten one's self-concept or self-esteem may cause greater distress than stressors that do not entail such threats (e.g., Thoits, 1983), and it is possible that arguments and other social stressors more often ensnare self-processes than do financial strains, transportation difficulties, and nonsocial stressors. Additionally, conflicts with intimate associates, such as spouses or friends, violate implicit rules of conduct and, particularly in the case of a friendship, may occur in the absence of well-established procedures for resolving disagreements and renewing relational commitments (Wiseman, 1986). Similarly, resolution of interpersonal tensions typically requires coordination and negotiation with one or more individuals, which largely precludes the possibility of unilateral action and increases the complexity of coping efforts. Finally, research on the determinants of perceived quality of life (e.g., Campbell, Converse, & Rodgers, 1976) clearly demonstrates that most people care deeply about their relationships with family members and friends; the level of satisfaction with one's social relationships has been found consistently to be among the strongest predictors of overall happiness and morale. Thus if stressors that jeopardize life domains in which people have significant investments cause the greatest dismay (Lazarus & Folkman, 1984), it is not surprising that social stressors often inflict more pain than do nonsocial stressors.

Comparisons of Positive and Negative Social Exchanges as Moderators of Adaptation to Stress

A third and still relatively small line of research on negative social exchanges represents a logical extension of the stress-buffering paradigm that has dominated investigations of social support. This extension considers the role of negative exchanges in hindering, or exacerbating, adaptation to life stress. An illustrative study of this type was recently reported by Okun, Melichar, and Martin (1990). The study participants were 110 community-residing older adults drawn from a local medical clinic. Interviews and self-administered questionnaires were used to assess daily stress experienced in the preceding 6 months, positive social ties, negative social ties, and psychological distress. Positive and negative social ties were operationalized in terms of positive versus negative feelings aroused by contact with each network member. Care was taken in constructing the daily stress inventory to avoid confounds with the measures of participants' social ties (cf. Thoits, 1982; Monroe, Bromet, Connell, & Steiner, 1986).

Regression analyses that controlled for participants' physical health and background characteristics (e.g., age, gender, income, marital status) revealed no significant main effect of positive social ties but did reveal a significant main effect of negative social ties (with more such ties related to greater psychological distress). A significant stress-buffering effect of positive social ties also emerged, but there was no evidence that negative social ties amplified the adverse effects of daily stress. Thus these data suggest that negative social exchanges detract from psychological health regardless of the presence or absence of other burdens and demands.

The study by Finch et al. (1989) described earlier included analyses that permit a comparison of stress-buffering versus stress-exacerbation effects, even though the study was not explicitly designed to examine adaptation to stress. The study examined the effects of supportive social ties and problematic social ties on the emotional health of three different subgroups of the older adult sample: (a) those who had suffered recent conjugal bereavement, (b) those who had suffered recent physical disability, and (c) matched controls who had not experienced recent life stress. Analyses indicated that neither the effects of positive social ties nor the effects of negative social ties differed in these three subgroups. Thus these results suggest that troublesome social exchanges do not necessarily aggravate the emotional distress of individuals who are already contending with serious life difficulties (nor do supportive exchanges necessarily alleviate their distress).

A study by Kiecolt-Glaser, Dyer, and Shuttleworth (1988) reached a somewhat different conclusion. The researchers contrasted 34 individuals experiencing a major, chronic life stress (caring for a relative with Alzheimer's disease) with a comparison group of 34 individuals not experiencing a major life stress. They found that negative social interactions predicted depression only among the group struggling with the chronic burden of caregiving; positive interactions had no effect on depression in this group. In the comparison group that was not experiencing life stress, neither positive nor negative interactions were related to depression levels.

Thus, the studies by Okun et al. (1990) and Finch et al. (1989) suggest that preexisting life stress does not increase one's vulnerability to negative social exchanges; those experiencing low stress react as strongly to negative social exchanges as do those experiencing high stress. In contrast, the findings of Kiecolt-Glaser et al. (1988) suggest that experiencing major life stress makes one uniquely vulnerable to negative exchanges. How these conflicting results should be reconciled is not entirely clear, although the dissimilar nature of the stressors studied may provide at least a partial account. More generally, however, the rather specialized nature of the samples investigated argues against drawing firm conclusions about the interactive effects of life stress and negative social exchanges.

A related line of research that warrants comment has contrasted positive social interaction and negative social interaction not as moderators of adaptation to life stress but, rather, as moderators of progress toward the attainment of personally valued goals. Emotional health is influenced, in part, by the nature of one's personal strivings and the degree of success one experiences in achieving personal goals (Emmons, 1986). Ruehlman and Wolchik (1988) accordingly reasoned that social relationships may contribute to psychological functioning not only by influencing adaptation to life stress but also by facilitating or hindering one's pursuit of important goals. In a study of 229 college students, Ruehlman and Wolchik (1988) assessed the extent to which the three most important members of each student's social network interfered with or facilitated the student's work on valued personal projects. Project hindrance and project support were evaluated in relation to two aspects of emotional health—psychological well-being and psychological distress. The researchers found that project hindrance was associated both with greater psychological distress and lower psychological well-being, whereas project support was associated with greater psychological well-being but was unrelated to psychological distress. Although the results do not provide a simple answer to the question of whether hindrance or support plays a larger role in the pursuit of personal goals, they do extend our knowledge of the diverse contexts in which negative exchanges moderate adaptational outcomes.

This discussion has highlighted several different strategies for analyzing the effects of negative social exchanges on psychological health and has reviewed preliminary evidence that indicates that these effects can be quite potent. These effects have emerged in a variety of different populations, including college students (e.g., Abbey, Abramis, & Caplan, 1985; Ruehlman & Wolchik, 1988), medical students (Brenner et al., 1989), pregnant adolescents (Barrera, 1981), married couples (Bolger et al., 1989), older adults (e.g., Okun et al., 1990; Rook, 1984), and individuals coping with serious life stresses, illness, or disability (e.g., Finch et al., 1989; Fiore et al., 1983; Kiecolt-Glaser et al., 1988; Manne & Zautra, 1989; Stephens et al., 1987). Strong effects have emerged using a variety of different procedures for measuring problematic interaction, including interview and questionnaire assessment of specific negative exchanges (e.g., Rook, 1984; Finch et al., 1989), daily diary records of negative exchanges (Bolger et al., 1989), behavioral observation of verbal interaction patterns (e.g., Manne & Zautra, 1989), ratings of the personal upset or negative affect aroused by others' actions (e.g., Fiore et al., 1983; Okun et al., 1990; Pagel et al., 1987; Stephens et al., 1987), and content analysis of open-ended comments obtained from focus group participants (Morgan, 1989). Moreover, these effects have survived controls for health, gender, marital status, education, and personality factors (e.g., Finch et al., 1989; Pagel et al., 1987; Rook, 1984; Stephens et al., 1987) and have emerged in some well-controlled longitudinal studies (e.g., Pagel et al., 1987). Considering the weight of the evidence, further work on the negative aspects of social relationships clearly seems warranted.

In thinking about directions for future research, it is apparent that many of the conceptual and methodological dilemmas that have challenged (and sometimes plagued) researchers interested in social support also challenge researchers interested in social conflict (Rook, 1990b). Indeed, an agenda for future research on negative social interaction may be derived by identifying parallel versions of the issues that have engaged social support researchers.

PARALLELS IN THE STUDY OF SUPPORTIVE SOCIAL EXCHANGES AND PROBLEMATIC SOCIAL EXCHANGES

Several of these conceptual and methodological parallels are summarized in Table 1. Considering the conceptual parallels first, more differentiated analyses of problematic interaction could be undertaken that contrast the effects of different kinds of negative exchanges (such as rejection vs. demands from others) and that contrast the effects of negative exchanges that involve different categories of social actors (such as kin vs. friends). Some work in this vein has already begun. For example, Abbey et al. (1985) contrasted the effects of social conflict with intimate associates versus casual associates, and Bolger et al. (1989) examined the distinctive effects of social conflict with several different categories of network members. Similarly, Norris et al. (1990) sought to determine which kinds of negative exchanges with family members cause the greatest distress among elderly individuals recovering from a stroke.

Determining what causes some people to experience a great deal of conflictual interaction represents a high priority for future research, just as the question of what causes some people to experience deficient social support has begun to be

Table 1 Conceptual and methodological parallels in the study of supportive exchanges and problematic exchanges

Study of supportive exchanges	Study of problematic exchanges
Conceptual issues	
What types of supportive exchanges can be distinguished conceptually and empirically?	What types of problematic exchanges can be distinguished conceptually and empirically?
Who are the primary sources of supportive exchanges (family members, friends, etc.)?	Who are the primary sources of problematic exchanges (family members, friends, etc.)?
What causes people to experience few supportive exchanges?	What causes people to experience many problematic exchanges?
Through what specific processes do supportive exchanges affect emotional and physical health?	Through what specific processes do problematic exchanges affect emotional and physical health?
Which specific health-related outcomes are most strongly related to supportive exchanges?	Which specific health-related outcomes are most strongly related to problematic exchanges?
Methodological issues	
How valid and reliable are self-reports of supportive exchanges?	How valid and reliable are self-reports of problematic exchanges?
Do associations between supportive exchanges and health-related outcomes reflect reverse causation or confounded factors?	Do associations between problematic exchanges and health-related outcomes reflect reverse causation or confounded factors?
Are associations between supportive exchanges and health-related outcomes linear or curvilinear?	Are associations between problematic exchanges and health-related outcomes linear or curvilinear?
How should the magnitude of effects of supportive exchanges be evaluated?	How should the magnitude of effects of problematic exchanges be evaluated?

widely investigated. The answers to these two questions may turn out to be closely related, although aggregate (vs. dyad-specific) measures of support and conflict have been found to be only weakly correlated (e.g., Finch et al., 1989; Kiecolt-Glaser et al., 1988; Norris et al., 1990; Pagel et al., 1987; Rook, 1984). This suggests that the factors that prevent or erode support may not be identical to those that provoke conflict.

Additional conceptual issues that have parallels in work on social support include the need to test alternative models of the interrelations of negative interactions, life stress, and adaptation (e.g., by contrasting main-effect and interactive models), and the need to investigate the cognitive, affective, and behavioral processes by which social conflict jeopardizes health and emotional well-being (cf. Cohen, 1988). Consideration of these alternative theoretical models and of the underlying or mediating processes would provide the basis for more refined conceptions of the outcomes that are affected by interpersonal tensions. For example, under some conditions, interpersonal conflict may provoke depression and social withdrawal (Evans, Palsan, Lepore, & Martin, 1989; Lepore, 1990). But, under other conditions, conflict may provoke anger and aggression. More elaborated conceptions of the nature of negative social exchanges and the processes that link such exchanges to emotional health would guide us in the choice of appropriate outcome measures in our research.

Methodological concerns that must be addressed in studies of problematic interaction and that have parallels in work on social support include: the need to evaluate the reliability and validity of self-reports of negative exchanges, the need to control for the effects of factors that may be confounded with negative exchanges, greater use of research designs that permit legitimate inferences about causal associations, greater attention to possible threshold effects or other curvilinear patterns, and greater efforts to document the magnitude of observed effects. Several of these issues have been discussed extensively elsewhere (e.g., Dooley, 1985; House & Kahn, 1985), but one issue that appears to have important and insufficiently appreciated implications warrants further comment here—the possibility of threshold effects.

The Possibility of Threshold Effects

Social support researchers have often argued that the benefits of social support may be most apparent when individuals who have no supportive relationships are compared with those who have at least one such relationship (Coyne & DeLongis, 1986; House, 1981; Kahn & Antonucci, 1980). That is, a critical threshold may exist beyond which increased levels of support contribute little to a person's psychological well-being. The same prediction could be made about the effects of negative social exchanges, yet few studies have included tests for such nonlinear patterns.

This is worrisome because when researchers have reported the distributions of positive and negative interactions in their samples, a sizable number of respondents have been found to disclaim having any negative interactions with others. For example, in my own work on the elderly (Rook, 1984, and research in progress), I have found that as many as 25–30% of the respondents report having no problematic interactions with members of their social networks. In contrast, very few respondents report having no supportive interactions with members of their networks. Higher figures have been reported in other studies of older adults, including figures as high as 58% (Okun et al., 1990) and 83% (Stephens et al., 1987, based on averaging percents specified for individual items in Table 1, p. 127); only a small fraction of the respondents in these studies reported having no supportive interactions. Likewise, other studies may have tended to underrepresent individuals with quite deficient levels of support because such individuals are often difficult to locate or, once located, are often reluctant to participate in research.

These differences in the clustering of respondents at the low end of the distributions of positive and negative exchanges could partly account for the disproportionate impact of negative exchanges on psychological functioning. That is, the data collected in these studies may have included the critical threshold for negative exchanges but may have excluded the critical threshold for positive exchanges. If this were so, it would not disconfirm the importance of negative social exchanges, but it would cast doubt on the inference that negative exchanges have more powerful effects than do supportive exchanges. In future studies that seek to compare the effects of supportive and problematic exchanges, researchers may wish to include explicit tests for possible threshold effects (see Veiel, 1987, for a discussion of analytic procedures for detecting threshold effects).

This section has considered some of the conceptual and methodological issues that confront researchers interested in social support and that, likewise, confront researchers interested in social conflict. Recognition of these parallel concerns serves to highlight significant gaps in our existing knowledge base regarding the manner in which negative social exchanges may affect emotional and physical health.

STUDYING THE JOINT EFFECTS OF SOCIAL SUPPORT AND SOCIAL STRAIN

Beyond the questions that have direct parallels in the social support literature, unique questions arise in attempting to consider how supportive and problematic social exchanges combine to affect health and well-being. For example, do positive and negative aspects of social interaction represent truly independent domains of experience, as previous research has suggested (e.g., Finch et al., 1989; Manne & Zautra, 1989; Norris et al., 1990; Rook, 1984; Ruehlman & Wolchik, 1988), or do positive and negative interactions covary systematically in certain kinds of relationships (cf. Abbey et al., 1985; Morgan, 1989) or in specific subgroups of the population? What implications stem from viewing positive and negative social exchanges as independent rather than interdependent phenomena? What theoretical models best characterize the additive and interactive effects of positive and negative exchanges? Does a high base rate of positive interaction cushion the painful effects of the comparatively rare negative interaction, or is the opposite true—is negative interaction more painful precisely when it represents a departure from a general pattern of harmonious interaction? If future research indicates that the effects of negative social exchanges often overshadow the effects of positive exchanges, how should such asymmetries best be explained? What significance should we ascribe to such asymmetries? Finally, should positive and negative exchanges be expected to influence the same or different dimensions of emotional and physical health (cf. Rook & Pietromonaco, 1987; Stephens et al., 1987)? This list of questions is by no means exhaustive, but illustrates the kind of thinking that will be required if we are to make the shift from a preoccupation with either supportive *or* problematic aspects of social relationships to a consideration of the complex *dual* nature of social bonds.

CONCLUSION

Social relationships provide a complex mix of uplifting and disheartening experiences. Neglecting either kind of experience will hinder our efforts to develop a comprehensive understanding of how social ties affect health and well-being. To complement other chapters in this volume, the current chapter has focused on the detrimental aspects of social bonds. Yet it is important not to exaggerate the prevalence or impact of interpersonal conflicts and tensions that people typically encounter in the everyday course of their lives. Researchers using a variety of different methods and studying a variety of different populations have consistently shown that, for most people, supportive social contacts outnumber troublesome social contacts (e.g., Brenner et al., 1989; Finch et al., 1989; Okun et al., 1990; Rook, 1984; Stephens et al., 1987). Levels of reported satisfaction with friendships and family relationships tend to be high in most studies (e.g., Antonucci, 1985; Campbell et al., 1976). Thus despite mounting evidence that negative social exchanges can cause considerable anguish, it would be unfortunate to "pathologize" social relationships.

A balanced perspective on the adaptive significance of social relationships requires acknowledgment of the important benefits that stem from supportive transactions with others as well as recognition of the distress that results from discordant transactions with others. Anchoring the study of social support in this broader context may increase our effectiveness in designing interventions to help those whose social relationships are deficient in some way. Most discussions of social network interventions focus on the need to help people forge new social ties that can function as sources of support and companionship (e.g., Gottlieb, 1983; Snow & Gordon, 1980). Yet some people may benefit more from efforts to help them disengage from chronically strained relationships or to improve the quality of such relationships. The past two decades of vigorous research on social support provide a strong base from which to elaborate a more complex understanding of how social relationships influence adaptation and, hopefully, to develop new insights about how social network interventions can be tailored to be most effective.

REFERENCES

Abbey, A., Abramis, D. J., & Caplan, R. D. (1985). Effects of different sources of social support and social conflict on emotional well-being. *Basic and Applied Social Psychology, 6,* 111–129.

Antonucci, T. C. (1985). Personal characteristics, social support, and social behavior. In R. H. Binstock & E. Shanas (Eds.), *Handbook of aging and the social sciences* (2nd ed., pp. 94–128). New York: Van Nostrand Reinhold.

Barrera, M., Jr. (1981). Social support in the adjustment of pregnant adolescents. In B. H. Gottlieb (Ed.), *Social networks and social support* (pp. 69-96). Beverly Hills, CA: Sage.

Bolger, N., DeLongis, A., Kessler, R. C., & Schilling, E. A. (1989). Effects of daily stress on negative mood. *Journal of Personality and Social Psychology, 57,* 808–818.

Brenner, G. F., Norvell, N. K., & Limacher, M. (1989). Supportive and problematic social interaction: A social network analysis. *American Journal of Community Psychology, 17,* 831–836.

Campbell, A., Converse, P. E., & Rodgers, W. L. (1976). *The quality of American life.* New York: Sage.

Cohen, S. (1988). Psychosocial models of the role of social support in the etiology of physical disease. *Health Psychology, 7,* 269–297.
Coyne, J. C. (1990). Doing without social support as an explanatory concept. *Journal of Social and Clinical Psychology, 9,* 148–158.
Coyne, J. C., & DeLongis, A. M. (1986). Going beyond social support: The role of social relationships in adaptation. *Journal of Consulting and Clinical Psychology, 54,* 454–460.
Coyne, J. C., Ellard, J. H., & Smith, D. A. F. (1990). Social support, interdependence, and the dilemmas of helping. In B. R. Sarason, I. G. Sarason, & G. R. Pierce (Eds.), *Social support: An interactional view* (pp. 129–149). New York: Wiley.
Coyne, J. C., Wortman, C. B., & Lehman, D. R. (1988). The other side of support: Emotional overinvolvement and miscarried helping. In B. H. Gottlieb (Ed.), *Marshaling social support: Formats, processes, and effects* (pp. 305–330). Newbury Park, CA: Sage.
Dooley, D. (1985). Causal inference in the study of social support. In S. Cohen & S. L. Syme (Eds.), *Social support and health* (pp. 109–125). New York: Academic Press.
Eckenrode, J., & Gore, S. (1981). Stressful life events and social supports: The significance of context. In B. H. Gottlieb (Ed.), *Social networks and social support* (pp. 43–68). Beverly Hills, CA: Sage.
Emmons, R. A. (1986). Personal strivings: An approach to personality and subjective well-being. *Journal of Personality and Social Psychology, 51,* 1058–1068.
Evans, G. W., Palsane, M. N., Lepore, S. J., & Martin, J. (1989). Residential density and psychological health: The mediating effects of social support. *Journal of Personality and Social Psychology, 57,* 994–999.
Finch, J. F., Okun, J. A., Barrera, M., Jr., Zautra, A. J., & Reich, J. W. (1989). Positive and negative social ties among older adults: Measurement models and the prediction of psychological distress and well-being. *American Journal of Community Psychology, 17,* 585–605.
Fiore, J., Becker, J., & Coppel, D. (1983). Social network interactions: A buffer or a stress? *American Journal of Community Psychology, 11,* 423–439.
Gottlieb, B. H. (1983). *Social support strategies: Guidelines for mental health practice.* Beverly Hills, CA: Sage.
Gottman, J. M. (1979). *Marital interaction: Experimental investigations.* New York: Academic Press.
Heller, K. (1979). The effects of social support: Prevention and treatment implications. In A. P. Goldstein & F. H. Kanfer (Eds.), *Maximizing treatment gains: Transfer enhancement in psychotherapy* (pp. 353–382). New York: Academic Press.
Homans, G. G. (1974). *Social behavior* (2nd ed.). New York: Harcourt Brace Jovanovich.
House, J. S. (1981). *Work stress and social support.* Reading, MA: Addison-Wesley.
House, J. S., & Kahn, R. L. (1985). Measures and concepts of social support. In S. Cohen & S. L. Syme (Eds.), *Social support and health* (pp. 83–108). New York: Academic Press.
House, J. S., Umberson, D., & Landis, K. R. (1988). Structures and processes of social support. *Annual Review of Sociology, 14,* 293–318.
Jacob, T. (1975). Family interaction in disturbed and normal families: A methodological and substantive analysis. *Psychological Bulletin, 18,* 35–65.
Kahn, R. L., & Antonucci, T. (1980). Convoys over the life course: Attachment, roles, and social support. In P. B. Baltes & O. Brim (Eds.), *Life-span development and behavior* (Vol. 3, pp. 253–286). Boston: Lexington.
Kaplan, B. M., & Toshima, M. T. (1990). The functional effects of social relationships on chronic illness and disability. In B. R. Sarason, I. G. Sarason, & G. R. Pierce (Eds.), *Social support: An interactional view* (pp. 427–453). New York: Wiley.
Kessler, R. C., McCleod, J. D., & Wethington, E. (1985). The costs of caring: A perspective on the relationship between sex and psychological distress. In I. G. Sarason & B. R. Sarason (Eds.), *Social support: Theory, research, and application* (pp. 491–506). Dordrecht, the Netherlands: Martinus Nijhoff.
Kiecolt-Glaser, J. K., Dyer, C. S., & Shuttleworth, E. C. (1988). Upsetting social interactions and distress among Alzheimer's disease family care-givers: A replication and extension. *American Journal of Community Psychology, 16,* 825–837.
Lazarus, R. S., & Folkman, S. (1984). *Stress, appraisal, and coping.* New York: Springer.
Leff, J., & Vaughn, C. (1981). The role of maintenance therapy and relatives' expressed emotion in relapse of schizophrenia. *British Journal of Psychiatry, 139,* 102–104.
Lepore, S. J. (1990). *Residential density and psychological health: The role of social support and social withdrawal.* Unpublished manuscript, University of California, Irvine.

Manne, S., & Zautra, A. J. (1989). Spouse criticism and support: Their association with coping and psychological adjustment among women with rheumatoid arthritis. *Journal of Personality and Social Psychology, 56,* 608-617.
Monroe, S. M., Bromet, E. J., Connell, M. M., & Steiner, S. C. (1986). Social support, life events, and depressive symptoms: A one-year prospective study. *Journal of Abnormal Psychology, 95,* 423-431.
Morgan, D. L. (1989). Adjusting to widowhood: Do social networks really make it easier? *Gerontologist, 29,* 101-107.
Norris, V. K., Stephens, M. A. P., & Kinney, J. M. (1990). The impact of family interactions on recovery from stroke: Help or hindrance? *Gerontologist, 30,* 535-542.
Okun, M. A., Melichar, J. F., & Hill, M. D. (1990). Negative daily events, positive and negative social ties, and psychological distress among older adults. *Gerontologist, 30,* 193-199.
Pagel, M. D., Erdly, W. W., & Becker, J. (1987). Social networks: We get by with (and in spite of) a little help from our friends. *Journal of Personality and Social Psychology, 53,* 793-804.
Riley, D., & Eckenrode, J. (1986). Social ties: Costs and benefits within differing subgroups. *Journal of Personality and Social Psychology, 51,* 770-778.
Rook, K. S. (1984). The negative side of social interaction. *Journal of Personality and Social Psychology, 46,* 1097-1108.
Rook, K. S. (1989). Strains in older adults' friendships. In R. G. Adams & R. Blieszner (Eds.), *Older adult friendships: Structure and processes* (pp. 166-194). Newbury Park, CA: Sage.
Rook, K. S. (1990a). Stressful aspects of older adults' social relationships: An overview of current theory and research. In M. A. P. Stephens, J. H. Crowther, S. E. Hobfoll, & D. L. Tennenbaum (Eds.), *Stress and coping in later life families* (pp. 173-192). Washington, DC: Hemisphere.
Rook, K. S. (1990b). Parallels in the study of social support and social strain. *Journal of Social and Clinical Psychology, 9,* 118-132.
Rook, K. S., Dooley, D., & Catalano, R. (1991). Stress transmission: The effects of husbands' job stressors on the emotional health of their wives. *Journal of Marriage and the Family, 53,* 165-177.
Rook, K. S., & Pietromonaco, P. (1987). Close relationships: Ties that heal or ties that bind? In W. H. Jones & D. Perlman (Eds.), *Advances in personal relationships* (Vol. 1, pp. 1-35). Greenwich, CT: JAI Press.
Ruehlman, L. S., & Wolchik, S. A. (1988). Personal goals and interpersonal support and hindrance as factors in psychological distress and well-being. *Journal of Personality and Social Psychology, 55,* 293-301.
Shinn, M., Lehmann, S., & Wong, N. W. (1984). Social interaction and social support. *Journal of Social Issues, 40,* 55-76.
Snow, D. L., & Gordon, T. W. (1980). Social network analysis and intervention with the elderly. *Gerontologist, 20,* 463-467.
Stephens, M. A. P., Kinney, J. M., Norris, V. K., & Ritchie, S. W. (1987). Social networks as assets and liabilities in recovery from stroke by geriatric patients. *Psychology and Aging, 2,* 125-129.
Suls, J. (1982). Social support, interpersonal relations, and health: Benefits and liabilities. In G. S. Sanders & J. Suls (Eds.), *Social psychology of health and illness* (pp. 255-277). Hillsdale, NJ: Erlbaum.
Thibaut, J. W., & Kelley, H. H. (1959). *The social psychology of groups.* New York: Wiley.
Thoits, P. A. (1982). Conceptual, methodological, and theoretical problems in studying social support as a buffer against life stress. *Journal of Health and Social Behavior, 23,* 145-159.
Thoits, P. A. (1983). Dimensions of life events that influence psychological distress: An evaluation and synthesis of the literature. In H. B. Kaplan (Ed.), *Psychosocial stress: Trends in theory and research* (pp. 33-103). New York: Academic Press.
Veiel, H. O. F. (1987). Buffer effects and threshold effects: An alternative interpretation of nonlinearities in the relationship between social support, stress, and depression. *American Journal of Community Psychology, 15,* 717-740.
Veiel, H. O. F., & Kühner, C. (1990). Relatives and depressive relapse: The critical period after discharge from in-patient treatment. *Psychological Medicine, 20,* 977-984.
Wiseman, J. P. (1986). Friendship: Bonds and binds in a voluntary relationship. *Journal of Social and Personal Relationships, 3,* 191-211.
Wortman, C. B., & Lehman, D. R. (1985). Reactions to victims of life crises: Support attempts that fail. In I. G. Sarason & B. R. Sarason (Eds.), *Social support: Theory, research, and application* (pp. 463-489). Dordrecht, the Netherlands: Martinus Nijhoff.
Zautra, A., & Reich, J. W. (1983). Life events and perceptions of life quality: Developments in a two-factor approach. *Journal of Community Psychology, 11,* 121-132.

12

Some Reflections on the Process of Social Support and Nature of Unsupportive Behaviors

Tirril O. Harris
University of London, United Kingdom

One point that has been made strongly in several contributions to this volume is the lack of attention paid to the nature of supportive behaviors relative to their complexity—especially given the importance of this in understanding how the words and actions of others may help in confronting stress. I will, therefore, comment on this subject, while referring to some detailed material on the role of lack of social support. The work in question focuses on the onset of clinical depression among women. By adhering to concrete examples, this might help to fill in one corner of the broad theoretical structure that exists in other chapters in this volume. The contextual style of measurement of stress adopted in this research and the situational measures of social support allow a focus on just such an aspect of potentially supportive (or unsupportive) behaviors by various types of support figures at particular points in time, rather than merely reflecting vague general perceptions, with all the possibilities of confounding by response bias that are described in other chapters.

In this sense, then, the measures used go some way toward meeting the requirements of the kind of exploration that has been recommended here. This approach, described in detail by Brown (Chapter 15), highlights the advantages of combining a flexible semistructured interviewing style with systematic rating procedures of high interrater reliability. These procedures afford the interviewer the opportunity to check and cross-check the information given in terms of the temporal sequence of stressors, and requests and provisions of different kinds of support. They also permit the calibration of rating standards in discussion with colleagues blind to key variables to minimize interviewer bias. This allows the interviewer to maintain a distinction between what "really" happened and how the women studied felt, thus approximating more closely the phenomenon of supportive (or unsupportive) behaviors rather than a general response set.

SOCIAL SUPPORT AND CLINICAL DEPRESSION: A THEORETICAL MODEL

The two studies discussed here were undertaken during the 1980s in London by the Royal Holloway and Bedford College research team. One was in a representative general population sample—in the North London Borough of Islington—of women with children at home and husbands in manual occupations, and the other

Provoking Agent ------------------------- Specific ------------------- Generalized ---------------- Depression
Hopelessness Hopelessness

(Severe Life Event/
Major Difficulty)

Vulnerability Factor -- Low Self-Esteem,
Helplessness

1. Lack of Intimacy
2. Early Loss of Mother
3. Three Plus Children at Home
4. Lack of Employment

Figure 1 Initial theoretical model of depression.

was in a recently collected consecutive series of women under 60 with depression, regardless of presence of children or social class, who were attending the psychiatric departments of three London hospitals during the years 1984–86. (For further details of the first sample see Brown, Craig, & Harris, 1985. The second sample is in the initial stages of analysis, and the present discussion represents only a preliminary report.) Although the longitudinal nature of these studies permitted the investigation of factors associated with the course of depression, these comments will focus on onset alone.

Previous work by the same team, both among psychiatric patients and in the general population (Brown & Harris, 1978), had given rise to a theoretical model of depressive onset as represented in Figure 1. Here, factors to the left represent empirically verified associations with depression and those to the right speculative hypotheses about intervening processes. It will be apparent that this model is a variant of the stress-buffering hypothesis of the role of social support, with the measure of provoking agent from the Life Events and Difficulty Schedule (LEDS; see Brown & Harris, 1978) representing the stressor and the measure of intimacy representing social support.

The nature of the speculative intervening psychological processes, and particularly the emphasis on hopelessness, reflects a cognitive perspective of depressive illness, very much along the lines of Beck's classic exposition (Beck, 1967), although the introduction of the notion of self-esteem has overtones of later psychoanalytic thinkers, such as Bibring (1953) and Fenichel (1946). Perhaps even more important, however, was the idea of the *generalization* of this hopelessness, as the mechanism through which a standard response to a stressor is transformed into a disordered one—an idea that was echoed in the notions of globality and stability in the later reformulated theory of learned helplessness (Abramson, Seligman, & Teasdale, 1978). This notion of generalization will prove a crucial reference point in the following discussion of the process of social support.

THE NATURE OF SUPPORTIVE AND UNSUPPORTIVE BEHAVIORS

A Summary of Initial Findings

One of the aims of the Islington study was to explore the area of social support in greater detail, and (as described by Brown, Chapter 15) the Self-Evaluation and

Social Support Schedule (SESS) was accordingly developed. At the start of the original Camberwell study, the rating of intimacy had not been given its deserved importance in comparison with other social network variables. As a result, although it had paid attention to frequency of contact and distinguished romantic from other relationships, it had been a relatively crude "yes/no" measure of the subject's general tendency toward confiding in that figure. The SESS not only distinguished such a general belief about confiding from actual behavior at a specific point in time, but it also examined the degree of confiding on a four-point scale; furthermore, it distinguished confiding from other aspects of the support process: the degree of active emotional support received in return, and negative verbal or behavioral responses that might vitiate confiding's otherwise protective effects.

As described by Brown in Chapter 15, one of the main features of the Islington study was its prospective nature, which allowed the measurement of self-esteem at a time (first interview) well before depressive onset (during follow-up), rather than risking the possibility of confounding (by the effects of the depression itself on the self-image) that attends cross-sectional research. But the longitudinal design also permitted a more thorough examination of the degree to which descriptions at the first interview of the supportiveness of a particular figure would in fact prove accurate at the time of a later crisis, or provoking agent, during follow-up.

At this time, the four aspects of crisis support mentioned earlier were measured for a number of different figures along with practical (or instrumental) support. Each potential support figure had at least one of these crisis-support records (or F-records, Table 1), and perhaps more if the subject had experienced several provoking agents, or if their supportiveness had changed for any reason during the interview period. The rater was routinely required to give a detailed written description on each F-record of the full circumstances of the support behaviors that occurred and was required to transcribe in detail the respondent's own comments about whether she found this behavior helpful. A rating of this "perceived helpfulness" was also made.

Brown's Chapter 15 describes the complications of analyzing this wealth of material on the large number of F-records obtained, and outlines features that are critical in terms of buffering or preventing depressive onset after a provoking agent. It may, however, be worth summarizing these features here. The support figure must be a core contact—that is, a spouse/partner/lover, or someone defined as a "very close other" at the first interview; both confiding and active emotional support must be at least moderate, and there must be no moderate or marked negative response of any kind. When these features were identified, there was no role for practical (or instrumental) support in preventing depression. This degree of crisis support from a noncore contact (e.g., a neighbor or a sister who was not very close) did not appear to have a protective effect.

It is tempting to keep this discussion at the level of concrete detail by summarizing these findings in the graphic metaphorical shorthand then in use by the team interviewers: "fire-engine support," where a competent stranger came in especially to cope with the crisis, was less helpful than "milk-van support." (In Britain, although milk is delivered in slow-moving electric vans, it comes every day to the household doorstep, and, of course, is encrusted with all the symbolism of infant care.)

Table 1 List of scales rated on the F-record

1. Subject identification
2. Identification of other (One record for *each* support member)
3. Identification of event/difficulty complex
   (Record all relevant severe events/major difficulties)
4. Relationship to other

1. Spouse/cohabitee	8. Mother
2. Partner (boy/girlfriend)	9. Father
3. Very close other	10. Sister
4. New very close other*	11. Brother
5. Confidant/main friend*	12. Child
6. New confidant/main friend*	13. Other relative
7. Acquaintance	14. Formal contact (e.g., priest)

5. Confiding in O (other)
   The degree to which the subject is able to talk to O about the crisis and her feelings concerning it (4-point scale).
6. Active emotional support from O
   The extent to which O offers sympathy, understanding, advice, encouragement, etc. concerning the crisis (4-point scale).
7. Practical support from O
   The extent to which O offers practical help, either in solving the crisis, or with the subject's other responsibilities (4-point scale).
8. Negative verbal response from O
   The extent to which O is critical or rejecting to the subject in relation to the crisis. Take number of negative comments into account (4-point scale).
9. Negative behavioral response from O
   The extent to which O's nonverbal behavior suggests O's commitment to the subject's point of view about the crisis is not unambiguous—e.g., despite saying he is sorry about the financial situation he continues to spend a great deal on drink (4-point scale).
10. Perceived helpfulness of support
    The extent to which the subject perceives O's responses as helpful (4-point scale).
11. Date of start of support
12. Date of end of support

*New since initial interview.

Particularly interesting was the finding that those women in a confiding relationship at the first interview who did not receive crisis support from that figure during follow-up (i.e., those "let down") were especially at risk for depression, even if they received crisis support elsewhere. This is reminiscent of Cohen's result, which suggests the ratio of received positive supportive behaviors to those expected is a critical mediator of the effectiveness of the program for quitting smoking; those receiving less than expected were the least successful (see Cohen, Chapter 8).

As explained earlier, the situational focus on support behaviors rather than on the respondent's perception of supportiveness allows an examination of any contrasts between the more subjective and the more objective features of the situation. Interestingly, where these did not coincide, the findings were quite contrary to what some workers have predicted. Earlier results in Canberra (Henderson, Byrne, & Duncan-Jones, 1981) had suggested that it would be those who received adequate crisis support, but who perceived it as unhelpful, who would be most likely to have experienced onset, with both depression and perception of support being the results of a prior "plaintive cognitive set" rather than directly associated with each other. However, the Islington sample suggested the exact opposite. It was those who had received only lukewarm support or support from a noncore contact (neither considered "adequate" in terms of the definition of crisis support), and who perceived it as moderately or markedly helpful, who were most likely to have suffered onset (Brown, Andrews, Harris, Adler, & Bridge, 1986).

Another interesting feature of this analysis was the exploration of the relationship between the various measures of social support and self-esteem. It seemed that self-esteem might not be the only mediator between lack of social support and the tendency to generalize hopelessness (Brown et al., 1986). The relationship between support and some kind of general level of hopefulness might be equally important and indeed on occasions prove to be more important. Thus women with helplessness or low self-esteem might well avoid hopelessness if they believed they could count on the help of other masterful people around them to remedy the situation. Figures 2 and 3 convey this perspective. Figure 2 shows how even with support an individual may have such a low initial level of general hopefulness that a provoking agent will cause her to cross the lower threshold critical for generalization toward Beck's negative cognitive triad. Figure 3 conveys how even a generally hopeful individual may succumb to onset if "let down" in a crisis. For example, a woman who is protected against depression by support from her very close friend after, say, hearing that her son was caught thieving, will cease to benefit from that protection once she is let down by her husband when he comments that she has only herself to blame for the son's behavior because of the way she has raised him (a marked negative verbal response).

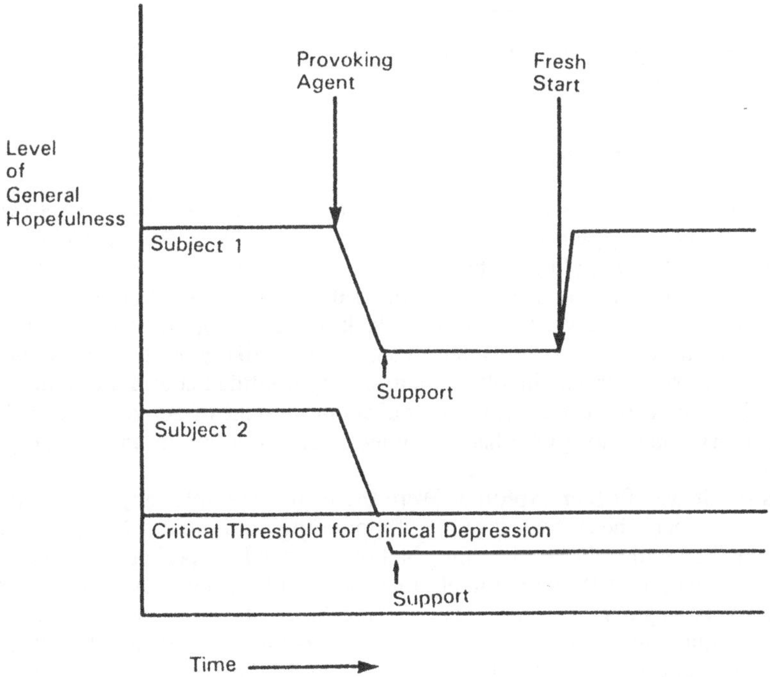

Figure 2 Diagram to illustrate possible differences in the support process between subjects.

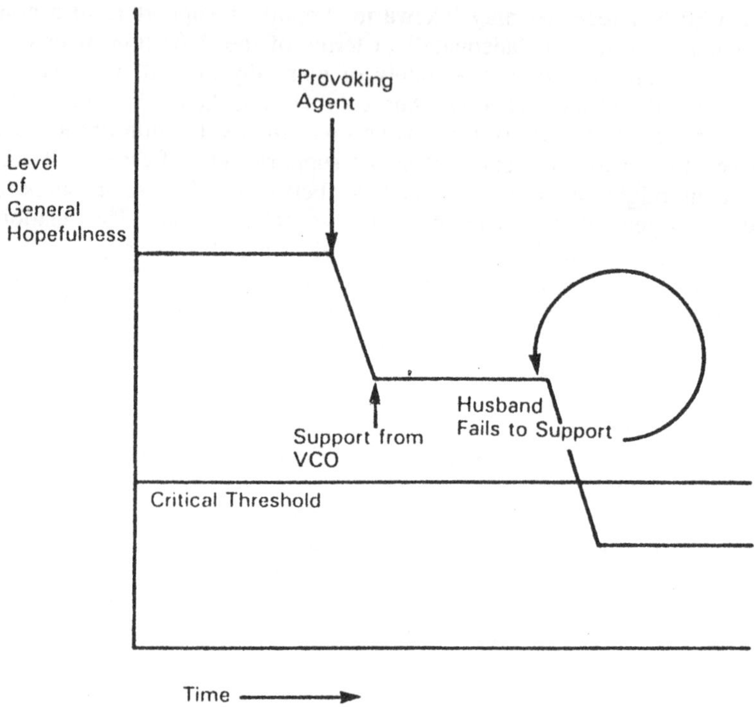

Figure 3 Diagram to illustrate possible process by which "let down" overrides support.

Further Exploration of the Data

Although these results offer much about the process by which crisis support might be protective (against depression), there is still a long way to go before the mechanisms of this hopefulness-maintenance are fully understood. To explore the data in more detail, I took as a starting point the insight that, even among women who had not been let down, the impact of lack of crisis support seems to vary with certain circumstances. Such women seemed more likely to become depressed when lack of crisis support involved them having confided substantially in at least one person, but without receiving an equivalent amount of active emotional support in return, than those who had refrained from confiding in anyone (see Table 2).

This result was further explored. Were there, for example, any systematic differences between these two groups of confiding and nonconfiding women—perhaps in the nature of the crises they had experienced, or perhaps in some aspect of their personalities? It seemed likely that the wealth of longhand descriptions on the F-records might give some leads, on the basis of which the current indices could be refined and new variables created for testing in other samples. With this in mind, I read through all the F-records relating to the key provoking agent that each subject had experienced in the follow-up year. Respondents tended to be more vocal when support had not been forthcoming than when it was adequate. In the

Table 2 Onset of depression in Islington by lack of core crisis support and being "let down"

	Confiding in someone	Not confiding in anyone	Total
Inadequate supportive context			
Lack of core crisis support	52 (12/23)	29 (9/31)	39 (21/54)[a]
Let down with core crisis support	50 (6/12)	N/A	50 (6/12)[a]
Total with inadequate supportive context	51 (18/35)	29 (9/31)	41 (27/66)[b]
With adequate supportive context	4 (3/80)	N/A	4 (3/80)[a,b]

[a] $p < .001$, 2 df.
[b] $p < .001$, 1 df.

latter instances, although praise was not stinted, descriptions were less detailed, usually amounting to simple comments: "She was always there for me when I felt like calling her" or "He was never too busy to hear me out." I concentrated on situations where there had been an inadequate supportive context, and Table 3 reflects the categories developed to deal with various possible reasons for this failure. Most of these reasons could apply both when there was and was not confiding on the subject's part; in other words, her expectation that she would be met by criticism or denial of the problem, leading her to feel there would be no point in trying to confide, could be placed in the same category as her actually receiving such negative responses after having confided.

Further Concrete Examples: Some Reasons for the Failure of the Supportive Context

The ordering of categories in Table 3 is purportedly hierarchical in terms of everyday notions of what constitutes truly sympathetic behavior; that is, behavior encouraging someone to "open the sluices of their heart," as Thomas Hardy put it (Hardy, 1886). A key principle in deciding this has been evidence that the support figure (or O for other person) has been "on the side of" the respondent (or S for subject), a notion clearly akin to Sarason, Sarason, and Pierce's (1990) idea of a sense of self-acceptance. However, such behaviors often seem overdetermined, falling into more than one category. This is conveyed by the overlapping vertical lines at the side of Table 3.

Divided Loyalties

As Argyle has reminded us in Chapter 2, one of the most obvious departures from such a situation of acceptance is when O's loyalties are divided between S and another person. One example was a son's complete refusal to see his mother's point of view when she became distressed at her other son's involvement with an older married woman, or a young woman whose father took her mother's side against her instead of trying to heal the breach when they broke off contact after an argument. In the latter case, S was fortunate that her husband, brother, and sister all took her side and, perhaps because of this, she managed to avoid depression—unlike the first. Situations of divided loyalties need not involve an actual (or even a

Table 3 Some reasons for the inadequacy of the supportive context

Everyday commonsense lack of sympathy

1. Divided Loyalties
   - O loyal to a 3rd in a potential/actual conflict with S.
   - O jealous of a 3rd whom S must nurture.
   - O oblivious to issue of loyalties, so gossips to a 3rd.
   - O takes S's side against a 3rd to an embarrassing excess.
2. O critical
   - O implies S is to blame as the source of the problem.
   - O blames S for perpetuating the problem.
   - O blames S for overreacting, but agrees there is a problem.
   - O denies problem, implicitly criticizing S's sensitivity.
3. O hard
   - O denies problem—so defensive that is incapable of recognizing it.
   - O has unusually resigned pessimistic outlook and thus copes.
   - O denies problem as a member of a different subculture.
4. O protects self
   - O denies problem and is unwilling to perform required tasks by pretending not to hear; asking S not to talk about it; focusing instead on own problems; and distancing self physically.
   - O denies problem and is unwilling to acknowledge its source is O.
   - O is co-victim, so avoids problem to avoid own pain.

Reasons with less lack of sympathy

5. S protects O
   - By not confiding in O because O is co-victim in the crisis and because O has other crises.
6. S protects self
   - By not confiding in anyone S saves face; S is not demeaned by support-seeking; S temporarily distracts self; and S saves O as a resource for the future.
7. O not present regularly enough at crucial time, though well disposed.

Kindly failures of support

8. O tries, but fails to protect S.
   - O tries to distract S, thus prevents S from confiding fully.
   - O takes S's side too strongly and loses credibility.
   - O hurries into looking on the bright side before S is ready.

S does not define situation as a serious enough crisis for confiding

9. S sees stressor as low-key

S refers to the subject or respondent; O refers to other, or support figure.

potential) conflict between S and a third person (although these were not infrequent).

Another slightly different version arises when the subject is involved in caring for a third party, and the potential support figure becomes jealous. Such examples frequently involve invalid relatives; ironically the invalid could well be O's relative rather than S's, yet S would still bear the brunt of O's resentment that she was spending time with the invalid rather than with him. Furthermore, the situations could involve ministering to psychological rather than physical distress: Thus one husband became cold and complaining when S moved in for a month to stay with her sister who had just been left a widow with three young children, and one lover's response to S's distress about her son's being in institutional care was "You know I'm not interested—I hate your son and he hates me."

A third variant of divided loyalties (or, at any rate, deficient loyalty) concerns behavior later on in the support process rather than being part of the direct response to S's confiding: O would later reveal her obliviousness to S's true needs by passing on tittle-tattle about S's intimate experiences to inappropriate people. Even if such Os were apparently friendly and sympathetic to S's face, support was rendered ineffective against depression by S's sense of being devalued in becoming an item of gossip.

A fourth version of divided loyalties can arise when O takes S's side against a third person too strongly. As a result of this, S may become embarrassed, no longer believe any of the reasons O gives for taking her side against the third person, and withdraw from such an "unreliable" O. Occasionally, the volubility of O's loyalty has the added effect of further alienating the third person from S, thus contributing to depressive onset not only via lack of support, but also through exacerbating the stressor (increasing the interpersonal long-term difficulty). Although I did not come across an example of this in Islington, it has been reported in other samples, and for completeness it is included in Table 3. Because O's motives for behaving in this way sometimes seem kindly and sometimes hypocritical, it has been listed both under "everyday lack of sympathy" and under "more kindly failures of support."

The Support Figure Is Critical

One of the most negative responses to intimate confiding is to convey that the sufferer has only herself to blame for the crisis—thus implying that somehow she does not deserve sympathy. One woman's mother told her that "she had made her bed and now she must lie in it" (concerning her marriage, which the mother had done nothing to discourage earlier). Another woman, who had suffered a bad marriage for years and finally got the courage to leave her husband, found that her normally supportive father thought this was going too far. However, he did not merely convey that he thought she should persevere with the marriage, but said she "should grow up and stick with it."

Criticism may not always be quite as explicit as this. It may be conveyed in a fraction of a second and may not involve direct censure, but only a certain surprise that S has allowed such an event to occur. Frequently, however, O will expostulate "how could you?" or refuse to speak to S for some time; unplanned pregnancies were often received in this way, especially by mothers and sisters, but also by close friends whose patience had been sorely tried in giving support through S's previous struggles. This last type of reaction is reminiscent of Cohen's point about the likelihood of support givers withdrawing as their assessment of S's need for support exceeds what they consider appropriate. It reminds us that when S experiences a large number of stressors that seem to form part of one complex, a previously supportive O may start to blame her less for causing than for perpetuating the situation. Thus one woman reported that her sister had lost sympathy with her over her financial hardship and the many crises it fostered: "Somehow she seems to think that by now I should be well off, though I'm sure I don't know how."

Another variant of critical support behavior focuses on criticism of S's reaction to the stressor rather than of her role in causing or prolonging it. This may be particularly common when S is a woman and O is a man, and gender stereotypes are bandied about, perhaps with insults about "whining," "creating unnecessary fuss," and "making mountains out of molehills." One husband told his wife she was "being silly" to get upset when their son was mugged, but fortunately she had a very understanding platonic male friend who saw her through the crisis. Another woman, whose father had stood by her staunchly through the vagaries of her ex-husband's attempts to oust her through an unfair divorce settlement, shattered the support with one remark when the ex-husband tried another maneuver. In order to marry his new wife as a Roman Catholic the ex-husband required S to sign an untrue statement about their previous religious practices. She was most unwilling, but her father suggested she should "do the decent thing" and permit him to remarry, thus implying that she was making too much of the contempt she felt she had been shown by the request. S herself was unsure whether her father had intended to be critical, or whether he was just being single-mindedly practical and had not realized how hurtful his remark had been.

The Support Figure Is Hard-Hearted

The last example raises the question of the ambiguity that often attends the comments of those who imply that "too much fuss" is being made. Although a hard-hearted comment of the kind dealt with in this third category can appear to be genuinely critical of S, it may sometimes issue from a genuine insensitivity on the part of O, who appears not to recognize the distressing nature of S's experiences. This ambiguity is represented in Table 3 by the vertical lines that overlap between the categories "critical," "hard-hearted," and "O protects himself." Although it is often difficult to reach a confident assessment of O's motives from S's account of O's behavior, it seemed that S's own assessment of these motives might well bear some relationship to the outcome. Various subcategories of this hard-heartedness have, therefore, been listed in Table 3. One husband tried to discourage S from having her 7-year-old son referred for psychological assessment and told her that there was really no reason to be concerned about his bad behavior, even though the boy's school was taking it seriously enough to suggest the referral. S saw his denial of the problem as an implicit criticism of her oversensitivity, whereas the interviewer judged that his response might have been defensive rather than critical. The key point, however, is that S, who did in fact become depressed, experienced this as criticism—apparently before the onset of her depression.

Another woman's son was expelled from school, and her ex-husband and her close friend both thought it was "a big laugh." Their response may well have been the result of different subcultural perspectives about the value of schooling rather than reflecting a humorous coping style, but S, who did not become depressed, did not share their attitude and seemed to have no understanding of its origins. Provoking agents involving children were especially likely to elicit reactions of this type where the problem was denied, but those concerning S's work conditions, neighbors, and involvement with other people's problems were also often involved. Financial stressors, on the other hand, usually fell into the next category.

The Support Figure Tries to Protect Himself

There are a number of potentially unpleasant consequences of giving crisis support. First, support givers might be required to perform various tasks, first and not least of which would be to set aside further time to continue listening; second, they might have to acknowledge their own role in causing or perpetuating the crisis; or third, in the case of the crisis affecting them as co-victims, they might have to spend time focusing on something liable to prove especially distressing to them. An example of the second consequence involved one woman's lover, who was clearly not penurious (because he made frequent trips home across the Atlantic). He would pretend not to hear when she tried to raise the topic of her troubled finances with him (the crucial provoking agent). Meanwhile, he was happy to continue to eat most of his meals at her home without contributing financially to their cost (an example of a negative behavioral response in the absence of a negative verbal response). A similar example involved a cohabitee who reacted to being verbally confronted about their joint money problems by staying out late every night in the pub, and coming home too late and too drunk for S—a chronic case of depression—to enter in any kind of effective discussion. (He thus further exacerbated the financial difficulty with his expenditure on drinks.)

In some circumstances, like this last example, all three of these versions of O's self-protection applied simultaneously, and in many at least two were relevant. Siblings would often be evasive and change the topic of conversation when S, who was bearing most of the brunt of nursing an elderly or invalid father, would report on his health or state of mind; and one husband conveyed that he would prefer S not to raise the issue of her possible terminal illness anymore. In this category, again Cohen's (Chapter 8) point about support not being forthcoming when there is no positive reinforcement is evident in the many instances where friends or relatives changed the topic of conversation to focus on their own problems—as if they felt that nothing could be achieved by listening to S. Compared to the previous three groupings in this category, where the support figures were protecting themselves, evading the topic appeared to be less often associated with depressive onset, and perhaps in general was experienced as less upsetting. One woman who saw her husband's behavior in this way told us: "Talking to him is like extracting a tooth—it has to be done gently. Sometimes I mind about this, but sometimes I don't."

The Subject Seeks to Protect Her Close Contacts by Not Confiding

This altruistic behavior usually occurs when O is the co-victim of a crisis, as was the case with one woman who became depressed after her child was killed in a car accident. She did not talk about it with her husband nor he with her. But examples may also be found when O is the source of the problem and S is the victim who wishes to be supportive of O. Thus one woman with a severe housing difficulty felt she could not confide in her husband because it would make him feel defensive about the way he had handled the mortgage. Another, whose electricity was cut off for some time as a result of continuing financial problems, explained that she had not raised the matter with her lover because he "tended to go missing if he heard too much about the past," and he had recently been diagnosed as having cancer of the throat. Another woman's husband had become sexually uninterested in her, and they now slept in separate bedrooms. He was also in pain and, although she had made no attempts to find out about this from the doctor, she saw his condition as a reason why she could not really talk to him "about him being the problem." (As may be seen later, none of the women involved in these last three examples became depressed.)

For obvious reasons, a husband's unemployment was frequently the provoking agent for support behaviors in this category. Another woman became depressed after her confidant was murdered by her (the confidant's) husband, who then shot himself. She told us she could not talk to her mother (her key support figure) about it as she, too, had been fond of this confidant and she did not want to upset her mother. This example, however, was another reminder of how these support behaviors are often overdetermined. She also told us that all she wanted was "just company, not to talk about it." In other words, she also seemed to be protecting herself—an example of the next category.

The Subject Protects Herself by Not Confiding in Anyone

The most frequent example of this type of situation involved S trying to escape her own painful feelings by avoiding consideration of their source (the stressor). Sometimes this was overlaid by an implicit criticism of the support figure's response style—as if it were almost too sympathetic for her to bear. Thus one woman who had recently been diagnosed as having cancer of the tongue avoided talking about it with her husband because he was "too much of a fusspot, and I'm liable to burst out crying if too much fuss is made." However, she would not tell her close woman friend that she had had the diagnosis, let alone talk further to her, despite the fact that this friend was not a "fusspot." This suggests she was also trying to distract herself from having to think about it with her friend.

Sometimes the women were trying to protect themselves by preventing others from knowing about a stressor, which might have shaming features for them. At other times the very act of confiding might be experienced as demeaning. One woman, whose daughter had demanded to return to live with her grandmother who had once looked after her for a couple of years, appeared to have both these reasons (involving shame) for not talking to her very close woman friend about the event. She added that she was a "very private person" and had also refused this friend's offers of practical help when she had to move out of her house. Another woman with a similar outlook about how it was "best not to get too close to anyone" was less reluctant to accept practical support after an operation for the deterioration of a longstanding health problem. But her refusal to confide her distress about this to others was also tempered with contempt: "What's the point of talking to them?" she said. "They're not doctors so they can't help me." Only one other woman in Islington conveyed a similar sense of the potential inferiority of her support figures (again where a medical problem was involved), and she too became depressed.

The Support Figure, Though Well Disposed, Is Not Present Regularly Enough to Give Adequate Support at the Crucial Time

When crisis support fails for this reason, the situation, as with the previous category, is clearly much less unsympathetic than when it is absent for reasons subsumed by the first five categories. Close friends and relatives who were left behind when S moved, or who themselves had to move away for reasons such as a partner's work or the need to care for an invalid relative, were usually unable to provide adequate support, although there were some striking examples of large expenditures on phone calls, which met our threshold for moderate active emotional support. Of course, instances where O or S were not geographically distant from each other, but O chose not to be present, would not be classified here, but in one of the first four categories.

Well-Intentioned Attempts at Supportive Behavior Prove Inappropriate

Although there were no examples of this category in the Islington sample, experience with other studies suggested it should be included for completeness.

Behavior of this type is not only "less unsympathetic" than the previous six categories, but almost kindly and only unfortunately misfiring. Again, ratings were investigator-based and not determined purely by what S thought was appropriate. On the other hand, as with all situational ratings, S's account of O's behavior in the context of S's own response to O was taken seriously. Thus when one S told me that O had started out spending a great deal of time with her, but would tell her after a few minutes that she must stop talking about the provoking agent because it wasn't good for her, it was judged that O's kindly attempt to distract S had been too constricting to prove supportive. Sometimes O did nothing so definite as this, but merely seemed to be hurrying her into looking on the bright side of the situation before this could reasonably be expected. (Bowlby's description of the process of resolving losses [1961] has been taken as the basis for judging what should count as "hurrying" here; he talks of the phases of protest and despair that a person must go through before such detachment can finally be reached after a loss.)

One example involved O saying, on the first day after S's husband had left her, "Well, it's really a good thing he has gone as you won't have to worry anymore when he's out late." Here it was possible to draw a distinction between those Os who could not wait to hasten S into a later phase of mourning and those who could move more or less at S's pace, perhaps encouraging her to progress if she was getting stuck, but conveying a basic acceptance of her emotional reactions. In some instances, the example was included in an earlier category (the first or third), because there was an element of criticism or hard-hearted denigration of S's values implied along with the hurrying. This was done, for example, for a close friend of one psychiatric patient who told her that "it was probably a good thing" that her drug-addict ex-husband had died from a heroin overdose, and professed surprise that S should be upset by the death.

The Subject's Appraisal of the Stressor Is So Low-Key That She Feels No Need to Confide in Anyone

The use of contextual measures of stress along with the situational ratings of support necessitates the creation of a final reason for the absence of adequate crisis support. This occurs when a woman chooses not to confide, not to protect herself or the other person, but because she sees the stressor as less severe than is indicated by the contextual assessment—that is, less severe than would be the average woman's reaction in her biographical circumstances. In her own terms, she thus has no need for support with it. This was distinguished from the other instances where S had chosen not to confide, because it probably represents the type of instance of lack of support least likely to be associated with depressive onset. There was only one such instance in Islington. A woman with a schizophrenic mother was told by a teacher that her daughter was behaving bizarrely at school, making strange grimaces all the time, and asked if she had had her checked by a medical professional. S did not take the suggestion seriously and did nothing that could either diminish (or indeed confirm) the distressing nature of this notion that was put into her head—that her daughter might turn out like her mother. Such defensive strategies are perhaps a version of one of the subvariants of the category of not confiding—dealing with temporary distractions—except that here S succeeds in doing so permanently. Nevertheless, this distraction did not reach the lengths of forgetting the event completely. She reported it quite readily without hesitation in answer to our standard LEDS questions at our interview 4 months later.

DEPRESSION AND THE NATURE OF UNSUPPORTIVE BEHAVIORS

In outlining the various reasons for the inadequacy of the supportive context, it became apparent that there is a tendency for particular categories to be associated with particular types of provoking agents. It was already apparent that depressive onset was more likely after some types of provoking agents (particularly those involving relationships) than after others (see Brown, Bifulco, & Harris, 1987), and it was therefore important to control for this before drawing even tentative conclusions about the relationship between depression and the various ways in which crisis support could fail.

Further Contextual Insights: Relationship Between Reasons for Inadequacy of the Supportive Context and Type of Provoking Agent

Table 4 shows the distribution of type of crucial provoking agent by case and noncase in Islington, as well as in the psychiatric patient sample. It is clear, especially in column 3, that marital provoking agents (such as a husband's loss of job through drinking) are the most frequent precursors of depression in both samples,

Table 4 Types of crucial provoking agents (CPA's) by depression group

	Islington sample			
Type of CPA	Noncases %	Onset cases of depression %	Percent with onset with that CPA type %	Psychiatric patients* %
Relationships				
Marital	17 (20/120)	37 (11/30)	37 (11/31)	44 (48)
Relative	6 (8/120)	7 (2/30)	20 (2/10)	7 (8)
Friend	2 (3/120)	0 (0/30)	0 (0/3)	2 (2)
Child	24 (26/120)	20 (6/30)	18 (6/32)	12 (13)
Death	4 (5/120)	13 (4/30)	44 (4/9)	10 (11)
Pregnancy/birth	4 (5/120)	10 (3/30)	38 (3/8)	4 (5)
Health/accidents				
Subject's	4 (5/120)	3 (1/30)	17 (1/6)	8 (9)
Another's	6 (7/120)	0 (0/30)	0 (0/6)	2 (2)
Other				
Work	3 (4/120)	0 (0/30)	0 (0/3)	7 (8)
Money	21 (26/120)	7 (2/30)	7 (2/28)	2 (2)
Housing	7 (9/120)	3 (1/30)	10 (1/10)	1 (1)
Miscellaneous	2 (2/120)	0 (0/30)	0 (0/2)	1 (1)
Total	100 (120)	100 (30)	20 (30/150)	100 (110)

*Borderline cases (14) excluded.

and that circumstances involving only housing or money problems (i.e., not directly brought about by the husband, such as his loss of job because the firm was closing down), although often rated severe, are more often negotiated without depression. Because of the intensely interpersonal nature of social support, the question arises as to whether the effects shown in Table 4 are simply reflections of the fact that failures of crisis support are most likely to occur after interpersonal stressors. Table 5 considers failures in support and type of provoking agent. (Lack of crisis support rather than inadequacy of supportive context was used in the psychiatric patient sample because, not being prospective, it could not provide a satisfactory measure of "let down," which could rule out the possibility of bias by current depression.)[1]

Although there is a tendency for the more material provoking agents to have elicited more support—in other words, fewer lacked crisis support—the pattern does not consistently dovetail with the trends with onset in Table 4. Although the proportion of death events followed by onset was among the higher percentages in Table 4, the proportion not supported (11%) was one of the lower percentages in Table 5. Although the proportion of provoking agents involving S's health followed by onset was on the low side of those in Table 4 (17%), the proportion unsupported was among the higher percentages in Table 5.

[1]There may be a tendency to romanticize the past in the light of the gloominess felt in the present, and we could not be as confident that the patient's retrospective reports of the degree of support offered by certain key figures before the provoking agents had occurred might not be romantically enhanced in this way. There was thus no way we could be confident in assessing whether or not it was reasonable for such women to have expected crisis support from these figures, and thus no completely trustworthy rating of their being let down when it was not forthcoming.

Table 5 Percentage of women with inadequate supportive context or lack of core crisis support for their crucial provoking agent (CPA) by type of CPA and depression group

	Islington sample			Patient sample
	Noncases	Onsets of depression	Total with a PA	% lack of core crisis support
Type of CPA	% inadequate supportive context			
Relationships				
Marital	45 (9/20)	100 (11/11)	65 (20/31)	58
Relative	13 (1/8)	100 (2/2)	33 (3/10)	86
Friend	100 (2/2)*	N/A	100 (2/2)*	100
Child	38 (10/26)	100 (6/6)	50 (16/32)	86
Death	0 (0/5)	25 (1/4)	11 (1/9)	55
Pregnancy	0 (0/5)	100 (3/3)	38 (3/8)	75
Health				
Subject's	69 (3/5)	100 (1/1)	67 (4/6)	22
Another's	33 (2/6)*	N/A	33 (2/6)*	50
Other				
Work	0 (0/2)*	N/A	0 (0/2)*	38
Money	35 (9/26)*	100 (1/1)	37 (10/27)*	100
Housing	22 (2/9)	0 (0/1)	20 (2/10)	100
Miscellaneous	50 (1/2)	N/A	50 (1/2)	0

*One instance omitted, as not known for crisis support; total = 4 missing.

One possible way to further explore the relationship between lack of support, type of provoking agent, and depression is to follow the initial insight in Table 2 about the apparent lower vulnerability of those who do not confide in anyone, and see whether the type of support failure differed by type of crucial provoking agent. Perhaps the examples of S's health difficulties that lacked crisis support were more benign in terms of depression (i.e., S had *chosen* not to confide in anyone, or the manner in which it was denied was less unsympathetic) than when support was lacking after a crisis with a relative (where perhaps confiding had taken place and been met by one of the most unsympathetic types of responses). This seemed quite possible in view of the masking of those let down in the presentation of Table 5, because they, by definition, always confided and were met by the more unsympathetic responses. Table 6 examines this possibility in the Islington data and uses the nine types of reasons for inadequacy of the supportive context along with the type of crucial provoking agent.

Not only does the rate of depressive onset vary along this dimension of everyday lack of sympathy, but so does the type of provoking agent. To examine these associations, a decision was made to consider the fourth category (trying to protect self) as less unsympathetic than the first three categories, and the dimension was thus dichotomized there rather than farther down the list as in Table 3. Using this division, 54% (19/35) of those who lacked a supportive context for one of the first three reasons (most unsympathetic) became depressed, as compared with only 23% (7/30) of the remainder ($p < .025$). Likewise, 67% (31/46) of the women who had experienced a provoking agent involving a relationship, a death, or a pregnancy had one of the most unsympathetic supportive contexts, as compared with only 21% (4/19) of those with less interpersonal provoking agents ($p < .001$).

The application of the scheme to this data revealed one feature not yet dealt with by the sympathy dimension. One young woman had to be excluded from Table 5 because her support context was difficult to classify due to a discrepancy (not usually encountered) between situationally supportive behavior and the subject's use of the term "very close." She had broken up with her boyfriend after learning of his infidelity, and had confided to a moderate extent in her mother and sister, whose marked active emotional responses could not be counted as adequately supportive because she had been adamant when seen earlier at first interview that they were not "very close others." She continued in this opinion at follow-up, despite their seemingly positive responses to her confiding, and her perception that these efforts were mildly helpful. She had confided in no one else, and thus received an overall rating of inadequate supportive context.

It was tempting to relate her vulnerability to depression (for she became a case) to some internal psychic phenomenon along the lines of Henderson and colleague's plaintive set (1981), which made her unable to feel "very close" to her kin and which prevented her from benefiting from their genuine sympathy. On the other hand, her descriptions of the history of her family relationships suggested that it might well have been correct to classify these two relatives as "unsympathetic" up until the time of the provoking agent. The mother had always made it clear that she thought S was inferior to her sister, and had not been in the habit of encouraging intimate confidences. She even recommended that she move away while the sister continued to live at home. The interviewer was puzzled and toyed with the notion of a "foul-weather friend," someone who only pays attention to a person when

Table 6 Onset of depression, type of crucial provoking agent, and predominant reason for inadequacy of supportive context in Islington sample

Type of CPA	1 Divided loyalties	2 O critical	3 O hard	4 O protects O	5 S protects O	6 S protects S	7 Not present regularly enough	8 Kindly failure of support	9 Crisis defined as too minor	Total
Marital	3/4*	4/6	2/4	—	0/1	—	1/4	—	—	10/19*
Relative	1/2	1/1	—	—	—	—	—	—	—	2/3
Friend	0/1	—	—	—	0/1	—	—	—	—	0/2
Child	0/1	1/3	2/5	0/1	1/2	0/1	2/2	—	0/1	6/16
Death	—	—	1/1	—	2/2	—	—	—	—	3/3
Pregnancy	—	1/1	2/2	—	—	—	—	—	—	3/3
S's health	—	—	—	—	0/3	1/1	—	—	—	1/4
Health of another	—	—	—	0/1	0/1	—	—	—	—	0/2
Work	—	—	—	—	—	—	—	—	—	—
Money	—	1/3	0/1	0/2	0/2	—	0/2	—	—	1/10
Housing	—	—	—	0/1	0/1	—	—	—	—	0/2
Miscellaneous	—	—	—	—	0/1	—	—	—	—	0/1
Total	4/8	8/14	7/13	0/5	3/14	1/2	3/8	—	0/1	26/65*
		54 (19/35)			$p = .025$			23 (7/30)		

*One possible example omitted (a case of depression; see text).

they are in trouble and then extracts confidences, almost as if to gloat over them. She speculated that to have to confide in people whom one has previously distrusted may be even worse than confiding in no one at all (Bernice Andrews, personal communication).

Before leaving Table 6, one query should perhaps be raised. The figure of 38% (3/8) onsets in the seventh category, where support was not forthcoming for geographical reasons, is difficult to interpret because of the small number involved. There did not seem to be any difference according to the recency of moving away by the key figure(s). It was important to consider that, because it could be argued that in instances where O had lived away for some time the relatively high risk of depression might relate less to lack of support than to some intrapsychic phenomenon producing both a liability to depression and an incapacity to establish effective ties with core contacts living closer.

In the patient sample (Table 7) it is the women, whose main reason for lack of crisis support is geographical, who seem to show the greatest number of depressed cases on the less unsympathetic side of the table, and there are many more of these than would be expected from the Islington figures. This might well relate to nosocomial factors. Many of the psychiatric patients in this category had no core contacts at all, let alone any who were geographically close. Women who have no close ties tend to be overselected in psychiatric patient samples, partly because general practitioners tend more often to refer on those cases of depression that they worry may be difficult to cope with at the community level than those whose close ties can ease the doctor's burden of care (Brown, Craig, & Harris, 1985). By contrast, the selection criterion for the Islington sample (the presence of children at home) would have underselected women who had never had any relationships with men, and would therefore also not give a true picture of the proportion whose inadequate supportive context stemmed from a total absence of core contacts. For the moment, it is probably fair to estimate that in most populations the percentage of depressive onsets in this category falls somewhere in between those in Tables 6 and 7.

Other features of Table 7, however, serve to reinforce the impressions gained from Table 6: depression is most frequently associated with situations in the top left quadrant, where relationships are involved and S is made to feel criticized, excluded, or isolated—both by the stressor and by the type of supportive behaviors associated with it.

Table 7 Onset of depression, type of crisis, and predominant reason for lack of core crisis support (psychiatric patients with a provoking agent and no crisis support)

	Predominant reason for lack of core crisis support of crisis				
	Most unsympathetic 1-3	Less unsympathetic 4-6	Not present regularly 7	Other	Total
Relationships, death, and pregnancy 1-6	26	3	20	1	50
Other crises 7-12	1	2	3	0	6
Total	27	5	23	1	56

Proposals for Further Analysis

Future study must involve investigating the possible association of these different types of support failure with aspects of S's personality and features of her personal history, including childhood features such as early inadequate parenting or sexual abuse, which may have brought about any of these. Particularly in the case of those in the category where the subject has no core contacts, and therefore cannot begin to qualify as "supported," it is always possible that prior personality determines both current lack of support and current depression, which are themselves only spuriously associated. An avoidant personality would be the most likely personality characteristic linked to those with no close ties, and already there are indications that nonoptimal confiders (many of whom only confide in noncore contacts because they possess no core contacts whom they could approach instead) show such avoidant features as attitudinal constraints (Andrews & Brown, 1988). An analysis of the patient sample, which has better data on personality, is still in progress, and will focus not only on avoidant tendencies but also on prior hostility, helplessness, nurturance, and defendedness, which may increase the probability of responses to S in the categories of divided loyalties, "O criticizes S," "S protects O," and "S protects S."

CONCLUSION

This discussion has been only a preliminary meander through data still in the process of being analyzed, and the text is confined only to the outcome of clinical depression. Although not intended to be definitive, it may draw attention to various mechanisms by which absence of support potentiates the depressogenic impact of severely threatening experiences. What has emerged so far has an encouragingly familiar ring: everyday common sense conceptions of what is more or less sympathetic coincide with risk of onset of depression. Moreover, the characteristics of the unsupportive behaviors promoting depression are echoed in the losses and interpersonal disappointments that proved to be the most common features of the events provoking onset. Unsupportive behaviors also often recapitulate the emotional themes of the postulated vulnerability and mediating factors—low self-esteem and hopelessness. The unsupportive behaviors implying that the subject deserves criticism or is unworthy of loyalty (the first three categories) predict depression better than the mere absence of supportive input (categories 4–8). These associations highlight the importance of minimizing the person's sense of being disapproved of, neglected, or abandoned, rather than merely alone, if the generalization of hopelessness is to be avoided and depression prevented.

REFERENCES

Abramson, L. Y., Seligman, M. E. P., & Teasdale, J. D. (1978). Learned helplessness in humans: Critique and reformulation. *Journal of Abnormal Psychology, 87,* 49–74.

Andrews, B., & Brown, G. W. (1988). Social support, onset of depression and personality: An exploratory analysis. *Social Psychiatry, 23,* 99–108.

Beck, A. T. (1967). *Depression: Clinical, experimental and theoretical aspects.* New York: Harper & Row.

Bibring, E. (1953). The mechanism of depression. In W. Gaylin (Ed.), *The meaning of despair.* New York: Science House.

Bowlby, J. (1961). Childhood mourning and its implications for psychiatry. *American Journal of Psychiatry, 118,* 481–497.
Brown, G. W., Andrews, B., Harris, T. O., Adler, Z., & Bridge, L. (1986). Social support, self-esteem and depression. *Psychological Medicine, 16,* 813–831.
Brown, G. W., Craig, T. K. J., & Harris, T. O. (1985). Depression: Disease or distress? Some epidemiological considerations. *British Journal of Psychiatry, 147,* 612–622.
Brown, G. W., & Harris, T. O. (1978). *Social origins of depression: A study of psychiatric disorder in women.* London: Tavistock.
Brown, G. W., & Harris, T. O. (1989). *Life events and illness.* New York: Guildford Press.
Fenichel, O. (1946). *The psychoanalytic theory of neurosis.* London: Routledge & Kegan Paul.
Hardy, T. (1886). *The mayor of Casterbridge.* London: Penguin.
Henderson, A. S., Byrne, D. G., & Duncan-Jones, P. (1981). *Neurosis and the social environment.* Sydney: Academic Press.
Sarason, I. G., Sarason, B. R., & Pierce, G. R. (1990). Social support: The search for theory. *Journal of Social and Clinical Psychology, 9,* 133–147.

V

ASSESSMENT AND ANALYSIS

13

Assessment of Social Support

Alan Vaux
Southern Illinois University, USA

In 1977 Dean and Lin wrote that a thorough search of the social support literature "failed to uncover any measures of social support with either known and/or acceptable properties of reliability and validity" (p. 409). A great deal of progress has been made in the assessment of social support since that statement. The field has advanced beyond "the plethora of idiosyncratic measures (often post hoc) exhibiting dubious relevance to unclear concepts" (Vaux & Harrison, 1985, p. 245), which characterized early research. We now have a good number of instruments that have been thoughtfully designed and subjected to some psychometric evaluation.

Yet much remains to be done. House and Kahn's (1985) conclusion "that measurement in this area is still in a fairly primitive state" (p. 102) remains quite accurate as we begin a new decade. First, reviews of the literature continue to reveal many measures consisting of just a few items. For example, over a third of the measures in community studies of the buffer hypothesis reviewed by Kessler and McLeod (1985) consisted of three or fewer items. Such brief measures almost certainly limit reliability, underrepresent the construct they are intended to measure, and attenuate observed empirical relationships.

Second, few measures have found wide acceptance. Most are used faithfully by the research team who developed them. Pragmatic concerns rather than psychometric quality or theoretical relevance seem to dominate many selection decisions. A good many researchers continue to develop new instruments, which are sufficiently redundant to be unhelpful, but sufficiently different to make synthesis of findings more difficult. Indeed, we can state with confidence that mono-operation bias is one problem not evident in the social support literature as a whole, though it remains a problem in individual studies.

Third, few measures have been subjected to anything like a thorough psychometric analysis. Instruments should show an appropriate form of reliability—internal consistency and/or stability over time. Instruments should show both convergent and discriminant validity in the form of a differential pattern of associations with measures of related constructs. Finally, they should show relationships with other variables that are consistent with theoretical predictions. Few, if any, social support measures have been so systematically examined.

Most importantly, as research and theory accumulate, the wealth of meaning in

The author wishes to thank Kelly Rhodes for her assistance in developing an earlier version of the tables summarizing characteristics of the measures.

social support—implicit in the earliest discussions of the topic—is increasingly being recognized, made explicit, and incorporated into both empirical studies and conceptual analysis. In short, that-which-must-be-assessed has grown in scope, depth, and specificity along with our knowledge.

My goal is to briefly review the progress that has been made in the assessment of social support and to outline an agenda for future work. This goal demands discussion of two issues as prerequisites: the scope of social support and the purposes that measures might serve. Only in this context can we assess the psychometric adequacy of measures, let alone address gaps in the armory of available instruments.

THE SCOPE OF SOCIAL SUPPORT

What is it that we wish to measure? A major obstacle to progress has been the sheer scope and complexity of the topic. As noted elsewhere (Vaux, 1988), social support reflects a wealth of ideas including "belonging, bonding, and binding; attributes of groups, relationships, and persons; and processes that are social, behavioral, cognitive, and affective in nature" (p. 33). Social support, per se, is simply not a viable theoretical construct and it cannot be measured. Rather, social support refers to a complex and dynamic process involving transactions between individuals and their social networks within a social ecology. Broadly, it is a process whereby people manage social resources to meet social needs and to enhance and complement their personal resources for meeting demands and achieving goals (Vaux, 1988).

From this model, we can identify a number of distinct social support constructs that are measurable. The key constructs include support resources, incidents, behavior, appraisals, and orientation. These are defined here. Support network resources are that subset of a person's social network to whom they routinely turn or could turn for assistance in dealing with demands or achieving goals. Support incidents are social situations in which goals and rules having to do with the provision and receipt of assistance have prominence. Support behaviors are specific acts of assistance occurring within the context of a relationship and during support incidents. Support appraisals are the person's subjective evaluative beliefs regarding network resources and the assistance that they provide. Finally, support orientation (or network orientation) is a relatively stable set of beliefs regarding the risks and utility of seeking help from the network, which likely influences the development, maintenance, and use of support resources, as well as resulting support appraisals.

Table 1 presents some basic theoretical propositions involving these constructs (for a more complete discussion, see Vaux, 1988, Chapters 1 & 3). These constructs, not some vague and wooly concept termed "social support," should be what measures are designed to operationalize. Indeed, in an implicit and imperfect fashion, they often are.

Unfortunately, the conceptual differentiation just outlined does not complete our task. Four other issues warrant serious attention: support mode, support source, research focus, and negative aspects of support.

Table 1 Some theoretical propositions

Support resources
Must be developed and maintained
Will show systemic properties
Will be influenced by personal and social factors
May self-activate or be mobilized
May be utilized on a routine and crisis basis
In response to chronic or acute difficulties
May be affective, cognitive, or practical
Supportive behaviors
May be preferred or requested
In response to stressors or distress
May be of several modes (emotional, practical, etc.)
May vary in quality, fit, and timing
Depends on personal, network, and context factors
May serve active or palliative coping functions
Support appraisals
May depend on quantitative and qualitative features of support network resources
May depend on quality, fit, and timing of supportive behavior
May be relatively stable except in times of crisis
May be the most critical aspect of the support process in terms of well-being

Support Mode

The earliest discussions of social support noted that people could help each other in a variety of ways. That is, assistance might involve different activities (e.g., listening, encouraging, advising, sharing tasks, etc.) and serve different functions (e.g., expressing appreciation or caring, informing, providing evaluative feedback, etc.). Simple distinctions (tangible vs. intangible, instrumental vs. expressive) have given way to more complex typologies, reviews of which suggest consensus on some six modes of support (Barrera & Ainlay, 1983; House, 1981; Vaux, Riedel, & Stewart, 1987). An overview of support mode typologies (both functions and activities) is presented in Table 2.

The importance of support mode in assessment cannot be overstated. Quite simply, help is context-specific. A favorite macabre image illustrates the point: picture a man offering sympathy to a drowning friend and, later, a rope to his widow. More seriously, specifying support modes is crucial. The buffer hypothesis was revised in recognition that a perfectly respectable form of helping might be disastrously mismatched to the context. In their influential review, Cohen and Wills (1985) proposed that support buffers the effects of stressors only when it matches the functional demands created by those stressors. I suggested that this was only one of several "support-specificity" models (Vaux, 1988), each of which requires measures of distinct modes of support to be tested. Yet, as we shall see, measurement instruments often ignore modes of support.

Source of Support

Again, early discussions recognized that people in disparate relationships, from beloved spouse to neighborhood acquaintance, might contribute support to a focal person. An individual's support resources are somewhat like an American football team. Certainly there are key players on whom most attention is focused. Yet most

Table 2 Forms of social support: Functions and Activities (compiled by the author)

			Functions			
Lin	——— Instrumental ———			——— Expressive ———		
Pattison	——— Instrumental ———			——— Affective ———		
Weiss		Social integration	Guidance	Attachment	Reassurance of worth	Social integration
Cobb				Love	Esteem	Belonging
House	—— Instrumental ——		Information (environment)	Emotional	Information (self-eval.)	—
Wills	—— Instrumental ——		Information	Motivational	Esteem	Social comparison
			Activities			
Caplan	Concrete aid	Practical service	Information prob. solving	Emotional mastery	Feedback	Rest and recuperation
Foa	Goods	Service	Information	Love	Status	—
Tolsdorf	——— Tangible assistance ———		Advice	Intangible support	Feedback	—
Hirsch	——— Tangible assistance ———		Cognitive guidance	Emotional support	Social reinforcement	Socializing
Gottlieb	——— Problem solving ———			Emotional sustenance	—	—
Barrera	Material aid	Behavioral assistance	Guidance	Intimate interaction	Feedback	Positive social int.
Vaux	Financial assistance	Practical assistance	Advice/ guidance	Emotional support	—	Socializing

team members serve some important function; there are a great many reserve players and some specialists who are crucial in a particular circumstance. The decision to focus on an intimate relationship or key confidants, or to cast a broader net that will include family, friends, workmates, and perhaps some "specialists" and "reserves," is an important one for the researcher. It is critical if the study of social support is to be linked with the research on close relationships and social roles. Again, measurement instruments have not always given adequate attention to source of support.

Research Focus

The focus of research is another important issue. Support may be viewed as a general process with particular manifestations or as a collection of unique processes pertaining to, for example, adapting to chronic illness, negotiating the transition of a divorce, resisting the debilitating effects of poverty, or quitting smoking. The former view facilitates theoretical integration and synthesis of empirical findings, but makes intensive study of a particular issue more difficult. The reverse is true of the "unique process" view.

The issue is comparable to that of "emic" and "etic" in cross-cultural research. These are complementary perspectives—both of which are valuable. We can promote synthesis and avoid disintegration of the field to the extent that global measures can be adapted to specific foci, such as support in the context of illness, unemployment, grief, caring for a handicapped family member, development of vocational identity, and so forth. Similarly, microanalytic studies that focus on the details of particular support exchanges or situations need to be integrated into the broader literature. Thus flexibility of application is an important feature of a measure.

Negative Aspects of Support

Social interaction does not always run smoothly. This is a complicated issue but, clearly, enhancing one's resources through social ties involves both liabilities and benefits (Eckenrode & Gore, 1981; Kessler, McLeod, & Wethington, 1985; Rook, 1984, Chapter 11). The social network may include individuals who actively undermine rather than support. The support network may include individuals who are unreliable or who provide support at great cost (conflict, demands). Maintaining network relationships or sharing the burdens of others may involve negative effects. Supportive behavior may be enthusiastic but inept. Normatively supportive relationships may be appraised as unsupportive. A number of writers have noted such processes or demonstrated them empirically. Yet, conceptual clarification and explication of relevant processes are still in the early stages and these issues have not been addressed in most measurement instruments.

Social support is both extremely broad and complicated in scope. Mapping out the conceptual territory is an essential prerequisite to evaluating instruments. The single most important question in assessment is "What is it that we are trying to measure?" Let us now turn to a related question.

GOALS OF ASSESSMENT

Why are we measuring social support phenomena? There are many goals of assessment in this area. Some of the more prominent include (a) epidemiological research; (b) studies of support in the context of particular stressors, relationships, or social situations; (c) evaluation of interventions targeting support; and (d) clinical assessment of individuals. These are not intended to exhaust all forms of social support research, but rather to illustrate some implications for measurement.

Epidemiological Research

Mainstream epidemiological research is concerned with the distribution of problems in populations (e.g., Lin, Dean, & Ensel, 1986). Quite similar is research in community psychology that is aimed at understanding variations in risk for psychological problems or in well-being. Much of this research involves large samples from which data are collected, most often, by survey through brief measures (cf. Kessler & McLeod's review of community studies, 1985). Here, global measures of support, focusing on the general quantity of support resources or on general support appraisals, are the norm. However, relatively extensive work has been done in developing theory-based instruments within the context (e.g., Lin et al., 1986; Turner, Frankel, & Levin, 1983). When brevity is important, the reliability, validity, and selection of measures become even more crucial.

Focused Studies

The study of particular stressors, relationships, and social situations requires some specificity in support measures. General measures of support resources, behavior, or appraisals may be a poor choice if research questions address, for example, support for controlled drinking, support within a marital or work relationship, or support in the workplace or neighborhood. Yet, as noted earlier, there is sense in adapting general measures rather than using a host of measures designed for ostensibly unique situations. Thus the most useful general measures are those that are adaptable and, in particular, that allow specification of support modes, support sources, and the stressor in relation to which support is available or provided. Measures that are not adaptable will be of little use in the study of particular stressors or relationships.

Regarding social situations, I will just note that that context has been largely ignored in the social support process. In particular, assessment of social support incidents is in its infancy. Quite often, focused studies will involve relatively small samples that can be assessed more intensively. When this is the case, there is a lot to recommend using both an adapted general measure and one tailored for the issue at hand. Such a strategy should greatly facilitate the synthesis of findings from different areas of social support.

Support Interventions

A number of issues arise in the evaluation of social support programs, whether support processes are the target of intervention or the medium through which change is sought (Gottlieb, 1983, Chapter 18; Vaux, 1988). Most important is that assessment should fit the component of the support process that is anticipated to change. This seems rather obvious, but the prevalence of misdirected measurement in program evaluation suggests that the point bears repeating. Programs that target communication with intimates should not be evaluated with broad measures of support resources. Those that target appraisals should assess appraisals. Those that target the development of relationships should not expect dramatic increases in network size overnight. As in the case of psychotherapy, change resulting from nonspecific programs may be very difficult to assess.

Intact true experiments are a rarity in social intervention. Quasiexperiments shift the burden of proof to comparisons over time. Thus data on the stability of support measures is very helpful in this context. The support process is a dynamic one. At least under some circumstances, aspects like network orientation or support appraisals may be relatively stable. But some fluctuation in resources—in network membership or the quality of component relationships—is to be expected, and enacted supportive behavior may change dramatically as stressors are encountered and managed. In short, data on the stability and fluctuation of measures are desirable.

Clinical Assessment

Finally, assessment might be undertaken for clinical purposes. Some likely issues include the following: Does an individual have a negative orientation that obstructs the use of rich support resources? Are a client's support appraisals negatively distorted? Does a client have a support network that will facilitate a difficult but healthy transition? Does the client have untapped support resources? Is the client inept at handling support incidents? Not only are support processes an important contextual consideration in individual change, but many traditional clinical issues can and no doubt will be reconceptualized as support issues. It is important that clinicians are familiar with the complexity of the processes involved, that they be persuaded of the usefulness of suitable assessment instruments, and that more normative data become available. The major problem here is that most assessment is conducted to answer a referral question. Assessment as a prelude to therapy is employed by a minority of more research-oriented clinicians. On the positive side, brevity is not a central concern and intensive individual assessment encourages the use of multiple instruments.

Social support instruments must serve a wide variety of purposes. These make different demands on measures. Some emphasize brevity, readability, and ease of administration. Others emphasize adaptability to specific research foci. Still others require sensitivity that allows detection of change over time. All these purposes are served best by measures that are based explicitly on theory, that have established reliability and validity, that are adaptable, and that both sample and yield scores reflecting different sources and modes of support in relation to either general or specific stressors or contexts.

OVERVIEW OF MEASURES

The issues mentioned previously relate to more traditional psychometric concerns. All measures should be reliable, but some need only be internally consistent, whereas others should show stability over time. Demonstrations of an instrument's validity should be tailored to the meaning of the relevant theoretical construct and related support processes, as well as to the pragmatics of intended use, such as length, complexity, and so forth. The obvious should not need stating: but often the description of constructs is implicit or ambiguous, the statement of processes is loose, and tests of validity are tangential.

With the aforementioned constructs, issues, and goals as a backdrop, I would like to note progress made in the assessment of social support. Current measures of support resources, behavior, and appraisals will be briefly reviewed in relation to available reliability and validity, and strengths and weaknesses (for a more complete review, see Vaux, 1988, Chapter 2). The measures included do not exhaust all those in use. Rather, they were selected to illustrate current efforts and, in particular, to note some special features and limitations, and to highlight where more work is most urgently needed.

Support Resources

Quite a few instruments address support network resources, either alone or with other support constructs. Some basic features of those selected here are presented in Table 3. These measures are diverse, with different strengths and weaknesses. Some of these differences are worth noting.

First, by design or accident, measures differ in the networks they identify. For example, the Social Network Questionnaire (SNQ: Hirsch, 1979) asks respondents to list "significant others." In contrast, the Social Relationship Scale (SRS: McFarlane, Neale, Norman, Roy, & Streiner, 1981) asks respondents to list persons with whom they discuss problems in each of six life domains. The Barrera (1981) and Vaux (1982) measures focus on networks providing particular modes of support (six and five, respectively). The Social Support Questionnaire (SSQ: Sara-

Table 3 Support resource measures—Basic features

Measures	Network nomination	Modes	Structural variables	Composition	Relationship quality	Adaptable to focused research	Format
SNQ Hirsch (1979)	Significant others with whom they will interact		Size, density, boundary density	Relationship type	—	Possibly	Questionnaire
SRS[a] McFarlane, Neale, Norman, Roy, & Streiner (1981)	Persons with whom problems in six areas of life are discussed	Emotional, advice, feedback	Size	Some data, but not usually scored	(Tables 7 & 8)	Yes, to particular life problems and possibly sources	Questionnaire
SSQ[b] Sarason, Levine, Basham, & Sarason (1983)	Broad sampling through 27 situations in which support is important	Emotional, primarily	Size	Some data, but not scored	(Tables 7 & 8)	Not easily because of unique items	Questionniare
SSNI Fischer (1982)	Specific questions to elicit persons outside the home who provide support	Counseling Companionship Practical assistance	Size	Relationships	(Tables 7 & 8)	Possibly	Interview
ASSIS[c,d] Barrera (1981)	Specific questions to elicit persons who provide six modes of support	Material aid Physical assistance Intimate interaction Guidance Feedback Social participation	Size Conflicted network size	Age, sex, ethnicity	Conflict	Yes to sources Possibly to specific stressors	Interview

SSR Vaux & Harrison (1985)	Specific questions to elicit persons who provide five modes of support	Emotional Socializing Practical assistance Financial assistance Advice/ guidance	Size (density) Mode-specific size	Relationship Setting Age, sex, or ethnicity	Closeness Reciprocity Complexity	Yes to sources Possibly to specific stressors	Questionnaire or telephone interview
MISS[e] Veiel (1990)	Specific questions to elicit persons actually or potentially providing support in everyday or crisis situations	Every day/crisis Emotional/ instrumental	Size both total & specific to four functional cagegories	Gender, age, role (kin, nonkin)	Complexity (frequency) (proximity)	Yes, designed to accommodate changes, both focusing and broadening with respect to sources, functions, stressors	Interview (translated into several languages)

[a,b,c]These measures also involve assessment of support appraisals.
[d,e]These measures also involve some assessment of enacted support behavior.

son, Levine, Basham, & Sarason, 1983) elicits network nominations through multiple items, designed to reflect "the great variety of situations in which social support might be important to people" (p. 129), though most appear to reflect emotional support networks. Barrera (1981), among others, has noted the importance of the initial procedure for eliciting network nominations. I, too, favor asking the respondent, through a series of relevant questions, to list people who provide particular modes of support.

Measures differ in the information they provide on structural aspects of support networks. All yield a network size score, though some provide mode-specific size scores (Vaux, 1982). Some measures focus almost exclusively on size, at least with respect to structural features. Others provide either crude (Vaux, 1982) or detailed assessment (Hirsch, 1979) of network density. Such structural features may be important: Hirsch and Reischl (1985) found that a denser parent-friend boundary was associated with poor or good adjustment among adolescents with or without, respectively, an arthritic or depressed parent. Structural features such as boundary density may be important, but are not provided by most resource measures.

Several measures yield information on the composition of the network in terms of characteristics such as age, sex, ethnicity, relationship, and context (e.g., Barrera, 1981; Vaux, 1982). Like others, I have proposed the resource value of a large and diverse network in terms of accessibility, stamina, expertise, information, and perspective, yet diversity has not often been examined in support network studies.

The quality of network relationships (as opposed to the support they provide) is not assessed by most of the measures. On the other hand, the Social Support Resources (SSR) measure (Vaux, 1982) taps the closeness, reciprocity, and complexity of each relationship, and these resource variables have been found to predict support appraisals. The Arizona Social Support Interview Schedule (ASSIS) (Barrera, 1981) is noteworthy in assessing network relationships that also involve conflict. Several of the measures assess the quality of the support provided in some fashion (e.g., SSQ, SRS, ASSIS), which is viewed here as a form of support appraisal.

Table 4 presents information on the reliability and validity of the instruments. A complete report on the validity coefficients for each measure is beyond the scope of this paper. Rather the table gives a sense of the kind of validity data available. Stability data, available for several measures, is encouraging, without leaving room for complacency. Relatively little data are available on the convergent validity of measures, even less on discriminant validity. Most of the measures have demonstrated associations consistent with theoretical predictions, particularly with respect to psychological distress.

Support Behavior

There are few measures of support behavior. Two are discussed here: the Inventory of Socially Supportive Behavior (ISSB) (Barrera, Sandler, & Ramsay, 1981) and the Social Support Behavior (SSB) Scale (Vaux, 1982). The measures have a number of features in common (Table 5). Both are multi-item instruments that assess several modes of support through specific acts. The ISSB was designed to assess enacted supportive behavior. The SSB, on the other hand, was designed to assess available supportive behavior, but has also been adapted as an enacted

Table 4 Support resource measures—Reliability and validity

Measure	Samples	Stability	Internal consistency	Convergent validity	Discriminant validity	Theoretically predicted relationships	Comments
SNQ Hirsch (1979, 1980)	College Women in transition	—	—	—	—	Denser boundary between family & friend networks was associated with more symptoms, poorer mood, lower self-esteem & lower enacted support	Procedure for assessing density is cumbersome, but has yielded some interesting findings
SRS McFarlane, Neale, Norman, Roy, & Streiner (1981)	College Community	.91 (1 week)	—	—	—	Variations in network size across marital status groups	Brief, fairly adaptable resources and stressors Little data on nature or quality of resources
SSQ Sarason, Levine, Basham, & Sarason (1983)	College	.90	.97	—	Modest association with support satisfaction	Associated with support satisfaction, extroversion (females), optimism, & low depression, hostility, & (for women) anxiety; also with greater internal locus of control, self-esteem, less cognitive interference while working on a frustrating task	Listing network members across all situations is time consuming, esp. if data on network composition and reln. quality are not scored Unclear which modes of support are sampled; yet the SSQ provides a useful measure of resources & appraisals

(*Table continues on next page*)

Table 4 Support resource measures—Reliability and validity (*Continued*)

Measure	Samples	Stability	Internal consistency	Convergent validity	Discriminant validity	Theoretically predicted relationships	Comments
SSNI Fischer (1982)	Community	—	—	—	—	Variations in mode-specific networks across demographic groups Associated with happiness	Brief measure developed for large scale surveys Multiple modes Limited yield
ASSIS Barrera (1981)	College Pregnant adolescents	Size (.88) Support need (.80) Conflicted network size (.54) 74% overlap in nominations (2 days)	.52	—	Modest associations with enacted support, behavior and satisfaction	Conflicted network size and support need were associated with distress Some buffer effects observed	Strong measure Multiple modes and yields a good deal of information on conflict and need
SSR Vaux & Harrison (1985)	College Community	Size (.72) Closeness (.31) Complexity (.48) Reciprocity (.46) (6 weeks)	Index of resources (.76)	—	Modest associations with support behavior & appraisals	Related to negative network orientation and loneliness	Multiple modes and yields a good deal of data (some mode-specific) including relationship quality

MISS Veiel (1990)	Discharged depressed patients College Parents of children with cancer	Many specific variables .70–88 (4 weeks) .42–.79 (6 months)	—	Association of kin vars. with PSS-family, & nonkin with PSS-friend (inconsistent across samples)	Modest associations among functional category scores (Across samples .44–.65 for kin, .42–.59 for nonkin variables) Differentiation of resource & appraisal components in factor analysis	Nonkin vars. associated with low loneliness and depression	Complex instrument designed to incorporate many facets of support process

Table 5 Support behavior measures—Basic features

Measure	Concept	Mode	Source	Adaptable to focused research	Rating	Format
ISSB Barrera, Sandler, & Ramsay (1981)	Activities directed at assisting others in mastering emotional distress, sharing tasks, giving advice, teaching skills, and providing material aid	Material aid Practical assistance Intimate interaction Guidance Feedback Social participation (Mode subscales vary with factor analysis)	Others	Yes with specific stressors and sources	Frequency of occurrence within previous month	Questionnaire
SSB Vaux (1982); Vaux, Stewart, & Riedel (1987)	Specific acts of assistance reflecting five modes	Emotional* Socializing* Practical assistance* Financial assistance* Advice/guidance*	Family* Friends*	Yes with specific stressors and sources	Likelihood that others would provide each form of assistance (available form) Checklist (enacted form)	Questionniare

*Indicates subscale scores yielded; otherwise content is sampled only.

measure. As enacted measures, both could be adapted to target particular time periods, assistance with particular stressors, or support from particular types of relationships. (The original form of the SSB asked about family and friends separately.) Although the ISSB reflects different modes of support behavior, designated subscales for these do not exist. Rather, Barrera and Ainlay (1983) and others have examined the structure of the instrument through factor analysis, the results of which have not always been consistent. In contrast, the SSB has designated subscales and yields scores for each mode of support behavior.

Table 6 presents some of the information available on the reliability and validity of the two measures. Both instruments have been studied fairly extensively. In particular, considerable effort was made to establish the predicted subscale structure of the SSB and the discriminant as well as convergent validity of the subscales.

Support Appraisals

Many support instruments fall into the support appraisals category (Table 7). Some of these involve ratings of satisfaction (Sarason et al., 1983), sufficiency (Barrera, 1981), or helpfulness (McFarlane et al., 1981), which are integrated with support resource measures. Many can stand alone or be used as part of a battery. Some address support appraisals within a focused set of relationships like the family or work group (Holahan & Moos, 1982), whereas others yield scores for subgroups like family and friends (Procidano & Heller, 1982; Vaux et al., 1986). Some have an elaborate theory-base and yield scores reflecting appraisals with respect to different functions or social needs (Cohen & Hoberman, 1983; Russell & Cutrona, 1984; Turner et al., 1983; Vaux, 1987).

Table 8 presents some of the reliability and validity information available on these measures. More work has been done with this category of instruments than any other. They have been related to an enormous variety of variables. Indeed, one criticism that can be made is that tests of validity have sometimes been unsystematic. The theoretical rationale for predicted relationships has not always been obvious. Again, discriminant validity data are rare. Nonetheless, a good deal of data upholds the quality of these measures.

CONCLUSION

Much progress has been made in the assessment of social support. Quite a few carefully constructed measures with some reliability and validity data have been published. Yet the complexity of social support processes demands quite an arsenal of measures, and quite a few instruments confuse support resources, behavior, and appraisals, thus providing a good measure of none. A good many measures fail to address such basic dimensions of the support process as mode or source; others sample content across these dimensions, but fail to provide mode- or source-specific scores. Finally, there is great need for measures that can serve general purposes, but that can be adapted to particular research foci.

We can draw several conclusions about the assessment of social support. (a) The majority of established measures focus on global support rather than support in relation to a particular stressor or life goal. (b) Assessment of support processes has been relatively macro-analytic: measurement of naturalistic support incidents

Table 6 Support behavior measures—Reliability and validity

Measure	Samples	Stability	Internal consistency	Convergent validity	Discriminant validity	Theoretically predicted relationships	Comments
ISSB Barrera, Sandler, & Ramsay (1981); Barrera (1981)	College Pregnant adolescents	.88 (2 days)	.93	(see SSB)	(see SSB) Mode scales derived through factor analysis	Life events, distress Life events, distress, network size, cohesive family climate	Samples modes but factor analyses yield inconsistent structure Should attempt to validate original designed scales
SSB Vaux (1982); Vaux, Riedel, & Stewart (1987)	College (several samples)	—	.85 (total) Subscales consistently above .90	Moderate with ISSB subscales	Modest to poor with ISSB subscales Confirmatory factor analysis	Items correctly classified Subscales sensitive to mode-specific deficiencies in role-adoption manipulation Modes varied by nature of stressor	Need more on the enacted version Also, brief version available with superior content saturation

Table 7 Support appraisal measures—Basic features

Measure	Dimensions of appraisal	Source	Ratings	Format
ASSIS[a] Barrera (1981)	Sufficiency of enacted support	Various, but not usually scored	Insufficient, optimal, or excessive	Questionnaire
SRS McFarlane, Neale, Norman, Roy, & Streiner (1981)	Helpfulness of network support	Various, but not usually scored	Helpfulness/unhelpfulness	Questionnaire
SSQ Sarason, Levine, Basham, & Sarason (1983)	Satisfaction with support in diverse situations	Various, but not usually scored	Satisfaction	Questionnaire
DIRF Hirsch (1979, 1980)	Satisfaction with interactions re emotional, socializing, tangible assistance, social reinforcement, cog. guidance	Family, friends	Satisfaction/dissatisfaction	Log
PSS Procidano & Heller (1983)	Perception that needs for support, information, and feedback are met	Family* Friends*	Agreement with items (T/F)	Questionnaire
FRI Holahan & Moos (1982)	Cohesiveness Expressiveness Conflict (subscale scores combined)	Family	Agreement with statements (T/F)	Questionnaire

(*Table continues on next page*)

Table 7 Support appraisal measures—Basic features (*Continued*)

Measure	Dimensions of appraisal	Source	Ratings	Format
WRI Holahan & Moos (1982)	Involvement Peer cohesion Supervisor support (subscale scores combined)	Work relationships	Agreement with statements (T/F)	Questionnaire
ISEL Cohen & Hoberman (1983)	Self-esteem* Appraisal* Belonging* Tangible*	Various, not usually scored	Agreement with statements (T/F)	Questionnaire
SPS Russel & Cutrona (1984)	Attachment* Integration* Opportunity for nurturance* Reassurance of worth* Reliable alliance* Guidance*	Various, not usually scored	Agreement with statements	Questionnaire
PSR Turner, Frankel, & Levin (1983)	Attachment* Integration* Reassurance of worth* Reliable alliance* Guidance*	Family* Friends* (alternate scoring based on factor analysis)	Agreement with items	Questionnaire
RKS Turner, Frankel, & Levin (1983)	Loved/cared for Respected* Involved*	Others	Comparison of self to others described in vignettes	Questionnaires Interviews
SSA[b] Vaux et al. (1986)	Loved/cared for* Respected* Involved*	Family* Friends*	Agreement with items	Questionnaire Telephone interview

[a]These measures also involve assessment of support resources.
[b]Scales reflecting these dimensions emerged in factor analyses with five samples (Vaux, 1987).
*Indicates subscale scores yielded; otherwise content is sampled only.

Table 8 Support appraisal measures—Reliability and validity

Measure	Samples	Stability	Internal consistency	Convergent validity	Discriminant validity	Theoretically predicted relationships	Comments
ASSIS Barrera (1981)	College Pregnant adolescents	.69 (2 days)	.33 .50	—	—	Related to fewer negative events, less need for support, & less distress	Useful measure of appraisals of enacted supported esp. focused research
SRS McFarlane, Neale, Norman, Roy, & Streiner (1981)	College	.78 (.54–.94) (1 week)	—	—	—	Varied across marital groups and non- vs. distressed couples	Useful as part of resource measure esp. in focused research
SSQ Sarason, Levine, Basham, & Sarason (1983)	College	.83 (4 weeks)	.94	—	SSQ-N & -S scores are fairly independent	Associated with lower anxiety, depression hostility, & neuroticism among women, and lower depression among men	Focus on satisfaction Broad sampling of situations though most are emotional support related
DIRF Hirsch (1979, 1980)	College	—	—	Global score related to interviewer ratings	Mode-specific appraisals are fairly indpendent (.22–.51)	Associated with low density and low boundary density networks	Focus on satisfaction Unique log methodology
PSS Procidano & Heller (1983)	College	.83	Family (.89) Friends (.90)	—	Subscales fairly independent (.24–.35)	Associated with low distress, few negative events, and various social assets	Complex appraisals

(Table continues on next page)

Table 8 Support appraisal measures—Reliability and validity (*Continued*)

Measure	Samples	Stability	Internal consistency	Convergent validity	Discriminant validity	Theoretically predicted relationships	Comments
FRI Holahan & Moos (1982)	Community	—	.89	—	—	Related to low depression, psychosomatic symptoms, & anxiety (inconsistent across gender)	Brief, simple format Focus on family is both strength & limitation
WRI Holahan & Moos (1982)	Community	Source instrument (WES) scales .69–.86 (1 month)	.88	—	—	Similar to above	Brief, simple, focus on workplace
ISEL Cohen & Hoberman (1983)	College	—	.60–.77 (self-esteem lowest)	—	Subscales fairly independent (.19–.56)	Related to support behavior, low depression Showed buffer effect in predicting depression	Complex multifaceted appraisals Unclear conceptual basis
SPS Russell & Cutrona (1984)	College Older adults	—	.61–.80 (various samples)	—	Subscales are intercorrelated (> .50)	Related to social network vars., satisfaction with relationships, loneliness Buffered life event effects on distress	Theory-based, brief, multifaceted Content saturation of scales needs improvement

PSR Turner, Frankel, & Levin (1983)	College Physically disabled Expatients	—	.75–.87 (family & friend scales)	Related to RKS	Social provisions not differentiated	Related to poor network resources, low anxiety, anger, and depression	Useful brief measure, but does not yield dimensional "provision" appraisals
RKS Turner, Frankel, & Levin (1983)	College New mothers Adults with hearing loss Expatients	—	.73–.87	Related to PSS	Separate from distress items in factor analysis	Related to network resources, low anxiety, anger, and depression	Novel vignette methodology
SSA Vaux et al. (1986)	College Community	Friend (.71) Family (.80) (6 weeks)	.84–.90 (for both sample types)	Related to seven other appraisal measures incl. mother reported FRI	Moderate patterns of divergence by source and dimensions of appraisal	Related to support resource and behavior, low depression, negative affect, loneliness, positive affect, life satisfaction, & happiness	Useful brief measure Adapted for various formats and settings

has been minimal. (c) The negative aspects of the social support process, though recognized, have not been well integrated into current measures. (d) There are a great many measures of support network resources, though many ignore distinct modes of support and most fail to exploit structural aspects of network analysis. (e) There are few measures of supportive behavior, though these tap distinct support modes and sources. (f) Measures of support appraisals abound, but often emphasize global satisfaction rather than an evaluative appraisal of social provisions or fulfilled social needs.

This author proposes several recommendations for the selection of instruments. (a) Researchers should include measures of support resources, behavior, and appraisals, whenever possible. (b) Researchers should consider carefully which component of the support process—resources, behavior, appraisals—is most relevant to their research question and select measures accordingly. (c) Generally, measures that sample or, better still, provide separate scores for several modes and sources of support should be selected. (d) When the research question concerns a particular mode (e.g., emotional) or source (e.g., family) of support, measures that have this focus, that include it, or that can be adapted should be selected. (e) In studies where measurement must be severely restricted, the focus should be on support appraisals, emotional support, and/or intimate ties. (f) Generally, in clinical assessment, priority should be given to network orientation, support appraisals, and support resources, in that order. (g) In social support interventions, measures should be selected to target the focus of change, but in nonfocused interventions priority should be given to support resource measures that would be sensitive to growth in the network and to quality of relationships.

I also offer some recommendations for research and instrument development. (a) As much as possible, the term "social support" should give way to more precise terms like support resources, behavior, and appraisals (or some such constructs). (b) Researchers should routinely pose research questions and discuss findings within the framework of such a multiconstruct perspective. (c) Both current measures and new measures need to be evaluated in terms of discriminant validity. (d) Brief versions and alternate presentation forms of existing instruments should be developed. (e) Negative aspects of the support process should be incorporated better into measures (e.g., conflicted network relationships, inept or mismatched support behavior, and negative appraisals). (f) Measures of support incidents need to be developed. (g) Whenever possible, multiple measures should be used in studies to facilitate secondary psychometric analyses.

Although gaps continue to exist, researchers generally have a choice of fairly good measures. Current instruments differ less in terms of known psychometric properties than in their scope, their match to particular constructs, their sampling and differentiation of support modes and sources, and their yield in terms of subscale scores. In selecting a measure, the critical question that researchers must ask themselves is, "What exactly is it that I wish to measure?"

REFERENCES

Barrera, M., Jr. (1981). Social support in the adjustment of pregnant adolescents: Assessment issues. In B. H. Gottlieb (Ed.), *Social networks and social support* (pp. 69–96). Beverly Hills, CA: Sage.

Barrera, M., Jr., & Ainlay, S. L. (1983). The structure of social support: A conceptual and empirical analysis. *Journal of Community Psychology, 11,* 133–143.

Barrera, M., Jr., Sandler, I. N., & Ramsay, T. B. (1981). Preliminary development of a scale of social support: Studies on college students. *American Journal of Community Psychology, 9,* 435–447.

Cohen, S., & Hoberman, H. M. (1983). Positive events and social support as buffers of life change stress. *Journal of Applied Social Psychology, 13,* 99–125.

Cohen, S., & Wills, T. A. (1985). Stress, social support, and the buffering hypothesis. *Psychological Bulletin, 93,* 310–357.

Dean, A., & Lin, N. (1977). The stress-buffering role of social support: Problems and prospects for systematic investigation. *Journal of Nervous and Mental Disease, 165,* 403–417.

Eckenrode, J., & Gore, S. (1981). Stressful life events and social supports: The significance of context. In B. H. Gottlieb (Ed.), *Social networks and social support* (pp. 43–68). Beverly Hills, CA: Sage.

Fischer, C. S. (1982). *Too well among friends. Personal network in town and city.* Chicago: The University of Chicago Press.

Gottlieb, B. H. (1983). *Social support strategies.* Beverly Hills, CA: Sage.

Hirsch, B. J. (1979). Psychological dimensions of social networks: A multimethod analysis. *American Journal of Community Psychology, 7,* 263–277.

Hirsch, B. J. (1980). Natural support systems and coping with major life changes. *American Journal of Community Psychology, 8,* 159–172.

Hirsch, B. J., & Reischl, T. M. (1985). Social networks and developmental psychopathology: A comparison of adolescent children of a depressed, arthritic, or normal parent. *Journal of Abnormal Psychology, 94,* 272–281.

Holahan, C. J., & Moos, R. H. (1983). The quality of social support: Measures of family and work relationships. *British Journal of Clinical Psychology, 22,* 157–162.

House, J. S. (1981). *Work stress and social support.* Reading, MA: Addison-Wesley.

House, J. S., & Kahn, R. L. (1985). Measures and concepts of social support. In S. Cohen & S. L. Syme (Eds.), *Social support and health* (pp. 83–108). Orlando, FL: Academic Press.

Kessler, R. C., & McLeod, J. D. (1985). Social support and mental health in community samples. In S. Cohen & S. L. Syme (Eds.), *Social support and health* (pp. 219–240). Orlando, FL: Academic Press.

Kessler, R. C., McLeod, J. D., & Wethington, E. (1985). The cost of caring. In I. G. Sarason & B. R. Sarason (Eds.), *Social support: Theory, research, and application.* The Hague, the Netherlands: Martinus Nijhoff.

Lin, N., Dean, A., & Ensel, W. (1986). *Social support, life events, and depression.* Orlando, FL: Academic Press.

McFarlane, A. H., Neale, K. A., Norman, G. R., & Roy, R. J. (1983). The process of social stress: Stable, reciprocating, and mediating relationships. *Journal of Health and Social Behavior, 14,* 160–173.

McFarlane, A. H., Neale, K. A., Norman, G. R., Roy, R. G., & Streiner, D. L. (1981). Methodological issues in developing a scale to measure social support. *Schizophrenia Bulletin, 7,* 90–100.

Procidano, M., & Heller, K. (1983). Measures of perceived social support from friends and from family: Three validational studies. *American Journal of Community Psychology, 11,* 1–24.

Rook, K. (1984). The negative side of social interactions: Impact on psychological well-being. *Journal of Personality and Social Psychology, 46,* 1097–1108.

Russell, D., & Cutrona, C. (August, 1984). The provisions of social relationships and adaptation to stress. Paper presented at the American Psychological Association meeting in Toronto.

Sarason, I. G., Levine, H. M., Basham, R. B., and Sarason, B. R. (1983). Assessing social support: The Social Support Questionnaire. *Journal of Personality and Social Psychology, 44,* 127–139.

Turner, R. J., Frankel, B. G., & Levin, D. M. (1983). Social support: Conceptualization, measurement, and implications for mental health. In J. R. Greenley (Ed.), *Research in community and mental health* (pp. 67–111). Greenwich, CT: JAI Press.

Vaux, A. (1982). Measures of three levels of social support: Resources, behavior, and feelings. Unpublished manuscript, Southern Illinois University.

Vaux, A. (1987). Appraisals of support: Love, respect, and involvement. *Journal of Community Psychology, 15,* 493–502.

Vaux, A. (1988). *Social support: Theory, research, and intervention.* New York: Praeger.

Vaux, A., & Harrison, D. (1985). Support network characteristics associated with support satisfaction and perceived support. *American Journal of Community Psychology, 13,* 245–268.

Vaux, A., Phillips, J., Holly, L., Thomson, B., Williams, D., & Stewart, D. (1986). The Social

Support Appraisals (SSA) Scale: Studies of reliability and validity. *American Journal of Community Psychology, 14,* 195–220.

Vaux, A., Stewart, D., & Riedel, S. (1987). Modes of social support: The Social Support Behaviors (SSB) Scale. *American Journal of Community Psychology, 15,* 209–237.

Veiel, H. O. F. (1990). The Mannheim Interview on Social Support: Reliability and validity from three samples. *Journal of Social Psychiatry and Psychiatric Epidemiology, 25,* 250–259.

14

Measuring Social Support: Issues of Concept and Method

R. Jay Turner
University of Toronto, Canada

INTRODUCTION

As the various contributions to the present volume show, the view that social bonds and supportive interactions are important to a person's health and well-being has been both long and widely shared. What is comparatively new is the availability of hard evidence on the subject and a diversity of opinion with respect to how social support should be conceptualized and measured.

This diversity, which was widely commented on in the literature nearly a decade ago, is even more obvious and potentially problematic today. Elaborations that represent a kind of conceptual imperialism are increasingly found. Social support has come to refer to an ever-widening domain of content that, it seems, will soon be coextensive with both the structural and the social aspects of all human relationships and interactions. Of course, these tendencies represent frames of reference, which, like theories, are never true or false but only more or less useful. In this author's view, the tendencies in the field toward greater inclusiveness or imperialism hinder more than help by impeding our capacity to communicate with one another about the object of our study, the inconsistencies in our results, and what the cumulative evidence suggests with respect to the role and significance of social support for health and well-being.

This discussion argues that there would be significant advantage to reserving the term "social support" to refer to perceived or experienced support, which has been most clearly described by Cobb (1976). From Cobb's point of view, what makes social support social in nature is that it is composed entirely of information belonging to one or more of three classes: (a) information leading the subject to believe that he or she is cared for and loved, (b) information leading the subject to believe that he or she is esteemed and valued, and (c) information leading the subject to believe that he or she belongs to a network of communication and mutual obligation in which one can count on others should the necessity arise. As Barrera (1981) has observed, "From this perspective it is a cognitive appraisal of support that is regarded as the central target of [measurement]" (p. 71). In other words, social support refers to the clarity or certainty with which the individual experiences being loved, valued, and able to count on others should the need arise.

Cobb (1979) argued the importance of distinguishing social support from support that is instrumental (counseling, assisting), active (mothering), or material (providing goods and/or services). However, there has been no suggestion from

Cobb that these other forms of support are not important or that they lack relevance for health and well-being. His view was, and presumably is, simply that it is worth distinguishing social support as self-relevant information from various support resources and support activities. From this perspective, then, social support can be usefully regarded as a personal experience rather than as a set of objective circumstances or even a set of interactional processes.

Cobb's emphasis on perceived support was substantially reflected in a number of constructs that were described at about the same point in time. These include Henderson's (1977, 1980) concept of "social bonds"; Cassel's (1976) reference to "meaningful social contact"; "the availability of confidants" as emphasized by Brown, Bhrolchain, and Harris (1975), by Lowenthal and Haven (1968), and by Miller and Ingram (1976); and "human companionship" as described by Lynch (1977). Implicit, if not explicit, in each of these formulations was the assumption that the experience of being supported by others represents a core human requirement. These scholars thus focused their interest on social support as a social-psychological variable with what Henderson (1980) has described as significant affective content and psychological function.

This interest is consistent with Thomas and Thomas' (1982) familiar admonition that situations that are defined as real are real in their consequences. It is an axiom of social psychology that events or circumstances in the real world affect the individual only to the extent and in the form in which they are perceived. As Ausubel (1958) has pointed out, "This does not imply that the perceived world is the real world but that perceptual reality is psychological reality and the actual (mediating) variable that influences behavior and development" (p. 277).

The available evidence seems highly consistent with this latter point. Indeed, a decade ago, House (1981) pointed out that the great bulk of evidence pointing to the significance of social support for health and well-being came from studies that focused on "emotional support"—his term for perceived support. He further acknowledged that emotional support was the common element across most conceptualizations, that it was what most people meant when they spoke of being supportive, and that, indeed, it seemed to be the most important dimension. Since that time, studies have repeatedly demonstrated that the most powerful correlations between measures that purport to index social support and psychological distress, among other outcomes, are found with measures of perceived or experienced social support.

Recently, Wethington and Kessler (1986) presented rather compelling evidence for the primacy of perceived over received support in buffering the effect of stressful events. They document "not only that perceptions of support availability are more important than actual support transactions but that the latter promotes psychological adjustment through the former, as much as by practical resolutions of situational demands" (p. 85). As House (1981) has noted, "social support is likely to be effective only to the extent perceived" (p. 27).

The foregoing considerations amount to a rather strong case for viewing experienced or perceived support as a central object of study and for reserving the term "social support" to refer to the perception or experience of being supported by others. Although it may seem that my view takes us back 10 years and ignores the substantial progress that has been made in specifying and measuring relevant aspects of social relationships and social interactions, this is far from the case. Indeed, I find myself in substantial agreement with the action implications of

Vaux's Chapter 13, with respect to future measurement requirements and future research directions. Specifically, I agree that our efforts should include attention to support resources, support incidents, and supportive behaviors, and that such things as the negative aspects of social interactions and relationships need to be taken into account. My argument is that, although these crucial matters must be recognized as important and related concepts, they also should be distinguished from the concept of social support.

From this perspective, then, research on the relationships between related behavioral and social resource concepts and physical or mental health provides information on the relevance and significance of social support because, on average, those with more resources, with richer networks, or with fewer enduring negative relationships will experience more support. However, social support cannot be reduced to availability of resources, system capacity or potential, or interactional processes, no matter how eloquently assessed. As Kessler (1982) has suggested with respect to network analysis, the central concern of research on these variables is not with a measurement of, but with a prediction of social support, and predictive factors should not be confused with the phenomena being predicted. To estimate the potential of varying social environments for, in Gottlieb's (1981) terms, "radiating supportive functions to its members" (p. 210) is to predict levels of social support, which surely must be measured on other grounds.

One of the most obvious and most important consequences of accepting this frame of reference is its implication for our research agenda. Accepting that the concept of social support refers to perceived or experienced support—and of the evidence that it is perceived support that is most persistently and powerfully associated with various health outcomes—focuses attention on perceived support as a highly significant dependent variable. Based on this perspective and observations such as those by Wethington and Kessler (1986), reliable measures of perceived social support represent the most useful and direct criteria for assessing the role and significance of network characteristics, other social resources, negative as well as positive encounters and relationships, and support transactions, more generally. Perceived support is thus both what matters for health and well-being and the central tool for identifying the most promising targets toward which preventive intervention efforts might be aimed.

Most investigators who have included social support among their objects of study appear to share, as a major objective, the goal of identifying those social factors and circumstances that make a difference for the health and well-being of humankind and that are, at least in principle, socially or programmatically modifiable. Accordingly, the ultimate goal of our research and thus of our measurement must be to identify the social circumstances, actions, and processes that influence the experience of being supported by others. The central point of this chapter is that this goal can best be obtained by making a clear distinction between social support as a social-psychological variable and the various factors, transactions, and processes that may contribute to, or detract from, the experience of being supported by others—and by recognizing that the effective measurement of perceived support provides the best lever by which to estimate the relative significance of potentially modifiable social factors for health and well-being.

In undertaking this research agenda, it is important to recognize that the fit between social resources and transactions and social support is unlikely to be any stronger than that typically observed between social stressors and psychological distress. Here, as with the stress process, it will be crucial to recognize that the link between social circumstances and processes and the experience of social support is likely to be mediated both by structural factors, such as gender, class, and ethnicity, and by one's personal history and personality. Clearly, systems and circumstances of support generating potential vary in the clarity with which support-relevant information is transmitted; also, individuals vary widely in their capacity or tendency to receive and incorporate messages sent. Accordingly, we should expect major variations in the strength of associations between various social resources and social transactions—and social support across personal dispositions and social statuses.

Nevertheless, it is clear that we must seek appropriate targets for prevention or intervention efforts in the domains of social organization, social process, and specific social actions. Accordingly, Vaux's call (Chapter 13) for the development of better and more reliable measures of a wide range of social resources, social transactions or helping behaviors, and social relationships generally must be emphatically seconded. Vaux's chapter provides an excellent review and summary of previous measurement efforts in these domains and thus represents a useful starting point for the development of new or improved strategies for indexing these various potential contributors to the experience of social support.

As argued previously, the effective and reliable measurement of perceived social support is a crucial element in the process of developing such measures and for assessing the significance of these factors, once measured, for health and well-being. This is so because, as Wethington and Kessler (1986) have shown, social resources, transactions, and supportive behaviors exert their influence largely, if not wholly, through their influence on perceived or experienced support. Fortunately, there is a growing number of measures of perceived or experienced support that appear to possess the formal properties that recommend their use in both field and clinical studies. Since many of these measures have been reviewed elsewhere in this volume, I will limit consideration to only two such indices with which the reader may not be familiar and that I have used personally within five major studies.

THE REVISED KAPLAN SCALE

Several of the efforts we have made to measure social support have followed directly from Cobb's (1976) conceptualization of the construct. The starting point for one of these efforts was an instrument developed by Kaplan (1977) as part of her honors thesis, done under Cobb's supervision. Kaplan proposed and partially tested a story-identification technique composed of 16 sets of vignettes. We evaluated several of these items within a series of pretests and one major field study, producing a nine-item scale that includes two entirely new sets of vignettes, five sets to which slight modifications were made from the Kaplan originals and two sets in their original form. Love support, esteem support, and network support are each assessed by three sets of vignettes. This instrument, which we have named the Revised Kaplan Scale, is reproduced as Appendix A to this chapter.

THE PROVISIONS OF SOCIAL RELATIONS (PSR) SCALE

In developing instruments for assessing perceived social support, we were also influenced by Weiss' (1974) conceptualization of the provisions of social relationships. We developed the present instrument in an effort to assess subjects' perceptions in relation to five of the "provisions" identified by Weiss (attachment, social integration, reassurance of worth, reliable alliance, and guidance). A total of 18 items were initially developed, which were pretested on a sample of 200 university students and subsequently employed in two major field studies briefly described in the upcoming text. Analysis of these data led us to drop 3 items resulting in a final 15-item scale, which is reproduced as Appendix B to this chapter.

For convenience, information on the characteristics and formal properties of these measures will be reported based on data from the two large field studies in which we employed both indices simultaneously.

Mental Health Study: A Follow-up of Ex-Psychiatric Patients in the Community

The central objective of this study was to assess community tenure and adaptation among a sample of discharged psychiatric patients. All respondents had been diagnosed as functionally psychotic during one or more hospitalizations. A total of 523 subjects living in southwestern Ontario were studied. Forty-one percent of the sample were male and 59% female. Subjects ranged in age from 19 to 65, with a mean age of 43.

Study of Physical Disability

One of the major objectives of this study was to assess the social and psychological adjustment of physically disabled community residents. Subjects were identified through the use of multistage cluster sampling followed by screening interviews involving more than 11,000 households. They are thus representative of disabled community residents in southwestern Ontario. Subjects had a wide array of disabilities, with varying degrees of impairment. Of the 989 subjects successfully interviewed, 46% were male and 54% female. Subjects ranged in age from 18 to 92, with a mean age of 56.

Findings

Table 1 presents the results of factor analytic studies of the Revised Kaplan Scale. Consistent with Cobb's (1976) conceptualization, we were interested in distinguishing the subdimensions of love, esteem, and network support within this scale. However, it is clear from these results that the items addressed to love support and those addressed to esteem support have the same underlying determinants and hence represent a single dimension. The Revised Kaplan is thus a two-dimensional scale. The love-esteem dimension is composed of six items, whereas the network dimension contains three items. Using Cronbach's (1951) alpha, tests of internal consistency of the nine-item summary measure yielded coefficients of 0.83 in the physical disability study and 0.81 in the mental health study. As might

Table 1 Rotated factor analyses on the Revised Kaplan Scale with oblique solution from two studies

Dimension of Kaplan scale	Item no.*	Physical disability study		Mental health study	
		Factor 1	Factor 2	Factor 1	Factor 2
Love	1	.62	−.05	.69	.00
	4	.34	−.25	.41	−.27
	7	.77	.00	.75	.00
Esteem	2	.49	−.16	.53	−.15
	5	.65	−.11	.67	.08
	8	.39	−.30	.75	.00
Network	3	.04	−.61	.11	−.61
	6	.07	−.83	−.09	−.86
	9	.10	−.59	.16	−.62

*Item no. refers to the order in which the items were originally administered. (From Turner, Frankel, and Levin, 1983; reprinted with permission.)

be expected from the factor analytic results, the internal reliabilities of the two subdimensions were also highly satisfactory. For the physical disability and mental health studies, respectively, the coefficients were 0.79 and 0.87 for the love-esteem dimension, and 0.73 and 0.78 for the network support dimension.

Tables 2 and 3 present factor analytic results on the PSR scale. Four factors with eigen-values greater than one were found in both the mental health and physical disability data sets. Although the resulting factors were virtually identical in both studies, several items loaded on more than one factor, and the factors did not

Table 2 Factor analyses on PSR scale from physical disability study using varimax rotation with orthogonal solution

Dimension	Item no.*	Four-factor solution				Two-factor solution	
		1	2	3	4	1	2
Friend support	1	.09	.19	.35	.28	.12	.45
	2	.07	.24	.27	.35	.10	.46
	4	.09	.12	.57	.08	.13	.41
	6	.08	.35	.31	.23	.10	.54
	7	.00	.61	.02	.13	−.02	.47
	11	.04	.74	.22	.07	.02	.67
	15	.13	.12	.59	.03	.16	.40
	16	.11	.49	.35	.14	.12	.62
	18	.18	.22	.13	.50	.24	.39
Family support	5	.84	.07	.01	.18	.85	.11
	8	.57	−.04	.00	.38	.62	.10
	10	.76	.00	.24	.09	.77	.17
	12	.69	.04	.30	.01	.68	.24
	14	.52	.07	.06	.13	.52	.12
	17	.89	.17	.01	.09	.88	.09
Dropped from scale	3	.10	.10	−.07	.36	—	—
	9	.09	.00	.17	.48	—	—
	13	.06	.05	.06	.46	—	—

*Item no. refers to the order in which the items were originally administered. (From Turner, Frankel, and Levin, 1983; reprinted with permission.)

Table 3 Factor analyses on PSR scale from mental health study using varimax rotation with orthogonal solution

Dimension	Item no.*	Four-factor solution 1	2	3	4	Two-factor solution 1	2
Friend support	1	.13	.60	.11	.09	.16	.59
	2	.06	.52	.19	.10	.09	.56
	4	.31	.60	−.09	.07	.32	.54
	6	.17	.56	.25	−.16	.18	.63
	7	.04	.52	.22	−.29	.04	.58
	11	−.10	−.68	−.29	.25	.10	.75
	15	.18	.59	.01	.08	.20	.55
	16	.10	.23	.22	.08	.13	.28
	18	.11	.37	.39	.17	.17	.44
Family support	5	.83	.16	.06	−.09	.81	.17
	8	.56	.04	.26	.12	.58	.12
	10	.73	.25	.01	.15	.75	.23
	12	−.68	−.35	.04	−.14	.68	.29
	14	.60	.09	.29	.01	.60	.16
	17	.88	.14	.08	.09	.90	.14
Dropped from scale	3	.03	−.03	.04	.30	—	—
	9	.13	.11	.26	.40	—	—
	13	.11	.17	.46	.14	—	—

*Item no. refers to the order in which the items were originally administered. (From Turner, Frankel, and Levin, 1983; reprinted with permission.)

seem to resemble the subdimensions of support suggested by Weiss' (1974) provisions of social relationships. Instead, most items appeared to factor in terms of sources of support. To further evaluate this pattern, factor analyses were run specifying only two factors. As can be seen in the righthand portion of Tables 2 and 3, all 15 items clearly factored into one of the two dimensions. The first factor contains six items assessing family support, whereas the second is composed of nine items addressing support from friends. Tests of the internal consistency of the family-support and friend-support factors and of the 15-item summary measure indicated satisfactory reliabilities, with alpha coefficients ranging from 0.75 to 0.87 across the two studies.

Thus despite the apparent inability of the PSR to reliably measure the "provisions" of social relationships specified by Weiss (1974), it represents a reliable and useful instrument for generally assessing perceived social support. Moreover, in providing a reliable distinction between family support and friend support, the two clear subscales that have emerged offer an opportunity to consider the relative significance of support from two primary sources.

Our field experience with both the Revised Kaplan Scale and the PSR scale has been uniformly positive. They are easy to administer and take a modest amount of time, whether an interview or questionnaire context is employed. Moreover, subjects respond very well to these scales, especially the Revised Kaplan. Indeed, the fact that subjects tend to be interested in and even enjoy the vignettes has led us to place them at the very end of questionnaires, to reduce information loss occasioned by the impatience or fatigue of respondents. However, this very positive feature of the Revised Kaplan Scale does not appear to extend to older subjects. We found some tendency among the elderly to experience irritation rather than enjoyment when confronted with the vignettes. Accordingly, we would recommend use of the PSR rather than the Revised Kaplan when studying subjects who are at or beyond retirement age.

The analyses just presented, and our experience with these two measures, suggest that both scales are promising as global indices of experienced social support; they may provide a basis for distinguishing and measuring some theoretically interesting and practically important subcomponents of the construct. Figure 1 presents zero-order correlations among and across components of these two measures of social support for the two major studies that have employed both measures. Two observations seem noteworthy. First, despite the extreme differences in the nature of the samples involved in the studies of ex-psychiatric hospital patients and physically disabled individuals, the correlations across these studies are highly consistent. Second, this pattern of midrange coefficients presents a picture of considerable cohesiveness both within and across these instruments. We see the evidence presented on the internal reliabilities of these measures, on their underlying factor structures, and on the interrelationships between each measure and their subcomponents as in the service of construct explication. Although there may very well be important components of perceived social support that are not represented

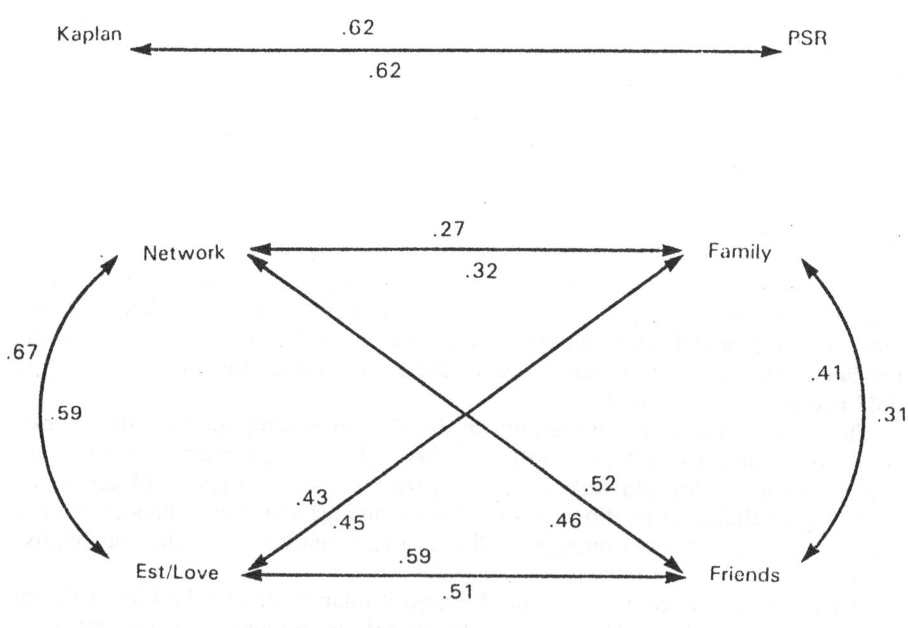

Figure 1 Correlations: Kaplan or PSR from the mental health and physical disability studies. (From Turner, Frankel, and Levin, 1983; reprinted with permission.)

here, these findings represent steps toward specifying the domain of content of this construct and therein its meaning.

PERCEIVED SOCIAL SUPPORT AND MENTAL HEALTH: THE ISSUE OF OPERATIONAL CONFOUNDING

The core argument in this chapter is that the term "social support" should be reserved for the perception or experience of being supported by others. Since perceived support appears to be what matters for emotional health and well-being, reliable measurement of this construct provides a powerful tool for assessing the role and significance of various supportive resources and actions. However, our focus on the perception or experience of social support raises a question of possible redundancy between measures of support and measures of psychological distress or well-being. It might well be argued that the perception of being loved and esteemed and able to count on others must be an integral part of emotional well-being or mental health, at least when broadly conceived.

To address the prospect of operational confounding, confirmatory factor analyses specifying only two factors were applied to each data set to assess whether these two apparently similar constructs can be empirically differentiated. The results of these analyses appear in Tables 4, 5, and 6. In these analyses both the Revised Kaplan Scale and the PSR scale were separately paired with psychological distress measures utilized in each study. In the disability study (Tables 4 and 5) we employed the anxiety and anger/aggression subscales of the "How I feel" instrument developed by Peterson and Kellman (1977) along with the Centre for Epidemiologic Studies Depression Scale (CES-D) (Radloff, 1977). The anxiety subscale contains seven items and has an internal reliability of 0.82, whereas the anger/aggression subscale contains six items and has a reliability coefficient of 0.78. Cronbach's alpha for the CES-D scale was 0.90.

Within the sample of ex-psychiatric patients (Table 6), psychological well-being was evaluated through use of the Brief Symptom Inventory (BSI). The BSI is a brief form of the well-known SCL-90. It is composed of 53 items, and each item is rated on the same five-point scale used with the SCL-90. This instrument is scored in terms of nine primary symptom dimensions: somatization, obsessive-compulsion, interpersonal sensitivity, depression, anxiety, hostility, phobic anxiety, paranoid ideation, and psychoticism. The psychometric characteristics of this instrument have been established and evidence for validity presented by its authors (Derogatis, Richels, & Roch, 1976; Derogatis & Cleary, 1977). Our own analyses of the internal reliabilities of the measured dimensions yielded highly satisfactory coefficients.

The results of these various factor analyses seem quite remarkable in their clarity and persuasive in their consistency. Except for 2 of the 15 PSR items, the most important determinant of the social support items in all the analyses, across both studies, is factor 2. Factor 1 shows little or no influence. Although factor 2 appears to account for some variance in two or three depression items, factor 1 is a major determinant of essentially all psychological distress items across all six analyses.

To more fully assess the discriminability of the social support and psychological

Table 4 Rotated factor loadings, with two orthogonal factors specified, on Kaplan support items and psychological distress (physical disability study)

Construct and items		Factor 1	Factor 2	Construct and items		Factor 1	Factor 2
Revised Kaplan	1	.07	.59	Revised Kaplan	1	.11	.61
	2	.05	.58		2	.04	.60
	3	.06	.56		3	.11	.55
	4	.05	.53		4	.05	.52
	5	.14	.49		5	.11	.49
	6	.02	.65		6	.07	.62
	7	.15	.68		7	.18	.68
	8	.004	.63		8	.008	.62
	9	.13	.59		9	.15	.58
Anxiety	1	.46	.08	CES-D	1	.52	.04
	2	.70	.07		2	.51	.00
	3	.66	.08		3	.79	.11
	4	.37	.06		4	.29	.15
	5	.71	.06		5	.52	.08
	6	.50	.11		6	.79	.10
	7	.67	.11		7	.52	.63
Anger/aggression	1	.39	.07		8	.39	.17
	2	.49	.02		9	.52	.22
	3	.69	−.10		10	.65	.12
	4	.51	.01		11	.48	.02
	5	.60	.06		12	.66	.16
	6	.40	.06		13	.47	.10
					14	.61	.20
					15	.30	.25
					16	.56	.21
					17	.62	.02
					18	.77	.09
					19	.37	.31
					20	.49	.07

(From Turner, Frankel, and Levin, 1983; reprinted with permission.)

distress dimensions, three additional sets of analyses were conducted. The analyses reported here were repeated using an oblique rather than an orthogonal solution. Analyses were also conducted that generated all factors with eigen-values greater than one, first specifying an orthogonal and then an oblique solution. All of these analyses produced results that were wholly consistent with those presented in Tables 4, 5, and 6. Although in some analyses both the support scales and distress measures divided into subscales, the distinction between support and distress remained constant throughout these analyses.

Thus on the question of some possible redundancy between our measures of social support and psychological distress, we view these results as demonstrating that social support is a separate and distinguishable dimension. Although it is accepted that experienced social support cannot be wholly divorced from the general domain of psychological well-being, there seems to be considerable support, both from previous research and from findings presented here, for the argument that the construct of social support warrants separate consideration in both theory and future measurement and research efforts.

Table 5 Rotated factor loadings, with two orthogonal factors specified, on PSR support items and psychological distress (physical disability study)

Construct and items		Factor 1	Factor 2	Construct and items		Factor 1	Factor 2
PSR	1*	.30	.28	PSR	1	.28	.28
	2	.25	.26		2	.20	.26
	4	.13	.31		4	.08	.32
	5	−.01	.80		5	.16	.77
	6	.11	.31		6	.11	.31
	7	.06	.20		7	.02	.20
	8	.16	.58		8	.23	.56
	10	−.01	.76		10	.06	.75
	11	.12	.29		11	.04	.32
	12	.01	.72		12	.04	.74
	14	−.04	.52		14	.07	.51
	15	.04	.33		15	.03	.33
	16	.11	.38		16	.07	.39
	17	−.03	.80		17	.12	.78
	18	.34	.38		18	.39	.34
Anxiety	1	.45	.09	CES-D	1	.52	.07
	2	.69	.12		2	.51	.01
	3	.64	.14		3	.79	.11
	4	.39	.10		4	.29	.16
	5	.70	.09		5	.51	.10
	6	.53	.05		6	.79	.10
	7	.66	.17		7	.53	.00
Anger/aggression	1	.41	.07		8	.40	.17
	2	.51	−.02		9	.51	.19
	3	.69	.14		10	.67	.09
	4	.53	−.01		11	.47	.06
	5	.62	.14		12	.66	.16
	6	.42	.05		13	.48	.10
					14	.59	.21
					15	.32	.21
					16	.56	.19
					17	.63	.01
					18	.77	.11
					19	.39	.23
					20	.52	.06

*Item nos. as originally administered. (From Turner, Frankel, and Levin, 1983; reprinted with permission.)

In this chapter, arguments have been presented to support the view that it would be useful to reserve the term social support to refer to the experience or perception of being supported by others. Moreover, it is contended that the effective and reliable measurement of perceived support is crucial to the process of identifying those circumstances, resources, and actions that represent promising targets for prevention or intervention efforts.

The presentation of the Revised Kaplan Scale and the PSR scale is not intended to suggest their superiority to other measures. Rather, they are simply examples of indices that possess the kinds of characteristics and formal properties that recommend them for possible use in field and clinical investigations. Indeed, my own thinking leads to a criticism of these measures because they lack the capacity to

Table 6 Rotated factor loadings, with two orthogonal factors specified, on social support items and psychological distress (physical disability study)

Construct and items		Factor 1	Factor 2	Construct and items		Factor 1	Factor 2
BSI	SOM	.65	−.15	BSI	SOM	.64	−.17
	DEP	.80	−.18		DEP	.78	−.27
	PHO	.73	−.11		PHO	.71	−.21
	COMP	.82	−.09		COMP	.80	−.19
	ANX	.85	−.09		ANX	.86	−.14
	PAR	.67	−.23		PAR	.68	−.24
	SEN	.81	−.14		SEN	.80	−.23
	HOS	.63	−.02		HOS	.64	−.07
	PSY	.82	−.19		PSY	.80	−.26
	ADD	.70	−.22		ADD	.69	−.23
PSR	1*	−.36	.40	Revised	1	−.13	.65
	2	.26	.35	Kaplan	2	−.11	.64
	4	.08	.56		3	−.19	.63
	5	−.01	.76		4	−.18	.61
	6	.28	.47		5	−.20	.52
	7	.09	.36		6	−.22	.64
	9	.15	.50		7	−.23	.67
	10	.08	.73		8	−.11	.62
	11	.22	.47		9	−.16	.70
	12	−.11	.72				
	14	.07	.57				
	15	.15	.47				
	16	.07	.27				
	17	.00	.79				
	18	.41	.32				

*Item nos. as originally administered. (From Turner, Frankel, and Levin, 1983; reprinted with permission.)

distinguish support received from one's spouse from support received from other sources. My hypothesis, based on some evidence and experience, is that support from one's spouse may differ, in nature and strength of effects, from support received from other sources. Although there seems much to recommend—these particular measures for assessing perceived support—additional items aimed at assessing the experience of support drawn from one's spouse may also be required.

REFERENCES

Ausubel, D. P. (1958). *Theory and problems of child development.* New York: Grune & Stratton.

Barrera, M., Jr. (1981). Social support in the adjustment of pregnant adolescents: Assessment issues. In B. H. Gottlieb (Ed.), *Social networks and social support* (pp. 69–96). Beverly Hills, CA: Sage.

Brown, G. W., Bhrolchain, M., & Harris, T. (1975). Social class and psychiatric disturbance among women in an urban population. *Sociology, 9,* 225–254.

Cassel, J. (1976). The contribution of the social environment to host resistance. *American Journal of Epidemiology, 104,* 107–123.

Cobb, S. (1976). Social support as a moderator of life stress. *Psychosomatic Medicine, 38,* 300–314.

Cobb, S. (1979). Social support and health through the life course. In M. W. Riley (Ed.), *Aging from birth to death* (pp. 93–106). Boulder, CO: Westview Press.

Cronbach, L. J. (1951). Coefficient alpha and the internal structure of test. *Psychosomatic Medicine, 16,* 297–334.

Derogatis, L. R., & Cleary, P. A. (1977). Confirmation of the dimensional structure of the SCL-90: A study of construct validation. *Journal of Clinical Psychology, 33,* 981–989.

Derogatis, L. R., Richels, K., & Roch, F. (1976). The SCL-90 and the MMPI: A study of construct validation. *Journal of Clinical Psychology, 33,* 981–989.

Gottlieb, B. H. (1981). Social networks and social support in community mental health. In B. H. Gottlieb (Ed.), *Social networks and social support* (pp. 11–42). Beverly Hills, CA: Sage.

Henderson, S. (1977). The social network, support and neurosis: The function of attachment in adult life. *British Journal of Psychiatry, 131,* 185–191.

Henderson, S. (1980). A development in social psychiatry: The systematic study of social bonds. *Journal of Nervous and Mental Disease, 168,* 63–69.

Henderson, S., Duncan-Jones, P., Adcock, S., Scott, R., & Steele, G. (1978). Social bonds in the epidemiology of neurosis: A preliminary communication. *British Journal of Psychiatry, 132,* 463–466.

House, J. S. (1981). *Work stress and social support.* Reading, MA: Addison-Wesley.

Kaplan, A. (1977). *Social support: Construct and its measurement.* B. A. thesis, Department of Psychology, Brown University.

Kaplan, B. H., Cassel, J. C., & Gore, S. (1977). Social support and health. *Medical Care, 15,* 47–58. (Suppl.)

Kessler, R. C. (1982). Life events, social supports, and mental health. In W. R. Gove (Ed.), *Deviance and Mental Illness* (pp. 247-271). Beverly Hills, CA: Sage.

Lowenthal, M. F., & Haven, C. (1968). Interaction and adaptation: Intimacy as a critical variable. *American Sociological Review, 33,* 20–30.

Lynch, J. (1977). *The broken heart.* New York: Basic Books.

Miller, P., & Ingham, J. (1976). Friends, confidants and symptoms. *Social Psychiatry, 11,* 51–57.

Mueller, D. P. (1980). Social networks: A promising direction for research on the relationship of the social environment to psychiatric disorder. *Social Science and Medicine, 14A,* 147–161.

Murawski, B., Penman, D., & Schmitt, M. (1978). Social support in health and illness: The concept and its measurement. *Cancer Nursing, 1,* 365–371.

Pagel, M. D., Erdly, W. W., & Becker, J. (1987). Social networks: We get by with (an in spite of) a little help from our friends. *Journal of Personality and Social Psychology, 53,* 793–804.

Petersen, A., & Kellam, S. (1977). Measurement of the psychological wellbeing of adolescents: The psychometric properties and assessment procedures of the How I Feel. *Journal of Youth and Adolescence, 6,* 229–247.

Radloff, L. S. (1977). The CES-D scale: A self-report depression scale for research in the general population. *Applied Psychological Measurement, 1,* 385–401.

Thomas, W. I., & Thomas, D. S. (1982). *The child in America: Behavior problems and programs.* New York: Knopf.

Turner, R. J., Frankel, & Levin. (1983). Social support: Conceptualization, measurement, and implications for Mental Health. *Research in Community and Community Health, 3,* 67–111.

Weiss, R. (1974). The provisions of social relationships. In Z. Rubin (Ed.), *Doing unto others* (pp. 17–26). Englewood Cliffs, NJ: Prentice-Hall.

Wethington, E., & Kessler, R. C. (1986). Perceived support, received support, and adjustment to stressful life events. *Journal of Health and Social Behavior, 27,* 78–90.

APPENDIX A: THE REVISED KAPLAN SCALE

We would like to know your thoughts and feelings about yourself and the people who matter to you. After reading each item, please check the box below that best applies to you.

Love-Esteem Dimension

*1.	Ronnie	Stuart	Peter
	People are devoted to Ronnie and love him.	People are usually fond of Stuart. They can be	People are not devoted to Peter. They do not

They always support him, listen to him, and sympathize with him. They care about him a lot.	sympathetic, but do not always listen to him nor always support him.	support him, listen to him, or sympathize with him. They do not care about him or love him.

Check one box.

☐	☐	☐	☐	☐
I'm like Ronnie.	I'm halfway between Ronnie and Stuart.	I'm like Stuart.	I'm halfway between Stuart and Peter.	I'm like Peter.

	John	David	Andy
2.	People rarely let John know that he is wanted. He does not really make a difference to them and they are rarely concerned about him. He does not matter to them.	People sometimes let David know that he matters. Sometimes they think that he makes a difference to them.	People constantly let Andy know that he is wanted. He really makes a difference to them. They are concerned about him and he matters.

Check one box.

☐	☐	☐	☐	☐
I'm like John.	I'm halfway between John and David.	I'm like David.	I'm halfway between David and Andy.	I'm like Andy.

	Steve	Gregory	Charles
4.	Steve rarely has close friends he can count on. He does not know that they will always be there for him to lean on, and he does not support them.	Gregory sometimes has close friends who are there for him and whom he can count on.	Charles always has close friends he can count on. He does not have to worry about whether they will be there for him to lean on. He gives them the same support.

Check one box.

☐	☐	☐	☐	☐
I'm like Steve.	I'm halfway between Steve and Gregory.	I'm like Gregory.	I'm halfway between Gregory and Charles.	I'm like Charles.

	Dennis	Brian	Edward
5.	People believe that Dennis will make the right decisions and do the right things. They have confidence and faith in him.	Some people have confidence and faith in Brian. Sometimes they think that he will make the right decisions and do the right things.	People rarely believe that Edward will make the right decisions or do the right things. They hardly ever have confidence in him.

Check one box.

☐	☐	☐	☐	☐
I'm like Dennis.	I'm halfway between Dennis and Brian.	I'm like Brian.	I'm halfway between Brian and Edward.	I'm like Edward.

	Hank	Michael	Anthony
7.	Hank knows that people care a lot about him. He has their attention and support.	Michael sometimes has people's attention and support. He sometimes feels that they care about him.	Anthony is uncertain that people care about him. He gets little attention or support.

Check one box.

☐	☐	☐	☐	☐
I'm like Hank.	I'm halfway between Hank and Michael.	I'm like Michael.	I'm halfway between Michael and Anthony.	I'm like Anthony.

	Patrick	Gordon	Joel
8.	Patrick is rarely admired and praised. There are very few people who think Patrick is important and worthy.	Gordon is sometimes admired and praised by some people. He is not always being reminded of his worth.	Joel is constantly being admired by people. They always praise him and think that he is important and worthy.

Check one box.

☐	☐	☐	☐	☐
I'm like Patrick.	I'm halfway between Patrick and Gordon.	I'm like Gordon.	I'm halfway between Gordon and Joel.	I'm like Joel.

Network Dimension

	Jonathan	Bill	Allen
3.	People always think that Jonathan is a	Bill has friends and is a good person to be with,	Allen is mostly alone. He rarely sees people

friend. They like talking with him and spending a lot of time with him. He always has lots of people around. He is seldom alone.

but he isn't always surrounded by people.

or spends time with them. He is most often by himself.

Check one box.

☐	☐	☐	☐	☐
I'm like Jonathan.	I'm halfway between Jonathan and Bill.	I'm like Bill.	I'm halfway between Bill and Allen.	I'm like Allen.

	Ronnie	Richard	Jeffrey
6.	Ronnie rarely spends time with other people. When he wants to do things, he hardly ever has anyone to do things with him.	Richard sometimes spends time with other people. When he wants to do things, sometimes there are other people around to do things with him.	Jeffrey is almost always with other people. Whenever he wants to do things, he knows that one or another of his friends will be there to do things with him.

Check one box.

☐	☐	☐	☐	☐
I'm like Ronnie.	I'm halfway between Ronnie and Richard.	I'm like Richard.	I'm halfway between Richard and Jeffrey.	I'm like Jeffrey.

	Ricky	Harold	Jason
9.	Ricky does not have a lot of different people to lean on. He does not belong to a group of people who know each other and who would help one another when needed.	Harold sometimes has people he can lean on. He belongs to a group of people who sometimes help one another when needed.	Jason knows that there are a lot of different people he can lean on. He belongs to a group of many people who know each other and who always help one another out when needed.

Check one box.

☐	☐	☐	☐	☐
I'm like Ricky.	I'm halfway between Ricky and Harold.	I'm like Harold.	I'm halfway between Harold and Jason.	I'm like Jason.

APPENDIX B: THE PROVISIONS OF SOCIAL RELATIONS (PSR) SCALE

Now I would like to know something about your relationships with other people. For each of the statements I read to you please use the scale on this card to tell me the number of the category that best describes your experience.

Family Dimension

*5. No matter what happens, I know that my family will always be there for me should I need them.
8. Sometimes I'm not sure if I can completely rely on my family.
10. My family lets me know they think I'm a worthwhile person.
12. People in my family have confidence in me.
14. People in my family provide me with help in finding solutions to my problems.
17. I know my family will always stand by me.

Friends Dimension

1. When I'm with my friends I feel completely able to relax and be myself.
2. I share the same approach to life that many of my friends do.
4. People who know me trust and respect me.
6. When I want to go out to do things I know that many of my friends would enjoy doing these things with me.
7. I have at least one friend I could tell anything.
11. I feel very close to some of my friends.
15. People who know me think I am good at what I do.
16. My friends would take the time to talk over my problems, should I ever want to.
18. Even when I am with my friends I feel alone.

Items Dropped from Scale

3. My friends don't know one another well.
9. My friends do not always approve of my attitudes and lifestyle.
13. There are some problems that I can't share with anyone.

Response Scale

1. very much like my experience.
2. much like my experience.
3. somewhat like my experience.
4. not very much like my experience.
5. not at all like my experience.

*Numbers denote the order in which items appear in the scale.

15

Social Support: An Investigator-Based Approach

George W. Brown
University of London, United Kingdom

There is now an impressive accumulation of ideas about social support. An excellent example is the 1985 edited volume *Social Support and Health* by S. Cohen and S. L. Syme (1985). My aim is not to add to these ideas, but to discuss the modest success of efforts to translate them into effective research. Although my colleagues and I have concluded that social support is important in the development of clinical depression (Brown, Andrews, Harris, Adler, & Bridge, 1986), our published accounts fail to convey the difficulty experienced in documenting this, and this would seem an appropriate occasion for this to be rectified.

Building on this experience, I will argue that it is insufficient to collect material about support in a precise way—although this is challenge enough. It is also necessary to deal with variability in support. Even when dealing with support at one point in time, different facets may not hold together; listening to the confidences of a person may not be matched by a show of emotional support. And, support may change with time. A satisfactory and close relationship may not predict support in a crisis 6 months later, and such support, given it occurs, may not be sustained for more than about a week.

I will also argue that aggregate measures that "average" support from a number of individuals can be highly misleading and mask evidence for the effect of a particular social relationship. Taking account of such variation led to an analysis of a complexity that is bound to lead some to question the validity of our conclusions. But without it, clear effects would not have emerged. Because life events are of importance in onset of depression, its study obviously provides something of a test case for the role of social support; therefore, if our conclusions cannot be sustained, the chance of documenting important etiological effects for other disorders must be in doubt.

THE RESPONDENT-BASED APPROACH TO MEASUREMENT

Etiological research in social psychiatry has faced the major challenges of dealing in some way both with meaning and with the intricacies of stress-diathesis formulations (or, as my colleagues and I have discussed it, with the relationship between stressors and vulnerability). Unfortunately, the respondent-based measures, almost universally employed, have largely proved ineffective. One consequence has been that life-event research, which made such a promising start with the classic work of Hinkle and Wolfe (1957) and Holmes and Rahe (1969), is largely moribund in North America.

A basic problem has been economic considerations. It is costly to collect good quality material from general population samples, and the necessary resources have not, on the whole, been offered by funding bodies. At the same time, there has been a general lack of recognition that sound research requires more or less equal investment in the tasks of instrument development, data collection, and analysis. One result has been the production of a great deal of data about stress and support, which has for the most part failed to lead to cumulative knowledge. Research has been cheap only at the level of the individual study. But looking at the research overall (not a task typically undertaken by funding bodies), noncumulative findings are far from economic. For the most part methodological concern in the field has been restricted to meeting conventional psychometric criteria, which are largely irrelevant for such broader issues.

The respondent-based and the alternative investigator-based approaches to data collection will therefore be described and contrasted. Although my treatment is perforce somewhat superficial, I hope to convey that there are critical differences and important choices to be made. Table 1 outlines the two approaches in terms of the material collected, based on distinguishing "internal" and "external" material, the former restricting itself to attitudes and feelings of the respondent.

The basic idea of the respondent-based tradition is that for either type of material, questions to the respondent should be sufficiently standard to make the presence of an interviewer largely irrelevant. (The approach is often via a self-completed questionnaire, and it is even possible to conceive of using a portable microcomputer to put questions and record precoded answers.) When an interviewer is present, a certain amount of leeway may be given to him or her (or in practice assumed by him or her) in the matter of question formulation; nonetheless, the job of measurement is essentially handed over to the respondent. It is the respondent who decides how terms such as "very much" or "highly dissatisfied" are to be interpreted. Irrespective of what might be said about an issue in the interview, it is the respondent who is the final arbiter in what rating point is utilized. Thus, it is possible for respondents to state (and thereby "rate"), say, that they are highly satisfied with the support provided, although by what they said as a

Table 1 Types of measure

Focus	Respondent-based measures	Investigator-based measures
"Internal" material	A. Attitudinal	D1. Attitudinal
"External" material	B. Frequency type C. Qualitative	D2. Attitudinal/behavioral E. Situational F. Contextual

On occasion, it is possible to combine D and E; see footnote 2.

whole and by their tone of voice (and perhaps facial expression), they may convey it was inadequate in a number of ways.

Nonetheless, the respondent-based attitudinal measures (A, Table 1) can undoubtedly be effective, although some caution should be shown, because at times they can give different results from the alternative investigator-based approach. (For an example dealing with self-esteem, see Brown et al., 1986; Brown, Andrews, Bifulco, & Veiel, 1990a; Brown, Bifulco, Veiel, & Andrews, 1990b; Brown, Bifulco, & Andrews, 1990c).

In the respondent-based tradition, the external measures suffer most obviously from imprecision—at least once they depart from the collection of simple frequency material of the kind whether the person has a telephone or car, or how much time a day he or she spends with a spouse (B, Figure 1). External material dealing with more qualitative aspects such as amount of confiding in a husband or severity of illness is likely to be imprecise as it is typically left to the respondent to decide what is meant by the questions (C, Table 1).[1]

Figure 1 illustrates what is probably a representative example of the respondent-based approach to such material. In a population inquiry in Camberwell using the alternative investigator-based measure of life events, a decline of 8% was found in reporting over a 21-week period before interview, compared with 62% in a study in Zurich (Brown & Harris, 1982; Schmidt, Scharfetter, & Binder, 1981). Because much the same events were covered, this extraordinary difference would appear to be a result of the way data were collected and rated. In other words, the Zurich group used a respondent-based approach where they included every incident mentioned in response to a list of standard questions (i.e., any illness, rather than one reaching a particular level of severity settled by the investigator). It is just this imprecision in dealing with the variability in qualitative material that is one of the central shortcomings of the respondent-based tradition. Although it would probably be too much to claim that gross imprecision is inevitable, it is endemic and energetic efforts to deal with the issue in the respondent-based tradition have been rare. Because questions employed to collect qualitative material are usually quite general, there is a good chance that internal and external material will be confounded; it is known, for example, that answers to general questions about the frequency of an activity tend to be biased in the direction of either any marked satisfaction or marked dissatisfaction (Brown & Rutter, 1966).

Table 2 presents some possible problems arising from a respondent-based approach in terms of three paradoxes. The first is that, given the difficulty of collecting accurate external material, a general question about attitudes may often provide a better indication of what actually occurred than several poorly focused ones dealing with the situation itself. The consequence of this lack of balance between internal and external measures can be a misleading emphasis on the importance of the "internal" as compared to the "external." It is hazardous to draw any conclusion about relative importance until the two forms of measure reach a state of more

[1]There is likely to be some overlap between the two approaches. For example, it is apparently common for an investigation in practice to break away from rigid rules regarding how the interview should be conducted and, for example, turn a rigidly designed clinical instrument such as the DIS (Robins, Helzer, Croughan, & Ratcliff, 1981) into a clinical-type interview where the interviewer not only adds a good number of additional probes, but also plays a major role in interpreting the respondent's answers. This may help to explain some of the puzzling discrepancies of results in the respondent-based tradition.

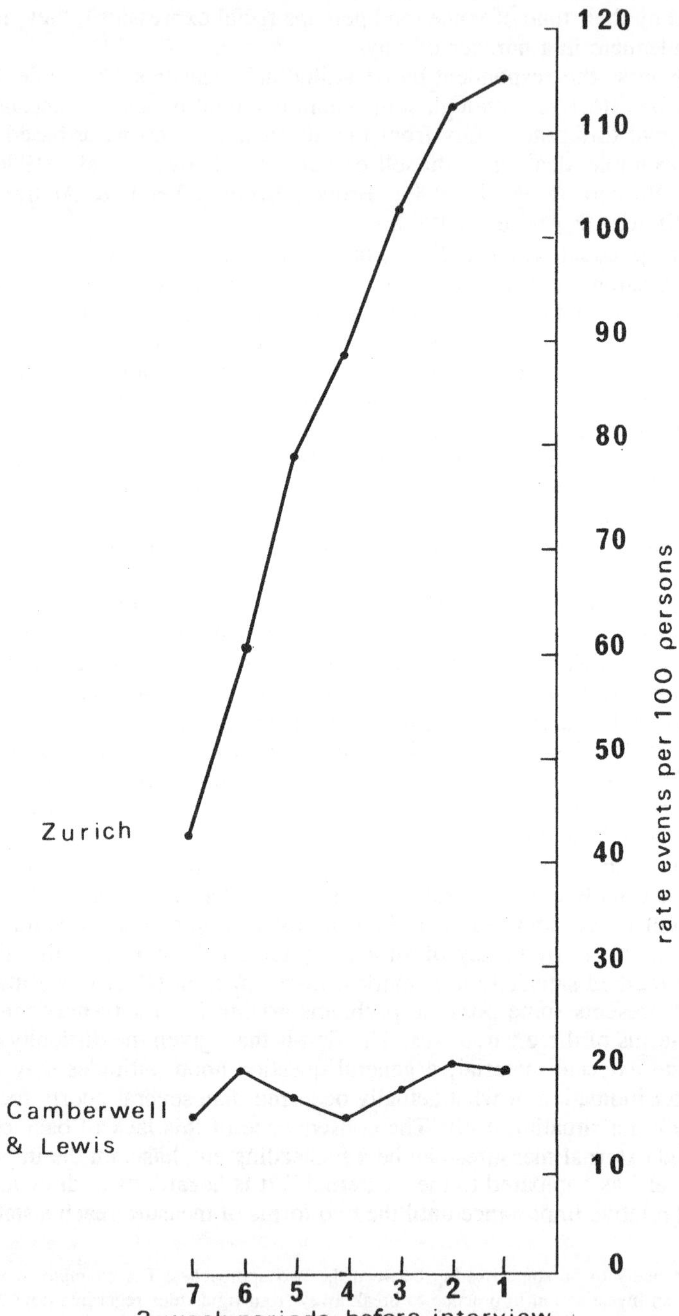

Figure 1 Rate of events in 3-week periods before interview for Zurich (n = 100) and Camberwell and Lewis (n = 659).

Table 2 Psychiatric epidemiological research and respondent-based measures: three paradoxes

	Internal versus external measures
Paradox:	Internal measures are often better reflections of what has occurred in behavioral terms than external measures.
Reason:	A respondent-based approach has great difficulty in dealing with external phenomena.
Consequence:	A misleading emphasis on attitudes and personality.
	Meaning
Paradox:	Internal measures are not always competent to deal with meaning.
Reason:	Contamination cannot be ruled out once a person is ill, and the difficulty of dealing with changes in meaning with a standardized instrument.
Consequence:	Reliance on insensitive objective measures—a birth is a birth.
	Time order
Paradox:	Longitudinal designs often fall short of dealing with time order.
Reason:	Inability to deal with occurrence within the period between T1 and T2 contacts.
Consequence:	Consideration of only stressors occuring before T1 to predict illness in T1 to T2 period.

or less equal precision. The claim by Henderson, Byrne, and Duncan-Jones (1981), that perceived rather than actual availability of social support was important, is almost certainly premature in these terms (see Henderson & Brown, 1988, for a full discussion of the issue).

The second paradox deals with meaning and suggests that attitudinal measures are not always the most effective way forward. Contamination, for example, is difficult to rule out once a person is "ill," and, probably equally as important, a respondent-based approach has difficulty in dealing with possible changes in meaning. Where support is concerned, it is usually left unclear, for example, whether we are interested in it from the perspective of the crisis itself or from how it was seen once the immediate crisis had subsided, which might well be after the onset of the disorder in question. Such difficulties have probably contributed to the popularity of checklist-type measures that bypass the question of personal meaning altogether; the birth of a child, for instance, is assumed to have a common impact (i.e., give the same "score") no matter what circumstances surround it (Brown, 1974, 1989).

A third paradox concerns the issue of time—something that has received surprisingly little attention. Longitudinal studies have typically failed to deal effectively with time order, the central issue they are designed to tackle. This largely arises from the difficulty of dealing with the order of "event" and "onset" in the period between first (T1) and follow-up (T2) contacts. With a highly structured approach to questioning, it is difficult to know whether a particular event preceded or followed an onset in this period. Only detailed questioning about event and onset is likely to reveal, for example, that the event occurring after onset was, in fact, anticipated by an earlier one occurring several weeks before onset (Brown & Harris, 1986). Because of such problems, longitudinal inquiries have considered only stressors occurring before T1; but, because relevant events often occur within a few weeks of onset, critical information will be lost if the period between T1 and T2 is just ignored. The problem arises equally with social support.

THE INVESTIGATOR-BASED APPROACH TO MEASUREMENT

The alternative investigator-based approach has been contrasted with the respondent-based type in Table 1 (compare the right and lefthand columns). Because the interviewer now plays a dominant role in collecting and rating material, it is essential to settle what is to be rated and the criteria for each scale point before data collection begins (i.e., in the life-event example given earlier, what would count as a serious illness, etc.). As will be seen, there are constraints on how much can be settled ahead of time for contextual ratings. Training, of course, is also necessary to reach satisfactory interrater reliability.

Internal material may be dealt with by means of straightforward rating of what the respondent reports (D1, Table 1). Obviously this may give a closely comparable result to that of a respondent-based self-report instrument, and I will therefore place emphasis on the possibility of dealing with attitudes by going beyond merely recording verbal statements to standard questions to take account of a wider range of phenomena, including *how* things are said and any inconsistency in reporting at different points of the interview (D2, Table 1). Such ratings are described as attitudinal/behavioral (rather than attitudinal), because they take account of observed emotional behavior in the interview itself—in terms of both what may be expressed spontaneously and what is reported in response to set questions.[2] The approach to collecting such material is still considered internal and differs from external material in the sense that it is only for the latter that an interviewer is instructed to question in detail about inconsistencies on the respondent's part to obtain as "true" a picture as possible of what occurred. No such view is taken of attitudinal material (of either type).

It is in the nature of attitudinal material to display inconsistency, and it is essential that the interviewer not refer directly to the fact, for example, that at one point the respondent said she was highly satisfied with her marriage, but later expressed a good deal of criticism. Such inconsistency and ambivalence is a part of psychological reality and the notion of there being just one "true" attitude must be eschewed—although on the basis of the material from the interview as a whole an interviewer may be able to judge the "dominant" one.

Two types of external material are collected. Although differing, both place importance on asking details about particular incidents—that is, in dealing with, say, violence in marriage, the interviewer would ask about recent examples of relevant behavior (including what the respondent sees as violent). The most straightforward of the two approaches is the situational (E, Table 1). The term is used to emphasize the importance of a full account of the relevant situation and the need to exclude consideration of the respondent's feelings when making the rating. (It is possible for a person to be considered to have received ample support, though complaining bitterly about it.) Using a reasonably full description of behavior and

[2]It is possible to take account of reported behavior outside the interview situation. However, if this is done, it will be necessary to develop a means for dealing with possible inconsistencies between feelings expressed within the interview situation and those that appeared to be implicit in the reported behavior. Emotional overinvolvement in the Expressed Emotion (EE) Index is a good example of a more inclusive approach. Although it emphasizes statements of attitude, emotional display, or dramatization in the interview, it also takes account of reported behavior, such as anxiety directly related to the targeted person's welfare (Leff & Vaughn, 1985).

situation, both presence of the phenomenon and frequency/amount is rated. As well as relevant definitions, there are anchoring examples of ratings to guide the investigator. The aim is to settle these definitions and examples before data collection begins.

Another characteristic of situational measures (to be kept in mind when considering the more complex contextual ratings) is that they are typically fairly restricted in the context taken into account. For example, a rating of emotional support received from a husband would ignore both whether any had been received from elsewhere and the kind of support received from the husband in the past before the study period. Support is judged within a quite limited temporal frame—as will be seen, in some instances, only with circumstances surrounding a particular life event. Within this limited time frame, a judgment is made of the match between the circumstances and the support received.

The other type of external measure, the contextual (F, Table 1), differs by taking more of the context into account. It is a more complex measure and because of this it is impossible to anticipate the range of examples that will be met in practice; although, if anchoring examples are extensive enough, a good deal of guidance is possible. However, because more is left to the judgment of the rater, it becomes particularly important to exclude any consideration of attitudinal material—or any other piece of information (such as whether the subject is depressed) that might produce bias in a causal inquiry. For a situational rating, it would be naive to claim that feelings are totally ignored; it would be more accurate to say that supporting external evidence is sought and the rater has no compunction in ignoring feelings if they are "inconsistent" with behavioral evidence. But almost certainly the interviewer would be influenced in his or her questioning about behavior by the strength of feelings expressed (e.g., "Why do you say that?"; "What made you dissatisfied?"). However, for contextual ratings, for the reason just given, a more rigid attempt is made to exclude all consideration of feelings and reported response. The rating is often formalized by the use of a rating team to reach a consensus rating by using the interviewer to present "edited" accounts that exclude all material about feelings (and information such as the presence of the medical disorder under study). Other raters present would then make the contextual rating based on the likely response of the average person in that situation without knowledge of that particular respondent's feelings and attitudes.

Although the primary reason for this more thorough attempt at exclusion in contextual ratings is methodological, there are more general reasons for attempting to exclude attitudinal material from ratings, including the less strict sense exemplified by situational ratings. It is, for example, common for parents of discharged schizophrenic patients to show little or no dissatisfaction about quite intolerable experiences (Brown et al., 1966). Leaving aside the issue of what is really felt (and the presence of depressive symptoms in many parents), there is clearly a need for a parallel measure of the external environment that goes beyond what the respondent chooses to express in terms of his or her feelings. The need for this has been recognized in the area of social support, although Cohen and Syme (1985) note that to their knowledge "there is no existing research in which investigators objectively determined the availability of existing resources" (p. 11).

Another reason for concentrating on behavioral aspects is that situational and contextual measures are likely to be better at picking up changes in internal characteristics insofar as this tends to be correlated with change in the external environment. As already noted, contextual measures have most often been employed to deal with the likely meaning of life events (Brown & Harris, 1989). Here, quite detailed biographical material is used to assess the respondent's plans and concerns that are relevant for the event, as far as these can be judged on the basis of behavior reports. The contextual rating itself is an estimate of the likely impact of the event on plans and concerns, and forms the basis for assessing the meaning of the event (Brown, 1989). The context explored, both past and present, is broader than with situational ratings. The narrow situational measures can often be made with little or no knowledge of the respondent as a person with plans and previous experiences; this will typically not hold for a contextual rating.

However, highly idiosyncratic needs of a person are deliberately ignored in both types of measure. Only attitudinal measures are capable of taking account of this—say that the respondent has an unusually excessive need for support, or seems to have extraordinarily low expectations of what is sufficient.

Despite the differences in the three types of measure (D, E, & F; Table 1), data collection is integrated in the sense that internal material will often be conveyed spontaneously when discussing behavior and the broader context. In the collection of all types of material, emphasis is placed on obtaining narrative accounts about the recent and, if necessary, distant past. These accounts are judged in terms of the sense they make as "stories," and questioning is ideally continued until the story holds together and matters are reasonably clear. (See Brown & Rutter, 1966; Rutter & Brown, 1966; and O'Connor & Brown, 1984; for details about the degree of interrater reliability that can be expected.) The general viability of the approach is perhaps best judged by the replicability of substantive findings that has been possible; see Leff and Vaughn (1988) for research on schizophrenia, and Brown (1989) for depression.

Table 3 outlines the relevance of the approach for the three paradoxes arising from the alternative respondent-based one. (a) Given improvement in external measures, analyses comparing internal and external measures are now a realistic possibility (e.g., a contrast of belief about a partner's effectiveness as a confidant [D, Table 1] and degree of actual confiding with partner [E, Table 1]). (b) Contextual measures offer much in dealing with methodological problems surrounding the study of the meaning. This is most easily seen in the study of life events, which are, of course, of central importance in the study of support (Brown & Harris, 1989). Furthermore, the exclusion of attitudinal material from situational measures means that internal and external measures of the same aspect of support are likely to provide significant theoretical insights. (c) Finally, the approach enables problems raised by the issue of time order to be realistically tackled. In terms of social support, it is particularly important in sorting out what occurred in the period immediately before onset. It is not unusual to find studies that make the unwarranted assumption that the quality of support has remained stable.

Insofar as an investigator-based account increases accuracy it becomes more realistic to consider the alternative possibility of real change. In fact, this can be done in the interview itself. First, it is possible to question about discrepancies: "But last time I saw you, you said you saw your sister . . . ." In this way it may well be possible to explain particular temporal discrepancies: "Yes, just after the New Year my sister became depressed about her marriage and called much less often." Because respondents typically give graphic and detailed accounts of what

Table 3 Potential advantages of investigator-based measures in terms of the three paradoxes

	Internal versus external measures
Strengths:	Development of common rating standards. Questions and probes can be used flexibly, and the recounting of stories encouraged. Both verbal and social aspects of speech can be utilized—whether expressed spontaneously or in response to a set question, and at any point of the interview.
Consequence:	Internal and external measures are of more or less equal accuracy, and can be more realistically compared.
	Meaning
Strengths:	Internal and external measures of the same phenomenon can be made. Contextual ratings to judge likely meaning—if necessary by consensus meetings.
Consequence:	Development of a methodological robust range of sensitive ratings concerning meaning and the environment.
	Time order
Strengths:	Intensive and flexible interviewing can date both environmental event, response to the event, and clinical course.
Consequence:	Causal inquiry is possible with retrospectively gathered material.

has occurred in such instances, it may be possible to make a good case for saying that a real change in behavior has or has not taken place.

The approach has other advantages; for example, with the use of tape recordings, new scales can be developed long after the original interview. However, Table 3 lists the major advantages—with the basic one being the flexibility in questioning that is possible (and necessary).

THREE STUDIES

By way of illustrating the discussion so far, I have first chosen, more or less at random, three papers: all were published in *Health Psychology* during 1989 and are excellent studies of their kind.

The first is the simplest. Support from a wife is shown to relate to both preoperative anxiety and postoperative recovery of coronary-bypass patients. Support is measured by whether or not a visit was made as often as 37% or more of the days spent in the hospital (Kulik & Mahler, 1989). It is a rare example of relevant behavior being observed, and in this sense fits into an investigator-based approach (E, Figure 1). The fact that a fifth of the wives were prevented from visiting because of distance or personal illness rather than through choice adds to the credibility of the author's conclusion that lack of support did influence medical outcome, because lack of contact is less likely to be related to characteristics of the patient and thereby a source of bias. Quality of marriage was quite unrelated to outcome—perhaps because it was a respondent-based measure using just one question dealing with whether it was excellent, good, fair, or poor (C, Table 1).

The other two studies are more ambitious, but utilize only respondent-based measures. The first concerns cardiac symptoms and distress in male patients seen in the hospital and subsequently at 3, 6, and 12 months following admission.

Structural modeling is used to link measures made at two points in time (Fontana, Kerns, Rosenberg, & Colonese, 1989). The authors note the similarity of the idea of support and loneliness, and a respondent-based measure is used as the sole support measure. This loneliness scale predicted symptomatology in the first two time comparisons but not the second two. Although it is an intriguing result, it is impossible to do more than speculate about what the loneliness questionnaire might represent. One of the shortcomings of such an instrument is the impossibility of gauging what lies behind a set of scores, as no material is collected about the thoughts, feelings, and behaviors on which the ratings are based.

The loneliness measure may also well have been confounded with depression in the patients. That is, although apparently intended as an external measure (C, Table 1), it is impossible to distinguish it from an internal one (A, Table 1). (Of course, if it is in fact merely attitudinal, the same point about confounding would equally hold.) Indeed, the study is gravely limited by the fact that all four of its central constructs—stressor, support, distress, and cardiac symptoms—could be influenced in this way. As the authors note, their findings may represent no more than the result of superordinate response bias such as defensiveness. As already noted, such measures have dominated the whole field of stress research and such a possibility is hardly a methodological quibble.

The last paper is in a number of ways the most sophisticated, although it again used only respondent-based measures with the limitations just outlined. In a prospective inquiry, 101 women whose children required medical attention were seen at initial contact and again 1 year later (Hobfoll & Lerman, 1989). The authors were concerned to relate (a) personal resources (self-esteem and mastery) and (b) intimacy in close relationships to (c) general support received 1 year later. Although the components of the various indices are quite sophisticated, only one overall score is used to represent them. For example, the third social support index uses a summated score based on five types of support (emotional assistance, being together when needed, information and advice, material assistance, and help performing a task) for up to 10 persons with whom the respondent reported feeling a close relationship. Such an aggregative measure greatly handicaps interpretation.

A key finding was that, among those with a child who had been ill on both occasions, there was a decrease in general support at time 2 among just those women who it had been predicted would do particularly well in terms of support because of the possession of either personal resources or intimacy at time 1. But measures are so confounded that the result is quite consistent with an actual *increase* in key support. Given the need to look after a badly handicapped child, support from a key tie such as spouse or mother might have increased in both amount and quality and that from others might have fallen—either because of an actual change or because they appear to be doing less when compared with the increased help from the key relative. But, because the various sources of support have been combined, it is impossible to explore such possibilities.

The problem of how best to combine the complex information typically collected about social support is critical for any type of data collection. Particularly important here are a number of issues concerning variation and change. For instance, Hobfoll and Lerman (1989) consider intimacy to be a "fairly stable construct" even though the correlation of initial and follow-up scores on its subscales are only .64, .49, and .56. The authors assume that the correlations will increase with better measurement. But why should such variation be seen in terms of measurement unreliability? It is equally possible that there have been real and important changes in the quality of social support over time. With the levels of reliability typically reached with respondent-based measures, there is no straightforward way of choosing between these two possibilities. The matter is obviously critical, if only by bringing to the fore the awkward fact that something like support may change over time. As already noted, the alternative approach to measurement is in a somewhat better position to tackle the problem. Although I do not wish to suggest that the investigator-based approach solves all the problems I have raised, recent research on the etiology and course of depression does illustrate some possible future applications, and at this point I will discuss in some detail a longitudinal study using the approach.

THE ISLINGTON LONGITUDINAL STUDY OF DEPRESSION

The Self-Evaluation and Social Support Schedule (SESS) and Crisis Support

The core of the study to be described consisted of a 1-year follow-up of a largely working-class sample of women living in Islington in North London with at least one child at home. The main instrument was the Self-Evaluation and Social Support Schedule (SESS), which employs both attitudinal (e.g., felt security in marriage) and situational measures (e.g., security characteristics of marriage). Many of the SESS scales in a broad sense deal with social support: the bulk of the 27 scales covering the marital relationship, for instance, are probably of some relevance for support. A marriage is described in terms of its identity-enhancing character (e.g., partner's expression of approval), security-increasing character (e.g., regularity of income, partner's predictability), felt security, expression of affective concern, positive quality of interaction, dependence on partner (e.g., degree to which he or she is leaned on), primary quality (e.g., degree to which it is characterized by fundamental acceptance), amount of confiding, belief about partner as confidant, partner's active emotional support in crises, closeness associated with sex, and so forth (O'Connor & Brown, 1984).

Other domains covered in similar detail are motherhood, housework, employment, other close ties, and further extrahousehold activity. It is the task of the interviewer to rate the material (usually from a tape recording) and each scale and scale point has appropriate definitions and anchoring examples. The majority are situational measures in the sense that the interviewer has to question fairly closely about relevant behavior and incidents, and feelings as such are ignored (E, Table 1). However, there are quite often parallel attitudinal scales dealing with both self-reported and spontaneously expressed feelings (D, Table 1).

Among those without depression of clinical severity at the time of first interview, 11% (32/303) developed depression in the follow-up year. For the great majority, this followed fairly closely a severely threatening event (29/32), most involving a significant loss or disappointment. These were often not the loss of a person as such but the loss of a cherished idea or goal (e.g., hearing a son had been charged with a serious offense). Because many studies have confirmed the importance of such events, the main focus of the Islington research was on the issue of vulnerability—why only one fifth of women with a severe event go on to develop depression (Brown, 1989). The analysis has been notable for the surprising number of factors of apparent importance. Moreover, although we finally concluded that quality of support was central for any theoretical understanding, initial forays pointed in quite the reverse direction. A situational measure about which we had set great store in the light of earlier research—confiding in husband at first interview—failed to predict who among married women would develop depression once a severe event had occurred (Brown et al., 1986). Even more surprising was that not 1 of the 17 attitudinal and situational scales associated with positive features of the marital relationship were of any use as predictors. To add to our puzzlement and confusion, scales reflecting negative features of the marriage almost without exception predicted onset extremely well.

Equally puzzling, this inconsistency in terms of negative and positive was not restricted to marital scales. It was, for instance, reflected in the central attitudinal measure of self-esteem (D2, Table 1): only an index based on negative comments predicted subsequent onset, with positive self-evaluation failing to do so (Brown et al., 1990).

We developed a number of rather farfetched (and quite interesting) ideas about what was going on, but it was only with a more sophisticated analysis of social support itself that a more persuasive explanation emerged. Before proceeding, it is necessary at this point to say more about the central measures of support. Most were situational rather than "attitudinal," and it should be assumed that these are being discussed unless explicitly stated.

Three types of *core* contacts were questioned about in detail at first interview: (a) spouse or cohabitee; (b) boyfriend/lover (usually only relevant for single mothers); and (c) very close others (VCOs), persons—other than a spouse cohabitee, boyfriend/lover, or a child at home if still a teenager—named at first interview in response to questions about to whom the respondent "felt very close."

A quite distinct exercise based on the follow-up interview focused on support actually given in the year following the first interview. The approach was more intensive than that at the first interview in the sense that a series of potential support figures were questioned about in relation to a particular severe event. Related severe events were covered by the rating (e.g., hearing a husband had cancer and the subsequent operation) as was any related major difficulty. Thus each person/severe event complex was given a separate record on which, in addition to a series of ratings, we recorded descriptive material and details of the subject's own feelings about the support received (Brown et al., 1986; Harris, Chapter 12). The detailed analysis of this follow-up material will be discussed later. At this point the outcome of a lengthy exercise will be anticipated and the index of crisis support that eventually emerged is described. Such support was considered present only when a core person (e.g., spouse/partner, boyfriend/lover, or VCO) met the following criteria with regard to a particular event/difficulty complex in the follow-up period: (a) The subject confided in them about the crisis, *and* (b) received in return emotional support, *and* (c) did not at same point experience a negative response concerning her behavior.

The use of this index enabled us to clarify the puzzling result already reported concerning the failure of first-interview positive scales to predict depression. Table 4 (dealing with the husbands of the married women) shows how the result becomes understandable when the crisis support measure was compared with support received at the time of the first interview. For women experiencing onset, the severe

Table 4 Confiding in husband at first interview, crisis support during the follow-up year, and onset of depression among those with a provoking agent (97 married Islington women)

Confiding in husband at first interview	Crisis support from husband during follow-up: Yes		Total
	Yes	No	Total
	% with onset	% with onset	% with onset
		"let down"	
Yes	a: 4 (1/28)	b: 37 (7/19)	17 (8/47)
No	c: 25 (2/8)	d: 24 (10/42)	24 (12/50)

Crisis support not known for 4.

event immediately before onset (and presumably provoking it) was selected for study and for other women the severe event nearest interview. Women who failed to receive the support from their husbands that they might reasonably have expected on the basis of the level of their confiding at the time of first interview were defined as "let down." It is important to deal with Table 4 in some detail. It shows, as would be expected, that those women who received no support from their husbands on either occasion had a high risk of developing depression (d). Women who were let down—in the sense of confiding in their husbands at the earlier point, but failing to obtain crisis support from them (b)—were at particularly high risk, and it was only those who received support on both occasions (a) who were at low risk. There were a few women who received unexpected support with the event from their husbands despite an earlier nonconfiding situation (c) and the risk of depression among them was still high.

As already noted, the association of first-interview lack of confiding and subsequent depression (righthand totals, Table 4) fell well short of statistical significance. However, as has now been made clear, it would be highly misleading to take this at face value as the high risk of depression among those let down suppresses any association. Once these women are omitted, the expected result emerges (a, Table 4). A further important point is not shown in Table 4, because, for the sake of simplification, crisis support from elsewhere has been omitted. Among the 42 women who received no support on either occasion from their husbands (d), there was an almost complete absence of depression for the 21 who received crisis support from someone named at the first interview as very close—usually a woman. (Only 1 of the 21, in fact, developed depression.) There was regrettably no hint of such protection where a woman had been let down by her husband (b).

There are, therefore, two ways of presenting results concerning support. Continuing with married women, if only crisis support is considered, and ignoring the notion of being let down, three times more of those not receiving than receiving crisis support from a husband or VCO developed depression—40% (12/30) and 12% (8/67), respectively ($p < .01$). The second way takes into account those let down. Here adequate support was defined as receiving crisis support as long as the woman was neither let down by her husband nor a VCO. Using this index the difference in risk of depression is 10-fold—43% (18/42) and 4% (2/55), respectively ($p < .001$). Those with an inadequate supportive context, in these terms, include two women who received crisis support from their husbands, but who were let down by a VCO, and both of those suffered onset. However, it should be noted that VCO here is used generically; a woman was not counted as "let down by VCO" if there was crisis support from at least one of her other VCOs.

So far only married women have been discussed and they were particularly prone to be let down. Support for single mothers was much more stable. Those who had a VCO in whom they were confiding at the time of first interview practically always received support in a crisis. Indeed, the overall high risk of depression among single mothers was related less to being let down than to the substantial number who lacked support in the first place (Brown et al., 1986). Only 7% (2/28) of those receiving crisis support developed depression, compared with 38% (8/21) who did not receive such support ($p < .05$). This result hardly changes when those (a small number) let down are taken into account.

For the women as a whole, ignoring marital status, the link of crisis support with onset was impressive—10% (9/92) with support developed depression once a provoking agent had occurred, compared with 39% (21/54) without support. But this does not consider the fact of being let down, especially the fact that when a woman was let down by her husband, crisis support from a VCO was unprotective. To take this into account, as already explained for married women, hierarchical rules were employed concerning when crisis support was canceled in this way to develop a second index, *adequacy of supportive context* (see Table 5 for details for married and single mothers). The association of this second index increases the basic link: once a provoking agent occurred only 4% (3/80) with an adequate supportive context developed depression, compared with 41% (27/66) without.

Aggregate Measures

Having dealt with the final indices, I will revert to the initial stages of the analysis that led up to the development of these indices. Given their success, it needs to be emphasized that the association between onset and the *individual* support measures were usually at best modest and most often nonexistent. This is summarized in Tables 6 and 7. (To maximize the chances of showing an association, findings are given for only those with a provoking agent and then at a 10% level of significance.) Results for married women and single mothers are presented separately because types of support could have different implications for them. The presentation has been simplified by the use of dichotomies, but the utilization of more categories does not change results in any important way. The measures are a mixture of aggregate (lack of social isolation) and specific (confiding in husband) ratings.

The first section of Table 6 deals with first-interview material concerning support: it shows that for married women not one measure related to onset. This was at least in part a result of the suppressing effect of being let down, which was common among the married.[3] For single mothers there is just one significant first-

[3]We also had the impression that this initial measurement of "active emotional support" from a husband was quite often inaccurate. With hindsight and in the light of follow-up material, a number of the married women appeared to display a certain amount of wish-fulfillment in their initial accounts. Indeed, it may require the occurrence of an important crisis quite close to the point of measurement for this rating to reach a reasonable degree of accuracy.

Table 5 Stages in defining adequate supportive context

1. Persons	
Core ties:	Husband/cohabitee.
	Boyfriend/lover.
	Very close other (VCO), someone named as "very close" at first interview, excluding both the above and teenage children at home.
2. Scales re particular event/difficulty complex in follow-up period	
Scales:	Confiding.
	Active emotional support.
	Negative response (to subject's confiding about crisis).
3. Definition of crisis support (CS) for each core the re selected event/difficulty complex in follow-up period	
Presence of confiding, presence of active emotional support, and absence of negative response.	
4. Definition of "let down"	
For husband/cohabitee/boyfriend/lover: lack of CS at follow-up when there was confiding at first interview.	
For VCO: lack of CS from all first interview VCOs (i.e., a woman was not considered let down if CS was received, say, from at least one VCO).	
5. Definition of adequate supportive context	
Married:	CS from husband/cohabitee and no let down by VCO.
	CS from VCO and no let down by husband.
Single mother:	CS from VCO and no let down by boyfriend/lover.
	CS from boyfriend/lover and no let down by VCO.

interview result and this is substantial: all but one of the onsets occurred among women without a "true" very close other. (A "true" VCO was defined as one who was confided in and seen quite often; see Brown et al., 1986, for details.) This marked difference between the two marital status groups relates to the fact, already noted, that the support in a crisis in the follow-up year was highly predictable for single mothers, and that for single mothers support from a VCO could not be overridden by being let down by a partner—by definition for single mothers all boyfriends/lovers were noncohabitating.

The second section of Table 6 concerns aggregate ratings about support in the follow-up year, concentrating on the key severe event/major difficulty complex. The results are, if anything, even more bleak. For married women only one of these aggregate measures was predictive, and this, involving formal contacts (e.g., with a doctor or social worker), was the *reverse* of what might be expected. The three measures that do show a trend involve the scales already discussed in relation to the crisis support index.[4] For single mothers none of the follow-up measures were related to onset: the clearcut first-interview result concerning "true" VCOs entirely disappears—doubtless because of the fact that it has been diluted by the use of an aggregate rating in which any lack of support from a VCO would be taken into account.

Table 7 turns to still more detailed material concerning support with a particular severe event/difficulty complex in the follow-up year. Some are specific and relate to just one person (e.g., husband, or the VCO giving the "highest" amount of support) and others are aggregate (e.g., overall rating of all personal contacts, or

[4]There were, in addition to the measures shown in Table 3, a series of ratings concerning general support irrespective of whether or not it was in response to a severe event or difficulty complex. These gave similar and, if anything, even worse results.

Table 6 Measures of "support" and onset of depression for women with a provoking agent (i.e., severe event or major difficulty) by marital status

	First interview support measures							
	Married				Single mother			
	Present % onset		Absent % onset		Present % onset		Absent % onset	
Close relatives in area study	17	(13/65)	19	(7/36)	16	(6/38)	36	(4/11)
Any contact with parent	21	(14/68)	18	(6/33)	18	(5/28)	24	(5/21)
Birth place in area of study	23	(16/60)	15	(6/41)	12	(2/17)	25	(8/32)
Social circle kin-based	20	(13/65)	17	(6/36)	15	(3/20)	24	(7/29)
Lack of social isolation	20	(12/60)	20	(8/41)	23	(5/22)	19	(5/27)
Lack of felt loneliness	18	(15/84)	25	(4/16)	18	(6/34)	27	(4/15)
Informal social participation	19	(12/63)	21	(8/38)	25	(7/28)	14	(3/21)
Positive quality of social/ recreational/activity	19	(14/74)	22	(6/27)	19	(6/31)	22	(4/18)
Confiding in husband	17	(8/48)	23	(12/53)	—		—	
Belief in husband as a confidant	19	(14/74)	22	(6/27)	—		—	
Husband's active emotional support	20	(11/56)	20	(9/45)	—		—	
Existence of very close other (VCO)	20	(17/83)	17	(3/18)	15	(6/40)	44	(4/9)
Existence of a "true" VCO (seen often and confided in)	24	(12/51)	16	(8/50)	4	(1/23)	35	(9/26)[c]
Existence of a boyfriend/lover	—		—		20	(4/20)	21	(6/29)

Aggregate ratings dealing with the quality of support as a whole in the follow-up year

	Present % onset		Absent % onset		Present % onset		Absent % onset	
Based on social network								
Confiding	18	(12/67)	27	(8/30)	22	(7/32)	18	(3/17)
Active emotional support	16	(10/64)	30	(10/33)	20	(6/30)	21	(4/19)
Negative response	50	(6/12)	21	(9/43)	14	(1/7)	17	(14/84)
Practical support	16	(5/31)	23	(15/66)	33	(5/15)	15	(5/34)
Based on formal contacts								
Confiding	35	(6/17)	18	(14/80)	20	(3/15)	21	(7/34)
Active emotional support	40	(6/15)	17	(14/82)[a]	28	(2/7)	19	(8/42)
Practical support	18	(2/11)	21	(18/86)	33	(2/6)	19	(8/43)

[a] $< .10$.
[b] $< .05$.
[c] $< .01$.

"mean" support from VCOs).[5] To simplify the presentation, only details of the emotional support scale are given, except for the scale dealing with perceived support. (Very similar results are obtained for the two other scales included in the crisis support index.) Results are now a little better. For married women, only measures dealing with core ties (e.g., husband/cohabitee or VCO) are related to onset. Support from a formal contact is again, if anything, inversely related to onset, and this may even hold for emotional support from noncore contacts. The clearest results emerge with the most specific type of measure—that is, when the

[5]The "highest" means the best support where there is more than one person in the category, and the average deals with all persons in a category.

Table 7 "Positive" ratings of terms of support in key crisis in follow-up year

		Emotional support				
		Positive		Not positive		% diff.
		% onset				
Married women						
Type of emotional support						
	1. Overall; all personal contacts	16	(10/64)	32	(10/33)	16
	2. Overall; formal contacts	40	(6/15)	17	(14/82)[a]	−23
Core	3. Husband/partner/boyfriend/lover	15	(6/40)	25	(14/57)	10
Core	4. Very close other; highest	16	(8/49)	25	(12/48)	9
Core	5. Very close other; mean	16	(7/44)	25	(13/53)	9
	6. Core; highest	16	(11/70)	33	(9/27)[a]	17
	7. Core; mean	16	(8/51)	26	(12/46)	10
	8. Noncore; highest	27	(4/15)	20	(16/81)	−7
	9. Noncore; mean	24	(5/21)	20	(15/75)	−4
	10. All; highest	15	(11/73)	33	(8/24)[b]	18
	11. All; mean	16	(9/58)	28	(11/39)	12
General support						
	Perceived helpfulness; highest	18	(13/73)	25	(7/28)	7
Single mothers						
Type of emotional support						
	1. Overall; all personal contacts	20	(6/30)	21	(4/19)	1
	2. Overall; formal contacts	25	(2/8)	20	(8/41)	−5
Core	3. Husband/partner/boyfriend/lover	13	(1/8)	22	(9/41)	9
Core	4. Very close other; highest	4	(1/23)	35	(9/26)[c]	31
Core	5. Very close other; mean	6	(1/17)	21	(9/42)	15
	6. Core; highest	7	(2/27)	36	(8/22)[b]	29
	7. Core; mean	6	(1/17)	28	(9/32)	22
	8. Noncore; highest	27	(4/15)	18	(6/34)	−9
	9. Noncore; mean	31	(4/13)	17	(6/36)	−14
	10. All; highest	21	(7/34)	20	(3/15)	1
	11. All; mean	27	(6/22)	26	(4/27)	1
General support						
	Perceived helpfulness; highest	21	(7/33)	19	(3/16)	2

[a] < .10.
[b] < .05.
[c] < .01.

highest support received from a core contact is taken. Associations tend to be attenuated if the average score is employed (compare rows 6 and 7).

For single mothers, only VCO ties are important. (The result concerning highest support is, in fact, the same as for the first-interview measure.) Indeed, as with the married mothers, emotional support from noncore ties tends to be inversely related to onset (rows 8 and 9), and the VCO result itself disappears when all ties are considered (rows 10 and 11).

Although the VCO result for single mothers is clear cut, the results for married women are still unsatisfactory; indeed, it was only when the crisis support index utilizing the three measures of confiding, emotional support, and lack of a negative response were considered together that substantial associations emerged. For single mothers, the measure of emotional support alone gave the same result as when combined with other components of the crisis support index, because for them emotional support almost always went with high confiding and lack of a negative response.

For methodological reasons, the greatest emphasis in dealing with support has been placed on situational measures. Obviously, it would have been more difficult to rule out possible contamination if attitudinal measures had been utilized. However, some attitudinal measures were collected (e.g., belief in husband as a confidant and feelings of loneliness in Table 6, and perceived helpfulness in Table 7), but there was no suggestion that they performed essentially any better. Indeed, if anything, evidence pointed in the reverse direction, attitudinal measures doing poorly. (This was made clear in an earlier publication in discussing the perceived helpfulness of core crisis support; see Brown et al., 1986, p. 821.)

It has been necessary to move away from first-interview measures because of the frequency of being let down among married women. When dealt with in the follow-up situation, clear-cut results have only emerged when particular individuals, particular aspects of support, and particular crises have been examined. Furthermore, for married women (where different facets of support were only modestly correlated), it was necessary to create a crisis support index taking three different aspects into account.

As already clarified, the crisis support index itself ignores the implications of the high risk associated with being let down and, as already described, a second (hierarchical-based) index of adequacy of supportive context was developed. This index enabled us to take account of the high rate of onset for a married woman, even when receiving crisis support from a VCO, if she had been let down by her husband. The results underline the point made earlier about the danger of using aggregate measures.

One reason for the almost universal use of aggregate measures, of course, is the daunting amount of material that can be collected about support even in a relatively modest interview. It is all too easy, whatever approach to data collection is employed, to generate a great deal of material about support, and understandably it has been tempting to cope with this by using indices combining different individuals and different aspects of support. (A comparable example in the field of stress research is the practice of aggregating life events into "scores.")

CONCLUSION

An approach to measurement has been outlined, which, I believe, is best able to explore the complex issues surrounding the study of social support, but which is not well represented in the methodological literature. It may be described as one with an epidemiological base, but still able to deal with case-history material; one that emphasizes systematic measurement, but retains the ability to develop new measures once material has been collected; one that deals with what respondents say about relevant phenomena, but also uses the investigator to judge what has taken place; and one that recognizes the possibility that special precautions have to be made if its empirical generalizations are not to be threatened by bias, and yet allows the respondent to talk at length and develop narrative and stories about relevant phenomena. However, it is possible to find signs of a growing recognition that the "hard" and "soft" aspects of social research must be brought together. Indeed, much of the intellectual rationale for this is probably already in place. Perhaps its chief enemy will remain its financial cost—although this can be greatly exaggerated (Brown & Harris, 1989), and without some change of heart by fund-giving bodies and thesis committees, it is likely to remain a minority activity. Having said this, a field of inquiry such as that of social support, bearing in mind that it can draw on some of the funding resources of medicine, stands as good a chance as any of promoting such an eclectic approach—and even, in time, adding a much needed experimental component.

Given the importance I have placed on the notion of "let down," it may be helpful to say more about it. Although the term conveys the kind of process we had in mind, we have on occasion slightly regretted its use as it suggests a greater coherence in the underlying phenomenon than is the case. We chose to define being "let down" in terms of discontinuity of support because it could then be easily operationalized. Unfortunately, this meant that for a handful of the women the term is probably inappropriate. For example, for the 16 women with an onset who were also let down by a husband or a VCO, 3 were not strictly let down. In one instance, the discontinuity in support was related to the fact that she felt unable to discuss with her husband her son's death following an accident (they had had a difficult relationship); a second said she was too caught up in the crisis to contact her VCO; and the third felt too ashamed to discuss the event with her mother. Fortunately, the term was not misleading for the majority, and in future research it should be easy enough to develop a more strictly accurate index.

The interpretation of the let-down result itself seems best incorporated into the findings concerning the role of severe events; that is, because both experiences probably serve to increase risk of depression by inducing feelings of hopelessness. If this were so, being let down would often represent a double blow and one likely to increase hopelessness (and probably decrease self-esteem) beyond the impact of the initiating event. On occasions, even when the event is severe, it might be the major or only reason for hopelessness.

It is also probably useful to emphasize the other side of the support indices, stressing the reception of adequate support. Those positive on the indices always received support as part of a long-term relationship and usually in the context of continuity of trust. (The few women receiving support only at follow-up [C, Table 4] were not rated as receiving adequate support.) Those not positive on the index certainly did not have such continuity.

Such an emphasis on support in a positive sense raises the question of why it should be important. The need for contact with others appears to have been critical in both the evolution of the central nervous system and in the behavior of social primates. Adler and Adler (1975) have described the positive consequences of contact-comfort in human beings in terms of "an absence of tension and feeling of well-being, which Sandler and Joffe (1968) believe to be a more potent reinforcing agent than either pleasure or the avoidance of pain" (p. 70). In an ethological context Chance (1988), on the basis of work with chimpanzees, has developed a similar theme in terms of a biological hedonic mode; and Weiss (1982) has identified heightened comfort and diminished anxiety as one of the key components of attachment in adolescence and adulthood. I point out this linking of the idea of support with the experience of contact-comfort in primates because of the possibility that, in defining some of the minutiae of supportive behavior, we may overlook the importance of the mere presence of (and perhaps physical contact with) a core tie.

Once a crisis has occurred, what may be critical is the continuation of some activation of the contact-safety system. This, rather than specific kinds of help, may be what is protective. Pearlin (1985) notes that "people embedded in primary relationships often think of themselves as entirely self-reliant, suggesting that emotional support is something built into such relationships rather than something that needs to be consciously sought from them" (p. 45). Perhaps part of the importance of indices, such as crisis support or adequacy of supportive context, is that such behavior is an effective way of perpetuating a sense of support-safety. Indeed, it is possible that, if there is good reason for the absence of the support figure (e.g., because he is serving in the armed services at sea), a protective effect may be possible at a distance. (Because such figures are typically either present or do not have "good" reasons for their absence, a direct test of this may be difficult.)

There might also be differences in the impact of kinds of support in relation to diagnostic condition. The actual presence of the person may be more important to ward off "anxiety" (as in the study of coronary bypass patients) than "depression." However, I would not want, in any case, to push the point about mere presence too far. Where there are obvious helpful things that can be done to alleviate a crisis, it may well not be enough. Nor do I wish to suggest that, even where presence in terms of contact-safety is critical, cognitive activity is never involved. The presence of a support figure (and the effect it has on biological processes) may make it easier for the person to remind herself of the existence of important long-term plans and goals (perhaps reflected in the tie with the person), and thus provide a sufficient influx of hope to prevent depression—at least of clinical severity.

As a further complexity, there are individual differences to be taken into account. Personality factors are doubtless sometimes critical in determining the kind of support network available to a person and how far it is experienced as protective. In the recent dimensional system discussed by Cloninger (1986, 1988), it is easy to see that those extreme on the personality dimension of "novelty seeking" will tend more often to disrupt ongoing supportive relationships than those high on "harm avoidance"; and the latter will be more affected by the absence of expected support than the former. There are, of course, many possibilities, some of which have been discussed in the Islington study in terms of the presence of a small group of "nonoptimal confiders" who were at particular risk for depression (Andrews & Brown, 1989). These subjects confided highly in at least one person at the time of crisis, but either received (a) no emotional support from anyone they confided in, or (b) received it only from a noncore tie. (In the study as a whole, the presence of the latter was unrelated to any lowering of risk.)

Such nonoptimal confiding was related to early inadequate parenting, and we were struck by two conflicting attitudes among the women. On the one hand, there was a certain reluctance about seeking support, often voiced as being the result of prior unpleasant experiences. On the other hand, this often went with an apparent naivete or romanticism about the amount of trust or confidence it was appropriate to place in would-be supportive ties. It seemed clear that some of the women needed to believe, in spite of contrary evidence, that those close to them were helpful and supportive.

It seems possible that for women with both early inadequate parenting and nonoptimal confiding we are dealing with the convergence of three linked processes. First, the women appeared to have had some difficulty in developing the kinds of relationships within which trust and dependence were realistic. This can be seen most clearly in their high ratings of attitudinal constraints about receiving support. It is possible that a fear of intimacy prevented some of the women from getting close to people who could genuinely reciprocate. Second, many of the women, because of their current circumstances, appeared to have very real difficulties in finding suitable support figures. For example, hardly any of the single mothers with early inadequate parenting had been born in the area, which may have limited their choices. Where support from both parents was concerned, even if they were living nearby, the chances of receiving genuine support from them was probably limited bearing in mind the quality of early care. Third, given that the women appeared to persist in banking on unsatisfactory relationships, there is perhaps an understandable tendency for them to romanticize particular relationships.

It is probably appropriate to study personality much along the lines of the kind of naturalistic approach I have described for the study of social support in general. Characteristics should not be assumed to be enduring; less than perfect test-retest correlations should not automatically be seen in terms of measurement error. Behavior should be seen, as much as possible, in context and, if possible, in terms of a person's whole life span. It is doubtful whether the effects of support are ever "pure"; a certain ineptness in seeking support, insofar as personality is involved, is likely to be influenced by temperament as well as early attachment experiences. Equally, a series of adverse experiences, perhaps prompted by such ineptness, is likely to have pushed a woman into current circumstances (say single motherhood) that increase her difficulties in a genuine sense. There may well be very real constraints in such circumstances on what can be done to obtain support—because of lack of money, current depression, isolation, and so forth (see Andrews & Brown, 1989).

MOVING BEYOND ONSET OF DEPRESSION

There are a number of other issues that ideally require discussion concerning support and depression. Of these, probably the most important is that the role of lack of support needs to be considered in terms of a number of other risk factors, such as the severity of the stressor and prior low self-esteem. The issue is too complex to deal with in this essay, but it is clear that, in coming to terms with the etiological role of social support, stressors and background risk factors such as low self-esteem cannot be viewed as independent. Effective analyses need to face a considerable degree of interrelationship between the different etiological factors with conditional or interactive factors likely to prove critical (Brown et al., 1990c), and here it is by no means clear that the current fashion of using structural equation modeling is necessarily the best way forward (Brown, 1989; Brown, Harris, & Lemyre, 1991). However, rather than attempt to pursue these complex matters I will, finally, comment on issues other than onset of depression.

There is no reason to believe that the lack of support that is important for onset of depression will be equally relevant once a depressive condition has taken a chronic course; the same point has been made about response to bereavement, where it has been argued (with interesting evidence) that, after the initial period of grief, a more active form of support is what is required and that a rather different range of ties may prove important (Bankoff, 1983). There is also some suggestion that for depression, at least support of relevance for men may be rather different from that relevant for women (Bolton & Oatley, 1986). Furthermore, to return to the issue of aggregative indices, these may be more useful for tackling issues other than onset—for example, in increasing the chances of a "positive" event occurring (such as getting a new job) that might help in recovery (Brown, Adler, & Bifulco, 1988). This may well be a function of the range of close ties capable of initiating the search for a job, the starting of divorce proceedings, the seeking of a reconciliation, and so forth.

There is a surprising absence of evidence that lack of support acts as a vulnerability factor, for onset of anxiety/phobic conditions, often found with depression, although the onset of anxiety-phobic conditions is highly related to the occurrence of severe events (i.e., involving danger rather than loss) (Finlay-Jones, 1989). Perhaps even more curious, there is evidence that women who have a history of receiving high levels of support may be particularly vulnerable to anxiety; in the rural Outer Hebrides depression was found to be highly related to lack of integration in the traditional way of life—measured by living on a small working farm and regular church attendance. Chronic anxiety showed the reverse gradient with the highest rates among the most integrated women (Prudo et al., 1981). Most of the anxiety conditions appear to have been provoked—often many years before—by the death of a close relative. There can be no question of the general supportiveness of the Hebridean way of life and it is possible that some of the women, because of this intense support, had not always been able to get a firm sense of themselves as a distinct person and therefore the death of someone close had a particularly adverse effect on their sense of security (Prudo, Brown, Harris, & Dowland, 1981).

Finlay-Jones (1989) recently published evidence that parental divorce in childhood relates to an increased risk of anxiety once a "danger" event has occurred, and it is possible that emotional experiences of importance for vulnerability to anxiety states may be found to be tied more to the past than to the current environment, and that the reverse holds for depression. It is also possible that the result reflects a quite different basis in the centralized nervous system for the two conditions. While anxiety and depressive states undoubtedly often occur together, recent work on the critical role of the amygdala in emotional experience is consistent with the possibility that processes relating to anxiety are more "automatic" in the sense of bypassing higher cortical centers (Le Doux, 1989).

Such examples also suggest the need to closely consider possible adverse effects of the human need for "security-safety." Some may place particular reliance on symbols of support—say the existence of a geographically distant parent or an all-protective God—only to find they are not helpful once a major loss occurs. It is also probably common to take for granted a core source of support/safety and fail to recognize the degree of one's dependence. In time this may well lead the person to abuse the relationship. It may, for instance, be used as a secure base for a variety of adventures, which in time serve to undermine the basis of the background support. Paradoxically, one of the major sources of "vulnerability" in women may prove to be (as a result of their child-rearing role) their greater awareness of their dependence. Given that the woman conveys this to her partner, it may better enable the partner to act without awareness of his dependence on her, which can lead to serious abuse of the relationship.

REFERENCES

Adler, H. M., & Adler, F. (1975). A group system hypothesis as an explanation of sociologic phenomena. *Social Psychiatry, 10,* 69–77.

Andrews, B., & Brown, G. W. (1988). Social support, onset of depression and personality: An exploratory analysis. *Social Psychiatry, 23,* 99–108.

Bankoff, E. A. (1983). Social support and adaptation to widowhood. *Journal of Marriage and the Family, 45,* 827–839.

Bolton, W., & Oatley, K. (1987). A longitudinal study of social support and depression in unemployed men. *Psychological Medicine, 17,* 453–460.

Brown, G. W., (1974). Meaning, measurement, and stress of life events. In B. S. Dohrenwend & B. P. Dohrenwend (Eds.), *Stressful life events: Their nature and effects.* New York: Wiley.

Brown, G. W. (1988). Causal paths, chains and strands. In M. Rutter (Ed.), *Studies of psychological risk: The power of longitudinal data.* Cambridge: Cambridge University Press.

Brown, G. W. (1989). Life events and measurement. In G. W. Brown & T. O. Harris, *Life events and illness.* New York: Guilford Press. London: Unwin & Hyman.

Brown, G. W., Adler, Z., & Bifulco, A. (1988). Life events, difficulties and recovery from chronic depression. *British Journal of Psychiatry, 152,* 115–128.

Brown, G. W., Andrews, B., Bifulco, A., & Veiel, H. (1990a). Self-esteem and depression: 1. Measurement issues and prediction of onset. *Social Psychiatry and Psychiatric Epidemiology, 25,* 200–209.

Brown, G. W., Andrews, B., Harris, T. O., Adler, Z., & Bridge, L. (1986). Social support, self-esteem and depression. *Psychological Medicine, 16,* 813–831.

Brown, G. W., & Bifulco, A. (1990). Motherhood, employment and the development of depression: A replication of a finding? *British Journal of Psychiatry, 156,* 169–179.

Brown, G. W., Bifulco, A., & Andrews, B. (1990c). Self-esteem and depression: 3. Aetiological issues. *Social Psychiatry & Psychiatric Epidemiology, 25,* 235–243.

Brown, G. W., Bifulco, A., Veiel, H., & Andrews, B. (1990b). Self-esteem and depression: 2. Social correlates of self-esteem. *Social Psychiatry and Psychiatric Epidemiology, 25,* 225–234.

Brown, G. W., Bone, M., Dalison, B., & Wing, J. K. (1966). *Schizophrenia and social care.* Maudesley Monograph, No. 17. London: Oxford University.

Brown, G. W., & Harris, T. O. (1986). Establishing causal links: The Bedford college studies of depression. In H. Katschnig (Ed.), *Life events and psychiatric disorders.* Cambridge: Cambridge University Press.

Brown, G. W., & Harris, T. O.(1982) Fall-off in the reporting of life events. *Social Psychiatry, 17,* 23–28.

Brown, G. W., Harris, T. O., & Lemyre, L. (1991). Now you see it, now you don't—Some considerations on multiple regression. In D. Magnusson, L. R. Bergman, G. Rudinger, & B. Torestad (Eds.), *Problems and methods in longitudinal research: Stability and change.* Cambridge: Cambridge University Press.

Brown, G. W., & Rutter, M. (1966). The measurement of family activities and relationships: A methodological study. *Human Relations, 19,* 241–263.

Chance, M. R. A. (1988). *Social fabrics of the mind.* Hove & London: Lawrence Erlbaum.

Cloninger, C. R. (1986). A unified biosocial theory of personality and its role in the development of anxiety states. *Psychiatric Developments, 3,* 167–226.

Cloninger, C. R. (1988). A unified biosocial theory of personality and its role in the development of anxiety states: A reply to commentaries. *Psychiatric Developments, 2,* 83–120.

Cohen, S., & Syme, S. L. (1985). *Social support and health.* London, New York: Academic Press.

Finlay-Jones, R. (1989). Anxiety. In G. W. Brown & T. O. Harris (Eds.), *Life events and illness.* New York: Guilford Press. London: Unwin & Hyman.

Finlay-Jones, R., & Brown, G. W., (1981). Types of stressful life event and the onset of anxiety and depressive disorders. *Psychological Medicine, 11,* 803–815.

Fontana, A. F., Kerns, R. D., Rosenberg, R. L., & Colonese, K. L. (1989). Support, stress and recovery from coronary heart disease: A longitudinal causal model. *Health Psychology, 8,* 175–193.

Henderson, A. S., & Brown, G. W. (1988). Social support: The hypothesis and the evidence. In A. S. Henderson & G. D. Burrows (Eds.), *Handbook of social psychiatry.* Amsterdam: Elsevier.
Henderson, A. S., Byrne, D. G., & Duncan-Jones, P. (1981). *Neurosis and the social environment.* London: Academic Press.
Hinkle, L. E., Jr., & Wolff, H. K. (1957). Health and social environment: Experimental investigations. In A. H. Leighton, J. A. Clauson, & R. N. Wilson (Eds.), *Explorations in social psychiatry.* New York: Basic Books.
Hobfoll, S. E., & Lerman, L. (1989). Predicting receipt of social support: A longitudinal study of parents' reactions to their child's illness. *Health Psychology, 8,* 61–77.
Kulik, J. A., & Mahler, H. I. M. (1989). Social support and recovery from surgery. *Health Psychology, 8,* 221–238.
Le Doux, J. E. (1989). Cognitive-emotional interactions in the brain. *Cognition and Emotion, 3,* 267–289.
Leff, J., & Vaughan, C. (1985). *Expressed emotion in families: Its significance for mental illness.* New York: Guilford Press.
O'Connor, P., & Brown, G. W. (1984). Supportive relationships: Fact or fancy? *Journal of Social and Personal Relationships, 1,* 159–175.
Pearlin, L. I. (1985). Social structure and processes of social support. In S. Cohen & S. L. Syme (Eds.), *Social support and health.* London & Florida: Academic Press.
Prudo, R., Brown, G. W., Harris, T. O., & Dowland, J. (1981). Psychiatric disorder in a rural and an urban population: 2. Sensitivity to loss. *Psychological Medicine, 11,* 601–616.
Rahe, R. H. (1969). Life crisis and health change. In P. R. May & J. R. Wittenborn (Eds.), *Psychotropic drug response: Advances in prediction.* Springfield, UK: Charles C. Thomas.
Robins, L. N., Helzer, J. R., Croughan, J., & Ratcliff, K. S. (1981). National Institutes of Mental Health interview schedule. Its history, characteristics & validity. *Archives of General Psychiatry, 38,* 381–389.
Rutter, M., & Brown, G. W. (1966). The reliability and validity of measures of family life and relationships in families containing a psychiatric patient. *Social Psychiatry, 1,* 38–53.
Sandler, J., & Joffe, W. G. (1968). Psychoanalytic psychology and learning theory in the role of learning. In R. Porter (Ed.), *Psychotherapy.* Boston: Little, Brown and Company.
Schmidt, I., Scharfetter, C., & Binder, J. (1981). Lebensereignisse in Abhangigkeit von soziodemographischen variablen. *Social Psychiatry, 16,* 63–68.
Weiss, R. S. (1982). Attachment in adult life. In C. M. Parkes & J. Stevenson-Hinde (Eds.), *The place of attachment in human behaviour.* New York: Basic Books. London: Tavistock Press.

16

Perceived Support and Adjustment to Stress: Methodological Considerations

Ronald C. Kessler
University of Michigan, USA

Despite a dramatic growth of interest in the effects of social support over the past decade, fundamental problems of research methods have not been resolved and still interfere with the advancement of work in this area. For example, controversy still exists over whether standard statistical approaches for estimating the stress-buffering effects of support are appropriate (Landerman, George, Campbell, & Blazer, 1989). This chapter focuses on one limited class of these methodological problems, involving the interpretation of the relationship between perceived support and adjustment to stress. I argue that issues of measurement, design, and analysis must all be addressed with an appreciation of the substantive complexities involved in interpreting the effects of perceived support if methodological roadblocks are to be removed in this area of research. The discussion of these methodological issues begins by reviewing what I consider to be the core substantive issues in interpreting the effects of perceived support. I then propose three types of research designs that I consider particularly promising avenues for future development. Measurement and analysis issues associated with these designs are also discussed.

BACKGROUND

It is now well established that perceptions of social support availability are associated with emotional adjustment to stress (Cohen, 1988; Cohen & Wills, 1985; House, Landis, & Umberson, 1988; Kessler & McLeod, 1985). It is less clear, however, how these protective effects come about or how one might intervene to enhance them. Given this uncertainty, social support researchers have increasingly turned their attention to identifying the specific interpersonal processes thought to underlie social support effects (Eckenrode, 1983; Gottlieb, 1988; Heller, Swindle, & Dusenbury, 1986; Reis, 1984).

Preparation of this manuscript was supported by Research Scientist Development Award K02 MH00507 from the U.S. National Institute of Mental Health. The author would like to thank his colleagues in the Psychosocial Factors in Mental Health and Illness Training Program for useful comments on an earlier version of this paper, which was presented at a seminar of the Training Program. He would also like to thank Niall Bolger, Roxanne Silver, Hans O. Veiel, Elaine Wethington, and Camille Wortman for useful discussions about the ideas presented here.

Although this line of investigation is too new to draw firm conclusions, naturalistic studies up to now have generally found that actual support transactions do not improve adjustment to stressful life experiences. Indeed, most studies have documented that support receipt is either associated with poor adjustment or, at best, leaves the recipient no better off than if support had not been received (Barrera, 1986; Sandler & Barrera, 1984; Sarason, Shearin, Pierce, & Sarason, 1987; Stokes, 1983).

We do not yet understand why receiving support appears to be ineffective in reducing distress, although three possibilities have been suggested as explanations. One possibility is that people who receive support are under more stress than those who do not receive support. Consistent with this view, Barrera (1986) has shown that the seemingly bad effect of receiving support is reduced when individual differences in stress severity are controlled. A second possibility is that getting help entails a cost to self-esteem (Fisher, Nadler, & Whitcher-Alagna, 1982; Shapiro, 1978). By this reasoning, received support may be ineffective because the cost to self-esteem counteracts the benefit of getting support. A third reason why received support may be ineffective is that people's attempts to give support may be miscarried; that is, their actions may make matters worse for the person under stress (Coyne, Wortman, & Lehman, 1988).

PERCEIVED SUPPORT AS A DETERMINANT OF ADJUSTMENT

One way to make sense of the fact that perceived support (but not received support) is associated with adjustment to stress is to posit that the stress-protective effects of perceived support are not mediated by actual support transactions. Several studies support this idea. For example, Brown (1978) has shown that people with the best social and personal resources are the least likely to report seeking support when they are under stress. This suggests that the perception that support is available if wanted is sufficient to help one deal with a stressful situation. More recently, Wethington and Kessler (1986) carried out a direct test of this idea by comparing the relationship of perceived support and support actually received when under stress with a measure of emotional adjustment to stress. They found that perceived support buffered stress, whereas received support had no independent buffering effect. The best psychological outcomes in their data were associated with perceiving that support is available but not seeking it.

One possible interpretation of this result is that the perception of support availability is itself the active ingredient that promotes adjustment to stress. Wethington and Kessler (1986) argued that the perception of having access to support could lead to objectively stressful situations being appraised as less threatening than they would be otherwise. Another possibility is that the perception of support availability could provide the kind of psychological safety net that helps motivate self-reliant coping efforts. Either of these processes could lead to an association between perceived support and adjustment to stress.

Some indirect evidence consistent with this view has been presented by Sarason, Pierce, and Sarason (1990). In two small studies with samples of college women, these authors and their students found a significant association between perceived social support and self-reported, problem-focused coping dispositions.

However, I am not aware of any research that has attempted to directly investigate this issue in the context of a genuine stress-buffering study. An important issue of study design arises in this context, because an adequate test would require the researcher to combine a conventional stress-buffering research design, which compares health outcomes between respondents who vary in exposure to stress with a focused design that considers support mobilization in the subsample of respondents who experienced serious stress. The design required to combine these two approaches would be similar to the one used by Wethington and Kessler (1986). In the ideal approach, longitudinal data would be collected with a baseline assessment of perceived support and an assessment of emotional functioning (or some other health outcome) at both baseline and follow-up. Measures of acute stress exposure would also be obtained. Respondents who reported the occurrence of serious acute stress at follow-up would be questioned retrospectively about appraisals and coping strategies.

The initial model to be estimated in these data would be a standard stress-buffering model, in which the impact of acute stress on change in emotional functioning between baseline and follow-up would be assumed to vary as a function of perceived access to support. Subsequent analyses would attempt to explain this stress-buffering effect as a result of the mediating effects of appraisal and coping. This test would not be straightforward, because appraisal and coping would only be measured in the subsample of respondents who reported a serious acute stress, whereas the stress-buffering model would be based on the entire sample. It is not clear how to handle the missing data problem posed by this difference in the sample bases.

Wethington and Kessler (1986) handled this problem by dichotomizing their sample into those respondents who reported one or more serious acute stresses (the "stress" subsample) and those who reported no such stresses (the "no stress" subsample). The stress-buffering model was reconceptualized in this approach as a model that implied a significant difference in the relationship between baseline perceived support and subsequent change in emotional functioning across these two subsamples. The task of explaining the stress-buffering effect of support, then, was reconceptualized as the task of explaining the difference in the relationship between perceived support and emotional adjustment in the stress and no stress subsamples. This was attempted by introducing control variables into the equation in the stress subsample for support received in response to the stress. It is important to recognize that the goal here is to explain the difference in the relationship between perceived support and emotional functioning in the two subsamples, not to explain the entire association between perceived support and emotional functioning in the stress subsample. Conventional significance tests can be used to test whether the significant difference in subsample associations disappears once controls are introduced into the stress subsample.

Although Wethington and Kessler (1986) were unable to explain the stress-buffering effect of perceived support by introducing a measure of support received in response to stress, it is important to recognize that their analysis was limited by the fact that information about received support was obtained retrospectively. Although this may not have been a problem for the measures of received support considered in their analysis, which consisted of fairly simple measures of the number of people who helped and the types of help they provided, it could be considerably more difficult to obtain accurate reports about more subtle dimensions of support provision or about appraisal and coping.

One way to handle this potential problem is to combine a baseline data collection in a large general population sample with a more focused longitudinal data collection in a subsample of respondents who experienced some serious stress. This would make it possible to obtain more fine-grained measures of appraisal, coping, and received support than in a single follow-up data collection. For example, Wortman and Silver (in press) recently described a longitudinal study of conjugal bereavement that illustrates this approach. Beginning with a baseline survey, which administered a variety of perceived support scales to a community sample of elderly married men and women, Wortman and Silver (in press) are monitoring death registries and administering a series of subsequent interviews to all baseline respondents who become widowed over a 5-year follow-up period. By obtaining information about appraisal, coping, and adjustment shortly after the death of a spouse and then continuing to monitor all widows in a series of follow-up interviews over a period of several years, they hope to obtain accurate information about cognitive and behavioral aspects of appraisal and coping that can serve as intervening variables to explain the stress-buffering effects of perceived support.

RECEIVED SUPPORT AS A DETERMINANT OF ADJUSTMENT

Although Wethington and Kessler (1986) failed to find an association between perceived support and adjustment to stress in their analysis of retrospectively reported support interactions, a more fine-grained longitudinal investigation might discover that this relationship is significant. This is particularly likely if poor adjustment to stress is associated with selective recall of support attempts, a possibility that has been suggested by some commentators (Cohen & Wills, 1985).

There is another type of genuine support effect, though, that would probably not be found even in a detailed longitudinal investigation such as the prospective widowhood study just described. This would occur if the support interactions that are most effective in promoting adjustment to stress are also the least visible to the support recipient. Lieberman (1986) suggested this possibility. In a discussion of Brown's (1978) community survey, which showed that the respondents who reported the most ready access to support seemed to adjust to stress without reporting the use of their support networks, Lieberman (1986) proposed that people who are deeply embedded in supportive networks might get support so smoothly and naturally that they fail to recognize it. Lieberman went on to suggest that this type of invisible support might actually be more effective than support that the recipient seeks out by virtue of the fact that invisible support circumvents the problem of self-esteem assault, which can be associated with support mobilization efforts.

This possibility poses a serious challenge to conventional research on social support processes because the self-report measures that are the mainstay of this research tradition are incapable of assessing the type of support that Lieberman (1986) suggests might be most important for adjustment. To test this notion, it is necessary to go beyond conventional reliance on the self-reports of support recipients and develop designs that include support providers in data collection efforts.

There are several examples in the literature of studies that interviewed both the people who experienced some stress and their supporters (e.g., Silver & Urbanowicz, 1990). There is some possibility for bias in these investigations because the support recipient is required to nominate the support providers who are later interviewed by the researcher, and truly invisible support could be overlooked by this approach. Another strategy is to interview a random sample of people in the stressed person's social network, generating the sampling frame in a series of questions that do not exclusively focus on supportive behaviors (Fischer et al., 1977), or to focus on one particular network member such as a spouse or parent.

Over the past few years, I have been involved in a program of research that has generated data that illustrate how the use of an informant can be used to study supportive interactions between husbands and wives. This work is based on a large general population sample of married couples who have been interviewed longitudinally to study sex differences in coping and adjustment to marital stress (Mattlin, Wethington, & Kessler, 1989). A subsample of these respondents were asked to complete a short daily diary questionnaire each day for a number of weeks (Bolger, DeLongis, Kessler, & Schilling, 1989). The diary included a checklist of 22 daily events; an inventory of 22 mood measures that formed scales of depression, anxiety, and hostility; and questions about giving support to and receiving support from one's spouse.

A preliminary analysis of these data showed that close to one third of the supportive actions reported by support providers in this diary sample were not reported by support recipients. Many of these involved "invisible" supportive actions—like a wife keeping the children away from her husband after he came home from a hectic day at work. The husband experienced this merely as a relaxing evening at home, not as an instance of support, whereas the wife saw herself as engaging in a supportive activity.

Regression analyses distinguishing the effects of visible and invisible support showed that there was a significant relationship between invisible support and adjustment to stress in terms of all three mood scales and a nonsignificant relationship between visible support and adjustment to stress. This pattern was similar for males and females and held up after controls for type of stress (Bolger, Kessler, & Schilling, 1990).

These results are very provocative, but they are not definitive for two reasons. First, we did not set out to investigate the visible-invisible distinction when we designed this data collection and, as a result, did not word the questions about giving and receiving support in such a way as to guarantee comparability of reports from recipients and support providers. Second, we did not obtain information about stress severity. It is likely that the visibility of supportive actions is related to stress severity, with the more severe stresses eliciting more visible support. Failure to control for this association could generate the results obtained in our analysis. This problem could be easily resolved, however, in a new data collection by obtaining information about stress severity. Given the enormous importance of self-report measures of support in the literature and the challenge to the centrality of these measures posed by the Bolger et al. (1990) analysis, I believe that the highest priority should be placed on replicating and extending this analysis in other investigations that include data obtained both from support recipients and support providers.

PERCEIVED SUPPORT AS A SOYRUIYS CORRELATE OF ADJUSTMENT

Regardless of how the results turn out in research on visible and invisible support, we still have to grapple with the fact that perceived support is a strong correlate of adjustment to stress for reasons that seem not to be associated with actual support transactions. The diary research just described showed this clearly in multivariate analyses, which documented that invisible support, powerful though it was in predicting adjustment to stress, did not explain the relationship between perceived support availability and adjustment.

As noted previously, one possible explanation is that the effect of perceived support could be mediated by appraisal and coping processes. Another possible interpretation is that the association between perceived support and adjustment to stress may be spurious. Several researchers have raised this possibility. Heller (1979) and Heller and Swindle (1983) have suggested that the putative effect of perceived support may be a result of social competence. Henderson, Byrne, and Duncan-Jones (1981) presented some data suggesting that neuroticism may have the same effect.

Attempts to isolate variables that clearly explain the effects of perceived support have focused primarily on personality variables. These attempts have been largely unsuccessful (Cohen, Sherrod, & Clark, 1986). However, it is important to recognize that most of these analyses have been based on simple additive models of personality effects. Models of this sort are unlikely to detect spuriousness. We know that higher-order interactions exist between perceived support and locus of control in predicting adjustment to stress (Sandler & Lakey, 1982; Lefcourt, Martin, & Saleh, 1984). This means that any personality determinant of support must (at a minimum) be considered a joint function of locus of control and some other aspects(s) of personality. A recognition of this fact will require future research on the determinants of support to adopt a more complex approach to personality measurement than in the past, focusing on what has recently been termed "conjunctive" effects among multivariate moderator variable profiles (Smith, Small, & Ptacek, 1990).

The research design decisions that are required to carry out work of this sort are fairly conventional. The more difficult issues involve conceptualization and measurement of presumed biasing variables. The latter issues are particularly difficult because the presumed biasing variables are only vaguely specified as some aspect of "competence" that could influence both success in forming and maintaining supportive interpersonal networks and success in adjusting to stress through mechanisms other than the actions of network members. It is not entirely clear how to move forward in conceptualizing or measuring this notion of competence.

These conceptualization and measurement problems can sometimes be bypassed to make a global test of spuriousness. For example, it might be possible in some situations to isolate a variable that is known to affect perception of support availability but not to affect adjustment to stress other than through its influence on this perception. An intervention aimed at making community residents aware of existing support programs would represent a variable of this sort. When such a variable is available, it could be used as an instrumental variable in a simultaneous equation system that separates out the reciprocal effects between perceived support and adjustment to stress (Kessler, 1987). This separation would effectively control for spuriousness in the relationship between perceived support and adjustment. This type of spuriousness is introduced by any third common cause even though the latter variable is not measured.

Another particularly intriguing example of a global test that allows the researcher to bypass direct measurement of presumed biasing variables involves a situation where genetic factors underlie the relationship between perceived support and adjustment to stress. A rationale for this possibility comes from research in the Swedish Adoption/Twin Study of Aging, which has recently documented that there are genetic influences on perceived support (Bergeman, Plomin, Pedersen, McClearn, & Nesselroade, 1990). Previous research has also documented genetic influences on perceptions about other interpersonal resources (Rowe, 1981; McClearn, Pedersen, Plomin, Nesselroade, & Bergman, in press). It is not implausible that these genetic factors could also be associated with adjustment to stress.

This possibility could be evaluated in an extension of conventional biometric genetic twin analysis. Heath, Neale, Hewitt, Eaves, and Fulker (1989) recently discussed the formal structure of such an evaluation and Kessler et al. (1990) presented an empirical example using this method. The methods and the results of the Kessler et al. (1990) analysis are briefly reviewed in this section. Because the methods of biometric twin analysis are quite complex, no attempt is made to provide a comprehensive review here, but rather to present an intuitive description of the design and analysis approach. The interested reader is referred to Heath et al. (1989) for a more technical discussion and exposition.

The Kessler et al. (1990) analysis made use of survey data from a large sample of female same-sex twin-pairs in the Virginia Twin Registry. The Virginia Twin Registry is a population-based registry, assembled by a systematic review of all birth records in the Commonwealth of Virginia. In 1987 and 1988, questionnaires were mailed to all caucasian female same-sex twins in the registry born between January 1, 1935, and April 7, 1971. A variety of perceived social support measures were included as part of this questionnaire, along with questions about exposure to 42 stressful life events and difficulties. The questionnaire also included the Center for Epidemiologic Studies Depression (CES-D) scale, a widely used 20-item measure designed to assess severity of depressive symptoms over a 1-week recall period (Radloff, 1977).

Preliminary analysis of these data showed that perceived friend support combined nonadditively with a summary measure of stressful life events to predict CES-D scores. The sign of this interaction was consistent with a stress-buffering interpretation; that is, the impact of stress on depressive symptoms was inversely related to perceived friend support. Rather than stop here, however, the twin structure of the data allowed this stress-buffering association to be investigated more thoroughly. The first step was to estimate a univariate model of additive genetic and environmental effects to evaluate the possibility that genes influence perceived friend support. This model assumed that the variance in perceived friend support is the result of an additive combination of genetic factors (A), environmental experiences shared by twins such as rearing environment, parental social class, school, and so forth (C), and environmental experiences unique to each member of a twin pair, including unreliability of measurement (E). This model can be identified statistically by beginning with the observed variances and covariances among separate subsamples of identical (monozygotic, MZ) and nonidentical (dizygotic, DZ) twin pairs. The identification constraints imposed on this covariance structure assume that: (a) genetic influences are perfectly correlated within MZ pairs and correlated .50 within DZ pairs, (b) the effects of common environment are correlated 1.0 within all pairs (both MZ and DZ), (c) the effects of A, C, and E are mutually uncorrelated, and (d) the magnitudes of the regressions of perceived friend support on the latent variables A, C, and E are equal regardless of twin order or zygosity. Loehlin (1989) presents a detailed discussion of the rationale behind these identification constraints. This type of model is overidentified, thus requiring estimation by means of maximum likelihood. Evaluation of model fit is made with likelihood-ratio chi-square tests.

Estimation of this model showed that genes explained a significant part of the variance in perceived friend support in the Virginia twin sample. The remaining variance was a result of unique environmental experiences not shared by twins. There was no significant influence of common environmental experiences on friend support in these data.

The documentation of a significant genetic influence on perceived friend support does not in itself demonstrate that the association between perceived friend support and adjustment to stress is spurious. It is possible that neither A nor E influences adjustment other than indirectly through perceived friend support. However, it is also possible that either A or C or both influence adjustment directly, over and above their indirect effects through perceived friend support. The twin structure of the data allows an empirical test to distinguish these two possibilities.

This test was carried out by dividing the sample into three subsamples for each zygosity, corresponding to pairs where both, only one, or neither co-twin experienced a major life event. Within each of these six subsamples, a bivariate model was estimated for the relationship between perceived friend support and CES-D. Consistent with the initial results documenting a stress-buffering effect of perceived friend support, this subsample analysis showed that the relationship between perceived friend support and CES-D was significantly stronger among twins who experienced a major life event than among those who had not and that these relationships did not differ by zygosity or as a function of the co-twins' stress exposure.

This analysis, in effect, used the same strategy discussed earlier in the review of Wethington and Kessler's (1986) work to reconceptualize the stress-buffering effect of perceived friend support as a subsample interaction involving the relationship between perceived friend support and CES-D. The test for spuriousness involved a decomposition of this subsample interaction by embedding the univariate additive genetic model for A and C effects on perceived friend support into a more general bivariate subsample model of A and C effects on CES-D. In essence, this procedure allowed Kessler et al. (1990) to determine whether the significantly elevated association between perceived support and CES-D among respondents who experienced a major life event was the result of an increase in the importance of only the A component of perceived support, only the C component, or of both components equally. If the association between perceived friend support and adjustment was spurious through A, the influence of the A component on CES-D would be significantly more elevated than that of the C component. If the association between perceived friend support and adjustment was not spurious, the effects of the A and C components on CES-D would be elevated to the same degree.

The analysis clearly showed that the A component was significantly more elevated than the C component. Indeed, it was only the association between the A component of perceived friend support and CES-D that showed any significant elevation among respondents who were exposed to a major life event. On the basis of this result, Kessler et al. (1990) concluded that the putative stress-buffering effect of perceived friend support was spurious.

It is important to recognize that this conclusion does not imply that genes directly influence either perceptions of network supportiveness or actual selection of supportive friends. A more likely interpretation is that genes directly affect some set of personality characteristics that, in turn, influence perceptions and selection. Nor should it be assumed that because genes are involved this means that perceptions and selection mechanisms cannot be changed by environmental influences. If some personality dispositions could be isolated that explain the effects of A on both perceived support and adjustment to stress, then these dispositions could be used as intervention targets without having to take into consideration the fact that they are partly determined genetically. The important point, from the methodological perspective, is that the twin structure of the data allowed an investigation of spuriousness in the relationship between perceived support and adjustment to stress without the researchers having to introduce explicit measures of third variables. In cases where no evidence of spuriousness is found, this approach could be an effective way of rejecting the possibility of spuriousness without having to resolve the complex problems of conceptualization and measurement that have so far plagued research in this area. An extension of this approach to other genetically informative designs (e.g., adoptees, halfsibs) and other measures of support could provide an extremely useful evaluation of this issue and provide basic information that could be analyzed to help provide some insights into likely sources of spuriousness.

CONCLUSION

As noted at the onset, the preceding discussion has not attempted to be comprehensive but rather to focus on a small set of research designs that I consider particularly promising for advancing our understanding of the relationship between perceived support and adjustment to stress. Issues of measurement and analysis were briefly mentioned in the context of these discussions about research design. No attempt was made to provide a technical discussion of analysis issues, because of limitations of space, and the reader was referred to accessible technical discussions of the analysis procedures recommended.

The first design that I discussed involves the integration of an analysis of the relationship between perceived support and adjustment to stress with more fine-grained studies of appraisal, coping, and received support. As far as I am aware, Wethington and Kessler (1986) are the only researchers to have reported an analysis of this sort. Their analysis was limited because all of their data came from a single cross-sectional survey rather than from a longitudinal investigation and because they had only a limited set of retrospectively reported measures of received support.

I believe that this integration of the stress-buffering paradigm with investigations of appraisal, coping, and support processes would provide a valuable corrective to current tendencies toward separating these two types of research. As noted at the beginning of my remarks, the mainstream of social support research is moving away from studies of perceived support availability toward more dynamic investigations of support transactions. Studies of perceived support, according to this line of thinking, have been successful in documenting a clear and consistent association between support and adjustment to stress, but are incapable of providing any insights into the support processes that bring about this relationship. An analysis of actual supportive actions, then, is thought to be required to advance our understanding.

I agree that we need research on what actually happens in supportive interactions. However, as this line of research continues to grow and our knowledge about support processes increases, it is becoming increasingly clear that the relationship between support processes and adjustment to stress is less powerful and less consistent than the relationship between perceived support and adjustment to stress. Support efforts are often miscarried and sometimes have unintended negative consequences (Coyne et al., 1988). Access to support can create social costs that, at times, can lead to greater emotional distress than if support had not been obtained at all (Lieberman, 1986). The provision of support can be stressful for the support provider, and this can interfere with the effectiveness of intervention efforts (Albrecht & Adelman, 1987). In short, social support is part of the broader fabric of interpersonal relations that can have either positive or negative effects on both the recipient and support provider.

Although it is important to continue research on the effects of actual support transactions, particularly the descriptive work that is being used to develop experimental support interventions (Sandler, Gersten, Reynolds, Kallgren, & Ramirez, 1988) and to isolate aspects of interventions that are experienced by recipients as stressful (Taylor, Falke, Mazel, & Hilsberg, 1988), it is also important to appreciate that the initial motivation for exploring the dynamics of support transactions was based on a belief that the relationship between perceived support and adjustment to stress resulted from an even stronger relationship between actual supportive behaviors and adjustment to stress. Although it is too early to know whether this belief will turn out to be correct, the evidence to date is that it is not. The effect of perceived support on adjustment to stress seems not to be mediated by actual supportive behaviors.

As a result, we need to continue exploring the meaning of perceived support. One very useful way of doing this is to combine conventional stress-buffering analyses with process analyses of appraisal, coping, and support in the way discussed earlier in this paper. This would allow a direct evaluation of the hypothesis that the effect of perceived support is mediated by received support. It would also allow an evaluation of the alternate hypothesis that the perception of support influences adjustment more directly, by influencing appraisals of threat and by facilitating active coping efforts.

I also argued that we need to expand studies of support processes to include the perspective of the support provider, and I discussed a research design that allows this to be done. Almost all studies of support processes have limited their focus to the reports of the support recipient. It is clear that this approach creates the opportunity for bias resulting from selective perceptions of supportiveness based on adjustment. Furthermore, by limiting the focus to the perceptions of the support recipient, we make it nearly impossible to explore the idea that some people are unsupportable.

An exclusive focus on the support recipient also makes it impossible to study the kinds of caregiver burdens that have been documented in the literature on chronic disease and family caregiving (e.g., Horowitz, 1985). There is good reason to believe that these burdens play an important part in determining the effectiveness of supportive interactions. Finally, an exclusive focus on the support recipient forecloses the possibility of exploring the intriguing possibility suggested by Lieberman (1982) and Bolger et al. (1990) that invisible support is more effective than visible support in promoting adjustment to stress. If this result is replicated, it would have enormously important implications for the design and analysis of nonexperimental investigations of support, because it would imply that self-reports about support transactions obtained from support recipients miss the most important elements of support for adjustment.

Finally, I argued that we need to expand our efforts to consider the possibility that the relationship between perceived support and adjustment to stress is spurious. This can be done either by introducing controls for presumed sources of spuriousness in multivariate analyses of expanded stress-buffering models, by using the method of instrumental variables, or by indirect tests of the sort provided by genetically informative designs. I illustrated the latter approach by discussing an analysis of data obtained from a general population sample of twins. In any of these cases, we need to recognize that past efforts to explore the issue of spuriousness have been inadequate and that more complex conceptions are required.

It is important to recognize that all the nonexperimental approaches to evaluating spuriousness reviewed in this last section of the paper are motivated by an implicit claim that they investigate fundamental processes that are, in effect, randomly assigned across individuals with respect to the dependent variable under investigation. In this sense, the persuasiveness of these approaches is grounded in an underlying claim that they approximate natural experiments. In cases where this claim is implausible, the only available option short of abandoning the research question is to use true experimentation aimed at manipulating perceived support or the environmental determinants of perceived support. This type of experiment is, ultimately, the only completely satisfactory way of resolving the spuriousness issue.

REFERENCES

Albrecht, T. L., & Adelman, M. B. (1987). Dilemmas of supportive communication. In T. L. Albrecht & M. B. Adelman (Eds.), *Communicating social support* (pp. 240–254). Newbury Park, CA: Sage.

Barrera, M. (1986). Distinctions between social support concepts, measures, and models. *American Journal of Community Psychology, 14,* 413–445.

Bergeman, C. S., Plomin, R., Pedersen, N. L., McClearn, G. E., & Nesslroade, J. R. (1990). Genetic and environmental influences on social support: The Swedish adoption/twin study of aging (SATSA). *Journal of Gerontology, 45,* 101–106.

Bolger, N., DeLongis, A., Kessler, R. C., & Schilling, E. (1989). The effects of daily stress on negative mood. *Journal of Personality and Social Psychology, 57,* 808–818.

Bolger, N., Kessler, R. C., & Schilling, E. (1990). Visible support, invisible support, and adjustment to daily stress. Submitted for publication.

Brown, B. B. (1978). Social and psychological correlates of help-seeking behavior among urban adults. *American Journal of Community Psychology, 6,* 425–439.

Cohen, S. (1988). Psychosocial models of the role of social support in the etiology of physical disease. *Health Psychology, 7,* 269–297.

Cohen, S., Sherrod, D. R., & Clark, M. S. (1986). Social skills and the stress-protective role of social support. *Journal of Personality and Social Psychology, 50,* 963–973.

Cohen, S., & Wills, T. A. (1985). Stress, social support, and the buffering hypothesis. *Psychological Bulletin, 98,* 310-357.

Coyne, J. C., Wortman, C. B., & Lehman, D. R. (1988). The other side of support: Emotional over-involvement and miscarried helping. In B. H. Gottlieb (Ed.), *Marshalling Social Support* (pp. 305-330). Beverly Hills, CA: Sage.

Eckenrode, J. (1983). The mobilization of social supports: Some individual constraints. *American Journal of Community Psychology, 11,* 509-528.

Fischer, C., Jackson, R. M., Stueve, C. A., Gerson, K., Jones, L. M., & Baldassare, M. (1977). *Networks and places: Social relations in the urban setting.* New York: Free Press.

Fisher, J. D., Nadler, A., & Whicher-Alagna, S. (1982). Recipient reactions to aid. *Psychological Bulletin, 91,* 17-54.

Gottlieb, B. H. (1988). Marshalling social support: The state of the art in research and practice. In B. H. Gottlieb (Ed.), *Marshalling social support.* Beverly Hills, CA: Sage.

Heath, A. C., Neale, M. C., Hewitt, J. K., Eaves, L. J., & Fulker, D. W. (1989). Testing structural equation models for twin data using LISREL. *Behavior Genetics, 19,* 9-35.

Heller, K. (1979). The effects of social support: Prevention and treatment implications. In A. P. Goldstein & F. H. Kanfer (Eds.), *Maximizing treatment gains: Transfer enhancement in psychotherapy* (pp. 353-382). New York: Academic Press.

Heller, K., & Swindle, R. V. (1983). Social networks, perceived social support, and coping with stress. In R. D. Felner, L. A. Jason, J. Moritsugu, & S. S. Farber (Eds.), *Preventive psychology: Research and practice in community intervention* (pp. 87-103). New York: Pergamon Press.

Heller, K., Swindle, R. W., & Dusenbury, L. (1986). Component social support processes: Comments and integration. *Journal of Consulting and Clinical Psychology, 54,* 466-470.

Henderson, S., Byrne, D. G., & Duncan-Jones, P. (1981). *Neurosis and the social environment.* New York: Academic Press.

Horowitz, A. (1985). Family caregiving for the frail elderly. In M. P. Lawton & G. Maddox (Eds.), *The Annual Review of Gerontology and Geriatrics* (pp. 194-246). New York: Springer.

House, J. S., Landis, K., & Umberson, D. (1988). Social relationships and health. *Science, 241,* 540-545.

Kessler, R. C. (1987). The interplay of research design strategies and data analysis procedures in evaluating the effects of stress on health. In S. V. Kasl & C. L. Cooper (Eds.), *Stress and health: Issues in research methodology* (pp. 113-139). New York: Wiley.

Kessler, R. C. & McLeod, J. D. (1985). Social support and mental health in community samples. In S. Cohen & S. L. Syme (Eds.), *Social support and health* (pp. 219-240). New York: Academic Press.

Kessler, R. C., Kendler, K. S., Heath, A., Neale, M. C., & Eaves, L. J. (in press). Social support, depressed mood, and adjustment to stress: A genetic epidemiologic investigation. *Journal of Personality and Social Psychology.*

Landerman, R., George, L. K., Campbell, R. T., & Blazer, D. G. (1989). Alternative models of the stress buffering hypothesis. *American Journal of Community Psychology, 17,* 625-642.

Lefcourt, H. M., Martin, R. A., & Saleh, W. E. (1984). Locus of control and social support: Interactive moderators of stress. *Journal of Personality and Social Psychology, 47,* 378-389.

Lieberman, M. A. (1982). The effects of social supports on responses to stress. In L. Goldberger & S. Breznitz (Eds.), *Handbook of stress: Theoretical and clinical aspects* (pp. 764-783). New York: Free Press.

Lieberman, M. A. (1986). Social supports—The consequences of psychologizing: A commentary. *Journal of Consulting and Clinical Psychology, 54,* 461-465.

Loehlin, J. C. (1989). Partitioning environmental and genetic contributions to behavioral development. *American Psychologist, 44,* 1285-1294.

Mattlin, J. A., Wethington, E., & Kessler, R. C. (1989). Situational determinants of coping and coping effectiveness. *Journal of Health and Social Behavior, 3,* 103-122.

Plomin, R., McClearn, G. E., Pedersen, N. L., Nesselroade, J. R., & Bergeman, C. S. (in press). Genetic influences on parents' perception of the family environment. *Journal of Marriage and the Family.*

Radloff, L. S. (1977). The CES Scale: A self-report depression scale for research in the general population. *Applied Psychological Measurement, 3,* 385-401.

Reis, H. T. (1984). Social interaction and well-being. In S. Duck (Ed.), *Personal relationships V: Repairing personal relationships.* New York: Academic Press.

Rowe, D. C. (1981). Environmental and genetic influences on dimensions of perceived parenting: A twin study. *Developmental Psychology, 17,* 203-208.

Sandler, I. N., & Barrera, M., Jr. (1984). Toward a multimethod approach to assessing the effects of social support. *American Journal of Community Psychology, 12,* 37–52.

Sandler, I. N., Gersten, J. C., Reynolds, K., Kallgren, C. A., & Ramirez, R. (1988). Using theory and data to plan support interventions: Design of a program for bereaved children. In B. H. Gottlieb (Ed.), *Marshalling social support: Formats, processes, and effects* (pp. 53–83). Newbury Park, CA: Sage.

Sandler, I. N., & Lakey, B. (1982). Locus of control as a stress moderator: The role of control perceptions and social support. *American Journal of Community Psychology, 10,* 65–80.

Sarason, B. R., Pierce, G. R., & Sarason, I. R. (1990). Social support: The sense of acceptance and the role of relationships. In B. R. Sarason, I. G. Sarason, & G. R. Pierce (Eds.), *Social support: An interactional view* (pp. 97–149). New York: Wiley.

Sarason, B. R., Shearin, E. N., Pierce, G. R., & Sarason, I. G. (1987). Interrelations among social support measures: Theoretical and practical implications. *Journal of Personality and Social Psychology, 52,* 813–832.

Shapiro, E. G. (1978). Embarrassment and help-seeking. In B. M. DePaulo, A. Nadler, & J. D. Fisher (Eds.), *New directions in helping: Volume 2, Help-seeking* (pp. 143–164). New York: Academic Press.

Silver, R. C., & Urbanowicz, A. (1990). A study of successful and unsuccessful support providers following bereavement. Paper presented at the Meetings of the American Psychological Association, Boston, MA.

Smith, R. E., Smoll, F. E., & Ptacek, J. T. (1990). Conjunctive moderator variables in vulnerability and resiliency research: Life stress, social support and coping skills, and adolescent sport injuries. *Journal of Personality and Social Psychology, 58,* 360–370.

Stokes, J. P. (1983). Predicting satisfaction with social support from social network structure. *American Journal of Community Psychology, 11,* 141–152.

Taylor, S. E., Falke, R. L., Mazel, R. M., & Hilsberg, B. L. (1988). Sources of satisfaction and dissatisfaction among members of cancer support groups. In B. H. Gottlieb (Ed.), *Marshalling social support: Formats, processes, and effects* (pp. 187–208). Newbury Park, CA: Sage.

Wethington, E., & Kessler, R. C. (1986). Perceived support, received support, and adjustment to stressful life events. *Journal of Health and Social Behavior, 27,* 78–89.

Wortman, C. B., & Silver, R. C. (in press). Effective mastery of bereavement and widowhood: Longitudinal research. In P. B. Baltes & M. M. Baltes (Eds.), *Successful aging research and theory.* London: Cambridge University.

17

Some Cautionary Notes on Buffer Effects

Hans O. F. Veiel
Central Institute of Mental Health, Mannheim, Germany

Much of the discussion about the effects of social support on health has revolved around the issue of stress-buffering versus direct (main) effects on health. (For overviews see Alloway & Bebbington, 1986; Cohen & Wills, 1985.) When social support is beneficial for a person's health in some proportion to his or her exposure to stress, it is called a buffer effect. A beneficial effect of support that is independent of concurrent stress levels is called a main effect. These two kinds of effects are not mutually exclusive. The presence of a stress-buffering effect is usually inferred when stress and support interact statistically in their association with health outcomes (i.e., when the association between stress and ill health is stronger at low levels of support than at high levels). There are a number of different approaches to measure this association (e.g., linear, nonlinear), and also to measure the differences in its strength (e.g., hierarchical and nonhierarchical). The first issue was the topic of a major controversy in the field (e.g., Tennant & Bebbington, 1978; Brown & Harris, 1978a), whereas the second has received comparably little attention.

Recently the controversy has died down somewhat, and there now seems to be a general agreement about adequate statistical procedures, and about how linear and nonlinear methods of examining main and buffer effects relate to each other (e.g., Everitt & Smith, 1979). The "buffer effect" has become a generally accepted paradigm that is usually not questioned and is routinely applied in most relevant empirical research (Alloway & Bebbington, 1986; Cohen & Wills, 1985). Yet, the suitability of the statistical methods that are used to empirically demonstrate buffer effects is far from proven. In this chapter I argue that the assertion of stress-buffering effects on finding a significant statistical interaction of support and stress is only warranted after a considerable number of possible artifacts have been ruled out.

The chapter discusses five issues relevant for the empirical investigation of stress-buffering effects of social support. Technical discussion is kept at a minimum. Readers interested in a more sophisticated treatment of the issues should consult Busemeyer and Jones (1983), Cleary and Kessler (1982), Kessler (1983), Reynolds (1978), Southwood (1978), Thoits (1982), and Veiel (1987, 1988). To simplify the arguments to follow, this author assumes that stress, support, and health measures are valid within the constraints specified, and that the direction of any effects is from stress and support to health, rather than the reverse.

AGGREGATE VERSUS SPECIFIC MEASURES[1]

The terms "social support," "stress," and "health" (or "mental disorder") denote broad classes of phenomena. For measures in each of these areas, a continuum of specificity exists: health outcome measures may refer to a specific, presumably homogeneous condition, such as subjectively experienced anxiety (e.g., the State-Trait Anxiety Inventory; Spielberger, Gorsuch, & Lushene, 1970), or they may consist of a conglomerate of all kinds of psychological, psychosomatic, and somatic symptoms (e.g., the General Health Questionnaire; Goldberg, 1972); stress indices may be obtained by summing up occurrences of many different, presumably stressful events, or they may represent a specific stress moment such as bereavement; social support indices may refer to a summary score of different social relationships and activities, or to a specific instance of confiding and emotional closeness after a severe stressful experience.

To examine how instrument specificity bears on the meaning of an observed statistical interaction effect of support and stress, let us consider two extreme but nonetheless quite realistic cases:

1. Stress operationalized by the death of a spouse, support by the presence of a narrowly defined confidant (Brown & Harris, 1978b), and health outcome by the onset of clinical depression.
2. Stress measured by a life event list, such as the prototypical Schedule of Recent Events (Holmes & Rahe, 1967), support measured by a summary index of Availability of Support (Henderson, Byrne, & Duncan-Jones, 1981), and mental health measured by a sum score on the General Health Questionnaire (Goldberg, 1972).

Let us assume that the association of stress and health in both cases is significantly lower under the respective conditions of high support than under conditions of low support, and also that this effect is not a methodological artifact of the kind discussed later. What does it mean? In case (1), it seems reasonable to conclude that the presence of an intimate and confiding relationship prevents the onset of depression after a severe bereavement, and several psychological mechanisms can be thought of that may be responsible for this effect. However, one cannot generalize to other stressors, support forms, and health outcomes; nor to stress, support, and health in general; and not even to such relatively narrow superordinate categories as "loss events," "emotional support," or "depressive symptomatology." This is because it is not at all clear—it is on the whole rather unlikely—that nonclinical symptom ranges, nonsocial "losses," and other social relationships are functionally similar to the conditions specified in case (1). Nonetheless, interaction effects obtained with specific measures are unambiguous within their proper domains and provide a firm ground for theory development.

[1]This section focuses on measures of support and stress as environmental rather than individual characteristics, and the basic question concerns the representativeness of such measures. The matter is different when global, subjective perceptions, or evaluations of support or stress are measured. Such perceptions or evaluations probably are highly organized intraindividual states or even traits, and they usually cannot be traced back to specific environmental conditions. Here the question of representativeness does not arise in the same way as when heterogeneous environmental variables are assessed (see also Brown, Chapter 15).

In case (2), all that can be said is that persons reporting many listed life events and a large number of positive social interactions tend to report less symptoms than those reporting comparable numbers of life events but fewer social interactions. Little can be derived regarding the psychological processes mediating this effect, because two similarly high scores on each measure can be—and frequently are—based on different sets of events, support experiences, or symptoms. There is no generally accepted definition of "social support" or of "psychosocial stress," and both terms have been plausibly said to denote areas of research rather than observable and/or definable empirical phenomena (Barrera, 1986; Lazarus, DeLongis, Folkman, & Gruen, 1985).

The basic problem with aggregate measures in these areas is that they sample from broad domains and can therefore only refer to their common denominators. The interpretation of the statistical interaction as reflecting stress-buffering processes is predicated on the assumption of equivalence of different life events, social experiences, and symptoms; and of one underlying, mediating psychological mechanism. These propositions do not seem generally tenable: different types of life events have different meanings and tend to engender different pathogenic processes (e.g., Craig & Brown, 1984; Finlay-Jones & Brown, 1981); the usefulness of some types of supportive transactions depends on individual needs and situational demands (e.g., Cohen & McKay, 1984); different classes of network members have different support functions (e.g., Veiel, Brill, Haefner, & Welz, 1988); and even genuinely supportive environments may have detrimental effects on health (Veiel & Kühner, 1990). It must be suspected that the common denominators of the items included in aggregate support and stress measures are small. Studies showing large buffer effects obtained with aggregate measures must therefore be suspected of having fallen prey to the methodological artifacts discussed later. It is revealing how often published empirical reports on stress-buffering effects obtained with aggregate measures refrain from offering explanations in terms of psychological and psychosocial processes that are responsible for the observed interaction effects.

Even if one can legitimately assume substantial common denominators of the domains covered by aggregate stress, support, and health measures, the absence of stress-buffering effects of support is hard to substantiate with such measures. Few stress or support instruments can claim to encompass all possible sources of stress or support, respectively, be it because of systematic omissions or because of measurement error. Despite their implicit claim to do so, aggregate stress measures such as life events sum scores are very unlikely to give a complete picture of the stress experienced by a particular individual. Life is inherently stressful, and the finding of main effects of social support on health may just mean that it actually buffers the effects of ubiquitous, but unmeasured, stress on health.

To summarize—basing the assertion of a stress-buffering effect of social support only on statistical interactions of aggregate measures is, I believe, insufficient. To do so one would also have to (a) rule out confounding effects and the methodological artifacts of the kind discussed later, and (b) provide a theoretical explanation in terms of the psychological processes involved. Conversely, in view of the many factors militating against detecting buffer effects with aggregate measures, a non-significant statistical interaction should not on its own be interpreted as the absence of a buffer effect.

The situation is much more clear-cut when specific measures are used, and the need for a plausible theoretical rationale a priori is much less urgent: the empirical data can better speak for themselves here. However, their generalization to other stress and support conditions and other outcomes needs explicit justification. There is no free lunch.

ADDITIVE VERSUS MULTIPLICATIVE EFFECTS[2]

Buffer effects are usually assumed to be present when stress and support measures interact statistically in their effect on health. In procedures based on the linear model (e.g., linear regression, analysis of variance), effects are assumed to combine additively, and interactions are defined as deviations from additivity. In ratio models (log-linear and logistic), main effects combine multiplicatively, and interactions represent deviations from such multiplicative combinations. (This holds with respect to the original measurements; the mathematical notations of the statistical procedures may well consist of purely additive terms of some nonlinear transformations of the original measurements. In structural analysis, which I will not explicitly refer to in this chapter, the distinction between measurement models and structural models makes this more clear; cf. Busemeyer & Jones, 1983; Newcomb, 1990). In ratio models, an interaction of the independent variables stress and support is assumed when the ratio between dependent variable levels at high and low stress is different on different levels of support. (Logistic and log-linear models differ slightly regarding how this ratio is defined.) As a number of papers has shown (Cleary & Kessler, 1982; Everitt & Smith, 1979), data structures that result in an interaction effect in linear analysis models are completely compatible with main effects in ratio models. It is now generally acknowledged that external (i.e., substantive or pragmatic) criteria must be applied when choosing one or the other model (cf. Rothman, 1978; Southwood, 1978).

However, there is another difference between the various methods commonly used to test for buffer effects. In linear regression analysis, buffer effects are generally tested with explicitly defined product terms of stress and support measures, which represent a restriction of possible interaction effects to the special case that the slope of the regression line linking health with stress changes as a linear function of support, and vice versa (Cohen, 1978). Nonlinear changes in the strength of the association between stress and health are modeled by product terms only approximately, if they are of uniformly positive or negative curvature, or even not at all, if they follow a U-shaped or even more complicated function.

In contrast, in the basic versions of analysis of variance and of most methods used to analyze tabular data, interactions are not explicitly specified. (Many statistical programs allow for interaction terms and most other kinds of effects to be explicitly specified, but this requires usually some degree of methodological sophistication; cf. Rindskopf, 1990.) Here, interactions are usually defined merely as discrepancies between observed cell values (or marginals) and the expected values assuming main effects (and lower-order interactions) only. Thus in cases where the association between stress and health does not change linearly with rising levels of support, but does so following U-shaped or threshold functions, it is mainly the error component that is increased in linear regression, which includes

[2]A more extensive and technical treatment of some issues in this and the following chapter can be found in Busemeyer and Jones (1983) and Kessler (1983).

products as interaction terms—whereas interaction effects may appear in standard analysis of variance or in tabular analyses.[3] However, there is a trade-off involved. The assumption of a specific shape of the interaction results, if correct, in much more powerful analyses. It is not commonly realized that a multiplicative combination of effects is the special case where significant interactions tend to appear in linear regression with products as interaction terms, but not in standard log-linear and logistic analysis models.

To summarize—the usual operationalization of interaction effects in linear regression (by product terms) generally shows the most powerful buffer effects in exactly those cases where ratio models (logistic and log-linear) show only main effects. In standard logistic and log-linear analyses all deviations from the (multiplicative) main effects model show up as interactions, as do all deviations from the additive model in standard analysis of variance. It would appear that combining linear regression with multiplicative models will give the researcher a much more complete picture of the data structure at hand than either method alone (Brown, Harris, & Lemyre, 1990; Kessler, 1983).

NONLINEAR ASSOCIATIONS AND CEILING AND FLOOR EFFECTS IN LINEAR REGRESSION[4]

Note these two noncontentious observations: (a) it is unlikely that the association of either stress or support with health is strictly linear, and (b) measures of stress and of social support are moderately correlated with each other.

The first observation is usually unproblematic for linear regression as long as the nonlinearity does not assume extreme proportions, in particular as long as the association is not U-shaped. If its slope is consistently positive, or consistently negative, the association will usually have a strong linear component, and the generally rather large error component in empirical data makes an empirical decision between linear and nonlinear models impossible in most cases.

What does the combination of (a) and (b) mean for the empirical investigation of buffer effects? As Kessler (1983) has demonstrated, linear regression analysis may produce misleading results in this case. The argument goes as follows: if some disorder is related to stress in a nonlinear, accelerating function, changes at low levels of stress have little effect on health, changes at medium stress levels have a stronger effect, and changes at high levels have the strongest effect. Since support and stress are negatively correlated, low levels of support co-occur preferentially with high levels of stress and vice versa. Because of the nonlinearity, the slope of the "real" nonlinear regression line linking stress and health is steeper at low levels of support than at high levels. In linear regression, therefore, their association would appear to change with changing levels of support, which is exactly how an interaction effect is defined (Figure 1).

The reverse case is also quite plausible: disorder as a decelerating function of stress, where changes at low stress levels have stronger effects on health than the same changes at high levels. Applying the above reasoning one would expect to

[3]This is only relevant when three or more categories (values) of the independent variables are considered. If there are only two categories, any deviation from the particular main effect model used will be captured by a specified interaction term.

[4]This chapter follows the arguments of Kessler (1983).

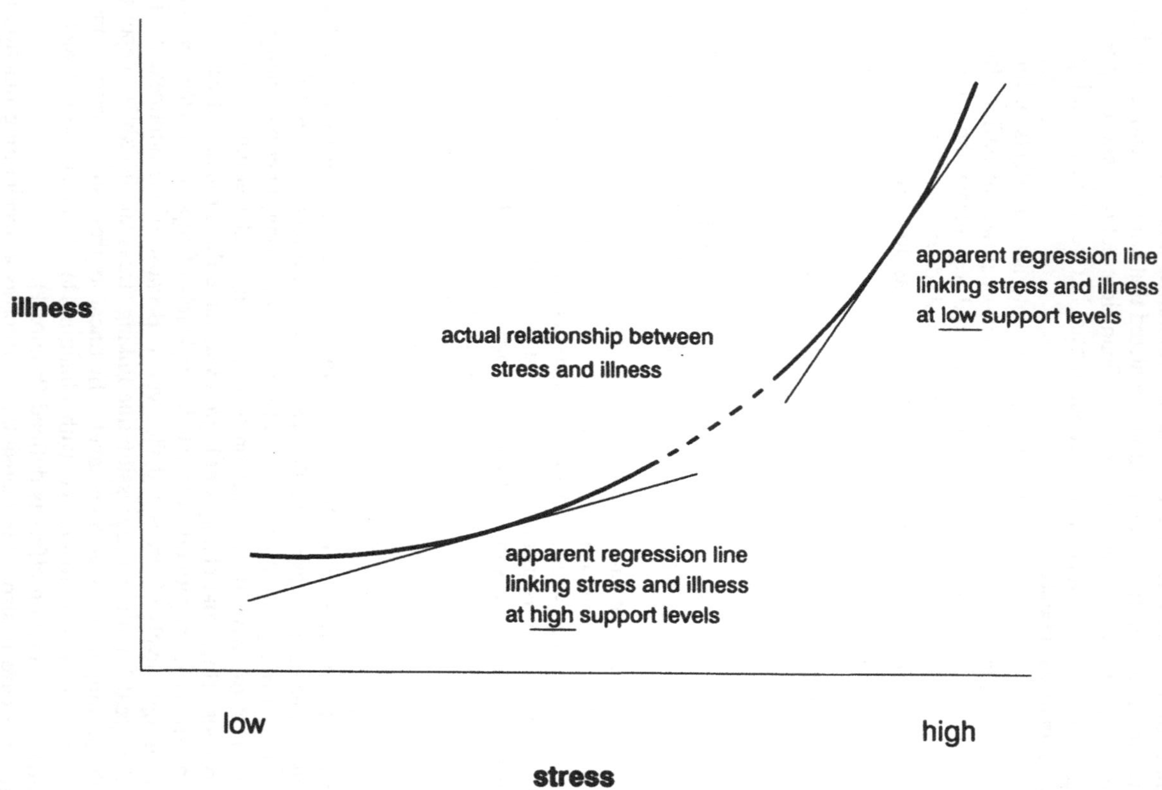

Figure 1 A curvilinear relationship between stress and illness, where low support co-occurs preferentially with high stress, and high support with low stress, produces different stress-illness regression slopes at high and low support levels: a spurious interaction effect (after Kessler, 1983).

find a negative buffering, or stress-enhancing effect of support. If support does indeed buffer the effects of stress, the real effect and the artifact would cancel each other out in this case.[5]

A similar situation exists not when the actual association between stress and health is nonlinear, but when there are floor and/or ceiling effects in the stress, support, or health measures. If the underlying relationships are strictly linear, and if there is a ceiling effect in the stress measure, the association of stress and health as measured will be a nonlinear one where the same scale differences at high stress levels are associated with greater differences on the health scales than at low stress levels. Consequently, because of the reasons given in the previous paragraph, spurious interactions of correlated stress and support measures will appear in linear regression analyses. In most cases, there is no independent yardstick for measuring the linearity of stress, health, or support scales. Given the pervasive correlation between stress and support, and the possible combinations of ceiling and floor effects in any of the three domains, the scope for spurious buffer effects can be imagined.

With typical correlations between support or stress and health outcomes between $r = .10$ and $r = .40$, violations of the linearity assumption of linear regression do not matter much as long as associations are not U-shaped, and as long as independent variables are not combined to form products: the large error component in the data will usually make nonlinear "true" associations indistinguishable from linear ones. Nonlinearities definitely do matter, however, when product terms are formed and entered into the regression equation. This is an intrinsic problem of products of monotonically transformable, observed (i.e., not error-free measured) predictor variables (cf. Busemeyer & Jones, 1983)—compounded by the fact that, in the case of stress and support, the respective measurement errors are also likely to be correlated.

MOBILIZATION AND SUPPRESSION OF SUPPORT

Longitudinal research designs are generally considered superior to cross-sectional ones when the direction of causality of an effect has to be empirically established. This is because when a variable X is measured before a variable Y, Y cannot have influenced X and any association between X and Y must be a result of direct or indirect effects of X on Y (or third variables influencing both X and Y). However, problems arise when synergistic effects are assessed with interaction terms involving variables measured at different points in time. This applies particularly to stress and support. Measures of social support that do not refer to a specific life event can only reflect support resources, or perceptions thereof, that are potentially useful for dealing with a subsequent life event.

Thoits (1982) examined what happens when the occurrence of stress changes the levels of available support. This is far from just an academic problem: fair-weather friends tend not to be available when the going gets tough, but sometimes we are able to mobilize much more support than we previously thought possible. (The former seems more frequent, though; cf. Dunkel-Schetter & Bennett, 1990.)

[5]Barrera (1988) discussed an additional possibility: when the interaction of stress and support itself is nonlinear, regardless of the bivariate relationships between support and illness and between stress and illness.

It is also of great relevance for evaluating buffer effects in prospective designs. Let us suppose that social support and symptoms are both measured at times A and B, some months apart. Because life events are rare, discrete, and largely random, their occurrence between A and B must be retrospectively assessed at time B. Buffer effects are commonly inferred from differential effects of one or several life events occurring in the A–B interval on changes in health between A and B, depending on the levels of (potential) support measured at time A. If the latter is an unbiased estimate of the support received by the subject during the A–B interval (when a life event occurs), then the procedure is perfectly adequate. However, if the occurrence of a life event changes the effective levels of support, statistical interactions may be biased. If stress mobilizes support in proportion to existing (perceived, potential) levels of support at time A, then the difference between low and high support levels appears greater at high levels of stress than at low levels. This will result in a spurious buffer effect, at least in linear regression analyses, if a support main effect is present (Figure 2).

On the other hand, severe life events may reduce effective support below what the subjects thought available at time A. If this reduction is particularly great at marginal support levels while high-level support remains unchanged, a spurious stress-buffering effect will again appear (Figure 3).

The reverse—stress-enhancing effect—occurs when the mobilization of support is greater at low levels, or when the reduction of support is greater at high levels as measured at time A. Such apparent stress-enhancing effects of support may mask real buffer effects. The negative consequences of being "let down" by an important support figure in the face of severe stress, which are discussed by Brown (Chapter 15), are an extreme example for this kind of effect. The basic problem here is that the level of support actually available when a severe life event occurs cannot be measured prospectively, and any systematic impact (mobilization, reduction) a life event has on support will lead to biased estimates of interaction effects. One solution is to measure both events and support retrospectively at time B, but then the methodological advantages of a prospective design are lost. This is clearly a no-win situation, and while doing this kind of prospective study one can but hope that support mobilization or reduction do not occur, or do so at random. (Although the latter would increase the error component of the data, random error can be dealt with statistically.)

THRESHOLD EFFECTS[6]

The previous two sections have focused on the problem of spurious interactions in linear regression analysis arising from nonlinear relationships that are present in the data. The common interpretation of epidemiological studies of health outcomes as reflecting etiologically relevant phenomena assumes that if a linear model is found to be appropriate for the relationship between stress, support, and health in the population, it can be transferred to intraindividual processes. This means that associations found to be linear in a population are assumed to be linear also within individuals over time; for example, illness levels rise in step with stress levels. At least in the case of depression, this assumption does not generally hold, since episodes of severe depression tend to develop rapidly with even minor experiences

[6]This section is based on a previously published paper (Veiel, 1987).

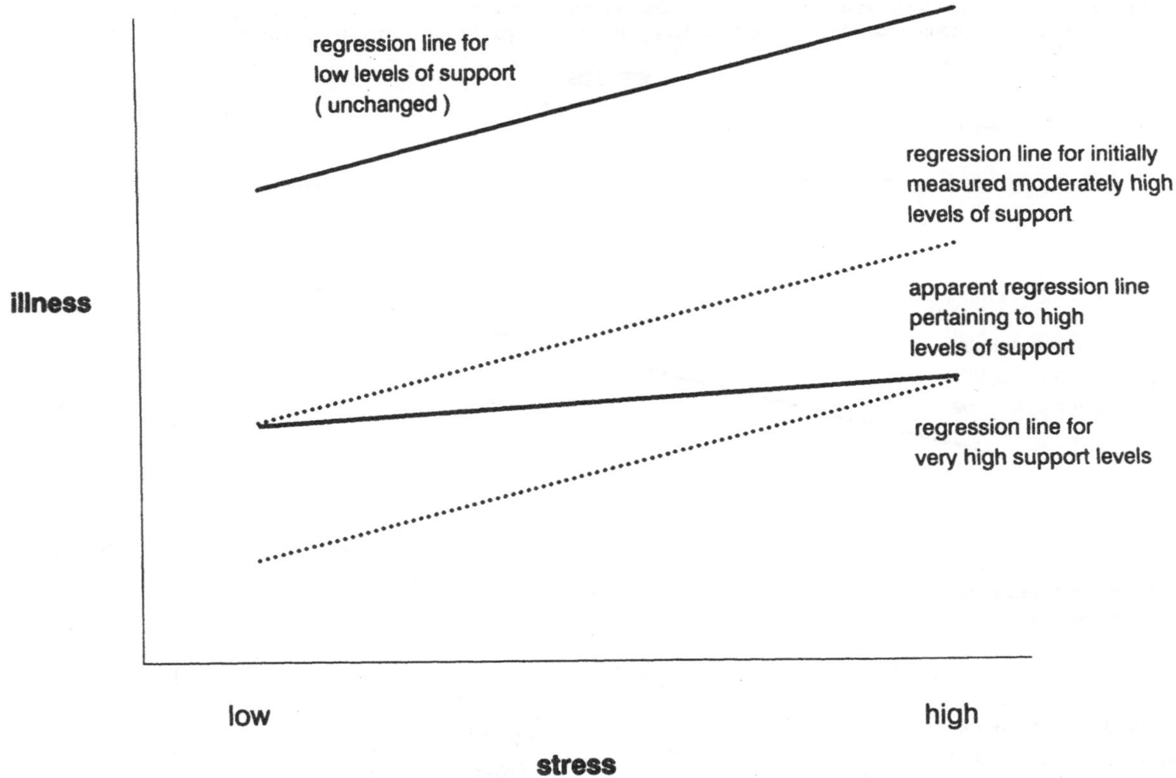

Figure 2 Mobilization of support. If initially (prospectively) measured support is medium-high, it is further increased (mobilized) when stress occurs, but not if initial support levels are low. The measurement of support is biased, which produces spurious interaction effects.

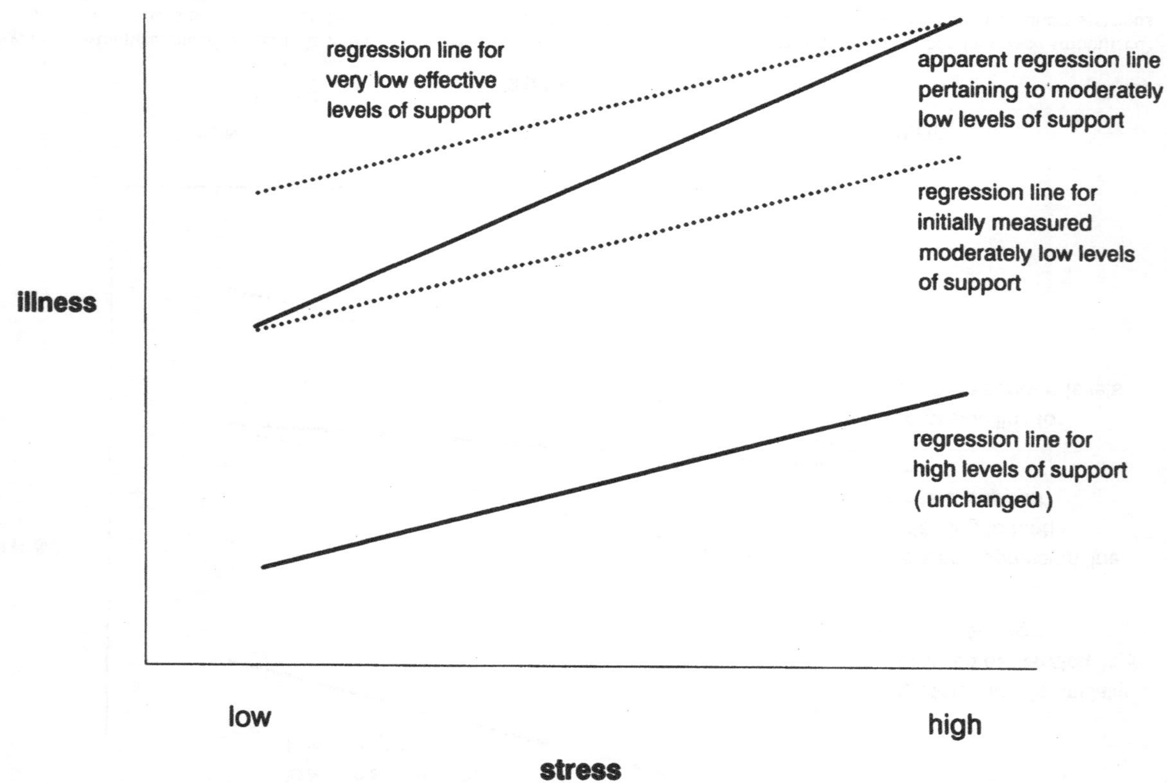

Figure 3 Reduction of support. If initially (prospectively) measured support is low, it is further reduced when stress occurs, but not if initial support levels are high. The measurement of support is biased, which produces spurious interaction effects.

of adversity ("the last straw"). In other words, in many individuals there is a (low) range of depressive symptom levels characteristic of subjective "well" states, and a (high) range of depressive symptom levels characteristic of subjective "depressed" states. Furthermore, the threshold of (objectively measurable) adversity at which the transition from the subjective "well" state to the subjective "depressed" state occurs probably differs considerably across different individuals. Although in a sizable proportion of individuals such a discontinuous association (threshold function) of depressive symptomatology and psychosocial adversity must be assumed, interindividual differences obliterate any trace of such threshold effects in samples and populations. Cross-sectional associations, therefore, may be perfectly linear.

Conditions usually subsumed under the category "stress" and the lack of social support can both be regarded as increasing the overall level of psychosocial adversity to which an individual is exposed. It can be demonstrated (Veiel, 1987) that when the relationship between depressive symptom levels and psychosocial adversity within individuals follows a threshold function, linear regression analysis of cross-sectional data will show spurious interactions, even when no true synergism exists. Sudden onset is particularly typical for depressive disorders, and data structures that are reflected in significant stress-by-support interactions in linear regression models are particularly frequent in studies where depression is the outcome variable of interest. Some investigators even found, in the same study, stress-buffering effects of support with depression as outcome, but not regarding other disorders (Veiel, 1987.)

It is important to keep in mind that the conditions leading to spurious interaction effects, and hence to the erroneous assumption of stress-buffering effects of social support, which are discussed here, stem from developmental discontinuities in an outcome variable (particularly depression), regardless of any actual synergistic effects of low support and high stress. If the effects of social support and stress are genuinely synergistic, statistical interaction effects should be present with any outcome variable that is dependent on psychosocial adversity (e.g., nonspecific distress symptoms, anxiety, or psychosomatic complaints). This is a convenient way of testing for stress-buffering effects of social support that are suspected to have resulted from developmental discontinuities of one outcome variable. (Other procedures for testing for spuriousness are described by Veiel, 1987.)

DICHOTOMIZATION OF INDEPENDENT VARIABLES[7]

It is generally acknowledged that linear regression is not the method of choice when the outcome variable is dichotomous (e.g., presence/absence of a disorder), and discriminant analysis, logistic regression, or log-linear analysis are more appropriate here. Very frequently in community mental health and epidemiological research, dichotomous outcome variables, such as the presence or absence of a disorder, are derived by labeling symptom levels above a predefined cutpoint as "cases," and levels below this cutpoint as "noncases." Similarly, essentially continuous distributions of stress and support levels are often artificially dichotomized

[7]This section is based on a previously published paper (Veiel, 1988). See also Reynolds (1978).

by defining conditions above a certain, predefined level as "support" or as a "major life event."

If the underlying relationships between support, stress, and disorder is consistent with a stress-buffering effect of social support as defined by a product term in linear regression models, it can be shown that in categorical analyses the cutpoints chosen for both the dependent (illness) and the independent variables (stress, support) crucially determine the size and presence of statistical interactions: the more the cutpoints between high adversity (high stress or low support) and low adversity (low stress or high support) are moved toward the high adversity end, the smaller are the observed statistical interactions between support and stress in ratio analysis models (they may even disappear completely), and the larger the observed interactions in linear analysis models. Data sets can be simulated that reflect a linear association between social support and depression of $r = -.25$, and between stress and depression of $r = .36$, with the product of social support and depression explaining about 3% of additional variance of depression.

If the depression variable is dichotomized to reflect a 10% base rate of depression, if stress and support are dichotomized so that the proportion of subjects in the respective categories is 40:60, 60:40, 80:20, and 90:10 (low stress/high stress, high support/low support), and if the risk of case depression is plotted as a function of both stress and support, the patterns shown in Figures 4 and 5 are obtained. Parallel lines indicate main effects only, and diverging lines indicate the presence of interaction effects. In the ratio model (Figure 4), interaction effects disappear with increasing inequality of category sizes, whereas in the linear model (Figure 5) the interaction effects actually increase. Thus the demonstration of buffer effects with dichotomized, essentially continuous stress and support measures depends both on the category boundaries and the analytical framework. If the interaction effect is U-shaped (i.e., when the effects of stress on health is lower at medium level of support than both at low and high support levels, which is the case, for example, in the empirical study by Parry & Shapiro, 1986), the choice of cutpoints on the support continuum even determines whether a stress-buffering effect or a stress-enhancing effect will be observed (cf. Veiel, 1988). Results of analyses based on categorizations of essentially continuous data, particularly regarding interaction effects, are obviously valid only for the specific categorization employed, and cannot be generalized to the whole continuum (i.e., to all other possible categorizations).

CONCLUSION

It has been shown that the choice of research designs, the properties of the instruments used to measure support and stress, the shape of the function linking psychosocial adversity and disorder, the outcome considered, and the analytical methods employed can all artificially produce statistical interactions that are usually interpreted as stress-buffering effects of social support. Similar conditions, at the same time, can also make "real" buffer effects disappear. Apparently, most kinds of violations of the assumptions made by the particular measurement and analysis model used can result in spurious statistical interactions, simulating or dissimulating stress-buffering effects of support. It would seem prudent, therefore, not to take at face value any buffer effect reported in empirical studies, and any contention that buffer effects are absent.

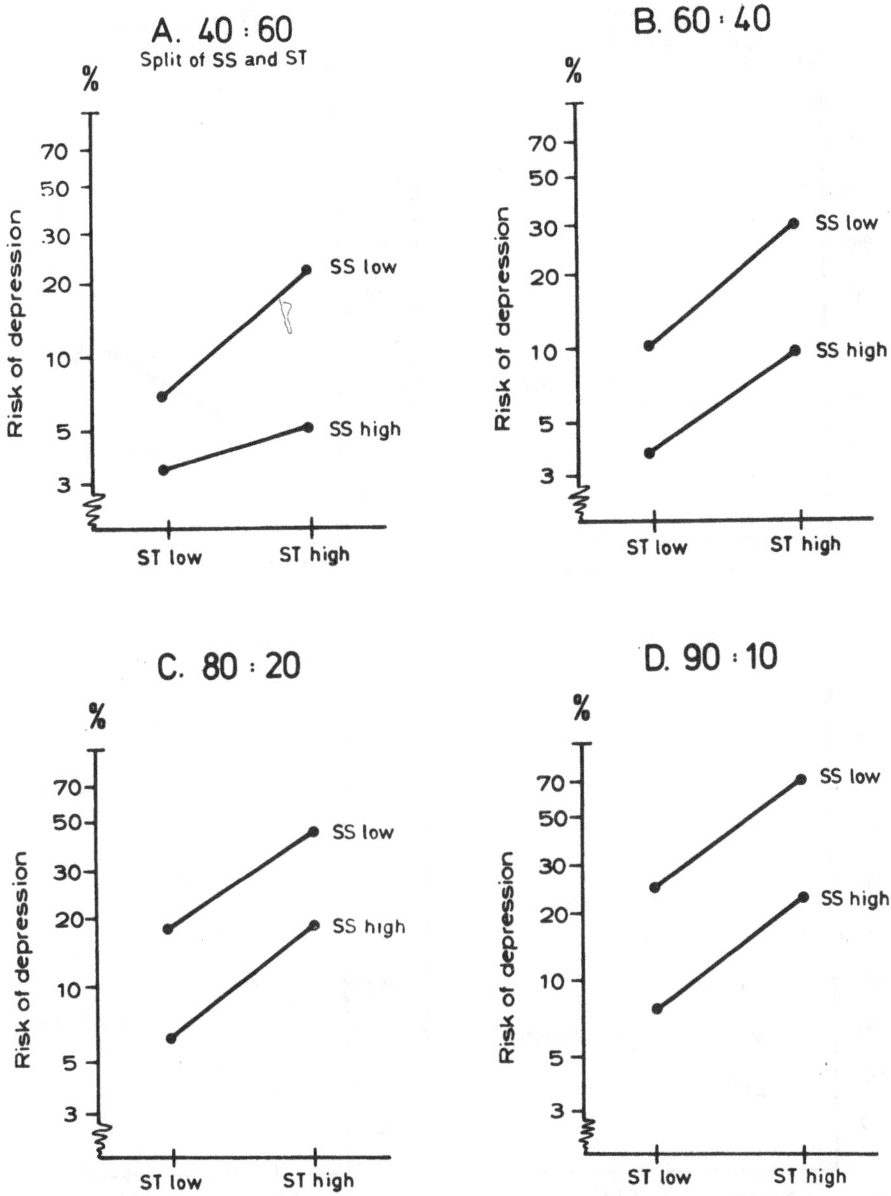

Figure 4 Dichotomization and ratio models. Continuous stress (ST) and support (SS) measures are dichotomized so that the high adversity (high stress; low support) categories contain 60%, 40%, 20%, or 10% of the total sample. The risk of depression is plotted as a function of both stress and support on a log scale. Diverging lines signify interaction effects. With increasingly uneven split of the independent variables, the interaction effects disappear. (See text for underlying true relationships.) (From Veiel, 1988; reprinted with permission.)

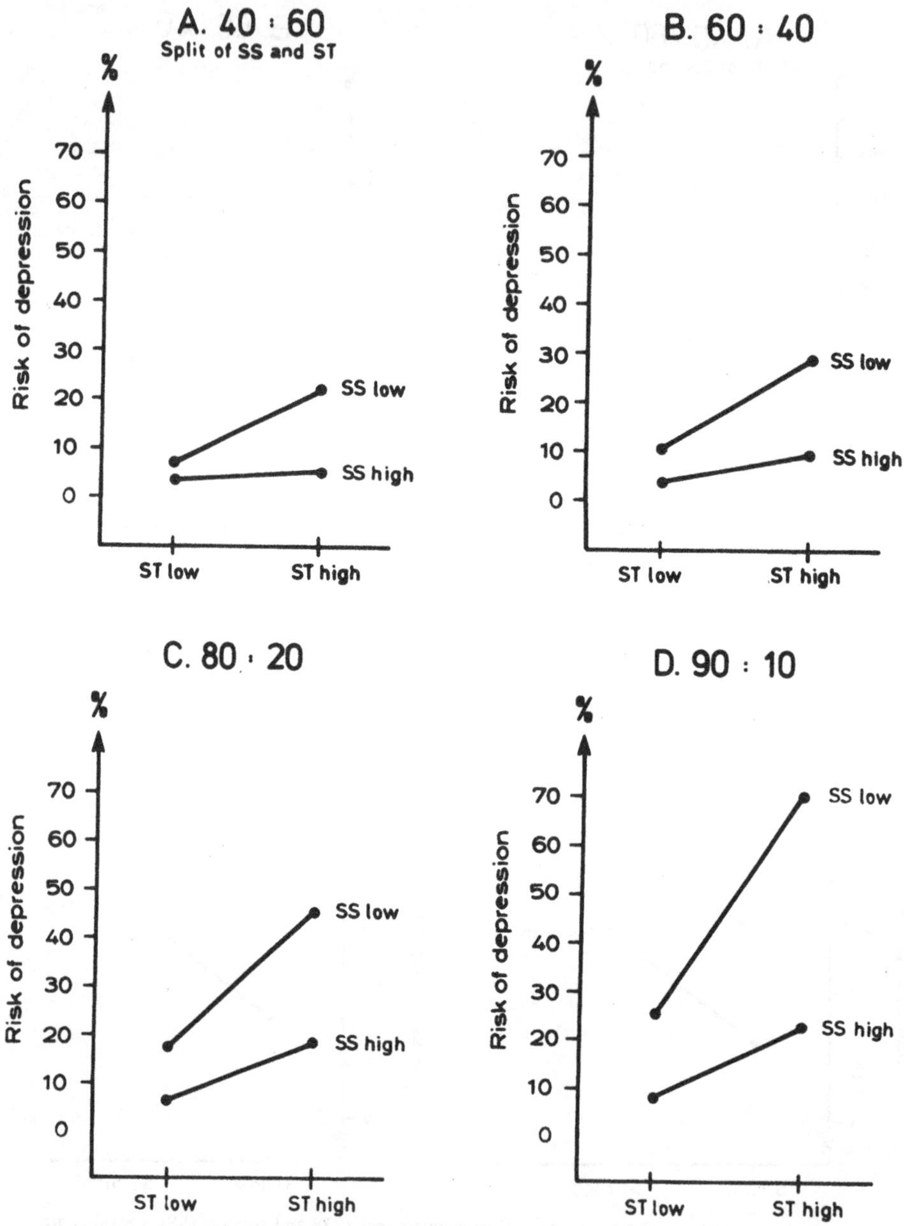

Figure 5 Dichotomization and linear models. Continuous stress (ST) and support (SS) measures are dichotomized so that the high adversity (high stress; low support) categories contain 60%, 40%, 20%, or 10% of the total sample. The risk of depression is plotted as a function of both stress and support on a linear scale. Diverging lines signify interaction effects. With increasingly uneven split of the independent variables, the interaction effects increase. (See text for underlying true relationships.) (From Veiel, 1988; reprinted with permission.)

What is usually interpreted as evidence of a buffer effect is better taken as a nonspecific indicator that the assumptions of the particular main effects model used have been violated. Synergistic effects are but one possible violation, and many more are possible on the measurement level (continuous vs. discrete variables, linearity, bias), on the level of univariate distributions, and on the level of bivariate associations (continuous vs. discontinuous associations). To contend that buffer effects are responsible for the observed deviations from a main effects model one would have to show, or at least convincingly argue, that none of the artifacts discussed previously are present.

Doing so successfully depends, in my view, on three interconnected prerequisites: (a) a theory that defines the kind of synergy to be expected between a particular stressor and a particular instance of social support, and a precise specification of the variables involved, with regard to both (b) their meaning and (c) their distribution.

In response to (a): Some time ago already, Southwood (1978) argued that theoretical considerations should guide the choice of linear, nonlinear, or interactive models to be tested. To expect that both the presence of a synergistic combination of two or more independent variables and its particular function can be empirically determined is to drive positivism to its extreme, and far beyond what error-fraught data in the social sciences could ever justify. The basic question to be answered before statistical tests for buffer effects are performed is the following: what (psychological, social) mechanisms are responsible for an expected buffer effect? The idea is to make the test for buffer effects a test for a specific theoretical proposition. This involves a statement about the stage in the stress-illness relationship in which the beneficial effect of social support occurs: is it expected to reduce actual stress levels (in which case buffer effects should be present with any kind of stress reaction), or does it interfere with the development of a specific disorder (in which case buffer effects should be present with some outcomes but not with others)? A statement about the expected psychological and social processes involved in an expected buffer effect must also specify how the particular stress and support measures are supposed to combine. The analytical model and the statistical tests to be selected follow directly.

In response to (b): The stress and support variables to be considered should be precisely defined and homogeneous to facilitate both the formulation of exact hypotheses about the kind of synergism to be expected and the interpretation of any obtained effect. This means that measures should not sample from broad domains, but define stressful conditions, supportive relationships, and disorders so that they have specific meanings. This makes it easier to specify possible synergistic combinations and to derive corresponding analytical models. (However, it also restricts the generalizability of the results.)

In response to (c): Care should be taken to ensure that the scales employed to represent the variables of interest meet the requirements of the analytical models used. In the case of linear regression, this is primarily the assumption of linearity of associations. However, in the stress and support domains, scale nonlinearity is extremely difficult to distinguish from substantive nonlinear associations. Because both have similar effects on tests for interaction in linear regression, a more comprehensive and practical prerequisite for testing interaction effects here is the linearity of the bivariate associations of both stress and support measures with health outcomes. In the case of categorical analyses, the categories should be discrete, if possible natural categories or, if this is not the case, it must be clear that the generalization to other possible categorizations has to be explicitly justified.

The same preparatory theoretical and methodological work as advocated previously for testing interactive buffer models should, ideally, also be done when testing for any kind of relationship between empirical variables. However, when only nonsynergistic relationships are of interest, the issue can be reduced to the question of whether an association is U-shaped or not: most other associations (linear, logarithmic, threshold, exponential, etc.) can be modeled reasonably well by linear or ratio models. The large error components typical for empirical data in the social sciences makes it impossible, in most cases, to decide between one or the other. It is only when synergistic combinations of effects are to be examined that the number of possible sources of artifacts explodes.

Given the complexity of the social and psychological worlds, theoretical specifications will always leave something to be desired, and artifacts of the kind discussed here should be guarded against by testing as many different models as feasible. Kessler (1983) and, more recently, Brown et al. (1990) have argued for doing so with regard to a decision between linear and ratio models. When examining possible buffer effects, models incorporating the various sources of artifact should also be explicitly tested. I have made some suggestions how to do this, and more specific methods are described in the literature cited.

REFERENCES

Alloway, R., & Bebbington, P. (1986). The buffer theory of social support—A review of the literature. *Psychological Medicine, 17,* 91–108.

Barrera, M. (1986). Distinctions between social support concepts, measures, and models. *American Journal of Community Psychology, 14,* 413–445.

Barrera, M. (1988). Models of social support and life stress—Beyond the buffering hypothesis. In L. H. Cohen (Ed.), *Life events and psychological functioning. Theoretical and methodological issues* (pp. 211–236). Newbury Park, CA: Sage.

Brown, G. W., & Harris, T. (1978a). Social origins of depression: A reply. *Psychological Medicine, 8,* 577–588.

Brown, G. W., & Harris, T. (1978b). *Social origins of depression.* London: Travistock.

Brown, G. W., Harris, T. O., & Lemyre, L. (1990). Now you see it, now you don't: Some considerations on multiple regression. In D. Magnusson, L. R. Bergmann, G. Rudiger, & B. Torestad (Eds.), *Problems and methods in longitudinal research: Stability and change.* Cambridge: Cambridge University Press.

Busemeyer, J. R., & Jones, L. E. (1983). Analysis of multiplicative combination rules when the causal variables are measured with error. *Psychological Bulletin, 93,* 549–562.

Cleary, P. D., & Kessler, R. C. (1982). The estimation and interpretation of modifier effects. *Journal of Health and Social Behavior, 23,* 159–169.

Cohen, J. (1978). Partialed products are interactions; Partialed powers are curve components. *Psychological Bulletin, 85,* 858–866.

Cohen, S., & McKay, G. (1984). Social support, stress and the buffering hypothesis: A theoretical analysis. In A. Baum, J. E. Singer, & S. E. Taylor (Eds.), *Handbook of psychology and health* (pp. 253-267). Hillsdale, NJ: Erlbaum.

Cohen, S., & Wills, T. A. (1985). Stress, social support, and the buffering hypothesis. *Psychological Bulletin, 98,* 310–357.

Craig, T. K. J., & Brown, G. W. (1984). Goal frustration and life events in the etiology of gastrointestinal disorder. *Journal of Psychosomatic Research, 28,* 411–421.

Dunkel-Schetter, C., & Bennett, T. L. (1990). Differentiating the cognitive and behavioral aspects of social support. In B. R. Sarason & I. G. Sarason (Eds.), *Social support: An interactional view.* New York: Wiley.

Everitt, B. S., & Smith, A. M. R. (1979). Interactions in contingency tables: A brief discussion of alternative definitions. *Psychological Medicine, 9,* 581–583.

Finlay-Jones, R., & Brown, G. W. (1981). Types of stressful life events and the onset of anxiety and depressive disorders. *Psychological Medicine, 11,* 803–815.

Goldberg, D. P. (1972). *The detection of psychiatric illness by questionnaire.* New York: Oxford University Press.

Henderson, S, Byrne, D. G., & Duncan-Jones, P. (1981). *Neurosis and the social environment.* Sydney: Academic Press.

Hobfoll, S. E. (1988). *The ecology of stress.* Washington, DC: Hemisphere.

Holmes, T. H., & Rahe, R. H. (1967). The social readjustment rating scale. *Journal of Psychosomatic Research, 11,* 213-218.

Kessler, R. C. (1983). Methodological issues in the study of psychosocial stress. In H. B. Kaplan (Ed.), *Psychosocial stress.* New York; Academic Press.

Lazarus, R. S., DeLongis, A., Folkman, S., & Gruen, R. (1985). Stress and adaptional outcomes: The problem of confounded measures. *American Psychologist, 7,* 770–779.

Newcomb, M. D. (1990). What structural equation modeling can tell us about social support. In B. R. Sarason & I. G. Sarason (Eds.), *Social support: An interactional view.* New York: Wiley.

Parry, G., & Shapiro, D. A. (1986). Social support and life events in working class women—Stress buffering or independent effects? *Archives of General Psychiatry, 43,* 315–323.

Reynolds, H. T. (1978). Some comments on the causal analysis of surveys with log-linear models. *American Journal of Sociology, 83,* 127–143.

Rothman, K. J. (1978). Occam's razor pares the choice among statistical models. *American Journal of Epidemiology, 108,* 347–349.

Southwood, K. E. (1978). Substantive theory and statistical interaction: Five models. *American Journal of Sociology, 5,* 1154–1203.

Spielberger, C. D., Gorsuch, R. L., & Lushene, N. (1970). STAI. *Manual for the State-Trait Anxiety Inventory.* Palo Alto, CA.

Tennant, C., & Bebbington, P. (1978). The social causation of depression: A critique of the work of Brown and his colleagues. *Psychological Medicine, 8,* 565–575.

Thoits, P. A. (1982). Conceptual, methodological, and theoretical problems in studying social support as a buffer against life stress. *Journal of Health and Social Behavior, 23,* 145–159.

Veiel, H. O. F. (1987). Buffer effects and threshold effects: An alternative interpretation of nonlinearities in the relationship between social support, stress and depression. *American Journal of Community Psychology, 15,* 717–740.

Veiel, H. O. F. (1988). Base-rates, cut-points, and interaction effects: The problem with dichotomized continuous variables. *Psychological Medicine, 18,* 703–710.

Veiel, H. O. F., Brill, G., Häfner, H., & Welz, R. (1988). The social supports of the suicide attempters: The different roles of family and of friends. *American Journal of Community Psychology, 16,* 839–861.

Veiel, H. O. F., & Kühner, C. (1990). Relatives and depressive relapse: The critical period after discharge from in-patient treatment. *Psychological Medicine, 20,* 977–984.

VI

SUPPORT INTERVENTIONS

18

Quandaries in Translating Support Concepts to Intervention

Benjamin H. Gottlieb
University of Guelph, Ontario, Canada

CHARACTERISTICS OF SUPPORT INTERVENTIONS

Based on my review of the literature and my experience with several human service organizations and academically based demonstration programs, I have developed a crude typology of support interventions (Gottlieb, 1988), which appears in Table 1. It is organized in terms of the level of intervention—some programs focusing on the individual, some on the relationship between two actors, some on the group or network level, and some on the institutional and community levels of intervention.

At the dyadic and group levels, it is useful to distinguish between strategies that augment or mobilize the support of existing social ties and strategies that graft new ties onto the individual's network. Some programs operate at more than one level of intervention, using either a sequential strategy in which, for example, a recent widow is first paired with a veteran widow and later enters a support group composed of six to eight other widows (Silverman, 1986), or adopting a simultaneous strategy where, for example, a teenaged mother develops a relationship with a home visitor and concurrently attends a center-based support group. In addition, interventions at one level can affect changes in support at another level, an example being Felner, Ginter, and Primavera's (1982) efforts to stabilize peer relationships in the junior high school by restructuring the course scheduling routine.

Although the typology exposes the protean character of support interventions, it also reflects the ambiguity surrounding their definition. In general, support interventions aim to optimize the psychosocial resources that people exchange with members of their primary social field. They accomplish this by effecting changes in the social field or in the individual's behavior (or outlook toward it) to improve the quality or quantity of needed supportive provisions, and ultimately to improve psychosocial functioning. Variations in the strategies of accomplishing this aim depend on a host of factors, including the particular coping challenges faced by the intended beneficiaries, the structure and resources of their existing social ties, the practical constraints that limit changes in the social environment, and, not least of all, the preferences of those planning the intervention.

Regardless of the particular strategy that is adopted, support interventions differ from other social interventions by virtue of their focus on creating a process of

Table 1 Preliminary typology of support interventions

Level of intervention	Examples
Individual	
Support provider	Promoting a network orientation to coping
	Promoting ways of coping that invite support
Support recipient	Controlling distress during supportive exchanges
Dyadic	
Support from key network member	Consultation to informal community caregivers
	Spouse-coach in the Lamaze method of childbirth
	Enlisting close associate in health habit change
	Lowering levels of expressed emotion (EE)
Introduction of new tie	Home visitor programs, including companions and friendly visitors
	Therapeutic partnerships between "fellow sufferers"
	Lay-helping alliances such as buddies, coaches, mentors, and preceptorships
Group	
Support from set of network members	Cultivation of natural-helping networks
	Network therapy and its variants
	Network/support assessment and development
Grafting on a set of new ties	Creation of support groups
	Family support programs such as Extend-a-Family and Family Clusters
	Psychosocial rehabilitation programs such as Fountain House and Lodge Society
Social system	
Role redefinitions	Expanded role for the primary nurse and high school homeroom teacher
Organizational policy/structural changes	Workplace daycare programs
	Network members room-in and assume care responsibilities in hospital
	Students in first year of high school stay together for core courses
Community	California's "Friends Can Be Good Medicine" campaign
	Radio talk/phone-in shows featuring self-help groups

(From Duck, 1988; reprinted by permission of John Wiley & Sons, Ltd.)

interaction with the social environment that meets people's psychosocial needs. Moreover, they concentrate on interactions in the primary social field, either with ongoing role partners or with those who are introduced from the outside and become temporarily or permanently allied in ways that have relationship meaning. The occasions for such interaction may be unexceptional, embedded in everyday life, or dramatic, occurring during times of exposure to acute or chronic stressors. The purpose of the intervention is to create a process of interaction that optimizes the fit between the psychosocial needs aroused by the demands people face and the social and emotional provisions they receive.

Unlike traditional psychotherapeutic practice, support interventions do not occur through direct interaction with a professional or other formal helping agent. That is, the beneficial effects conferred by support interventions do not arise from the instruction or training provided by a professional or from the latter's ability to create the conditions that promote psychological insights gained through dialogue with or modeling of the professional. Support interventions typically involve direct interaction with the social environment, and their ameliorative effects result from the resources conveyed through this interaction. These resources include information about the self and the environment, as well as tangible aid and companionate care and comfort. The role of the professional is therefore indirect, involving efforts to carefully match the resources of the social environment to the psychosocial needs of the individual. As revealed in the typology of support interventions, these efforts may entail changes in the structure or composition of the social environment, changes in the individual's behavior or attitudes toward it, and changes in the quality and frequency of interaction between the individual and one or more members of the social field.

Additional examples of support interventions include mentoring relationships between youths at risk of dropping out of school and college students, friendly visitors who offer companionship to nursing home residents, middle-aged daughters who attend weekly group meetings to discuss the care they provide to their elderly relatives, and efforts to restructure the social networks of parents of autistic children to increase the range and frequency of the network's support.

The conduct of support programs entails three major activities: (a) creating the conditions conducive to the expression of needed support, (b) determining whether the support actually arises, (c) and discerning its impact. It is noteworthy that some initiatives end after completing only the first of these three activities. That is, they concentrate only on support as a dependent variable, presuming that, once mobilized, it will have beneficial effects. Programs that view support as an end in itself typically attempt to increase people's social participation or to compensate for particular deficits in their social field. For example, the Big Brothers/Sisters organization introduces a new parental figure to children in single-parent families, whereas programs for the chronically mentally ill and other marginalized populations aim to increase their community ties (e.g., Gottlieb & Coppard, 1987). But once these new ties are introduced, the support that should arise is not gauged and any positive and negative effects are not monitored, reflecting an incomplete evaluation cycle.

However, there is a need for intervention studies that focus only on these two programmatic activities. For example, recent studies of the factors that prevent people from obtaining social support suggest the need for interventions to change the ways people cope, modulate their distress so they do not alienate would-be helpers, and alter their beliefs about the efficacy of help-seeking (Dunkel-Schetter, Folkman, & Lazarus, 1987; Eckenrode, 1983; Lehman, Ellard, & Wortman, 1986). In short, by planning interventions that alter the determinants of support and evaluating only their proximal effects on the expression of support, we can learn about the social-psychological contingencies governing this type of intervention. At the organizational level, interventions that alter institutional policies, practices, or structures presumed to limit people's access to support can be equally instructive. By permitting a parent to "room" with a hospitalized child, or by creating a set of smaller learning environments in the middle school (Carnegie Council on Adolescent Development, 1989), and then documenting the support that arises, we can gain insights into systemic barriers to the expression of support.

Finally, support interventions can complement professional treatment, can be embedded within a larger program, or can stand on their own. This will be determined by the needs of the intended beneficiaries and the aims of the program planners. For example, as a complement to professional treatment, a group of occupational therapists are attempting to restructure the social networks of young adult schizophrenic patients who have been referred to them by psychiatrists. Although the physicians are largely involved in managing the patients' medications, the occupational therapists are using "Social Network Therapy" (Gottlieb & Coppard, 1987) to stabilize and specialize the support of the patients' social fields.

A primary preventive initiative recently introduced in several disadvantaged communities in the Province of Ontario, Canada, illustrates one way in which a support strategy can be embedded in a larger social program. Here, parent groups and home visitors are used to foster supportive relationships among the families that use the preschool and the maternal and infant development programs that have been created expressly for this new community initiative. The conceptual framework underlying this demonstration program explicitly views family support as one of several necessary ingredients of a comprehensive approach to reducing the incidence of behavioral and emotional problems in low-income communities (Ontario Ministry of Community and Social Services, 1989).

TRANSLATING SUPPORT CONCEPTS TO INTERVENTION

The task of choosing the appropriate type or level of support intervention is of enormous practical significance to those planning programs. In several program reports, the rationale for choosing to convene support groups rather than to introduce a mentor, home visitor, or peer helper was typically omitted, and the grounds for the decision to intensify or modify the support of a key associate who is presently in the network rather than to graft a new tie onto the network were not discussed. A common failing of these support interventions is that they do not base their decision about how to improve the program participants' social support on an assessment of the social network and support that exist before the intervention, on a determination of the acceptability of different support strategies to the participants, or on preintervention analyses of the relationship between various support dimensions and measures of functioning and morale. For example, in Heller, Thompson, Trueba, Hogg, and Vlachos-Webber's (1991) account of a support intervention with low-income elderly women, peer telephone dyads were introduced before data were gathered, which revealed that perceived family support and not perceived friend support was related to initial levels of mental health. Although the intervention strategy may have been informed by the general literature on the social ties of elderly people, it was not predicated on an assessment of the specific kinds and sources of support needed by the particular population selected for intervention.

This leads to the more general question as to whether the voluminous literature on social support offers a theory or any scraps of a theory that might be called on in the planning and execution of interventions. My own answer is that it provides only general guidance by calling attention to issues of fit between the nature and duration of the stressful demands people face, the types and sources of support they need, and the enveloping conditions and culture in which they live. This general guidance has been given full expression by Cutrona and Russell (1990), who recently scoured the empirical literature to determine whether there is any basis for what they call a "theory of optimal matching" between stressful demands and individual components of support. They note that: "If we could match support components to stress, we could design better social support-based interventions. We could design programs to promote the most beneficial kinds of supportive interactions, given the clientele's particular circumstances . . ." (p. 319). In short, Cutrona and Russell (1990) suggest that the planning of support programs is best informed by mobilizing the support necessary to meet the particular emotional and instrumental needs that are aroused by the demands people face or by the changes they wish to make.

Practically, the steps entailed in translating these goodness of fit notions to intervention are complicated by three facts. First, because the demands people face at different stages of coping are dynamic in nature, giving rise to a fluid set of emotional and instrumental needs, the support that is called for must be specialized in content and carefully synchronized in time (Jacobson, 1986). As I will illustrate through the example provided by the work of Cohen et al. (1988) on smoking cessation, support interventions that are based on a theory of optimal matching are difficult to implement because of the stringent demands they make for change in the social environment and in the individual's interaction with it.

Second, although the theory of optimal matching suggests what types of support can meet the stressful demands placed on individuals, it does not address the complex problems entailed in engineering interactions that communicate these types of support. In my discussion of this issue, I will argue that contextual factors determine the meaning or appraisal of support, making it impossible to introduce theoretically relevant types of support without careful consideration of relational and social-psychological dynamics.

Third, because Cutrona and Russell's (1990) conclusions about optimal stress-support matches are derived from studies of people's interactions with members of their natural social networks, they may not apply to support programs in which new relationships are introduced from the outside. The discussion that follows elaborates on these three points.

In the analysis by Cohen et al. (1988) of the role of social support in smoking cessation, they call on notions of optimal matching to show how different kinds and functions of support operate at different stages of change in smoking behavior. Specifically, they maintain that the support mechanism operative at the first three stages—when the individual makes the initial decision to quit, actually quits, and shows early maintenance of abstinence—involves ". . . specific behaviors performed by others that reinforce the decision to quit and make the quitting process easier" (p. 216). In addition, during the second and third stages, stress-buffering support is also needed, and is gauged by measures of perceived rather than actual support. Throughout all the stages, support also consists of reduced or absent contact with network members who smoke, measured by the smoking status of close associates and the proportion of the network that does not smoke. Although the review by Cohen et al. (1988) of the empirical literature reveals that the effects of these varied types of support on outcomes at each stage are mixed, their analysis exemplifies the kind of matching that Cutrona and Russell (1990) recommend as the basis for planning interventions.

But there are many vexing complications that arise in linking theory and practice in this and other intervention contexts. Foremost among them is the problem of gaining the kind of access to the social environment that is required to alter the behaviors of network members that are relevant to the various stages of smoking cessation. It is unrealistic to expect the smoker's daily associates to adhere to a set of theoretically derived supportive requirements that entail altering specific kinds of health-related interactions and communications, and, at times, even to avoid contact altogether. In fact, in two studies that attempted to train spouses to provide relevant support for smoking cessation to their partners, no significant differences were found between spouses who were trained and those not trained, either in the frequency of supportive interactions or in follow-up abstinence rates (Lichtenstein, Mermelstein, Kamarck, & Baer, 1985; McIntyre-Kingsolver, Lichtenstein, & Mermelstein, 1986). These findings led Cohen et al. (1988) to conclude that it is not only very difficult to influence the support process in close, long-term relationships, but also that natural relationships can be placed at risk by the requirements that support interventions may place on them. For example, ". . . spouses who go out of their way to tolerate withdrawal symptoms and to reinforce positive behaviors may feel that their own needs and desires are being ignored in the process and manifest their dissatisfaction in other possibly hostile ways" (Cohen et al., 1988, p. 230). Paradoxically, support interventions may actually add strain to existing relationships by overburdening them with demands for particular expressions of support.

The second slippage between optimal matching theory and intervention practice stems from difficulties in ensuring that theoretically relevant types of support are actually expressed by providers in vivo, and interpreted by recipients in the ways intended. A number of recent studies of support recipients suggest that network associates often miscarry their support, even when they know what kinds of support may be most helpful (Dakof & Taylor, 1990; Dunkel-Schetter, 1984; Dunkel-Schetter & Wortman, 1982; Lehman, Ellard, & Wortman, 1986; Peters-Golden, 1982; Wortman, 1984; Wortman & Dunkel-Schetter, 1979). Research by Lehman et al. (1986) is persuasive regarding this point because it reveals that network members operate on the basis of an intuitive theory of optimal matching, holding beliefs about the support that would be helpful to a bereaved person that correspond to the support wanted and appreciated by bereaved people. However, these authors show that these ideas often fail to be converted into practice when people actually interact with the bereaved, resulting in unhelpful and unwanted communications. For example, network members miscarry their support by minimizing the event's emotional impact, avoiding open communication about the event, criticizing their associate's ways of coping, offering him or her unsolicited advice, and encouraging him or her to make a more rapid recovery. Lehman et al. (1986) speculate that the combined threat, anxiety, and feelings of responsibility aroused during face-to-face interaction with the distressed are responsible for the gap between enlightened knowledge of the support that would be helpful and its delivery.

It follows that intervention programs must carefully monitor the providers' expressions of support, and whenever possible, first eliminate or minimize the factors that may distort their expression. Even if such quality assurance of the provider's behaviors is undertaken, it is possible that the types of support intended for the recipient will be misread by the recipient. This may occur because the context of the communications, including the relationship between the two parties and the social-psychological conditions under which they interact, affect interpretations of their meaning. Among the social psychological factors that color the recipient's appraisals of the support that is proffered, the most influential are the attributions made about the provider's motives for helping, the ego-relevant costs of accepting help, and the loss of or threat to autonomy implied by the expressions of support (Coyne, Wortman, & Lehman, 1988; Fisher, Nadler, & Whitcher-Alagna, 1982). If context brings meaning to communications, it follows that words or behaviors intended to communicate a particular type of support may have different supportive meaning to different people. Moreover, a particular behavioral and verbal script may communicate different supportive messages to one individual when it is enacted by people with whom he or she has different relationships.

The implication for intervention is that optimal matches between stressful demands and particular types of support are more likely to occur when the contextual factors that affect people's appraisals of support are taken into account. This means that careful attention must be paid to the relationship between the two parties, recognizing that it shapes the meaning of the various types of support (e.g., esteem support, practical aid, advice, emotional support), which are optimally matched to the recipient's needs.

A third reason why Cutrona and Russell's (1990) conclusions about optimal matches cannot inform intervention is because they are derived from studies in which support is expressed through interaction with natural network members. Because the meaning of support is likely to depend on the meaning of the relationship with the supporter, it stands to reason that the support expressed by new ties introduced from the outside will be perceived differently than the support offered by network members. For example, the same utterances and gestures that convey emotional support from a close friend may be appraised as ingratiating when they are communicated by a home visitor charged with the task of developing rapport with a teenaged mother.

In addition to the difficulties in translating optimal matching theory to intervention practice, another impediment of prior research on social support to the planning and conduct of support programs is its emphasis on perceptions rather than transactions. The past emphasis on what Coyne and DeLongis (1986) refer to as the "cognitization" of social support and what Lieberman (1986) calls the "psychologizing" of the construct has tended to obscure the interpersonal dynamics that unfold during the help-seeking and coping process (Gottlieb, 1985). For the purpose of planning interventions, knowledge is needed about the ways people elicit support and, reciprocally, about the ways the social environment is structured and the contingencies affecting its response to both direct appeals for aid and signals of needed aid. In their discussion of the process of mobilizing social support, Ecknrode and Wethington (1990) underscore the need for research on the cues that elicit support from others, including the visibility and chronicity of the stressor and the nature and intensity of the distress. Chronic stressors may be less reliable cues of the need for support than acute stressors because they reflect relatively unchanging problems and, by definition, have neither a clear onset nor a marked offset. In this context, changes in levels of distress are clearer signals of the need for support. By gaining a better understanding of how chronic stressors inhibit both help-seeking and help-giving, interventions that aim to strengthen the support in the networks of persons in chronically stressful circumstances, such as family caregivers to the elderly and parents of handicapped children, can be mounted more effectively.

Coyne, Ellard, and Smith (1990) raise fundamental questions about the meaning of measures that evaluate the perceived support in relationships, and particularly about their relation to actual supportive transactions. On the one hand, high ratings of perceived support may mean that stress-related transactions with the partner have gone so smoothly that there has been no need for explicitly supportive exchanges. On the other hand, they may mean that when strains occur in the interpersonal coping process, the partner has extended valued support. In their research on the coping process of couples after one partner's heart attack, they found that ". . . being supported was probably better construed as being freed from particular worries, concerns, and conflicts that might otherwise burden coping efforts, rather than as a cognition that guided their coping" (p. 134). They found that explicitly supportive exchanges occurred only when long-established routines broke down and when the partners experienced conflict about how to make lifestyle changes that would minimize the risk of another heart attack. These observations suggest that if measures of perceived support can reflect either "judgments about the quality of mutual commitment and responsiveness" (p. 131) or assessments of the quality of supportive transactions, then low ratings have uncertain implications for intervention. They may imply either strategies to repair relationships or strategies to improve the help and support that is expressed when harmonious relations break down under stress.

The strongest basis for planning support interventions lies in an examination of the interactional dynamics that shape judgments of perceived support. The first aim of intervention is either to embed people in temporary or more enduring relationships that are characterized by mutual responsiveness or to involve them in a social process that generates the specialized types of support that they cannot otherwise obtain. Although the intervention may also result in heightening the participants' psychological sense of support, its first purpose is to arrange social conditions so that an interactional process occurs that is experienced as supportive. As Rutter (1987) observes, the protective effects of social support lie in the process rather than in the variable. By carefully steering and recording the interpersonal transactions that arise in the conduct of support interventions, the needed process dimension can be added to emergent theory.

IMPLICATIONS FOR THE IMPLEMENTATION STAGE OF SUPPORT PROGRAMS

In a number of reports of support interventions involving the introduction of new social ties, issues surrounding the creation of meaningful relationships between the support providers and recipients have proved to be consequential in determining the outcomes. For example, Lieberman and Videka-Sherman's (1986) studies of self-help groups for bereaved widows and widowers revealed that the benefits derived from participation only accrued to those who formed new friendships characterized by mutual exchange. The fact that there was no significant improvement among members who were exposed to the mutual aid process but who did not form new ties led Lieberman (1986) to conclude that self-help groups ". . . are social linkage systems where people form relationships, and in that sense, they provide social support. But it is unrealistic to assume that because they provide social support, it is this characteristic that is the essential condition for their positive impact" (p. 464).

More direct evidence that perceptions of support are contingent on the forging of meaningful relationships is found in the intervention by Heller et al. (1991). They found that their efforts to establish friendships among elderly women through the creation of telephone dyads did not result in the inclusion of the new telephone partner in the list of friends or in a significant increase in levels of perceived friend support. Commenting on this finding, Heller et al. (1991) state: ". . . it is possible that telephone friendships were too limiting, and did not allow sufficient contact for the development of intimacy and mutual sharing" (p. 68). On the basis of her review of a variety of family support programs for disadvantaged populations, Schorr (1988) observes that: "Every program successfully serving high risk populations has some attributes which are fragile, involve complex human relationships, and do not lend themselves to mass production. Just as teacher-proof curricula have not worked, there are no 'community-proof' or 'people-proof' programs . . ." (p. 276).

By implication, support programs are not "relationship-proof," because support is not a commodity or resource that can be dispensed to providers and then extended to those in need. As noted earlier, the proposition that behavior gains its supportive meaning from relationships is verified by evidence of network members' specialization with respect to support (Coyne & DeLongis, 1986; Lieberman, 1986), variability in people's evaluation of the helpfulness of the same supportive gestures in the hands of different categories of associates (Dakof & Taylor, 1990), and evidence that support from certain relationships is indispensable and cannot be compensated for or replaced by other relationships (Brown, Andrews, Harris, Adler, & Bridge, 1986). In fact, Brown et al. (1986) reported a particularly high risk of depression among married mothers who anticipated receiving but failed to obtain crisis support from particular close ties.

If the meaning and effectiveness of support are colored by the character of relationships, then the most popular support programs—those that introduce new ties—face the challenge of creating personal contexts that lend supportive meaning to the transactions that take place. In the implementation stage, they must build relationships with features that are likely to germinate support, while embedding these relationships in a program environment that invites participation and retention. To date, specific program practices that aim to optimize the likelihood that a supportive relationship will be formed have concentrated on selecting support providers who are able to produce the traditional Rogerian conditions deemed to be conducive to interpersonal rapport and who match the recipient along such dimensions as ethnicity, income, race, and education. In their review of the criteria used to select lay helpers in four preventively oriented informal support programs, Ireys, Halper, and Bauman (1989) find that the personal characteristics prized across all these programs are the warmth and empathy shown by the prospective lay helpers. The programs differ in their reliance on measures of personality, helping skills, and prior experience as bases for selecting lay helpers. However, high attrition rates in these programs point to either a failed chemistry of relationships or to other conditions in the program environment that detract from its appeal.

Other program reports reveal that the recruitment and retention of program participants depend on the success of shaping an interpersonal context and a larger program environment that is psychologically attractive. In their discussion of implementation issues in Family Support and Education programs, Weiss and Halpern (1990) note widespread difficulties in sustaining the involvement of families. They conclude that: "More research is needed about what program components maximize participation . . . and about what personal and contextual issues affect parents' participation in different types of family support and education interventions" (p. 95).

In the implementation stage of support programs it is critical to create conditions that welcome people to the doorstep, make it comfortable for them to cross over the threshold, and foster easy interaction with people with whom it is hoped they will form relationships that take on supportive meaning. Here, the literature on the help-seeking and support mobilization process can contribute some knowledge, or at least offer some hypotheses about the beginning context of support programs that can be systematically tested. It offers ideas about how to make the program context more psychologically acceptable, preempting unspoken messages that typically stand in the way of recruitment and retention of participants. More generally, it can provide a theoretical foundation for the implementation stage of support programs.

First, efforts should be made to avoid the stigmatizing consequences of targeting programs to identified "at risk" or "red-tagged" populations. By assigning mentors only to youths who are deemed likely to drop out of school, or by introducing home visitors only to "red-tagged" parents who show early warning signs of abusing their children, programs are likely to reinforce whatever negative self-perceptions already exist among these populations and call the community's attention to them. Universal rather than targeted recruitment strategies are therefore more acceptable.

Second, programs should operate in a style that places a premium on opportunities for reciprocity and mutuality, calling attention to what people bring to the program rather than to their deficiencies. This applies with extra force to support interventions because they not only risk damaging the self-esteem of the beneficiary, but also pose a threat to the network in which the individual is embedded. In effect, they may convey the message that the individual's associates have let him or her down by failing to render the supportive provisions that are needed.

Third, if there is any truth to the notion that unsolicited support confers greater value on relationships than support that must be requested, then conditions must be arranged that make help-seeking less salient and interdependence more prominent. By establishing a social context that blurs the distinction between the provider and the recipient of support, and is characterized by spontaneous and mutual exchanges, issues of subordinate and superordinate status become irrelevant (Lenrow & Burch, 1981).

All three of these aspects of the program context that affect its psychological acceptability come into play in Ireys, Facchini, Stein, and Bauman's (1990) penetrating analysis of the difficulties encountered in developing a support program for mothers of children diagnosed with serious chronic illnesses. Briefly, the initial program strategy involved deploying a group of trained volunteers, called Family Advocates, to provide support for a period of one year to a group of low-income, ethnically diverse mothers. These lay helpers were selected because they were also raising a child with a serious health problem, and were deemed by the staff to be competent caregivers. The main functions of the advocates were to be empathic sources of support, and to assist families to identify and use needed services. This was to be accomplished largely through weekly phone calls supplemented by face-to-face meetings at both the clinic where the children were served and in the mothers' homes. It is noteworthy that the program was planned to operate for a period of one year mainly because of the importance accorded to the initial process of relationship formation.

In examining the reasons why this program was terminated after three months, Ireys et al. (1990) mainly underscore problems in defining the relationship between the advocates and the mothers to whom they were assigned, and in creating auspicious social psychological conditions for the intervention. Specifically, they note that, by spending much of their time assessing how to help the mothers, the advocates ". . . conveyed a message that [they] were there to 'help' and therefore the mother was expected to have a 'problem' that the advocates could help her solve" (p. 11). Accordingly, in the training of the next generation of family advocates, less emphasis was placed on what can be described as the social work functions of the role, in favor of ". . . increased role playing and practice in developing new relationships . . . with increased attention to forming realistic expectations about the length of time needed for a relationship to develop . . ." (p. 12). Second, Ireys et al. (1990) implicate several social psychological features of the program context in its failure, observing that the mothers had virtually no opportunity to reciprocate aid, interpreted the extra support as a sign of their own incompetence, and were the victims of a social comparison process that backfired. On the latter score, the authors maintain that because the advocates emphasized their similarity along the problem dimension and their superiority along the coping dimension, the intended beneficiaries suffered ill effects.

Although role ambiguity—knowing what it means to act like a friend without being a friend—a social comparison process gone awry, and a targeted and problem-centered approach to a population at risk but not symptomatic, all detracted from the process of relationship formation, issues of reciprocity proved to be particularly important. This insight emerged from a subsequent series of ethnographic home interviews conducted by project staff to capture the mothers' own views of sources of stress and support in their parenting role. Serendipitously, the interviewers reported that when the mothers were cast in the role of "expert informer" and asked to share their experiences for the benefit of both the interviewer and other parents raising chronically ill children, they disclosed a great deal of information, including their own difficulties, reported benefiting from the interviews, and showed signs of forming a meaningful relationship with the interviewers. On this basis, a new process of program implementation was designed and is presently being tested. Although still targeted to a select group of vulnerable parents, the mothers who serve as home visitors are being trained to place equal emphasis on providing service, and acting as a kind of support clearinghouse for the mothers. That is, they will elicit ideas about ways of handling family problems and then share them during individual home visits to the mothers, thereby building in an indirect mechanism of reciprocation.

Other reports about the conditions that make for a hospitable start-up for support programs reinforce the importance of the social comparison process, issues of reciprocity, universal access rather than targeted selection of beneficiaries, and the spontaneous receipt rather than the solicitation of support. For example, in another report from the group conducting support interventions at the Albert Einstein College of Medicine, Coupey, Doctors, and Boeck (1987) describe the problems encountered in creating a peer counseling program for minority, inner city youths who suffer from chronic medical illnesses. Their initial efforts to recruit both counselors and counselees met several kinds of resistance. First, because the main criterion they used to recruit counselors was a diagnosis of chronic illness, few youths came forward. Apparently, they did not see themselves as ill and did not feel that their chronic condition should be the chief qualification for establishing a counseling relationship with a peer. Here, the process of recruiting support providers proved to be as stigmatizing as it was for the recipients in the program by Ireys et al. (1990). Once recruitment was extended universally, to both well and ill children, the youths' enthusiasm for the training depended on the promise of being assigned to the experimental condition in which they would actually put the training to use. The driving force of the intervention was the motivation to be of use to others, not to receive training, much less to receive service from others.

Similarly, Freedman's (1988) observations of several programs, in which elderly mentors were paired with teenage mothers, delinquent youths, and students at risk of dropping out of school, led him to conclude that the relationships that lasted the longest and proved to be the most satisfying were characterized by reciprocity. They involved elders who viewed the mentoring relationship as a way of leading more socially fulfilling lives and youths who perceived it as a way of acting on their instincts and abilities to be helpful. Moreover, certain properties of this relationship reflect some of the desirable social-psychological features of helping transactions enumerated by Fisher, Nadler, and Whitcher-Alagna (1982). As volunteers rather than paid professionals, the elders' aid is freely tendered rather than constrained by role obligations, and these relationships do not trigger the kinds of threatening social comparisons that would be aroused by contact with peers who were handling their problems more adeptly or who had not experienced the same problems at all.

Experience reveals that there are several social-psychological conditions that make for an inhospitable start-up in dyadic support programs involving the introduction of a new social tie. They include the beneficiaries' lack of opportunity to reciprocate aid, the use of a targeted and problem-centered approach to a population that is at risk but not symptomatic, the introduction of support agents whose emphasis on establishing a quasiprofessional helping relationship is interpreted by the recipients as a sign of their own incompetence, and a miscarried social comparison process.

The latter topic has also proved to be of inordinate importance in support interventions that introduce an entire set of new ties into people's lives. In fact, support groups are the most ubiquitous type of support intervention, widely implemented on behalf of clients experiencing various acute life events and role transitions, such as marital separation, the death of a loved one, new parenthood, and the diagnosis of a serious illness. Here, the public interactions and the covert social-psychological processes that affect relationship formation and the expression of mutual aid are complicated by the existence of numerous bases for and targets of social comparison. Although participants may share a common life event or transition, there is evidence that the group's composition has important implications for the covert downward and upward social comparisons members make. Similarities and differences among the members in stressor severity and the circumstances under which it occurs, differences in the participants' stage of coping with it and apparent mastery of it, and differences in the meaning it has, are ultimately consequential for mutual identification and relationship formation (Gottlieb, 1986, 1988; Wood, Taylor, & Lichtman, 1985). There is a need for studies that systematically vary group composition along these dimensions, examining how the resulting social comparisons mediate group cohesion, the formation of relationships, and both actual and perceived social support.

CONTEXTUAL DETERMINANTS OF THE TYPE, DOSAGE, AND OUTCOMES OF SUPPORT INTERVENTIONS

The growing literature on support groups spotlights a final analytical gap that deserves attention and returns to the question raised at the outset of this chapter, namely the grounds for choosing one support intervention over another. It concerns the match between the intervention and the sources, types, and timing of the support that is needed. If a support group is being considered as a strategy of intervention, then the circumstances must justify the mobilization of a new set of social ties. Specifically, it is important to determine whether there is something special about the character of the adversity or about people's responses to it that creates the kind of deficiency in the social environment for which a set of new ties can compensate. My review of the literature on support groups suggests that this strategy of intervention is warranted when people experience off-time or nonnormative events that leave them with few associates with whom they can share and compare the experience, when the stressors prevent people from maintaining their social field, and when the events have radiating effects on network members that give needs for their own protection priority over the protection of others. These conditions apply in a number of stressful contexts, but are particularly reflected in the circumstances faced by intergenerational family caregivers who consist largely of middle-aged daughters who assume the responsibility for the care and support of a dependent elderly relative.

First, middle-aged women who assume the caregiving role find themselves without relevant support from members of their own networks because they face an off-time, nonnormative event (Neugarten & Hagestad, 1976). Daughters who assume responsibility for the care of elderly relatives lack age-similar peers with whom to compare notes about their handling of the role.

Second, there is evidence that, over time, the demands of the role tend to engulf other spheres of life, forcing these caregivers to relinquish other valued activities and identities. As the demands for constant care increase, the caregivers become role captives, reducing the support they gain from their associates because of the narrowing of their field of interaction. For example, in a study of 103 intergenerational caregivers, Gottlieb, Chrisjohn, and McHugh (1990) found that objective dislocations that involved reduced interaction with others were causally related to depressive affect because they undermined both perceptions of control and perceptions of support.

Third, there is evidence that the support caregivers receive from the closest ties with whom they continue to interact, mainly family members, either dissipates rapidly or sours because the family members are themselves attempting to grapple with the problems at hand. The ways they come to terms with the difficulties may conflict with or disrupt the caregiver's way of coping and, conversely, the caregiver's emotional reactivity may be threatening if it interferes with other family members' reliance on palliative modes of coping. Such conflicting coping behaviors among family members are illustrated in a recent study of parents of children with serious chronic illnesses (Gottlieb & Wagner, 1991). The mothers reported that support from their husbands was precluded because of the latter's adoption of a self-defensive posture of stoicism, emotional composure, and preoccupation with the managerial dimension of caregiving.

Support groups are apposite in other stressful contexts that create these sorts of deficiencies and strained interactions with the natural social environment. For example, Weiss (1976) observed that an organization called Parents Without Partners compensated for the absence of a sustaining community composed of similarly placed friends. Weiss writes that, following marital separation, the transition to single parent status forced many women to ". . . relinquish friendships they had made during their marriages because of differences in schedules and in concerns, unwillingness to visit in the evening when husbands were home, envy of the married friends, or beliefs that the married friends feared that they might just possibly seduce the friends' husbands" (p. 179). Kalter, Schaefer, Lesowitz, Alpern, and Pickar (1988) report that support groups for children whose parents have separated compensate for absent parental support, noting, "The people they depend on most for understanding, comfort, and reassurance are themselves often attempting to cope with their own social and emotional disequilibrium . . ." (p. 168). Similarly, Sandler, Gersten, Reynolds, Kallgren, and Ramirez (1988) designed a short-term support group for children bereaved by the death of a parent because they found that deficiencies in the family care environment, rather than a deficient mourning process, led to psychological problems. In comparing cancer patients who do and do not attend support groups, Taylor, Falke, Shoptaw, and Lichtman (1986) report that those attending are significantly more likely to feel that family members do not truly understand what they are going through and expect too much from them.

Although these particular contextual factors may warrant support group interventions, and therefore need to be assessed before the intervention is chosen, demographic variables and individual differences must also be considered because they may affect people's participation in and benefit from this type of program. Moreover, even if conditions create the kind of deficiencies in the natural social environment that make support groups advisable, program planners must still decide how to compose and structure the groups in ways that optimize expressions of support.

Finally, contextual factors are not only relevant to the choice of a support group intervention, but also have implications for determining the dosage and gauging the effects of the intervention. With respect to the former topic, the literature on support groups for caregivers reveals that an average of six sessions are held over a period ranging from 2–5 months. Such a short-lived group is unsuited for people in chronically stressful circumstances that socially or emotionally isolate them from natural sources of support. Because they need the continuing support of peers, a higher dosage of support is required. In fact, the authors of virtually every published report observe that the participants wanted to continue meeting together following the last group session and that some of them did so, either on a group or individual basis.

A longer period of exposure to the group process might also spur formation of the kind of dyadic relationships that Lieberman and Videka (1986) report are necessary conditions for significant changes to occur. Although they were unable to establish exactly when these relationships develop, they found evidence of their existence at the end of one year of group participation. In short, because, by definition, the network deficiencies arising in chronically stressful contexts are not self-limiting, the support group should not be designed as if an acute crisis or short-lived transition had occurred, requiring only temporary supplemental support.

As for the intervention's effects, if outcomes are contingent on dosage, then it should not be surprising that short-term support groups have shown equivocal effects on physical and mental health outcomes (Toseland & Rossiter, 1989). Changes in these dependent variables are more likely to be observed following prolonged exposure to the intervention. In the short term, it would be more appropriate to develop evaluative measures that are capable of tapping the intermediate cognitive and emotional changes that dampen the perceived stress of caregiving. Leads about these proximal changes can be gleaned from the participants' reports of the short-term benefits and value of the group. For example, the participants report increased acceptance of their own feelings and limitations, an increased ability to find meaning in the caregiving role, less apprehensiveness and more hopefulness about the future, a heightened sense of self-efficacy, and, generally, an increased ability to make sense of what is happening in their external and emotional lives. Collectively, they speak to the psychological processes that improve their appraisals of themselves and their situation, and thereby reduce the strain of caregiving. By developing psychometrically sound measures of these short-term psychological gateways to change, we can gain greater insight into the processes mediating between the burdens and demands of caregiving and the more distal health outcomes.

CONCLUSION

Because the culture of intervention programs differs so strongly from the natural ecology in which supportive transactions take place, theoretical propositions derived from one context provide weak guidance for action in the other. To learn how to mobilize or augment support through the introduction of new ties, we must experiment with different ways of creating the interpersonal and environmental conditions conducive to the expression and acceptance of support. For example, we can vary the ways we introduce and interpret the program, placing a premium on universal rather than targeted recruitment and on reciprocal rather than asymmetrical exchanges of support. We can also vary the bases on which we match the participants to one another, examining the effects on the social comparisons that arise and the relationships that develop. Above all, through systematic study of intervention trials, we can discern how the interactions occurring in different types of intentionally created relationships take on supportive meaning, and how they confer measurable benefits, particularly those desired by the parties involved.

REFERENCES

Brown, G. W., Andrews, B., Harris, T., Adler, Z., & Bridge, L. (1986). Social support, self-esteem, and depression. *Psychological Medicine, 16,* 813–831.

Brown, G. W., Harris, T. O., & BiFulco, A. (1986). Long-term effects of early loss of parent. In M. Rutter, C. E. Izard, & P. B. Read (Eds.), *Depression in young people: Developmental and clinical perspectives* (pp. 251–297). New York: Guilford Press.

Carnegie Council on Adolescent Development. (1989). *Turning points.* New York: Carnegie Council on Adolescent Development.

Cohen, S., Lichtenstein, E., Mermelstein, R., Kingsolver, K., Baer, J. S., & Kamarck, T. W. (1988).

Social support interventions for smoking cessation. In B. H. Gottlieb (Ed.), *Marshaling social support: Formats, processes, and effects* (pp. 211-240). Newbury Park, CA: Sage.
Coupey, M., Doctors, S., & Boeck, M. A. (1987). *Preventive intervention research with adolescents: A study of a peer counseling program for teenagers with a chronic health impairment.* Paper presented as part of a symposium: Stress and Coping in Chronic Illness of Children and Adolescents. Society for Research in Child Development, Baltimore, MD.
Coyne, J. C., & DeLongis, A. (1986). Going beyond social support: The role of social relationships in adaptation. *Journal of Consulting and Clinical Psychology, 54,* 454–460.
Coyne, J. C., Ellard, J. H., & Smith, D. A. F. (1990). Social support, interdependence, and the dilemmas of helping. In B. R. Sarason, I. G. Sarason, & G. R. Pierce (Eds.), *Social support: An interactional view* (pp. 129–149). New York: Wiley.
Coyne, J. C., Wortman, C. B., & Lehman, D. (1988). The other side of support: Emotional overinvolvement and miscarried helping. In B. H. Gottlieb (Ed.), *Marshaling social support: Formats, processes, and effects* (pp. 305-330). Newbury Park, CA: Sage.
Cutrona, C. E., & Russell, D. W. (1990). Type of social support and specific stress: Toward a theory of optimal matching. In B. R. Sarason, I. G. Sarason, & G. R. Pierce (Eds.), *Social support: An interactional perspective* (pp. 319–366). New York: Wiley.
Dakof, G. A., & Taylor, S. E. (1990). Victims' perceptions of social support: What is helpful from whom? *Journal of Personality and Social Psychology, 58,* 80–89.
Duck, S. (Ed). (1988). *Handbook of personal relationships.* New York: Wiley.
Dunkel-Schetter, C. (1984). Social support and cancer: Findings based on patient interviews and their implications. *Journal of Social Issues, 40,* 77–98.
Dunkel-Schetter, C., Folkman, S., & Lazarus, R. (1987). Correlates of social support receipt. *Journal of Personality and Social Psychology, 53,* 71–80.
Dunkel-Schetter, C., & Wortman, C. B. (1982). The interpersonal dynamics of cancer: Problems in social relationships and their impact on the patient. In H. S. Friedman & M. R. DiMatteo (Eds.), *Interpersonal issues in health care* (pp. 69–100). New York: Academic Press.
Eckenrode, J. (1983). The mobilization of social support: Some individual constraints. *American Journal of Community Psychology, 11,* 509–528.
Eckenrode, J., & Wethington, E. (1990). The process and outcome of mobilizing social support. In S. Duck & R. C. Silver (Eds.), *Personal relationships and social support* (pp. 83–103). Newbury Park, CA: Sage.
Felner, R. D., Ginter, M., & Primavera, J. (1982). Primary prevention during school transitions: Social support and environmental structure. *American Journal of Community Psychology, 10,* 277–290.
Fisher, J. D., Nadler, A., & Whitcher-Alagna, S. (1982). Recipient reactions to aid. *Psychological Bulletin, 91,* 27–54.
Freedman, M. (1988). *Partners in growth: Elder mentors and at-risk youth.* (Available from Public/Private Ventures, 399 Market St., Philadelphia, PA, 19106.)
Gottlieb, B. H. (1985). Social support and the study of personal relationships. *Journal of Social and Personal Relationships, 2,* 351–375.
Gottlieb, B. H. (1986). Put them together and what have you got. *Journal for Specialists in Group Work, 11,* 121-127.
Gottlieb, B. H. (1988). Support interventions: A typology and agenda for research. In S. Duck (Ed.), *Handbook of personal relationships* (pp. 519–541). Chichester, UK: Sage.
Gottlieb, B. H., Chrisjohn, R., & McHugh, A. (1990). *Perceived support and reactance as mediators of the impact of the dislocations of caregiving on depressed mood.* Unpublished manuscript, Department of Psychology, University of Guelph, Guelph, Ontario.
Gottlieb, B. H., & Coppard, A. E. (1987). Using social network therapy to stabilize the support systems of the chronically mentally ill. *Canadian Journal of Community Mental Health, 6,* 117–131.
Gottlieb, B. H., & Wagner, F. (1991). Stress and support processes in close relationships. In J. Eckenrode (Ed.), *The social context of coping* (pp. 165–188). New York: Plenum.
Heller, K., Thompson, M. G., Trueba, P. E., Hogg, J. R., & Vlachos-Weber, I. (1991). Peer support telephone dyads for elderly women: Was this the wrong intervention? *American Journal of Community Psychology, 19,* 53–74.
Ireys, H., Facchini, R., Stein, R., & Bauman, L. (1990). *Implementing a lay prevention program for mothers of chronically ill children: How field experiences led to revisions in program theory.*

Working paper 90-07. Preventive Intervention Research Center, Albert Einstein College of Medicine, Bronx, NY.

Ireys, H., Halper, R., & Bauman, L. (1989). *Lay helpers as agents of prevention: Developing program theory for preventive lay intervention with children and parents.* Working paper 89-27. Preventive Intervention Research Center, Albert Einstein College of Medicine, Bronx, NY.

Jacobson, D. E. (1986). Types and timing of social support. *Journal of Health and Social Behavior, 27,* 250–264.

Kalter, N., Schaefer, M., Lesowitz, M., Alpern, D., & Pickar, J. (1988). School-based support groups for children of divorce. In B. H. Gottlieb (Ed.), *Marshaling social support: Formats, processes, and effects* (pp. 165–186). Newbury Park, CA: Sage.

Lehman, D. R., Ellard, J. H., & Wortman, C. B. (1986). Social support for the bereaved: Recipients' and providers' perspectives on what is helpful. *Journal of Consulting and Clinical Psychology, 54,* 438–446.

Lenrow, P. B., & Burch, R. W. (1981). Mutual aid and professional services: Opposing or complementary? In B. H. Gottlieb (Ed.), *Social networks and social support* (pp. 233–258). Newbury Park, CA: Sage.

Lichenstein, E., Mermelstein, R. J., Kamarck, T. W., & Baer, J. S. (1985). *Partner support and smoking cessation: Replication and extension.* Unpublished manuscript, Oregon Research Institute, Eugene, OR.

Lieberman, M. A. (1986). Social supports—The consequences of psychologizing: A commentary. *Journal of Consulting and Clinical Psychology, 54,* 461–465.

Lieberman, M. A., & Videka-Sherman, L. (1986). The impact of self-help groups on the mental health of widows and widowers. *American Journal of Orthopsychiatry, 56,* 435–449.

McIntyre-Kingsolver, K. O., Lichtenstein, E., & Mermelstein, R. J. (1986). Spouse training in a multicomponent smoking cessation program. *Behavior Therapy, 17,* 67–74.

Neugarten, B., & Hagestad, G. (1976). Aging and the life course. In R. Binstock & E. Shanas (Eds.), *Handbook of aging and the social sciences.* New York: Van Nostrand Reinhold.

Ontario Ministry of Community and Social Services. (1989). *Better beginnings, better futures.* Report available from the Children's Services Branch, Ontario Ministry of Community and Social Services, Queen's Park, Toronto, Ontario.

Peters-Golden, H. (1982). Breast cancer: Varied perceptions of social support in the illness experience. *Social Science and Medicine, 16,* 483–491.

Rutter, M. (1987). Psychosocial resilience and protective mechanisms. *American Journal of Orthopsychiatry, 57,* 316–331.

Sandler, I., Gersten, J. C., Reynolds, K., Kallgren, C. A., & Ramirez, R. (1988). Using theory and data to plan support interventions: Design of a program for bereaved children. In B. H. Gottlieb (Ed.), *Marshaling social support: Formats, processes, and effects* (pp. 53–84). Newbury Park, CA: Sage.

Schorr, L. (1988). *Within our reach.* New York: Doubleday.

Silverman, P. R. (1986). *Widow to widow.* New York: Springer.

Taylor, S. E., Falke, R. L., Shoptaw, S. J., & Lichtman, R. R. (1986). Social support, support groups, and the cancer patient. *Journal of Consulting and Clinical Psychology, 54,* 608–615.

Toseland, R. W., & Rossiter, C. M. (1989). Group interventions to support family caregivers: A review and analysis. *The Gerontologist, 29,* 438–448.

Weiss, H. B., & Halpern, R. (1990). *Community-based family support and education programs: Something old or something new?* (Available from National Center for Children in Poverty, Columbia University, 154 Haven Ave., New York, NY 10032.)

Weiss, R. S. (1976). The contribution of an organization for single parents to the well-being of its members. In G. Caplan & M. Killilea (Eds.), *Support systems and mutual-help* (pp. 177–186). New York: Grune & Stratton.

Wood, J. V., Taylor, S. E., & Lichtman, R. R. (1985). Social comparison in adjustment to breast cancer. *Journal of Personality and Social Psychology, 49,* 1169–1183.

Wortman, C. B. (1984). Social support and the cancer patients. *Cancer, 53* (Suppl. 10), 2339–2360.

Wortman, C. B., & Dunkel-Schetter, C. (1979). Interpersonal relationships and cancer: A theoretical analysis. *Journal of Social Issues, 35,* 120–155.

VII

CONCLUSION

19

Comments on Concepts and Methods

Hans O. F. Veiel
Central Institute of Mental Health, Mannheim, Germany
Urs Baumann
Universität Salzburg, Austria

The preceding chapters, in their diversity of topics and approaches, sketch what may be regarded as the purview of social support research. They demonstrate the impressive degree of sophistication that good research in the field has reached, particularly with regard to health correlates of support, as shown by Schwarzer and Leppin in Chapter 5 on physical disorders and Henderson in Chapter 6 on depression. Overall, the research attests to the basic importance of the support concept for epidemiological and etiological research in mental health.

The different contributions illustrate the enormous heterogeneity of the field, which is probably without parallel among the more established areas of psychological, sociological, and psychiatric research. The discrepancy and sometimes even incompatibility of the approaches advocated by different researchers indicate that basic conceptual and epistemological issues are yet to be resolved. In this discussion, we will try to summarize some of these issues by drawing on the ideas developed in the main body of this volume. Most of these issues have been discussed before, but they bear restating. Together, they sketch an agenda for conceptual and methodological research in the area.

SOCIAL PSYCHOLOGY, SOCIAL CONSTRUCTS, AND SOCIAL SUPPORT

Part I of this volume makes clear that social support—the phenomenon as well as the concept—cannot be regarded in isolation, and that the connections between social support and other, more established concepts of social research need to be examined more systematically. Argyle (Chapter 2) shows how supportive transactions are often tied to specific social roles, and how each social role fosters particular forms of support. Laireiter and Baumann (Chapter 3) and Thoits (Chapter 4) show that the relationship between the support concept and other, broader, and partially superordinate constructs, such as social network, social adjustment, or social integration, is far from clear (cf. Laireiter & Baumann, 1988; Katschnig, 1983). As argued in the Introduction, the present confusion in the support area is, to a considerable extent, a result of a lack of clarity of the concept itself. The empirical efforts that currently predominate in the field should therefore be complemented, we believe, by approaches aimed at the clarification of the semantic relationship between social support and other social-psychological constructs, and at establishing the position of social support vis-a-vis more established and elaborated social-psychological theoretical systems, such as role theory.

PERCEPTIONS AND EVALUATIONS VERSUS STRUCTURES AND BEHAVIORS

Turner, in his chapter on assessment strategies (Chapter 14), strongly advocates a definition of support that is restricted to individual states, and Sarason, Sarason, and Pierce (Chapter 10) demonstrate how close such a subjective support concept comes to being a personality construct. In contrast, Brown (Chapter 15) stresses the necessity of focusing on actual relationships and transactions free of subjective biases (cf. Lieberman, 1986; Gottlieb, 1985; Pearlin, 1989). Kessler's discussion (Chapter 16) finally suggests that support perceptions and actual support behaviors may have little to do with each other; they are largely uncorrelated, and their associations with health are disparate.[1]

The differences between the subjective-evaluative and the structural-behavioral perspectives are fundamental and can hardly be overstated. It is of both practical and methodological consequence to determine whether the basic health-promoting factors are trait-like cognitive sets (global support convictions) that are only indirectly responsive to social experiences, whether these global support convictions can be modified by specific transactions or relationships, or whether supportive social transactions promote health without mediation by cognitive processes.

Thus for planning and conducting social support interventions, remedial or preventive, it is crucial to know whether cognitive or structural-social variables are the ones that matter. For example, support deficits in depressed individuals require different therapeutic strategies, depending on whether they represent perceptual distortions or actually impoverished social relationships. The assessment of individual support beliefs and of presumably supportive structures and behaviors evidently require different methods, which roughly correspond to the psychological and sociological traditions of collecting empirical data.

The discrepancy between structural-behavioral and subjective-cognitive aspects directly bears on how "social support" is to be defined. If actual transactions or relationships as well as perceptions are to be called "social support" despite their disparity, the meaning of the term cannot be taken for granted or derived empirically, but must be spelled out explicitly for the context in which it is to be used. Unless their conceptual and empirical commonalities are well established, beliefs of being supported and presumably supportive social structures and behaviors should be kept strictly separate, conceptually and operationally (see later discussion).

UNITS OF ANALYSIS

Negative interactions are an integral part of many social relationships, as Sarason et al. (Chapter 10) note, regardless of their supportive aspects. Rook (Chapter 11) shows that the effects of negative interactions on health are pervasive and

[1]The term "perceived support" is frequently used for subjective convictions of being supported. In view of the very large subjective component of such convictions, the term "believed support" would probably be more accurate.

frequently overshadow those of supportive ones. Harris (Chapter 12) illustrates how negative comments or attitudes may invalidate—even quite inadvertently—otherwise adequate and helpful crisis support. She also shows how expectations of support can determine whether a particular situation or transaction is supportive, and whether the failure of supportive provisions to materialize constitutes a stressful event. Such support expectations may be tied to particular role relationships (e.g., "friend"), which, as Argyle (Chapter 2) shows, tend to have typical support modes.

Support beliefs are equally unlikely to be based on supportive transactions alone. Insofar as they reflect ongoing interactions and behaviors (rather than stable personality traits), support beliefs are likely to be influenced by both negative and supportive interactions, and by cognitive sets reflecting the previous history of such interactions. This may be one reason for the discrepancy between measures of "perceived" and "received" support mentioned by Kessler (Chapter 16).

It can be argued, we believe, that presumably supportive behaviors derive their support value from other, not obviously related behaviors and from actual or apparent attitudes and motives. In other words, it is the context, and particularly the characteristics of the support provider, that largely determine the support value of specific behaviors. The question must therefore be raised whether it is useful to examine support behaviors or transactions in isolation, or whether supportive persons or even roles should be taken as units of analysis and assessment (cf. Veiel, 1985).

THE DIMENSIONALITY OF STRESS AND SUPPORT

Life event and support measures are typically correlated with each other to about the same degree as are different support measures (cf. Sarason, Shearin, Pierce, & Sarason, 1987; Thoits, 1982). The idea that stress and social support are but two poles of a dimension of social stress, rather than two orthogonal dimensions, has been discussed before (e.g., Barrera, 1986; Dohrenwend & Dohrenwend, 1981; Thoits, 1982). With the emergence of the buffer hypothesis as the master paradigm in research on stress and support, this idea was apparently relegated to a kind of footnote in the research canon: the very notion of a buffer effect implies that support and stress are two different classes of phenomena. However, buffer effects do not prove that stress and support represent separate dimensions, but rather presuppose it (cf. Veiel, Chapter 17). Models and hypotheses regarding the combined effects of stress and support usually treat them as separate constructs; empirical studies using operationalizations of these constructs therefore invariably confirm this premise, whether or not a buffer effect is found.

Whether it makes sense to assume categorical differences between social stress and lack of support is both a conceptual and a measurement issue. The assumption of categorical differences between stress and support comes naturally when stress is operationalized as the verifiable occurrence of a life event, and support as a subjective perception. However, in this case the distinction between stress and lack of support is confounded with the distinction between the subjective-individual and objective-environmental perspectives discussed earlier. The latter distinction is arguably the more important one. (It should be interesting to examine if preexisting support beliefs interact with received support to enhance their beneficial effects.)

When stress and support are both measured as global perceptions, it would take a rather intrepid researcher to claim that these variables are independent of each other. When both are operationalized as social-environmental variables, a categorical distinction between stress and support seems defensible if a specific supportive behavior is contingent on the experience of stress (crisis support). In all other cases, the issue is much less clear.

Taken in isolation, a particular behavior may be identified as supportive, but Harris (Chapter 12) shows how much this is in effect context-dependent, and in the previous section we have argued that single behaviors may not be the appropriate unit of analysis. The independence of positive and negative everyday interactions that is sometimes reported (cf. Rook, Chapter 11) makes sense for the behavioral level only. When the stressfulness or supportiveness of persons or relationships, rather than of single behaviors, are considered, the notion of independence of positive and negative relationship aspects is of little practical value.

The categorical distinction between social stress and support, from which social support research derived much of its initial momentum, may be largely artificial, and a one-dimensional view may sometimes more adequately reflect the true state of affairs.

ASSESSMENT STRATEGIES

The conceptual issues identified earlier have obvious implications for the construction and use of assessment instruments.

The necessity of assessing network structures and interaction patterns unbiased by subjective conditions is eloquently argued by Brown (Chapter 15; cf. Lieberman, 1986; Pearlin, 1989; Wellman, 1985). Such an assessment should, ideally, be based on direct observations, or network members should be used as sources of data, as Kessler (Chapter 16) advocates. Both approaches tend to be expensive, and may not always be feasible. (How does a researcher observe supportive transactions when a major life event occurs unexpectedly?) If social network and interaction patterns cannot be directly observed and if network members cannot be used as independent sources of data, perceptual and evaluative biases can be reduced in two ways: (a) by using very specific assessment items targeting single network members and circumscribed behaviors and situations, thereby anchoring each item in a concrete bit of reality (cf. Phillips & Fischer, 1981; Veiel, 1990); and/or (b) by relying on the expertise of the investigator and his or her abilities to judiciously use collateral sources of information for filtering out respondent biases (Brown, Chapter 15).

These solutions are not without problems of their own. Breaking down complex transactions and relationships into concrete elements may make their assessment more immune to subjective biases but may miss essential supportive qualities, as we have argued earlier. This problem does not arise with the investigator-based approach, whose results, on the other hand, depend heavily on the quality of the investigator. To a large extent, the investigator is the assessment instrument here, which provokes a number of questions regarding his or her reliability and validity, and regarding the replicability of the resulting assessments, for which there can be no general answer. The investigator-based approach runs against the persistent decades-old trend in psychology and psychiatry toward standardization of assessment instruments by reducing the scope for investigator biases as much as possible, which may explain the controversial reception it has received in the field.

In contrast to the generally recognized need for an unbiased assessment of supportive network structures, the necessity for unbiased assessment of subjective convictions of support does not figure prominently in the literature. What is often billed as "perceived support" (e.g., Lakey, 1989) are scores obtained with instruments frequently containing relatively factual items alongside subjective-evaluative ones (cf. Vaux, Chapter 13). Scores obtained in this manner, as are most social support scores used in current research, are basically hybrids with unknown proportions of subjective-individual and social-environmental components. This is a characteristic that support measures share with life event questionnaires, and that distinguishes them from typical psychological tests; here, the subjects are asked to report on their own feelings or attitudes.

As the relationship between "perceived" (or "believed") and "received" support is unclear, and probably anything but straightforward, and as they seem to have disparate effects on health, empirical research would yield a much greater payoff if the two were unconfounded. In particular, the social and interactional determinants of subjective support beliefs, and the examination of support processes and interactions, would be greatly facilitated. The refinement of assessment instruments to measure either subjective, intraindividual states, or objective social structures, unconfounded by each other, would seem to deserve attention.

DEFINING SOCIAL SUPPORT

We began this volume with the question of what *is* social support, or what distinguishes supportive from nonsupportive behaviors, situations, or people, and we referred to the chapters in the main body of this volume for discussion. The bewildering diversity of the approaches to the topic "social support" that the authors reveal seems to preclude any comprehensive answer. The question must be asked whether we need a social support concept at all. As Argyle (Chapter 2) makes clear, many of the phenomena meant to be captured by the term are quite adequately described and/or explained by less global concepts such as friendship, doing things together, or confiding. Cohen's (Chapter 8) comprehensive model of support and stress makes such fundamental distinctions between different kinds, modes, dimensions, and so forth of support that their common denominator looks rather small. Hobfoll, Lilly, and Jackson's (Chapter 9) conceptualization of social support as a resource like any other seems to obviate the necessity of a separate concept of "support." At the other end of the research spectrum, Gottlieb (Chapter 18) illustrates the difficulties that arise when social support is to be translated into intervention goals and procedures: the latter have to be precise and specific, and a general concept of support is therefore of little help. Thus it would seem that neither for the explanation of the health-promoting effects of the social environment, nor for the practical application of the respective insights, is a general support concept needed.

Nonetheless, we believe that researchers would be ill-advised to adapt the conceptual agnosticism that has spread in the field in recent years and that is expressed in statements such that social support is too vague and unspecific a concept (Barrera, 1986) to serve a useful purpose in guiding empirical research, or that support is but a meta-construct (Vaux et al., 1986), which is to say that it means everything and nothing. The apparent lack of explanatory power of the support concept is largely a consequence of its atheoretical nature and of its globality: there is no differentiated conceptual frame of reference from which specific meanings could be derived and within which inconsistencies could be resolved. We believe that current social support research would profit if its concepts and empirical findings are discussed in a framework of a sociology/psychology of interpersonal relationships, which can accommodate different dimensions or qualities of such relationships.

As an example, we endorse Barrera's (1986) argument that one should distinguish between social embeddedness, enacted support, and perceived support. However, in our view Barrera does not go far enough. To maximize the payoff of empirical studies, we suggest that researchers should clearly differentiate between (a) subjective beliefs and actual occurrences; (b) everyday support (social integration, social embeddedness), potential crisis support, and actual (enacted) crisis support; and (c) behaviors, persons, and networks as units of analysis. Measures and operationalizations, of course, should also be correspondingly narrow and circumscribed, which might have the welcome side effect of reducing the great number of currently available support scales. (The proliferation of assessment instruments seems to be an intrinsic characteristic of contemporary social science, however, and the chances of a reversal of this trend seem slim.) Although the field has recently begun to move in this direction, there is still a long way to go.

The adoption of more circumscribed support concepts would greatly help in reducing the Babylonian confusion in the field. It would also be easier to link empirical findings to more established and elaborated bodies of knowledge in psychology, sociology, and psychiatry. The potential benefit to be derived by such linkage is shown by the work of Sarason et al. (Chapter 10), who have availed themselves of the methodology and the accumulated knowledge of psychological assessment to elucidate the structure and determinants of support perceptions and beliefs. Similarly productive links may be established between research on support networks and sociological network theory (e.g., Bernard, Johnson, & Killworth, 1990), or between research on the mobilization of support structures (e.g., Eckenrode, 1983) and social-psychological research on helping behavior (e.g., Fisher, Nadler, & Whitcher-Alagna, 1982), to mention but a few possibilities.

How social support research will develop in the future remains to be seen. The question is whether social support will be developed into more than a convenient, but vague, label for research efforts that are, at best, only loosely connected. If the support field is to be spared the fate of life event research, which has largely become stagnant and sterile, a number of conceptual issues have to be resolved. On the preceding pages, we have identified some of the more important ones, in our view, in the hope that they can be addressed more explicitly in further research.

REFERENCES

Barrera, M. (1986). Distinctions between social support concepts, measures, and models. *American Journal of Community Psychology, 14,* 413–445.

Bernard, H. R., Johnsen, E. C., & Killworth, P. D. (1990). Comparing four different methods for measuring personal social networks. *Social Networks, 12,* 179–215.

Dohrenwend, B. S., & Dohrenwend, B. P. (1981). Life stress and illness: Formulation of the issues. In B. S. Dohrenwend & B. P. Dohrenwend (Eds.), *Stressful life events and their contexts.* New York: Prodist.

Eckenrode, J. (1983). The mobilization of social supports: Some individual constraints. *American Journal of Community Psychology, 11*, 509-528.
Fisher, J. D., Nadler, A., & Whitcher-Alagna, S. (1982). Recipient reactions to aid. *Psychological Bulletin, 91*, 27-54.
Gottlieb, B. (1985). Theory into practice: Issues that surface in planning interventions which mobilize support. In I. G. Sarason & B. R. Sarason (Eds.), *Social support: Theory, research and applications.* Den Haag: Martinus Nijhoff.
Gottlieb, B. H. (1985). Social support and the study of personal relationships. *Journal of Social and Personal Relationships, 2*, 351-375.
Katschnig, H. (1983). Methods for measuring social adjustment. In T. Helgason (Ed.), *Methodology in evaluation of psychiatric treatment.* Cambridge: Cambridge Press.
Laireiter, A., & Baumann, U. (1988). Klinisch-psychologische Soziodiagnostik: Protektive Variablen und soziale Anpassung. *Diagnostica, 34*, 190-226.
Lakey, B. (1989). Personal and environmental antecedents of perceived social support developed at college. *American Journal of Community Psychology, 17*, 503-519.
Lieberman, M. A. (1986). Social supports—The consequence of psychologizing: A commentary. *Journal of Consulting and Clinical Psychology, 54*, 461-465.
Pearlin, L. I. (1989). The sociological study of stress. *Journal of Health and Social Behavior, 30*, 241-256.
Phillips, S. L., & Fischer, C. L. (1981). Measuring social support networks in general populations. In B. P. Dohrenwend (Ed.), *Stressful life events and their contexts.* New York: Prodist.
Sarason, B. R., Shearin, E. N., & Pierce, G. R. (1987). Interrelations of social support measures: Theoretical and practical implications. *Journal of Personality and Social Psychology, 52*, 813-832.
Thoits, P. A. (1982). Conceptual, methodological, and theoretical problems in studying social support as a buffer against life stress. *Journal of Health and Social Behavior, 23*, 145-159.
Veiel, H. O. F. (1985). Dimensions of social support: A conceptual framework for research. *Social Psychiatry, 20*, 156-162.
Veiel, H. O. F. (1990). The Mannheim interview on social support: Reliability and validity data from three samples. *Social Psychiatry and Psychiatric Epidemiology, 25*, 250-259.
Wellman, B. (1985). From social support to social network. In I. G. Sarason & B. P. Sarason (Eds.), *Social support: Theory, research and applications.* Den Haag: Martinus Nijhoff.

Subject Index

For Product Safety Concerns and Information please contact our
EU representative GPSR@taylorandfrancis.com Taylor & Francis
Verlag GmbH, Kaufingerstraße 24, 80331 München, Germany